EMERGENCY
MEDICAL TECHNICIAN WORKBOOK
EMT in Action

Barbara Aehlert, RN
Southwest EMS Education, Inc.

McGraw-Hill
Higher Education

Boston   Burr Ridge, IL   Dubuque, IA   New York   San Francisco   St. Louis
Bangkok   Bogotá   Caracas   Kuala Lumpur   Lisbon   London   Madrid   Mexico City
Milan   Montreal   New Delhi   Santiago   Seoul   Singapore   Sydney   Taipei   Toronto

McGraw-Hill
Higher Education

EMERGENCY MEDICAL TECHNICIAN WORK BOOK: EMT IN ACTION

Published by McGraw-Hill, a business unit of The McGraw-Hill Companies, Inc., 1221 Avenue of the Americas, New York, NY, 10020. Copyright © 2009 by The McGraw-Hill Companies, Inc. All rights reserved. No part of this publication may be reproduced or distributed in any form or by any means, or stored in a database or retrieval system, without the prior written consent of The McGraw-Hill Companies, Inc., including, but not limited to, in any network or other electronic storage or transmission, or broadcast for distance learning.

Some ancillaries, including electronic and print components, may not be available to customers outside the United States.

This book is printed on acid-free paper.

1 2 3 4 5 6 7 8 9 0 QPD/QPD 0 9 8

ISBN 978-0-07-727945-5
MHID 0-07-727945-X

Vice President/Editor in Chief: *Elizabeth Haefele*
Vice President/Director of Marketing: *John E. Biernat*
Publisher: *Linda Schreiber*
Sponsoring editor: *Claire Merrick*
Managing developmental editor: *Sarah Wood*
Marketing manager: *Kelly Curran*
Lead media producer: *Damian Moshak*
Media producer: *Benjamin Curless*
Director, Editing/Design/Production: *Jess Ann Kosic*
Senior project manager: *Rick Hecker*
Senior production supervisor: *Janean A. Utley*
Designer: *Srdjan Savanovic*
Senior photo research coordinator: *Lori Hancock*
Media project manager: *Mark A. S. Dierker*
Outside development house: *Julie Scardiglia*
Interior design: *Kay Lieberherr*
Typeface: *10/12 ITC New Baskerville*
Compositor: *Aptara*
Printer: *Quebecor World Dubuque Inc.*
Cover credit: *Rick Brady*

Photo credits: All photo credits © The McGraw-Hill Companies, Inc./Rick Brady, photographer except for the following. Page 83 (top): © Courtesy of City of Tempe Fire Department, Tempe, Arizona; Page 241 (second from top): Trauma.org Image; Page 241 (bottom): Courtesy of Stephen Corbett, MD, from Atlas of Emergency Medicine, 2nd edition, McGraw-Hill Company, Inc.; Page 293: EMSC Slide Set (CD-ROM), 1996, Courtesy of the Emergency Medical Services for Children Program, administered by the U.S. Department of Health and Human Service's Health Resources and Services Administration, Maternal and Child Health Bureau.

The Internet addresses listed in the text were accurate at the time of publication. The inclusion of a Web site does not indicate an endorsement by the authors or McGraw-Hill, and McGraw-Hill does not guarantee the accuracy of the information presented at these sites.

About the Author

Barbara Aehlert is President of Southwest EMS Education, Inc., in Phoenix, Arizona, and Pursley, Texas. She has been a registered nurse for more than 30 years, with clinical experience in medical/surgical and critical care nursing and, for the past 21 years, in prehospital education. Barbara is an active CPR, First Aid, ACLS, and PALS instructor. She is Director of Field Training for Southwest Ambulance in Mesa, Arizona, and an active member of the Pursley, Texas, Volunteer Fire Department.

Contents

Preface

This workbook provides you with an opportunity to review and master the concepts and skills introduced in your textbook, *Emergency Medical Technician: EMT in Action,* First Edition. Chapter by chapter, the workbook provides the following:

Reading Assignment
Provides corresponding textbook page numbers for review prior to completing the workbook exercises.

Sum It Up
A bulleted list of the key information covered in the chapter.

Tracking Your Progress
Readers can check off the objectives they have mastered after learning the chapter content.

Quiz Content
Includes a full range of question types: true or false, multiple choice, sentence completion, matching, and short answer. Each quiz allows the reader to ensure that he or she has mastered the information presented in the text chapter or appendix.

Quiz Answers
Provided at the end of each chapter.

Together, your textbook and this workbook form a complete learning package. *Emergency Medical Technician: EMT in Action,* First Edition, will help you prepare to provide safe and immediate patient care and to work effectively as part of an EMS team.

Contributors

Lynn Browne-Wagner, RN
LBW, LLC
Phoenix, AZ

Randy Budd, RRT, CEP
City of Mesa Fire Department
Mesa, AZ

Major Raymond W. Burton (Retired)
Plymouth Academy/Plymouth County Sheriff's
  Academy
Plymouth, MA

Holly Button, CEP
City of Mesa Fire Department
Mesa, AZ

Suzy Coronel, CEP
Sportsmedicine Fairbanks
Fairbanks, AK

Janet Fitts, RN, EMT-P
Educational Consultant
Prehospital and Emergency Medical Services
Pacific, MO

Paul Honeywell, CEP
Southwest Ambulance
Mesa, AZ

Travis Kidd, EMT-P
Orange County Fire/Rescue
Orlando, FL

Andrea Legamaro, RN
Southwest EMS Education, Inc.
Dallas, TX

Terence Mason, RN
City of Mesa Fire Department
Mesa, AZ

Kim McKenna, RN, EMT-P
Director of Education
St. Charles County Ambulance Service
St. Peters, MO

Sean Newton, CEP
City of Scottsdale Fire Department
Scottsdale, AZ

Jeff Pennington, CEP
City of Gilbert Fire Department
Gilbert, AZ

Gary Smith, MD
Medical Director: Apache Junction, Gilbert,
  and Mesa Fire Departments
Apache Junction, Gilbert, and Mesa, AZ

Edith Valladares
Director, Foreign Languages and Academic ESL
Central Piedmont Community College
Charlotte, NC

Reviewers

Terrell Buckson, BS, NREMT-P
MIEMSS
Baltimore, MD

Rick Criste
Fayetteville Technical Community College
Fayetteville, NC

Lyndal M. Curry, M.A., NREMT-P
University of South Alabama
Mobile, AL

Bradley Dean, BBA, NREMT-P
Davidson County Emergency Services
Lexington, NC

Lawrence A. Linder, MA. NREMTP
Hillsborough Community College
Tampa, FL

Keith Monosky, MPM, EMT-P
Assistant Professor, Department of Emergency Medicine
George Washington University
Ashburn, VA

Nikhil Natarajan, NREMT-P, CCEMT-P, I/C
SUNY Ulster
Stone Ridge, NY

Kenneth Navarro
University of Texas Southwestern Medical School
Dallas, TX

Keith A. Ozenberger, BS, LP
University of Texas Medical Branch
Galveston, TX

Brad J. Scoggins
University of Texas Medical Branch
Galveston, TX

William Seifarth
MIEMSS
Baltimore, MD

Tom Vines
Carbon Co. SAR/Mainrod
Red Lodge, MT

Preparatory

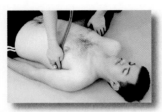

READING ASSIGNMENT ▶ Read Chapter 1, pages 3 to 26 in your textbook.

Sum It Up

- An EMT is a member of the EMS team who provides prehospital emergency care.
- A healthcare system is a network of people, facilities, and equipment designed to provide for the general medical needs of the population.
- The EMS system is part of the healthcare system. It consists of a coordinated network of resources that provides emergency care and transportation to victims of sudden illness and injury.
- There are four levels of nationally recognized prehospital professionals: EMR, EMT, AEMT, and Paramedic. EMRs and EMTs provide Basic Life Support. AEMTs and Paramedics provide Advanced Life Support.
- Every EMS system must have a medical director. A medical director is a physician who provides medical oversight and is responsible for making sure that the emergency care provided to ill or injured patients is medically appropriate.
- Medical oversight may be on-line or off-line. On-line medical direction is direct communication with a physician by radio or telephone, or face-to-face communication at the scene before a skill is performed or care is given. Off-line medical direction is the medical supervision of EMS personnel using policies, treatment protocols, standing orders, education, and quality management review.
- Quality management is a system of internal and external reviews and audits of all aspects of an EMS system. Quality management is used to identify areas of the EMS system needing improvement. This system helps to make sure that the patient receives the highest quality medical care.
- The phases of a typical EMS response include detection of the emergency, reporting the emergency (the call made for assistance, dispatch), dispatch/ response (medical resources sent to the scene), on-scene care, care during transport, and transfer to definitive care.
- The roles of an EMT include personal, crew, patient, and bystander safety; gaining access to the patient; performing a patient assessment to identify life-threatening conditions; continuing care through additional EMS resources; providing initial patient care based on the assessment findings;

assisting with additional emergency care; documenting the emergency per local and state requirements; and acting as a public safety liaison.

- The responsibilities of an EMT include personal health and safety; maintaining a caring attitude and composure; maintaining a neat, clean, and professional appearance; maintaining up-to-date knowledge and skills; and maintaining current knowledge of local, state, and national issues affecting EMS.

- EMTs are subject to state laws that specify the medical procedures and functions that can be performed. Recognition as a nationally registered EMT, which is known as certification, requires successful completion of a written and practical skills examination. Participating in CE courses or an EMT Refresher Course is required for recertification.

▶ Tracking Your Progress

After reading this chapter, can you:	Page Reference	Objective Met?
• Define EMS systems?	9	☐
• Differentiate the roles and responsibilities of the EMT from other prehospital care providers?	11	☐
• Describe the roles and responsibilities related to personal safety?	20	☐
• Discuss the roles and responsibilities of the EMT toward the safety of the crew, the patient, and bystanders?	20	☐
• Define quality management and discuss the EMT's role in the process?	16	☐
• Define medical direction and discuss the EMT's role in the process?	13	☐
• State the specific statutes and regulations in your state regarding the EMS system?	10	☐

True or False

Decide whether each statement is true or false. In the space provided, write *T* for true or *F* for false.

_____ **1.** The passage of the Highway Safety Act of 1966 was the first national commitment to reducing the number of highway-related injuries and deaths.

_____ **2.** The patient, patient's family, or bystanders may view the attention you pay to your personal hygiene and appearance as a reflection of the care that you will provide.

_____ **3.** A scene size-up is performed to sort patients by the seriousness of their injuries.

_____ **4.** Your contact with the patient, family, bystanders, and other members of the healthcare team must be respectful and professional, even in stressful or chaotic situations.

Multiple Choice

In the space provided, identify the letter of the choice that best completes the statement or answers each question.

_____ 5. Which of the following levels of prehospital professionals have the ability to assess patients, give intravenous medications, and perform advanced airway procedures?
   a. Emergency Medical Responder and Emergency Medical Technician
   b. Emergency Medical Technician and Advanced Emergency Medical Technician
   c. Emergency Medical Responder and Paramedic
   d. Advanced Emergency Medical Technician and Paramedic

_____ 6. A treatment protocol may be defined as
   a. communication with a physician when providing emergency care to an ill or injured patient.
   b. your best guess as to the treatment to be provided to an ill or injured patient.
   c. a list of steps to be followed when providing emergency care to an ill or injured patient.
   d. a set of guidelines developed by the DOT to be used when providing emergency care to an ill or injured patient.

_____ 7. States use the standards set by which of the following organizations to evaluate the effectiveness of their EMS system?
   a. NHTSA
   b. Federal Communications Commission
   c. American College of Surgeons
   d. American College of Emergency Physicians

_____ 8. You and your EMT partner respond to a motor vehicle crash in which two patients are found trapped inside a vehicle. The patients are assessed, and medical control is then contacted by telephone. This communication is an example of
   a. on-line medical control.
   b. off-line medical control.
   c. prospective medical control.
   d. retrospective medical control.

_____ 9. A 30-year-old man has experienced severe injuries as a result of a motor vehicle crash. To which of the following specialty centers should the patient be transported for definitive care?
   a. Stroke Center
   b. Rehabilitation Center
   c. Poison Center
   d. Trauma Center

_____ 10. The four nationally recognized levels of prehospital professionals, _from least to most advanced_, are
   a. Paramedic, Advanced Emergency Medical Technician, Emergency Medical Technician, and Emergency Medical Responder.
   b. Emergency Medical Technician, Emergency Medical Responder, Advanced Emergency Medical Technician, and Paramedic.
   c. Emergency Medical Responder, Advanced Emergency Medical Technician, Emergency Medical Technician, and Paramedic.
   d. Emergency Medical Responder, Emergency Medical Technician, Advanced Emergency Medical Technician, and Paramedic.

_____ 11. Which of the following organizations contributes to the development of professional standards and verifies the skills and knowledge of EMS professionals by preparing and conducting examinations?
   a. The National Association of State EMS Directors
   b. The National Association of Emergency Physicians
   c. The National Registry of Emergency Medical Technicians
   d. The National Council of State EMS Training Coordinators

Questions 12-13 pertain to the following scenario.

You arrive on the scene of a motor vehicle crash involving a minivan. You observe heavy damage to the vehicle.

_____ 12. Your *primary* concern at the scene of this emergency should be

    a. the well-being of the patient.

    b. personal safety.

    c. bystander safety.

    d. determining the total number of patients.

_____ 13. Before approaching the patient, you should

    a. await the arrival of personnel with more advanced medical training.

    b. contact a physician for instructions about how to proceed.

    c. put on PPE and size up the scene.

    d. determine the location of the nearest hospital.

_____ 14. The EMS system is usually activated by using

    a. pagers.

    b. telephones.

    c. citizen band radios.

    d. emergency alarm boxes.

_____ 15. The process by which a physician directs the emergency care provided by EMS personnel to an ill or injured patient is called

    a. medical oversight.

    b. certification.

    c. system regulation.

    d. resource management.

_____ 16. While on the scene of a motor vehicle crash, you note that the patient has an open femur fracture and is bleeding profusely. With continued assessments, you note the patient's blood pressure is dropping rapidly. You recognize that the patient is in need of ALS care. You notify the dispatcher that ALS assistance is required. She informs you that the ALS unit is on the way with an estimated time of arrival in 6 minutes. The closest appropriate facility is about 15 minutes away. Based on this information, your best course of action will be to

    a. explain to the patient that the ALS unit is on the way and return to your station.

    b. radio the ALS unit and determine a location to meet so you may pick up the ALS provider and then continue transporting the patient to the hospital.

    c. wait at the scene until the ALS unit arrives.

    d. radio the ALS unit and have them meet you at the hospital.

Sentence Completion

In the blanks provided, write the words that best complete each sentence.

17. A(n) _____ _____ _____ system is a network of resources that provides emergency care and transportation to victims of sudden illness or injury.

18. A(n) _____ is an unexpected illness or injury that requires immediate action to avoid risking the life or health of the person being treated.

Matching

Match the key terms in the left column with the definitions in the right column by placing the letter of each correct answer in the space provided.

_____ 19. Emergency transportation

_____ 20. Extrication

_____ 21. National EMS Education Standards

_____ 22. Healthcare system

_____ 23. Patient assessment

_____ 24. Standard of care

_____ 25. National EMS Scope of Practice Model

_____ 26. Personal space

_____ 27. Quality management

_____ 28. On-line medical direction

_____ 29. Enhanced 9-1-1

_____ 30. Statutes

A. Direct communication with a physician (or his designee) by radio or telephone or face-to-face communication at the scene before performing a skill or administering care

B. A system of internal and external reviews of all aspects of an EMS system; this system is used to identify the aspects that need improvement to ensure that the public receives the highest quality of prehospital care

C. The invisible area immediately around each of us that we declare as our own

D. The process of moving a patient from the scene of an emergency to an appropriate healthcare facility

E. Laws established by Congress and state legislatures

F. A document that defines four levels of EMS professionals and what each level of EMS professional legally can and cannot do

G. A system that routes an emergency call to the 9-1-1 center closest to the caller and automatically displays the caller's phone number and address

H. A network of people, facilities, and equipment designed to provide for the general medical needs of the population

I. To remove from entrapment

J. The minimum level of care expected of similarly trained healthcare professionals

K. A document that specifies the competencies, clinical behaviors, and judgments that each level of EMS professional must meet when completing their education

L. The process of evaluating a person for signs of illness or injury

Short Answer

Answer each question in the space provided.

31. In 1996, NHTSA published the *EMS Agenda for the Future*. This document proposed continued development of 14 EMS attributes. List the 14 attributes identified in this document.

    1.

    2.

    3.

    4.

    5.

    6.

    7.

    8.

    9.

    10.

    11.

    12.

    13.

    14.

32. List the four Cs that you should use when giving a verbal report to another healthcare professional about the patient care you have provided.

    1.

    2.

    3.

    4.

33. List five areas that are typically included in an EMS quality management program.

    1.

    2.

    3.

    4.

    5.

34. List five traits of an EMS professional.

    1.

    2.

    3.

    4.

    5.

35. List four responsibilities of an EMT.

    1.

    2.

    3.

    4.

Answer Section

Chapter 1

True/False

1. True

The Highway Safety Act of 1966 charged the DOT NHTSA with the responsibility of improving EMS. The act provided funding for the development of national highway safety programs and established standards for training EMTs.

Objective: N/A

2. True

If you are courteous, respectful, and present a professional appearance, they are reassured that you will provide quality patient care. If your appearance is untidy or you are ill-mannered, they may assume that the care that you will provide will be of poor quality.

Objective: N/A

3. False

Upon arriving at the scene, EMTs quickly size up the scene to find out if it is safe to enter. A scene size-up is done to:

- Find out if the scene is safe
- Identify the mechanism of injury or the nature of the illness
- Identify the total number of patients
- Request additional help if necessary

Objective: Describe the roles and responsibilities related to personal safety.

4. True

As an EMT, others will look to you as the person in control of the situation. Even though you may feel anxious, you must be able to adapt to these situations, remain calm, and display confidence.

Objective: N/A

Multiple Choice

5. d

An EMR is a person who has the basic knowledge and skills necessary to provide lifesaving emergency care while waiting for the arrival of additional EMS help (formerly called First Responder). AEMTs and Paramedics can perform all EMT skills and have received additional training in patient assessment, providing IV fluids and medications, advanced airway procedures, and monitoring heart rhythms.

Objective: Differentiate the roles and responsibilities of an EMT from other prehospital care professionals.

6. c

A treatment protocol is a list of steps to be followed when providing emergency care to an ill or injured patient. For example, a patient experiencing a heat-related illness may be treated by using the steps outlined in a Heat-Related Emergencies treatment protocol.

Objective: Define medical direction and discuss the EMT's role in the process.

7. a

In 1988, NHTSA began a statewide EMS system TAP. This program identified 10 essential parts of an EMS system and the methods used to assess these areas. States use the standards set by NHTSA to evaluate how effective their EMS system is.

Objective: N/A

8. a

On-line medical direction is direct communication with a physician by radio or telephone—or face-to-face communication at the scene—before performing a skill or administering care.

Objective: Define medical direction and discuss the EMT's role in the process.

9. d

A Trauma Center is a specialty center where specially trained personnel and equipment are available 24 hours a day to care for patients with serious injuries.

Objective: Discuss the roles and responsibilities of the EMT toward the safety of the crew, the patient, and bystanders.

10. d

The 4 nationally recognized levels of prehospital professionals, *from least to most advanced*, are Emergency Medical Responder, Emergency Medical Technician, Advanced Emergency Medical Technician, and Paramedic.

Objective: Differentiate the roles and responsibilities of an EMT from other prehospital care professionals.

11. c

The National Registry of EMTs provides examinations for certification and registration that may be required by your state. Recognition as a nationally registered EMT requires successful completion of a written and practical skills examination.

Objective: N/A

12. b

Although the patient's well-being is an important concern at the scene of an emergency, your personal safety must be your primary concern, followed by the safety of your crew, patients, and bystanders.

Objective: Describe the roles and responsibilities related to personal safety.

13. c

When you arrive at the scene and before you begin patient care, size up the scene. You should first determine if the scene is safe. You should then identify the mechanism of the injury or the nature of the illness, identify the total number of patients, and request additional help if necessary. Before approaching the patient, put on appropriate PPE. This helps reduce your risk of exposure to potentially infectious body fluid substances or other infectious agents.

Objective: Describe the roles and responsibilities related to personal safety.

14. b

EMS is usually activated by dialing 9-1-1. Other methods of activating an emergency response include emergency alarm boxes, citizen band radios, amateur radios, local access numbers, and wireless telephones.

Objective: N/A

15. a

Medical oversight is the process by which a physician directs the emergency care provided by EMS personnel to an ill or injured patient. It is also referred to as *medical control* or *medical direction*.

Objective: Define medical direction and discuss the EMT's role in the process.

16. b

You should determine the quickest way to provide the care the patient needs. You need to pick up the ALS provider on the way to the hospital so you do not delay patient care. Delaying this patient's care may result in severe blood loss, permanent damage, and a life-threatening condition. Having the ALS unit intercept while transporting the patient is necessary in this situation to ensure the highest level of medical care is provided. It is the quickest way to allow the patient to receive definitive care.

Objective: Discuss the roles and responsibilities of the EMT toward the safety of the crew, the patient, and bystanders.

Sentence Completion

17. An **Emergency** **Medical** **Services** system is a network of resources that provides emergency care and transportation to victims of sudden illness or injury.

Objective: Define EMS systems.

18. An **emergency** is an unexpected illness or injury that requires immediate action to avoid risking the life or health of the person being treated.

Objective: N/A

Matching

19.	D	**25.**	F
20.	I	**26.**	C
21.	K	**27.**	B
22.	H	**28.**	A
23.	L	**29.**	G
24.	J	**30.**	E

Short Answer

31. In 1996, NHTSA published the EMS Agenda for the Future. Because it also recommended directions for future EMS development in the United States, this paper is often called a *vision document.* This document reviewed the progress made in EMS over 30 years and proposed continued development of 14 EMS attributes. They are:

    1. Integration of Health Services

    2. EMS Research

    3. Legislation and Regulation

    4. System Finance

    5. Human Resources

    6. Medical Direction

    7. Education Systems

    8. Public Education

    9. Prevention

    10. Public Access

    11. Communication Systems

    12. Clinical Care

    13. Information Systems

    14. Evaluation

    Objective: N/A

32. When transferring patient care to a healthcare professional with medical training equal to or greater than your own, first identify yourself as an EMT. Then give the receiving healthcare professional a brief explanation about what happened, the position in which the patient was found, your assessment findings, the emergency care you gave, and the patient's response to the treatment given. Remember the 4 Cs when giving a verbal report:

    1. *C*ourteous

    2. *C*lear

    3. *C*omplete

    4. *C*oncise

    Objective: N/A

33. Quality management involves the constant monitoring of performance and is an important part of EMS. It includes:

- Obtaining information from the patient, other EMS professionals, and facility personnel about the quality and appropriateness of the medical care you provided
- Reviewing and evaluating your documentation of an emergency call
- Evaluating your ability to properly perform skills
- Evaluating your professionalism during interactions with the patient, EMS professionals, and other healthcare personnel
- Evaluating your ability to follow policies and protocols
- Evaluating your participation in continuing education opportunities

Your commitment to and participation in the quality management process is important in improving the EMS system. When your medical director or another healthcare professional provides you with feedback about an area monitored by the process, be sure to maintain a positive and professional attitude. Use the information shared as an opportunity for personal and professional growth.

Objective: Define quality management and discuss the EMTs role in the process.

34. Personal traits of an EMS professional include the following:

- Professional appearance, attitude, and conduct
- Professional oral and written communications
- Mastery of EMS knowledge and skills
- Confidence and leadership abilities
- Compassionate patient advocate
- Good moral character
- The ability to adapt to situations by using sound judgment

Objective: N/A

35. Responsibilities of the EMT include the following:

- Personal health and safety
- Composure and a caring attitude
- Neat, clean, and professional appearance
- Up-to-date knowledge and skills
- Current knowledge of local, state, and national issues affecting EMS

Objective: Differentiate the roles and responsibilities of an EMT from other prehospital care professionals.

2 The Well-Being of the Emergency Medical Technician

READING ASSIGNMENT ▶ Read Chapter 2, pages 27 to 53 in your textbook.

Sum It Up

- As an EMT, you will encounter many stressful situations. Whatever the situation, you must act professionally. It is important that you learn how to recognize the signs and symptoms of stress in yourself and others.

- Critically ill or injured patients may experience grief, which is a normal response to a loss of any kind. The five stages of grief are denial, anger, bargaining, depression, and acceptance. Remember that a person going through grief may skip a stage, go through more than one stage at the same time, or go through each stage more than once. Cultural factors will influence how a person experiences grief.

- Patients may experience any number of emotions in response to their illness or injury. As an EMT, you must be respectful of each patient. Listen with empathy to the patient's concerns but do not give the patient false hope or false reassurance. In dealing with the patient's family or friends or with bystanders, you may need to use many of the same approaches you use in dealing with patients.

- Some patients may not want aggressive efforts aimed at reviving them when they are dying. These patients may have an advance directive or a DNR order. An advance directive is a legal document that details a person's healthcare wishes when he becomes unable to make decisions for himself. A DNR order is written by a physician. It instructs medical professionals not to provide medical care to a patient who has experienced a cardiac arrest.

- The signs of obvious death include decapitation (beheading), putrefaction (decomposition), dependent lividity, and rigor mortis. If a person shows signs of obvious death, do not disturb the body or scene. The police or medical examiner will need to authorize removing the body. You should document the victim's position and his injuries. You should also document the conditions at the scene as well as statements of persons at the scene.

- As an EMS professional, you will experience personal stress and will encounter patients and bystanders in severe stress. A stressor is any event or condition that has the potential to cause bodily or mental tension. In order to be an effective EMT, you must learn to recognize the physical, behavioral, mental, or emotional signs of stress.

- You should manage stress through lifestyle changes. These changes include developing good dietary habits, exercising, and practicing relaxation techniques. You should also seek to create balance in your life, including time with family and friends.
- Professional help may be needed to help you cope with stress. Many organizations have employee assistance programs that offer confidential counseling to prehospital professionals.
- CISM is a program that assists emergency workers in coping with stressful situations. The results of some studies raise doubts about the effectiveness of CISM.
- An EMT is responsible for ensuring the safety of the crew, the patient, and bystanders. However, an EMT's first priority is ensuring his own safety at all scenes. This responsibility includes protecting one's self against disease transmission, which includes using personal protective equipment and having the proper vaccinations. It also involves safety at hazardous materials scenes, motor vehicle crashes and rescue scenes, and violent scenes.

▶ Tracking Your Progress

After reading this chapter, can you:	Page Reference	Objective Met?
• List possible emotional reactions that you may experience when faced with trauma, illness, death, and dying?	28	☐
• Discuss the possible reactions that a family member may exhibit when confronted with death and dying?	36	☐
• State the steps in your approach to the family confronted with death and dying?	36	☐
• State the possible reactions that your family may exhibit?	40	☐
• Recognize the signs and symptoms of critical incident stress?	41	☐
• State possible steps that you may take to help reduce/alleviate stress?	39	☐
• Explain the need to determine scene safety?	42	☐
• Discuss the importance of BSI precautions?	43	☐
• Describe the steps you should take for personal protection from airborne and bloodborne pathogens?	44	☐
• List the PPE necessary for each of the following situations: hazardous materials, rescue operations, violent scenes, crime scenes, electricity, water and ice, exposure to bloodborne pathogens, exposure to airborne pathogens?	46, 50, 51	☐

True or False

Decide whether each statement is true or false. In the space provided, write *T* for true or *F* for false.

_____ 1. An emergency is what the patient perceives it to be.

_____ 2. BSI precautions include handwashing; using PPE; and proper cleaning, disinfecting, and disposing of soiled materials and equipment.

Multiple Choice

In the space provided, identify the letter of the choice that best completes the statement or answers each question.

_____ 3. A normal response that helps a person cope with the loss of someone or something that had great meaning to them is known as
   a. stress.
   b. definition.
   c. grief.
   d. anger.

_____ 4. During the _____ stage of the grieving process, the person may use phrases such as, "Not me!" or "This can't be happening."
   a. denial
   b. anger
   c. bargaining
   d. depression

_____ 5. A stressor is an event or condition that has the potential to cause bodily or mental tension. Dealing with an agitated, combative, or abusive patient is an example of
   a. an environmental stressor.
   b. a psychosocial stressor.
   c. a personal stressor.
   d. a physical stressor.

_____ 6. When dealing with hazardous materials, it is important to remember that the placard represents which of the following combinations?
   a. Flammable, explosive, radioactive, combustible
   b. Flammable, radioactive, explosive, poisonous
   c. Explosive, poisonous, flammable, sterilization
   d. Poisonous, flammable, radioactive, disinfection

_____ 7. The process of washing a contaminated object with soap and water is known as
   a. cleaning.
   b. disinfection.
   c. sterilization.
   d. asepsis.

_____ 8. The direct or indirect contact with infected blood, body fluids, tissues, or airborne droplets is known as
   a. an infection.
   b. a pathogen.
   c. an exposure.
   d. dependent lividity.

_____ 9. Hepatitis A is an example of which communicable disease?
   a. Airborne
   b. Bloodborne
   c. Sexually transmitted
   d. Foodborne

_____ 10. Which of the following is the best example of direct contact?
   a. Contact with a needle used on a patient
   b. Contact with a patient's drinking glass
   c. Contact with a patient who is coughing
   d. Contact with drainage from a patient's open wound

_____ 11. When dealing with stressful situation, you notice your palms are sweaty, you have a headache, and your heart is pounding. These are examples of which type of stress response?
   a. Mental
   b. Emotional
   c. Physical
   d. Behavioral

_____ 12. Which of the following statements regarding handwashing is correct?
   a. Vigorous handwashing is unnecessary if adequate soap is used.
   b. Be sure to use a towel to turn off the faucet when you are finished washing your hands.
   c. It is best to leave all jewelry on during handwashing to get it thoroughly clean.
   d. When wearing gloves, it is not necessary to wash your hands after caring for your patient.

_____ 13. You should wear a HEPA mask when providing care to a patient known or suspected to be infected with
   a. tuberculosis.
   b. measles.
   c. hepatitis B.
   d. tetanus.

_____ **14.** HBV and HIV are examples of
   a. airborne diseases.   **c.** foodborne diseases.
   b. bloodborne diseases.   **d.** sexually transmitted diseases.

Sentence Completion

In the blanks provided, write the words that best complete each sentence.

15. _____ are germs capable of producing disease, such as bacteria and viruses.

16. An _____ is an illness that results when the body is invaded by germs capable of producing disease.

17. A(n) _____ disease is an infection that is spread by droplets produced by coughing or sneezing.

Matching

Match the key terms in the left column with the definitions in the right column by placing the letter of each correct answer in the space provided.

_____ **18.** Dependent lividity

_____ **19.** Advance directive

_____ **20.** Depression

_____ **21.** Rigor mortis

_____ **22.** Empathy

_____ **23.** Stressor

_____ **24.** Do Not Resuscitate order

_____ **25.** Putrefaction

A. To understand, be aware of, and be sensitive to the feelings, thoughts, and experience of another

B. Instructions written by a physician that notify medical professionals not to provide medical care to a patient who has experienced a cardiac arrest

C. Any event or condition that has the potential to cause bodily or mental tension

D. A legal document that details a person's healthcare wishes when he becomes unable to make decisions for himself

E. The decomposition of organic matter, such as body tissues

F. The settling of blood in dependent areas of the body (those areas on which the body has been resting)

G. A normal response to the loss of a significant other or the loss of some bodily function

H. Stiffening of body muscles that occurs after death

Short Answer

Answer each question in the space provided.

26. List four possible responses to stress that the family and friends of an EMS professional may exhibit.
   1.
   2.
   3.
   4.

27. List five signs of cumulative stress.
   1.
   2.
   3.
   4.
   5.

28. You receive a call for a woman who is about to give birth at home. What items of PPE should you use in this situation?

29. What is the single most important method you can use to prevent the spread of communicable disease?

30. List three lifestyle changes you can take to help reduce stress.

1.

2.

3.

31. You are called to the scene of a motor vehicle crash. A patient requires removal from one of the vehicles involved in the crash. List four items of protective clothing that should be worn during this situation.

1.

2.

3.

4.

Questions 32-34 pertain to the following scenario.

You respond to a residence for a possible drowning. You arrive to find law enforcement personnel performing CPR on a 3-year-old male. The child was found floating facedown in the pool. He was last seen 10 or 15 minutes ago.

32. The child's mother has arrived on the scene. Describe the possible reactions of the child's mother to this situation.

33. The child is transported to the hospital. Despite continued efforts to resuscitate him, the child is pronounced dead. List the possible emotional reactions that you may experience because of this situation.

34. The mother has been told of her child's death. List the five stages of the grief process in the order that most people experience them.

1.

2.

3.

4.

5.

Answer Section

Chapter 2

True/False

1. True

   What a patient considers an emergency may not appear to be an emergency to a person with medical training. It is important for you as the EMS professional to provide the best emergency care you can for every patient without questioning the validity of the complaint.

   Objective: N/A

2. True

   BSI precautions refer to self-protection against all body fluids and substances. Precautions include handwashing and using personal protective equipment. They also include the proper cleaning, disinfecting, and disposing of soiled materials and equipment.

   Objective: Discuss the importance of BSI precautions.

Multiple Choice

3. c

   This is the definition of grief. Grief is most often associated with death but can be present with any change if the person feels a significant loss.

   Objective: List possible emotional reactions that the EMT may experience when faced with trauma, illness, death, and dying.

4. a

   During the denial stage of the grief process, the person is unable or refuses to believe the reality of what has happened. Denial is a defense mechanism often used as a buffer against the shock of dying or dealing with an illness or injury.

   Objective: Discuss the possible reactions that a family member may exhibit when confronted with death and dying.

5. b

   Dealing with an agitated, combative, or abusive patient is an example of a psychosocial stressor.

   Objective: N/A

6. b

   A placard is a 4-sided, diamond-shaped sign. It is displayed on trucks, railroad cars, and large containers that carry hazardous materials. The placard will also contain a class or division number that indicates whether the material is flammable, radioactive, explosive, or poisonous.

   Objective: Explain the need to determine scene safety.

7. a

   The use of soap and water to wash a contaminated object is known as cleaning. To disinfect an object you must use a chemical solution such as alcohol or chlorine. The process that uses boiling water, radiation, gas, chemicals, or superheated steam to destroy all of the germs on an object is sterilization.

   Objective: Describe the steps the EMT should take for personal protection from airborne and bloodborne pathogens.

8. c

   An exposure is direct or indirect contact with infected blood, body fluids, tissues, or airborne droplets. An accidental exposure to infectious material can occur when your skin is pricked or cut, allowing the entry of germs. Germs can also enter your body through nicks or scrapes on your skin or through mucous membranes (such as your eyes, nose, and mouth). An exposure to a communicable disease does not automatically result in infection. Dependent lividity is the settling of blood in dependent areas of the body.

   Objective: Discuss the importance of BSI precautions.

9. d

Hepatitis A is an example of a foodborne disease that is spread by improper handling of food or by poor personal hygiene.

Objective: Discuss the importance of BSI precautions.

10. d

Contact with drainage from a patient's open wound is an example of direct contact transmission. Coughing is an example of airborne or droplet transmission. Contact with a needle or drinking glass are examples of indirect contact transmission.

Objective: Discuss the importance of BSI precautions.

11. c

These are all physical signs of stress.

Objective: Recognize the signs and symptoms of critical incident stress.

12. b

It is important to remember to use a towel when turning off the faucet after washing your hands. The faucet contains germs, and it is important not to touch any part of the sink once your hands are clean. You must wash your hands before and after each patient contact and wash for at least 10 to 15 seconds (longer if exposed to blood or body fluids). Jewelry must be removed before handwashing. Even if gloves were worn during patient care, you must wash your hands after patient care is complete and the gloves have been removed.

Objective: Discuss the importance of BSI precautions.

13. a

If you know or suspect that your patient has tuberculosis, wear an N-95 or HEPA mask.

Objective: Describe the steps the EMT should take for personal protection from airborne and bloodborne pathogens.

14. b

Bloodborne diseases are spread by contact with the blood or body fluids of an infected person. Examples include HBV, hepatitis C, HIV, and syphilis. When caring for patients, assume that all human blood and body fluids are infectious. For your safety, use appropriate BSI precautions during *every* patient contact.

Objective: Describe the steps the EMT should take for personal protection from airborne and bloodborne pathogens.

Sentence Completion

15. **Pathogens** are germs capable of producing disease, such as bacteria and viruses.

Objective: N/A

16. An **infection** is an illness that results when the body is invaded by germs capable of producing disease.

Objective: N/A

17. An **airborne** disease is an infection that is spread by droplets produced by coughing or sneezing.

Objective: N/A

Matching

18.	F	22.	A
19.	D	23.	C
20.	G	24.	B
21.	H	25.	E

Short Answer

26. Possible responses to stress that the family and friends of an EMS professional may exhibit include the following:

1. Lack of understanding of prehospital care
2. Fear of separation or being ignored
3. Frustration caused by the "on-call" nature of the job and the inability to plan activities
4. Frustration caused by wanting to share

Objective: State the possible reactions that the family of the EMT may exhibit.

27. Cumulative stress (also called *burnout*) is common in EMS. It results from repeated exposure to smaller stressors that build up over time. Cumulative stress may include not getting enough sleep for several days in a row, job-related problems, or family and relationship issues. Signs of cumulative stress may include the following:

• Physical and emotional exhaustion
• A negative attitude toward others
• A disrespectful attitude toward patients
• Increased absences

- Emotional outbursts
- Decreased work performance

Objective: Recognize the signs and symptoms of critical incident stress.

28. You will need gloves, gown, mask, and a face shield when caring for this patient because of the high risk of blood and body fluid exposure.

    Objective: List the PPE necessary for exposure to bloodborne pathogens.

29. Handwashing is the single most important method you can use to prevent the spread of communicable disease. BSI precautions should be used with handwashing to ensure proper protection against communicable disease for you and your patient.

    Objective: Discuss the importance of BSI precautions.

30. 1. Develop good dietary habits
    2. Exercise
    3. Practice relaxation techniques

    Objective: State possible steps that the EMT may take to help reduce/alleviate stress.

31. Personal protective clothing that should be worn during this situation includes the following (any four):

    - Puncture-proof gloves
    - Turnout gear
    - Helmet
    - Eye protection (such as heavy goggles)
    - Boots with steel toes

    Objective: List the PPE necessary for rescue operations.

32. People react differently to situations involving illness and injury. The child's mother may express anger, rage, despair, crying, feelings of guilt, or she may show little reaction.

    Objective: Discuss the possible reactions that a family member may exhibit when confronted with death and dying.

33. Despite your best efforts to resuscitate a patient, you may experience emotions such as anger, anxiety, frustration, fear, grief, and feelings of helplessness when a patient dies. These emotions are common and expected, and you should not feel embarrassed or ashamed when a situation like this affects you.

    Objective: List possible emotional reactions that the EMT may experience when faced with trauma, illness, death, and dying.

34. The five stages of grief:

    1. Denial
    2. Anger
    3. Bargaining
    4. Depression
    5. Acceptance

    Objective: Discuss the possible reactions that a family member may exhibit when confronted with death and dying.

READING ASSIGNMENT ▶   Read Chapter 3, pages 54 to 68 in your textbook.

Sum It Up

- The scope of practice includes the emergency care and skills an EMT is legally allowed and expected to perform. These duties are set by state laws and regulations. As an EMT, your ethical responsibilities include treating all patients with respect and giving each patient the best care you are capable of giving. You must also determine if the patient is competent (that is, if he can understand the questions you ask him and the consequences of the decisions he makes about his care).

- A competent patient must give you his consent (permission) before you can provide him with emergency care. Expressed consent is one in which a patient gives specific permission for care and transport to be provided. Expressed consent may be given verbally, in writing, or nonverbally. Implied consent is consent assumed from a patient requiring emergency care who is mentally, physically, or emotionally unable to provide expressed consent.

- Mentally competent adults have the right to refuse care and transport. As an EMT, you must make sure that the patient fully understands your explanation and the consequences of refusing treatment or transport. In high-risk situations in which the patient's injuries may not be obvious, you must contact medical direction or call ALS personnel to the scene to assess the patient.

- An advance directive is a form filled out by the patient. It outlines the patient's wishes for their care if they are not able to express their wishes. A DNR order is written by a physician and details the patient's wishes for care when he is terminally ill.

- Assault is considered threatening to, attempting to, or causing a fear of offensive physical contact with a patient or other person. Battery is the unlawful touching of another person without consent. Because each state has its own definitions of assault and battery, you should check your local protocols concerning these terms.

- Abandonment is terminating patient care without making sure that care will continue at the same level or higher. You can also be charged with abandonment if you stop patient care when the patient still needs and desires additional care.

- When a healthcare professional is negligent, he fails to act as a reasonable, careful, similarly trained person would act under similar circumstances. Negligence includes the following four elements:
  1. the duty to act,
  2. a breach of that duty,
  3. injury or damages (physical or psychological) that result, and
  4. proximate cause (the actions or inactions of the healthcare professional that caused the injury or damages).
- A medical identification device is used to alert healthcare personnel to a patient's particular medical condition. This identification device may be in the form of a bracelet, a necklace, or an identification card.
- If you are sent to a crime scene, you must wait for law enforcement personnel to declare that the scene is safe to enter. After you are certain the scene is safe and you ensure your safety, your first priority will be patient care. You should be alert and document anything unusual on the call.
- An organ donor is a person who has a signed legal document to donate his organs in the event of his death. The patient may have an organ donor card or may have indicated his intent to be a donor on his driver's license.

▶ Tracking Your Progress

After reading this chapter, can you:	Page Reference	Objective Met?
• Define the EMT-Basic scope of practice?	56	☐
• Discuss the importance of DNR (advance directives) and local or state provisions regarding EMS application?	60	☐
• Define consent and discuss the methods of obtaining consent?	58	☐
• Differentiate between expressed and implied consent?	58	☐
• Explain the role of consent with regard to minors in providing care?	59	☐
• Discuss the implications for the EMT in patient refusal of transport?	59	☐
• Discuss the issues of abandonment, negligence, and battery and their implications to the EMT?	62, 63	☐
• State the conditions necessary for an EMT to have a duty to act?	63	☐
• Explain the importance, necessity, and legality of patient confidentiality?	64	☐
• Discuss the considerations of the EMT in issues of organ retrieval?	66	☐
• Differentiate the actions that an EMT should take to assist in the preservation of a crime scene?	66	☐
• State the conditions that require an EMT to notify local law enforcement officials?	66	☐

True or False

Decide whether each statement is true or false. In the space provided, write T for true or F for false.

_____ **1.** The emergency care and skills an EMT is legally allowed and expected to perform are set by state laws and regulations.

_____ **2.** Individuals who violate rules regarding a patient's protected health information may face criminal and civil penalties.

_____ **3.** A potential organ donor should not be treated differently from any other patient who requires your care.

_____ **4.** An EMT's scope of practice is universal and doesn't vary despite the agency or location served.

_____ **5.** Informed consent requires that the patient be of legal age and able to understand the consequences of his decision.

Multiple Choice

In the space provided, identify the letter of the choice that best completes the statement or answers each question.

_____ **6.** Terminating patient care without making sure that care will continue at the same level or higher is called
   a. breach of duty.
   b. abandonment.
   c. damages.
   d. failure to act.

_____ **7.** You are dispatched to a private residence for an "ill man." You arrive to find a 30-year-old man unresponsive on the living room floor. The patient's 14-year-old daughter states she arrived home a few minutes ago and found her father in this condition. She immediately called 9-1-1 and then called her mother, who is at work. Your general impression reveals the patient appears to be unresponsive. You can see that he is breathing. There are no obvious signs of trauma. Select the *correct* statement about this situation.
   a. You cannot provide care for this patient if he is unable to give you verbal consent to treat him.
   b. You can provide care for this patient on the basis of the child's request that you provide care for her father.
   c. You may provide care for this patient by reason of implied consent.
   d. You may provide care for this patient only if medical direction authorizes you to do so.

_____ **8.** You are called to the scene of a patient who is not breathing and has no pulse. The patient has an advance directive. The document is illegible and does not appear to have a physician's signature. What should you do next?
   a. Do not resuscitate the patient. The presence of the document is enough validation that the patient is a DNR.
   b. Begin CPR and resuscitation efforts until clarification of the advance directive can be performed.
   c. Call an ALS crew to the scene to confirm the patient is dead.
   d. Perform chest compressions only. The patient should not receive any other resuscitation measures.

_____ **9.** The unlawful touching of another person without consent is called
   a. battery.
   b. assault.
   c. negligence.
   d. abandonment.

Sentence Completion

In the blanks provided, write the words that best complete each sentence.

10. _____ _____ _____ refers to the emergency care and skills an EMT is legally allowed and expected to perform when necessary.

11. A written document that specifies a person's healthcare wishes when he becomes unable to make decisions for himself is known as a(n) _____ _____.

Matching

Match the key terms in the left column with the definitions in the right column by placing the letter of each correct answer in the space provided.

_____ 12. Negligence

_____ 13. Protocols

_____ 14. Breach of duty

_____ 15. Ethics

_____ 16. Protected health information

_____ 17. Standing orders

_____ 18. Proximate cause

_____ 19. Competence

_____ 20. Comfort care

_____ 21. Duty to act

A. Written instructions that authorize EMS personnel to perform certain medical interventions before establishing direct communication with a physician

B. Written instructions to provide emergency care for specific health-related conditions

C. Measures used to ease the symptoms of an illness or injury; also called *palliative care* or *supportive care*

D. Principles of right and wrong, good and bad, which affect our actions and lead to consequences

E. A deviation from the accepted standard of care that results in further injury to the patient

F. A patient's ability to understand the questions you ask of him and understand the implications of the decisions he makes concerning his care

G. Information that relates to a person's physical or mental health, treatment, or payment that identifies the person, gives a reason to believe that the individual can be identified, or is transmitted or maintained in any form

H. Actions or inactions of the healthcare professional that cause an injury or damages

I. Violating the standard of care that applies in a given situation

J. A formal contractual or an implied legal obligation to provide care to a patient requesting services

Short Answer

Answer each question in the space provided.

22. When can patient care be transferred to another healthcare professional?

23. List the four elements that must be proved in a negligence case.
    1.
    2.
    3.
    4.

24. A 48-year-old man was involved in a high-speed motor vehicle crash. The patient was not restrained. He is alert and oriented to person, place, time, and event. Obvious injuries include minor bleeding from a cut on his forehead and a large bruise on his chest. The patient is refusing treatment and transport to the hospital. What information must you give the patient regarding his refusing care?

25. Briefly explain how you should obtain expressed consent from a patient.

26. You are called to the scene of a patient who has suffered a gunshot wound to the leg after a domestic dispute. You are about to get out of the ambulance and begin assessment of the patient when the patient's spouse returns, waving a gun and threatening to shoot. Law enforcement personnel on the scene are attempting to gain control of the patient's spouse. You and your partner decide to leave the scene until scene safety is restored. Is this considered abandonment?

Answer Section

Chapter 3

True/False

1. True

The scope of practice includes the emergency care and skills an EMT is legally allowed and expected to perform. These duties are set by state laws and regulations.

Objective: Define the EMT-Basic scope of practice.

2. True

HIPAA went into effect in 2003. This law was passed by Congress in 1996, partly to ensure the confidentiality of a patient's health information. Individuals who disobey HIPAA privacy rules face criminal and civil penalties.

Objective: Explain the importance, necessity, and legality of patient confidentiality.

3. True

An organ donor is a person who has signed a legal document to donate his organs in the event of his death. This document may be an organ donor card that the patient carries in his wallet. Alternately, the patient may have indicated his intent to be a donor on his driver's license. Family members may also tell you that the patient is an organ donor. A patient who is a potential organ donor should not be treated differently from any other patient who requires your care.

Objective: Discuss the considerations of the EMT in issues of organ retrieval.

4. False

Some states will modify an EMS professional's scope of practice to fit the needs or desires of the state. As a result, what is accepted EMS practice in one state may not be so in another.

Objective: Define the EMT-Basic scope of practice.

5. True

Expressed consent is a type of consent in which a patient gives specific permission for care and transport to be provided. Expressed consent may be given verbally, in writing, or nonverbally. Expressed consent must be informed consent. This means that you must give the patient enough information to make an informed decision; otherwise the patient's expressed consent may not be considered valid. You must tell the patient what you are going to do, how you will do it, the possible risks, and the possible outcome of what is to be done.

Objective: Differentiate between expressed and implied consent.

Multiple Choice

6. b

Abandonment is terminating patient care without making sure that care will continue at the same level or higher. You can be charged with abandonment if you turn the patient over to another healthcare professional who has less medical training than you. You can also be charged with abandonment if you stop patient care when the patient still needs and desires additional care.

Objective: Discuss the issues of abandonment, negligence, and battery and their implications for the EMT.

7. c

Implied consent is consent assumed from a patient requiring emergency care who is mentally, physically, or emotionally unable to provide expressed consent. Implied consent is sometimes called the doctrine of implied consent. Implied consent is based on the assumption that the patient would consent to lifesaving treatment if he were able to do so. It is effective only until the patient no longer requires emergency care or regains competence to make decisions.

Objective: Differentiate between expressed and implied consent.

8. b

In this situation, you have a doubt about the legality of the order. It is best to err on the side of caution and begin resuscitation.

Objective: Discuss the importance of DNR (advance directives) and local or state provisions regarding EMS application.

9. a

This is the definition of battery. To protect yourself from possible legal action, clearly explain your intentions to your patient and obtain his consent before beginning patient care.

Objective: Discuss the issues of abandonment, negligence, and battery and their implications to the EMT.

Sentence Completion

10. **Scope of care** (also called *scope of practice*) refers to the emergency care and skills an EMT is legally allowed and expected to perform when necessary.

Objective: Define the EMT-Basic scope of practice.

11. A written document specifying a person's healthcare wishes when he becomes unable to make decisions for himself is known as a(n) **advance directive.**

Objective: Discuss the importance of DNR (advance directives) and local or state provisions regarding EMS application.

Matching

12.	E	17.	A
13.	B	18.	H
14.	I	19.	F
15.	D	20.	C
16.	G	21.	J

Short Answer

22. Patient care may be transferred to another healthcare professional if that person accepts the patient and if his medical qualifications are equal to or greater than yours.

Objective: Discuss the issues of abandonment, negligence, and battery and their implications to the EMT.

23. The four elements that must be proved in a negligence case are the following:

1. You had a duty to act.
2. You breached that duty.
3. Injury and/or damages were inflicted.
4. Your actions or lack of actions caused the injury and/or damage.

Objective: Discuss the issues of abandonment, negligence, and battery and their implications to the EMT.

24. You must inform the patient of the following:

- The nature of his injury
- The treatment that needs to be performed
- The benefits of that treatment
- The risks of not providing that treatment
- Any alternatives to treatment
- The dangers of refusing treatment (including transport)

Objective: Discuss the implications for the EMT in patient refusal of transport.

25. To obtain expressed consent, you must:

- Identify yourself and your level of medical training
- Explain all treatments and procedures to the patient
- Identify the benefits of each treatment or procedure

Objective: Differentiate between expressed and implied consent.

26. If a scene is unsafe, it is not abandonment if you leave the scene for your safety with the intention of returning as soon as the scene is made safe.

Objective: Discuss the issues of abandonment, negligence, and battery and their implications to the EMT.

4 The Human Body

READING ASSIGNMENT ▷ Read Chapter 4, pages 69 to 99 in your textbook.

Sum It Up

- The body's most basic building block is a cell. The human body contains billions of cells. Clusters of cells form tissues. Specialized types of tissues form organs, such as the brain and the liver. An organ system (also called a *body system*) consists of tissues and organs that work together to provide a specialized function. The circulatory and respiratory systems are examples of organ systems.

- Organ systems work together to maintain a state of homeostasis (balance). These systems need a constant internal environment to perform the required functions of the body.

- In your role as an EMT, it is important to know the terms used to describe body positions and directions. You must be able to use these terms correctly so that you can describe the position in which a patient is found and transported. You will also need to know body positions so that you can place a patient in a specific position based on the patient's condition.

- A body cavity is a hollow space in the body that contains internal organs. Knowing the body cavities and the organs found within each cavity will help you describe the location of the injury or symptoms of a sick or injured patient.

- The musculoskeletal system gives the human body its shape and ability to move and protects the major organs of the body. It consists of the skeletal system (bones) and the muscular system (muscles).

- The respiratory system supplies oxygen from the air we breathe to the body's cells. It also removes carbon dioxide (a waste product of the body's cells) from the lungs when we breathe out. This system is made up of an upper and a lower airway. The upper airway includes the nose, the pharynx (throat), and the larynx (voice box). The lower airway consists of structures found mostly within the chest cavity, such as the trachea (windpipe) and the lungs.

- The circulatory system is made up of the cardiovascular and lymphatic systems. This system has three main functions: (1) to deliver oxygen-rich blood and nutrients to body tissues, (2) to help maintain body temperature, and (3) to protect the body against infection. The cardiovascular system consists of the heart, blood, and blood vessels. The lymphatic system consists of lymph, lymph nodes, lymph vessels, tonsils, the spleen, and the thymus gland.

- The nervous system is a collection of specialized cells that transfer information to and from the brain. The two main functions of the nervous system are to control the voluntary (conscious) and involuntary (unconscious) activities of the body, and to provide for higher mental function (such as thought and emotion). The nervous system has two divisions: (1) the CNS and (2) the PNS. The PNS has 2 divisions. The somatic (voluntary) division has receptors and nerves concerned with the external environment. It influences the activity of the musculoskeletal system. The autonomic (involuntary) division has receptors and nerves concerned with the internal environment. It controls the involuntary system of glands and smooth muscle and functions to maintain a steady state in the body. The autonomic division is divided into the sympathetic division and parasympathetic divisions. The sympathetic division mobilizes energy, particularly in stressful situations. This is called the *fight-or-flight response*. Its effects are widespread throughout the body. The parasympathetic division conserves and restores energy; its effects are localized in the body.
- The integumentary system is made up of the skin, hair, nails, sweat glands, and oil (sebaceous) glands. The skin is the largest organ of the body. It protects the body from the environment, bacteria, and other organisms and plays an important role in temperature regulation.
- The digestive system brings nutrients, water, and electrolytes into the body (ingestion). It chemically breaks down food into small parts so absorption can occur (digestion). It moves nutrients, water, and electrolytes into the circulatory system so they can be used by body cells (absorption). It also eliminates undigested waste (defecation). The primary organs of the digestive system are the mouth, pharynx, esophagus, stomach, small intestine, large intestine, rectum, and anal canal. The accessory organs are the teeth and tongue, salivary glands, liver, gallbladder, and pancreas.
- The endocrine system is a system of glands that secrete chemicals (hormones) directly into the circulatory system. It influences body activities and functions. The endocrine system works closely with the nervous system to maintain homeostasis.
- The reproductive system makes cells (sperm, eggs) that allow continuation of the human species. The urinary system produces and excretes urine from the body.

▶ Tracking Your Progress

After reading this chapter, can you:	Page Reference	Objective Met?
• Identify the following topographic terms: medial, lateral, proximal, distal, superior, inferior, anterior, posterior, midline, right, left, midclavicular, bilateral, midaxillary?	70	☐
• Describe the anatomy and function of the respiratory system?	81	☐
• Describe the anatomy and function of the circulatory system?	87	☐
• Describe the anatomy and function of the musculoskeletal system?	74	☐
• Describe the anatomy and function of the nervous system?	91	☐
• Describe the anatomy and function of the endocrine system?	95	☐

True or False

Decide whether each statement is true or false. In the space provided, write *T* for true or *F* for false.

_____ **1.** Hemoglobin is an oxygen-carrying protein in red blood cells.

_____ **2.** The chambers of the heart that have the thickest walls are the ventricles.

Multiple Choice

In the space provided, identify the letter of the choice that best completes the statement or answers each question.

_____ **3.** You find a man lying face down in an alley. What is the medical term for this position?
 a. Supine
 b. Prone
 c. Lateral recumbent
 d. Shock position

_____ **4.** Which of the following are bones of the forearm?
 a. Humerus and femur
 b. Tibia and radius
 c. Fibula and humerus
 d. Radius and ulna

_____ **5.** Select the correct statement about the circulatory system.
 a. The upper chambers of the heart are called the ventricles.
 b. The heart contains four 1-way valves that make sure blood flows in the proper direction.
 c. The walls of the heart are made up of skeletal muscle.
 d. The lower chambers of the heart are called the atria.

_____ **6.** White blood cells
 a. help the body fight infection.
 b. are also called erythrocytes.
 c. are irregularly shaped blood cells that have a sticky surface.
 d. gather at the site of an injured blood vessel and stop the flow of blood.

_____ **7.** Which of the following arteries is found in the upper extremity?
 a. Brachial artery
 b. Posterior tibial artery
 c. Femoral artery
 d. Carotid artery

_____ **8.** Where does the exchange of oxygen and carbon dioxide between the air and blood occur?
 a. Trachea
 b. Alveoli
 c. Bronchioles
 d. Larynx

_____ **9.** Which of the following are parts of the upper airway?
 a. Trachea, bronchioles, lungs
 b. Nose, bronchioles, pharynx
 c. Nose, pharynx, larynx
 d. Lungs, larynx, pharynx

Questions 10–11 pertain to the following scenario.

Your ambulance crew responds to a 2-year-old female who slipped and fell. Upon arrival you find the patient crying in her mother's arms. There is an approximately 1-inch laceration on the back of the patient's head. Bleeding is controlled with moderate direct pressure.

_____ **10.** The laceration is located at the
 a. coccyx.
 b. manubrium.
 c. frontal region of the sacrum.
 d. occipital region of the cranium.

_____ **11.** When this patient struck the ground, shock absorption for the brain was provided by
 a. the maxilla.
 b. the ossicles.
 c. the cervical spine.
 d. cerebrospinal fluid.

Questions 12–13 pertain to the following scenario.

Your rescue crew responds to a domestic dispute. Upon arrival, you find a 23-year-old man bleeding from a stab wound to the chest.

_____ 12. A 2-inch-long laceration is found on the front of the patient's chest next to his right nipple. Which of the following accurately describes the location of the wound?

    a. Right midaxillary line

    b. Anterior chest wall; lateral to the sternum

    c. Posterior chest wall; inferior to the scapula

    d. Anterior chest wall; superior to the right clavicle

_____ 13. Which of the following findings would be consistent with this patient's going into shock (hypoperfusion)?

    a. Slow pulse rate, increased blood pressure

    b. Rapid pulse rate, restlessness, and anxiety

    c. Unequal pupils, nausea, and vomiting

    d. Fever, increased blood pressure, and rapid pulse rate

Matching

Match the key terms in the left column with the definitions in the right column by placing the letter of each correct answer in the space provided.

Body Cavities

_____ 14. Thoracic cavity

_____ 15. Abdominal cavity

_____ 16. Body cavity

_____ 17. Pelvic cavity

_____ 18. Pleural cavities

_____ 19. Spinal cavity

_____ 20. Cranial cavity

_____ 21. Pericardial cavity

A. Surrounds the heart

B. Surrounds the lungs

C. Located in the head; contains the brain

D. Extends from the bottom of the skull to the lower back; contains the spinal cord

E. A hollow space in the body that contains internal organs

F. Located below the diaphragm and above the pelvis

G. Body cavity below the abdominal cavity

H. Located below the neck and above the diaphragm; contains the heart, major blood vessels, and lungs

_____ 22. Pulse

_____ 23. Appendicular skeleton

_____ 24. Homeostasis

_____ 25. Tissue

_____ 26. Aorta

_____ 27. Physiology

_____ 28. Cerebellum

_____ 29. Systolic blood pressure

_____ 30. Cells

_____ 31. Xiphoid process

_____ 32. Perfusion

_____ 33. Corpus callosum

Anatomy and Physiology

A. The largest artery in the body

B. The basic building blocks of the body

C. Upper and lower extremities (arms and legs), shoulder girdle, and pelvic girdle

D. A thick bundle of nerve fibers that joins the 2 hemispheres of the brain

E. The second largest part of the human brain

F. The pressure in an artery when the heart is pumping blood

G. The regular expansion and recoil of an artery caused by the movement of blood from the heart as it contracts

H. "Steady state"

I. Cells that cluster together to perform a specialized function

J. The flow of blood through an organ or a part of the body

K. The study of the normal functions of an organism

L. A piece of cartilage that makes up the inferior portion of the breastbone

_____ 34. Posterior

_____ 35. Midline

_____ 36. Lateral

_____ 37. Medial

_____ 38. Distal

_____ 39. Inferior

_____ 40. Proximal

_____ 41. Anterior

_____ 42. Superior

Directional Terms

A. Farthest from the point of attachment to the body

B. The front portion of the body or body part

C. Above or in a higher position than another portion of the body

D. In a position lower than another

E. Nearer to the point of attachment to the body

F. Toward the midline of the body

G. Toward the side of the body

H. A line down the center of the body that divides the body into right and left sides

I. The back side of the body or body part

Short Answer

Answer each question in the space provided.

43. List the formed elements of the blood.

44. Name the parts of the central nervous system.

45. Label the following on the figure to the right:

Right side, left side, superior, inferior, medial, lateral, proximal leg, distal leg, and midlineMatching

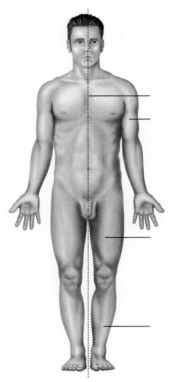

Anterior view

46. Label the following:

Abdominal cavity, abdominopelvic cavity, cranial cavity, diaphragm, dorsal cavity, heart, left lung, left pleural cavity, mediastinum, pelvic cavity, pericardial cavity, right lung, right pleural cavity, thoracic cavity, ventral cavity, and vertebral canal. Some terms may be used more than once.

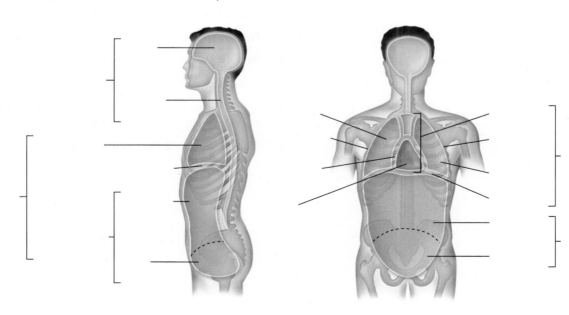

47. Label the following:

Calcaneus, carpus, clavicle, costal cartilages, femur, fibula, frontal bone, humerus, mandible, maxilla, metacarpal bones, occipital bone, parietal bone, patella, pelvic girdle, phalanges, radius, ribs, scapula, sternum, tarsus, temporal bone, tibia, ulna, vertebral column, and zygomatic bone. Some labels will be used more than once.

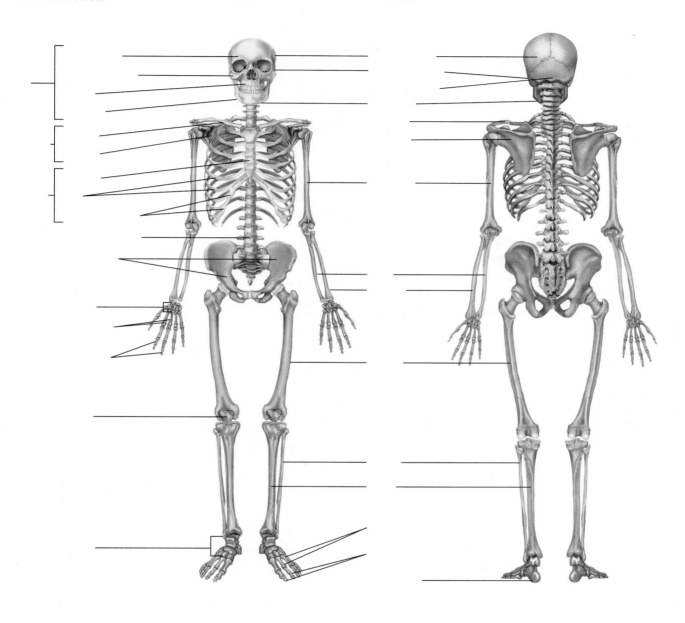

48. Label the following bones of the skull: frontal bone, mandible, maxilla, parietal bone, temporal bone, and zygomatic bone.

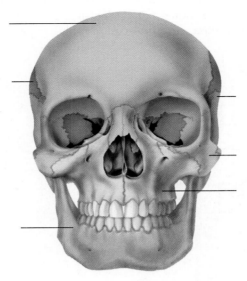

49. Label the following: atlas, axis, C7, cervical vertebrae, coccyx, L1, L5, lumbar vertebrae, S1, S5, sacrum, T1, T12, and thoracic vertebrae. Some terms may be used more than once.

Anterior view   **Posterior view**

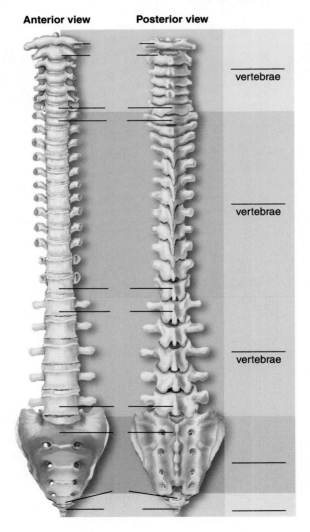

vertebrae

vertebrae

vertebrae

50. Label the following: body, clavicle, costal cartilage, false ribs, first thoracic vertebra, floating ribs, manubrium, 7th cervical vertebra, sternal angle, sternum, suprasternal notch, true ribs, and xiphoid process. Number ribs 1 through 12.

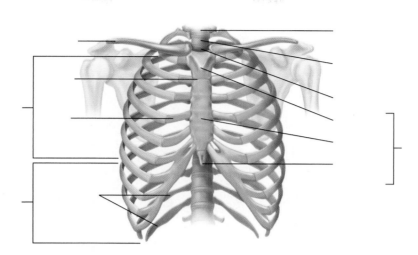

51. Label the following structures of the respiratory system: bronchus, epiglottis, esophagus, frontal sinus, hard palate, larynx, left lung, nasal cavity, nostril, oral cavity, pharynx, right lung, soft palate, and trachea.

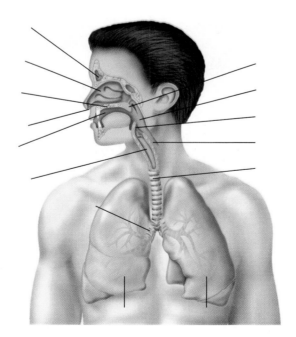

52. On the following drawing, use arrows to show normal blood flow through the heart and lungs. Label the following: aorta, descending aorta, from lung, inferior vena cava, left atrium, left ventricle, right atrium, right ventricle, superior vena cava, to lower body, to lung, to upper body. Some terms will be used more than once.

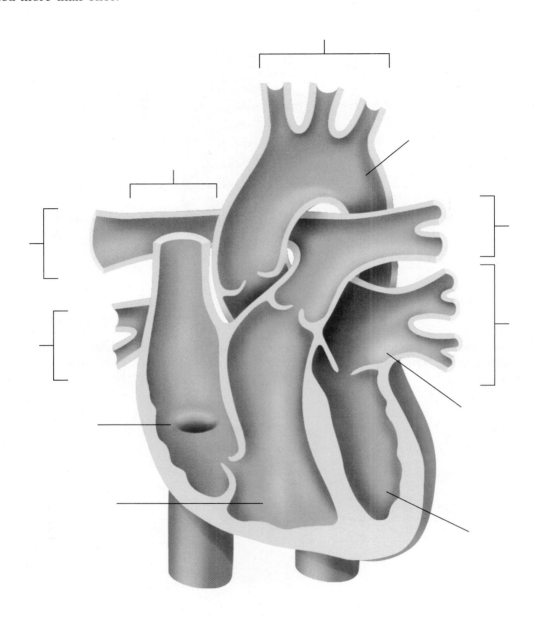

53. Label the following major arteries and veins: aorta, axillary artery, brachial artery, coronary arteries, dorsalis pedis artery, femoral artery, inferior vena cava, left and right carotid arteries, popliteal artery, radial artery, subclavian arteries, superior vena cava, tibial artery, and ulnar artery.

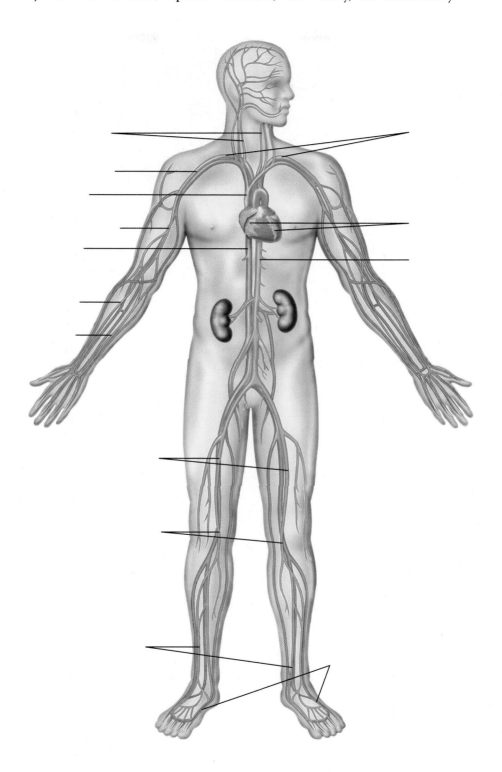

54. Label the following areas of the brain: brainstem, cerebellum, cerebrum, corpus callosum, diencephalon, hypothalamus, medulla oblongata, midbrain, pons, and thalamus.

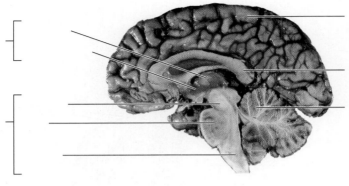

© Branislav Vidic

Answer Section

Chapter 4

True/False

1. True

Red blood cells (erythrocytes) contain hemoglobin. Each red blood cell has about 250 million hemoglobin molecules. Hemoglobin is an iron-containing protein that chemically bonds with oxygen. Thus, hemoglobin is the part of the red blood cell that picks up oxygen in the lungs and transports it to the body's cells. Hemoglobin is red and therefore gives blood its red color.

Objective: Describe the anatomy and function of the following major body systems: respiratory, circulatory, musculoskeletal, nervous, and endocrine.

2. True

The ventricles are larger and have thicker walls than the atria (the heart's upper chambers) because the job of the ventricles is to pump blood to the lungs and body.

Objective: Describe the anatomy and function of the following major body systems: respiratory, circulatory, musculoskeletal, nervous, and endocrine.

Multiple Choice

3. b

A person lying face down and flat is in a prone position. A person lying flat on his back (face up) is said to be in a supine position. If a person is found on his side, he is in a lateral recumbent position. If he is found on his left side, he is in a left lateral recumbent position. If he is on his right side, he is in a right lateral recumbent position. The shock position is lying on the back with the feet elevated approximately 8-12 inches.

Objective: Identify the following topographic terms: medial, lateral, proximal, distal, superior, inferior, anterior, posterior, midline, right and left, midclavicular, bilateral, and midaxillary.

4. d

The forearm contains two bones: the radius (lateral, thumb side) and the ulna (medial side). The ulna is the longer of the two bones.

Objective: Describe the anatomy and function of the following major body systems: respiratory, circulatory, musculoskeletal, nervous, and endocrine.

5. b

The heart has four hollow chambers. The two upper chambers are the right and left atria. The job of the atria is to receive blood from the body and lungs. The two lower chambers of the heart are the right and left ventricles. The ventricles are larger and have thicker walls than the atria because their job is to pump blood to the lungs and body.

The heart contains four 1-way valves that make sure blood flows in the proper direction. Cardiac muscle, found in the walls of the heart, produces the heart's contractions and pumps blood. Cardiac muscle is found only in the heart and has its own supply of blood through the coronary arteries.

Objective: Describe the anatomy and function of the following major body systems: respiratory, circulatory, musculoskeletal, nervous, and endocrine.

6. a

White blood cells (leukocytes) attack and destroy germs that enter the body. Red blood cells (erythrocytes) deliver oxygen to the cells, gather up carbon dioxide and then transport it to the lungs, where it is removed from the body when we exhale. Platelets are irregularly shaped blood cells that have a sticky surface. When a blood vessel is damaged and starts to bleed, platelets gather at the site of injury. The platelets begin sticking to the opening of the damaged vessel and seal it, stopping the flow of blood.

Objective: Describe the anatomy and function of the following major body systems: respiratory, circulatory, musculoskeletal, nervous, and endocrine.

7. a

The subclavian arteries branch into the axillary and brachial arteries in the upper arm. A brachial pulse can be felt on the inside of the arm between the elbow and the shoulder. This artery is used when determining a blood pressure with a blood pressure cuff and stethoscope.

Objective: Describe the anatomy and function of the following major body systems: respiratory, circulatory, musculoskeletal, nervous, and endocrine.

8. b

The trachea (windpipe) is located in the front of the neck. It is kept permanently open by C-shaped cartilages. The trachea branches into large airway tubes called the right and left mainstem bronchi. Each bronchus is joined to a lung, so 1 tube leads to the right lung and the other leads to the left lung. The mainstem bronchi branch into bronchioles. Bronchioles end in microscopic tubes called *alveolar ducts*. Each alveolar duct ends in several alveolar sacs. At the end of each alveolar duct, the collections of air sacs (alveoli) looks like a cluster of grapes. Alveoli are the sites where gases—oxygen and carbon dioxide—are exchanged between the air and blood.

Objective: Describe the anatomy and function of the following major body systems: respiratory, circulatory, musculoskeletal, nervous, and endocrine.

9. c

The respiratory system is divided into the upper and lower airways. The upper airway is made up of structures outside the chest cavity. These structures include the nose, the pharynx (throat), and the larynx (voice box). The lower airway consists of parts found almost entirely within the chest cavity, such as the trachea (windpipe) and the lungs.

Objective: Describe the anatomy and function of the following major body systems: respiratory, circulatory, musculoskeletal, nervous, and endocrine.

10. d

The occipital region of the cranium (skull) is the back of the head. The upper sides of the head are the parietal regions, the sides above and in front of the ears are the temporal regions, and the forehead is the frontal region. The coccyx is the tailbone. The manubrium is the uppermost portion of the sternum (breastbone). The sacrum is the section of the spine below the lumbar region.

Objective: Describe the anatomy and function of the following major body systems: respiratory, circulatory, musculoskeletal, nervous, and endocrine.

11. d

Cerebrospinal fluid circulates throughout the central nervous system (the brain and the spinal cord) and acts as a shock absorber, much like the fluid that surrounds an egg yolk. The maxilla is the upper jawbone, and the ossicles are the small bones of the middle ear that aid in hearing—the malleus (hammer), incus (anvil) and stapes (stirrup). The cervical spine is the uppermost section of the spinal column. The cervical spine of patients who have sustained a blow to the head should be stabilized to protect the spinal cord.

Objective: Describe the anatomy and function of the following major body systems: respiratory, circulatory, musculoskeletal, nervous, and endocrine.

12. b

Anterior refers to the front surface, and the sternum is the breast bone. Lateral to the sternum means to the outside (toward either side). The midaxillary line is an imaginary line drawn down the side of the body (armpit to ankle). The posterior chest wall refers to the back of the chest, and inferior to the scapula is below the shoulder blade. Superior to the clavicle is above the collarbone.

Objective: Identify the following topographic terms: medial, lateral, proximal, distal, superior, inferior, anterior, posterior, midline, right and left, midclavicular, bilateral, and midaxillary.

13. b

One of the first signs of shock is an altered mental status. This change in mentation can be very subtle, such as restlessness, anxiety, or agitation. Other signs of shock include cool, pale, clammy skin; rapid, shallow breathing; rapid pulse; nausea and vomiting; subnormal temperature; and decreasing blood pressure.

Objective: Describe the anatomy and function of the following major body systems: respiratory, circulatory, musculoskeletal, nervous, and endocrine.

Matching

Body Cavities

14.	H	**18.**	B
15.	F	**19.**	D
16.	E	**20.**	C
17.	G	**21.**	A

Anatomy and Physiology

22.	G	**28.**	E
23.	C	**29.**	F
24.	H	**30.**	B
25.	I	**31.**	L
26.	A	**32.**	J
27.	K	**33.**	D

Directional Terms

34.	I	**39.**	D
35.	H	**40.**	E
36.	G	**41.**	B
37.	F	**42.**	C
38.	A		

Short Answer

43. Red blood cells, white blood cells, platelets

Objective: Describe the anatomy and function of the following major body systems: respiratory, circulatory, musculoskeletal, nervous, and endocrine.

44. Brain and spinal cord

Objective: Describe the anatomy and function of the following major body systems: respiratory, circulatory, musculoskeletal, nervous, and endocrine.

45.

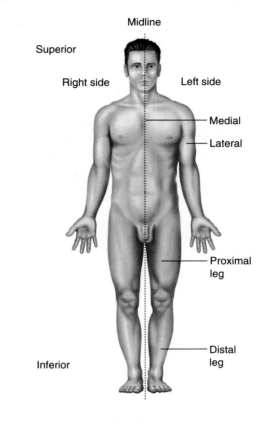

Anterior view

Objective: Identify the following topographic terms: medial, lateral, proximal, distal, superior, inferior, anterior, posterior, midline, right and left, midclavicular, bilateral, and midaxillary.

46.

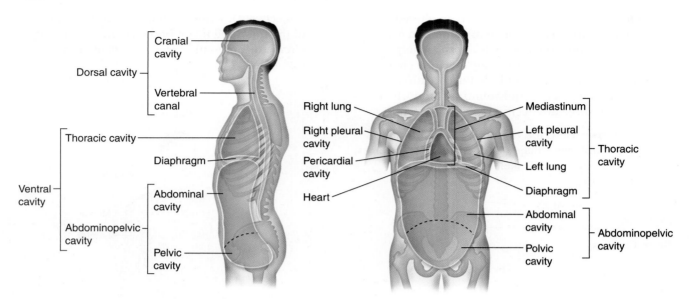

Objective: Identify the following topographic terms: medial, lateral, proximal, distal, superior, inferior, anterior, posterior, midline, right and left, midclavicular, bilateral, and midaxillary.

47.

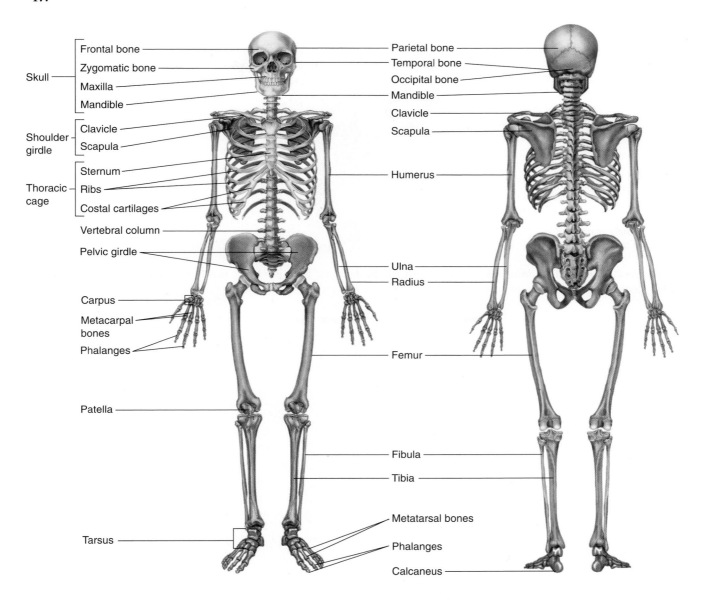

Objective: Describe the anatomy and function of the following major body systems: respiratory, circulatory, musculoskeletal, nervous, and endocrine.

48.

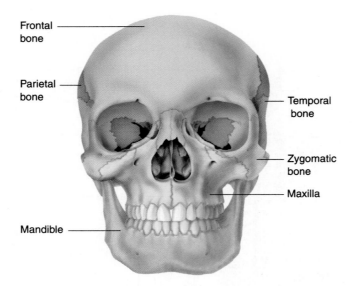

Frontal bone

Parietal bone

Temporal bone

Zygomatic bone

Maxilla

Mandible

Objective: Describe the anatomy and function of the following major body systems: respiratory, circulatory, musculoskeletal, nervous, and endocrine.

49.

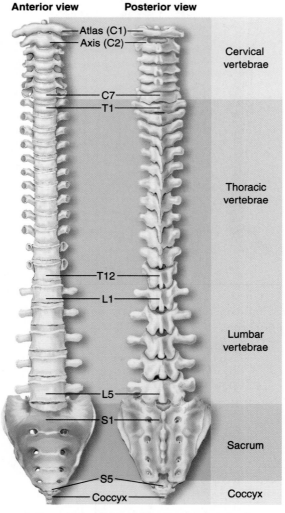

Anterior view   Posterior view

Atlas (C1)
Axis (C2)

Cervical vertebrae

C7
T1

Thoracic vertebrae

T12

L1

Lumbar vertebrae

L5

S1

Sacrum

S5

Coccyx

Coccyx

Objective: Describe the anatomy and function of the following major body systems: respiratory, circulatory, musculoskeletal, nervous, and endocrine.

50.

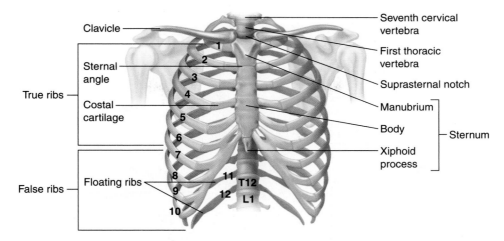

Clavicle

Sternal angle

Costal cartilage

True ribs

Floating ribs

False ribs

1
2
3
4
5
6
7
8
9
10
11
12
T12
L1

Seventh cervical vertebra

First thoracic vertebra

Suprasternal notch

Manubrium

Body

Xiphoid process

Sternum

Objective: Describe the anatomy and function of the following major body systems: respiratory, circulatory, musculoskeletal, nervous, and endocrine.

51.

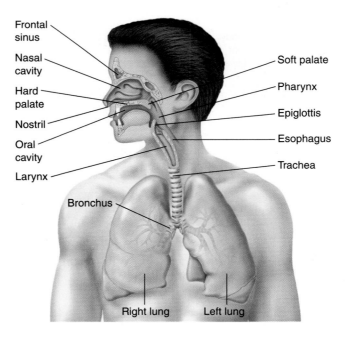

Frontal sinus

Nasal cavity

Hard palate

Nostril

Oral cavity

Larynx

Bronchus

Right lung

Left lung

Soft palate

Pharynx

Epiglottis

Esophagus

Trachea

Objective: Describe the anatomy and function of the following major body systems: respiratory, circulatory, musculoskeletal, nervous, and endocrine.

52.

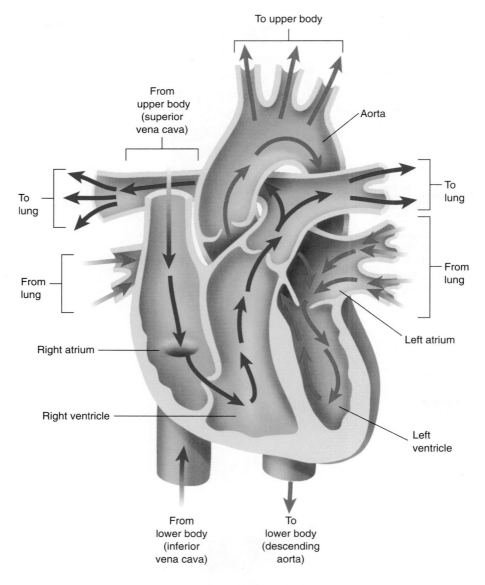

To upper body

From
upper body
(superior
vena cava)

Aorta

To
lung

To
lung

From
lung

From
lung

Right atrium

Left atrium

Right ventricle

Left
ventricle

From
lower body
(inferior
vena cava)

To
lower body
(descending
aorta)

Objective: Describe the anatomy and function of the following major body systems: respiratory, circulatory, musculoskeletal, nervous, and endocrine.

53.

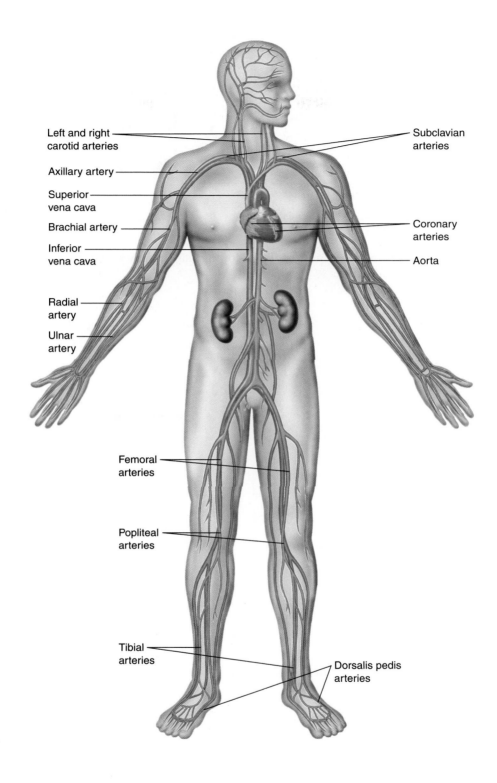

Left and right
carotid arteries

Axillary artery

Superior
vena cava

Brachial artery

Inferior
vena cava

Radial
artery

Ulnar
artery

Subclavian
arteries

Coronary
arteries

Aorta

Femoral
arteries

Popliteal
arteries

Tibial
arteries

Dorsalis pedis
arteries

Objective: Describe the anatomy and function of the following major body systems: respiratory, circulatory, musculoskeletal, nervous, and endocrine.

54.

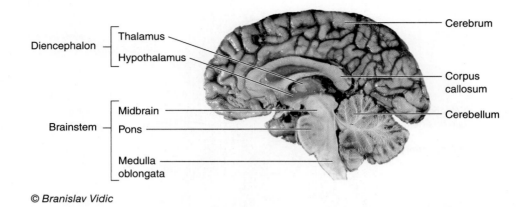

Diencephalon
- Thalamus
- Hypothalamus

Brainstem
- Midbrain
- Pons
- Medulla oblongata

Cerebrum

Corpus callosum

Cerebellum

© Branislav Vidic

Objective: Describe the anatomy and function of the following major body systems: respiratory, circulatory, musculoskeletal, nervous, and endocrine.

5 Baseline Vital Signs and SAMPLE History

READING ASSIGNMENT ▶ Read Chapter 5, pages 100 to 118 in your textbook.

Sum It Up

- Vital signs are assessments of breathing, pulse, temperature, pupils, and blood pressure. Measuring vital signs is an important part of patient assessment. Vital signs are measured to:
  — Detect changes in normal body function
  — Recognize life-threatening situations
  — Determine a patient's response to treatment
- Additional vital signs include pulse oximetry, end-tidal carbon dioxide, and pain assessment. Pulse oximetry is a method of measuring the amount of oxygen saturated in the blood.
- A sign is any medical or trauma condition displayed by the patient that can be seen, heard, smelled, measured, or felt. A symptom is any condition described by the patient.
- SAMPLE is an aid to remind you of the information you should get from the patient:
  — **S**igns and symptoms
  — **A**llergies
  — **M**edications
  — (Pertinent) **P**ast medical history
  — **L**ast oral intake
  — **E**vents leading to the injury or illness
- OPQRST is a memory aid that may help identify the type and location of a patient's complaint.
  — **O**nset
  — **P**rovocation/Palliation
  — **Q**uality
  — **R**egion/Radiation
  — **S**everity
  — **T**ime
- The Wong-Baker FACES Pain Rating Scale is a tool used to assess pain in children 3 years of age or older.

▶ Tracking Your Progress

After reading this chapter, can you:	Page Reference	Objective Met?
• Identify the components of vital signs?	102	☐
• Describe the methods to obtain a breathing rate?	105	☐
• Identify the attributes that should be obtained when assessing breathing?	105	☐
• Differentiate between shallow, labored, and noisy breathing?	105	☐
• Describe the methods to obtain a pulse rate?	102	☐
• Identify the components of the extended vital signs?	113	☐
• Identify the information obtained when assessing a patient's pulse?	104	☐
• Differentiate between a strong, weak, regular, and irregular pulse?	106	☐
• Describe the methods to assess the skin color, temperature, and condition (capillary refill in infants and children)?	106	☐
• Identify normal and abnormal skin colors?	106	☐
• Differentiate between pale, blue, red, and yellow skin color?	106	☐
• Identify normal and abnormal skin temperature?	107	☐
• Differentiate between hot, cool, and cold skin temperature?	107	☐
• Identify normal and abnormal skin conditions?	107	☐
• Identify normal and abnormal capillary refill in infants and children?	107	☐
• Describe the methods to assess the pupils?	108	☐
• Identify normal and abnormal pupil size?	108	☐
• Differentiate between dilated (big) and constricted (small) pupil size?	108	☐
• Differentiate between reactive and nonreactive pupils and equal and unequal pupils?	108	☐
• Describe the methods to assess blood pressure?	108	☐
• Define systolic pressure?	109	☐
• Define diastolic pressure?	109	☐
• Explain the difference between auscultation and palpation for obtaining a blood pressure?	110	☐
• Identify the components of the SAMPLE history?	115	☐
• Differentiate between a sign and a symptom?	102, 116	☐
• State the importance of accurately reporting and recording the baseline vital signs?	102	☐
• Discuss the need to search for additional medical identification?	116	☐

True or False

Decide whether each statement is true or false. In the space provided, write *T* for true or *F* for false.

_____ **1.** Equality of pulses is determined by assessing and comparing pulses on both sides of the body.

_____ **2.** Retaking a blood pressure too quickly may produce an inaccurate reading.

Multiple Choice

In the space provided, identify the letter of the choice that best completes the statement or answers each question.

Questions 3-8 pertain to the following scenario.

Your rescue crew is called to the home of an 11-month-old male child with difficulty breathing. His parents inform you that their child has had a cold for the last two days and has recently begun coughing a harsh, high-pitched cough.

_____ 3. Which of the following is a sign of this patient's difficulty breathing?
   a. He has had a cold for the last two days.
   b. He is not currently taking any medications.
   c. His respiratory rate is faster than normal for his age.
   d. His parents inform you that this has happened once before.

_____ 4. A normal respiratory rate for this patient would be
   a. 6-8 breaths per minute.   c. 12-20 breaths per minute.
   b. 10-12 breaths per minute.   d. 20-40 breaths per minute.

_____ 5. When assessing this patient's capillary refill, you would expect that the skin of his nail beds would return to normal color after being pressed within
   a. 2 seconds.   c. 5 seconds.
   b. 3 seconds.   d. 6 seconds.

_____ 6. Your partner palpates this patient's blood pressure. She informs you that the palpated pressure is "104." This finding represents the patient's
   a. pulse pressure.   c. systolic blood pressure.
   b. secondary pressure.   d. diastolic blood pressure.

_____ 7. The patient's blood pressure should be recorded as
   a. 104/0.   c. 104/P.
   b. 0/104.   d. 104/104.

_____ 8. After assessing this patient, you come to the conclusion that he is "stable." Vital signs should be assessed at least every
   a. 1-2 minutes.   c. 15 minutes.
   b. 3-5 minutes.   d. 30 minutes.

_____ 9. Which of the following is considered a symptom?
   a. Swelling   c. Open wound
   b. Dizziness   d. Flushed skin

_____ 10. A sphygmomanometer is a device used to measure a patient's
   a. Hearing   c. Respirations
   b. Heart rate   d. Blood pressure

_____ 11. Your patient's blood pressure is 90/54. The bottom number (54) refers to the
   a. pulse rate.
   b. number of seconds necessary to assess the blood pressure.
   c. force exerted by blood on the arterial walls during relaxation of the heart.
   d. force exerted by blood on the arterial walls during contraction of the heart.

_____ 12. When assessing the type and location of a patient's pain or discomfort, which memory aid is particularly helpful?
   a. APGAR   c. OPQRST
   b. SAMPLE   d. DCAPBTLS

_____ 13. Your rescue crew is called to the home of a 24-year-old woman complaining of vaginal bleeding. She states she is 6 weeks pregnant and the bleeding began about 3 hours ago. You note the patient's skin is pale, cool, and moist. These signs suggest
   a. shock.   c. liver disease.
   b. hepatitis.   d. high blood pressure.

_____ 14. "Are you seeing a physician for any medical condition?" is a question asked in which part of the SAMPLE history?

a. S   c. M

b. A   d. P

_____ 15. Your patient's pulse is irregular. Which of the following statements is correct regarding counting this patient's pulse?

a. Count for 15 seconds and multiply by 2

b. Count for 30 seconds and multiply by 4

c. Count for 60 seconds

d. An irregular pulse must be measured by using a machine to get an accurate reading

_____ 16. A pulse that is weak and thready means that the pulse is

a. hard to feel and fast.

b. difficult to feel and slow.

c. easily felt and the pressure is equal for each beat.

d. difficult to obliterate with pressure.

_____ 17. Attributes that should be assessed when evaluating a patient's pulse include

a. rate, rhythm, and speed.   c. rate, speed, and strength.

b. rate, rhythm, and quality.   d. rate, rhythm, and regularity.

Questions 18–21 pertain to the following scenario.

You respond to a local elementary school for a 10-year-old female patient with a history of asthma. The school nurse informs you the patient was playing during recess when she experienced a sudden onset of difficulty breathing. The patient has used her asthma medication inhaler twice without relief.

_____ 18. Upon auscultation of lung sounds, you note the patient has a continuous, high-pitched musical sound on expiration. This sound is consistent with

a. snoring.   c. gurgling.

b. crowing.   d. wheezing.

_____ 19. While assessing pulses, your partner notes the patient does not have a palpable radial pulse; however, a strong brachial pulse is present. Brachial pulses are felt by palpating

a. on either side of the throat.

b. proximal to the thumb on the wrist.

c. in the crease between the pelvis and thigh.

d. on the medial aspect of the upper arm, midway between the shoulder and elbow.

_____ 20. During inhalation, you note the skin between the patient's ribs appears to "sink in." This sign is called

a. grunting.   c. intercostal retractions.

b. gastric distention.   d. subcutaneous emphysema.

_____ 21. Upon further examination of this patient, you note that she is using her abdominal muscles to assist with exhalation and the shoulder and neck muscles to assist with inhalation. This finding is called

a. a pneumothorax.   c. accessory muscle use.

b. gastric distention.   d. paradoxical chest wall movement.

_____ 22. When treating an unstable patient, vital signs should be assessed and recorded

a. every 5 minutes.   c. every 30 minutes.

b. every 15 minutes.   d. only during the initial assessment and upon transfer of care.

Sentence Completion

In the blanks provided, write the words that best complete each sentence.

23. A _____ is a medical or trauma condition of the patient that can be seen, heard, smelled, measured, or felt.

24. You should never check the _____ pulse on both sides of the body simultaneously.

25. A symptom is a(n) _____ finding because it is dependent on (subject to) the patient's interpretation and description of his complaint.

Matching

Match the key terms in the left column with the definitions in the right column by placing the letter of each correct answer in the space provided.

_____ **26.** Mottling

_____ **27.** Systolic pressure

_____ **28.** Snoring

_____ **29.** Binaurals

_____ **30.** Objective findings

_____ **31.** Wheezing

_____ **32.** Pulse oximetry

_____ **33.** Central pulse

_____ **34.** Diastolic pressure

_____ **35.** Stridor

_____ **36.** SAMPLE

_____ **37.** Gurgling

_____ **38.** Subjective findings

_____ **39.** Respiration

_____ **40.** Vital signs

_____ **41.** Cyanosis

_____ **42.** Sphygmomanometer

_____ **43.** Anisocoria

_____ **44.** End-tidal carbon dioxide detector

_____ **45.** Stethoscope

A. Blue-gray color of the skin or mucous membranes that suggests inadequate oxygenation or poor perfusion

B. A high-pitched whistling sound heard on inhalation or exhalation

C. Assessments of breathing, pulse, temperature, pupils, and blood pressure

D. The pressure in an artery when the heart is pumping blood

E. A device used to take a blood pressure

F. A memory aid that serves to remind healthcare professionals of the information that should be gathered when obtaining a patient history

G. A pulse found close to the trunk of the body

H. A patient's interpretation and description of his complaint

I. Sound that results from partial obstruction of the upper airway by the tongue

J. An instrument used to hear sounds within the body, such as respirations

K. A medical or trauma condition of the patient that can be seen, heard, smelled, measured, or felt

L. The pressure in an artery when the heart is at rest

M. The sound heard as air passes through moist secretions in the airway

N. An irregular or patchy skin discoloration that is usually a mixture of blue and white; usually seen in patients in shock, with hypothermia, or in cardiac arrest

O. The exchange of gases between a living organism and its environment

P. A device that measures a person's exhaled carbon dioxide

Q. A method of measuring the amount of oxygen saturated in the blood

R. The metal pieces of the stethoscope that connect the earpieces to the plastic or rubber tubing

S. A harsh, high-pitched sound (like the bark of a seal) that is associated with severe upper airway obstruction

T. Unequal pupil size that is normal in about 2-4% of the population

Short Answer

Answer each question in the space provided.

46. List four possible causes of a slow heart rate.
1.
2.
3.
4.

47. List three words that may be used to describe the strength of a pulse.
1.
2.
3.

48. List the meaning of each letter of the OPQRST memory aid.

O =
P =
Q =
R =
S =
T =

49. List three possible causes of flushed skin.
1.
2.
3.

50. On the drawing below, label each of the following arterial pulse points: brachial, carotid, dorsalis pedis, femoral, posterior tibial, and radial. Then indicate if it is a central or a peripheral pulse.

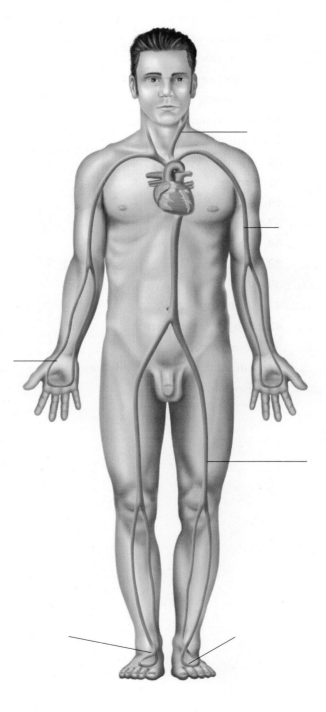

Answer Section

True/False

1. True

   Pulses are normally equal bilaterally. Pulses may be unequal in strength because of extremity injury or clot formation, among other causes.

   Objective: Identify the information obtained when assessing a patient's pulse.

2. True

   Retaking a blood pressure too quickly may produce a falsely high systolic or low diastolic reading. Wait 2-3 minutes before reinflating the cuff.

   Objective: Describe the methods to assess blood pressure.

Multiple Choice

3. c

   A sign is something you observe about a patient through sight, touch, or listening. The child's history of a cold and prior similar episodes is, however, important and should be included in your report.

   Objective: Differentiate between a sign and a symptom.

4. d

   The normal respiratory rate for an infant (younger than 1 year of age) is 20-40 breaths per minute. Abnormally slow breathing in a child is an ominous sign of impending respiratory collapse. The normal range of respirations for adolescents and adults is 12-20 breaths per minute. The normal range for a toddler and preschooler is 20-30 breaths per minute. The normal range for a school-age child is 16-30 breaths per minute. Remember that when assessing an infant's respiratory rate you must count the number of respirations during 1 full minute.

   Objective: Identify the attributes that should be obtained when assessing breathing.

5. a

   Capillary refill can be beneficial when assessing the perfusion of a child. For patients older 6 years of age, capillary refill tends to be less accurate. Normal capillary refill is less than 2 seconds. Delayed refill may be indicative of hypoperfusion (shock).

   Objective: Identify normal and abnormal capillary refill in infants and children.

6. c

   Measure blood pressure in children more than 3 years of age. In children less than 3 years of age, a strong central pulse is considered an acceptable sign of adequate blood pressure. When a blood pressure is obtained by palpation, the diastolic pressure cannot be measured. Pulse pressure is the difference between the systolic and diastolic blood pressure.

   Objective: Explain the difference between auscultation and palpation for obtaining a blood pressure.

7. c

   Document the patient's palpated blood pressure as the systolic pressure over a capital *P*, such as 110/P.

   Objective: Explain the difference between auscultation and palpation for obtaining a blood pressure.

8. c

   For stable patients, vital signs should be reassessed *at least* every 15 minutes. More frequent assessments provide more detailed information about the patient's status. Unstable patients should be reassessed *at least* every 5 minutes.

Objective: State the importance of accurately reporting and recording the baseline vital signs.

9. b

A symptom is a condition described by the patient. Shortness of breath, nausea, abdominal pain, chills, chest pain, and dizziness are examples of symptoms.

Objective: Differentiate between a sign and a symptom.

10. d

A blood pressure cuff (sphygmomanometer) is used to measure a patient's blood pressure.

Objective: Describe the methods to assess blood pressure.

11. c

The bottom number in an auscultated blood pressure is the diastolic pressure, the pressure in the arteries between heartbeats (relaxation of the heart muscle). The top number is the systolic pressure, which represents the force exerted against the arterial wall during contraction of the heart. The heart muscle receives its blood supply during the relaxation of the heart (between beats).

Objective: Define diastolic pressure.

12. c

OPQRST is a helpful memory aid for the assessment of a patient's complaint of pain or discomfort. It stands for *o*nset (when did the problem start), *p*rovoking/*p*alliating factors (what makes the problem worse or better), *q*uality (how is the pain described), *r*egion/*r*adiation (where is the pain and does it radiate), *s*everity (on a scale from 0 to 10, how does this problem rate), and *t*ime (how long ago did the problem begin).

APGAR is a memory aid for the assessment of a newborn child. SAMPLE is a history-gathering acronym. DCAPBTLS is a memory aid that is useful when assessing injured patients.

Objective: Identify the components of the SAMPLE history.

13. a

Pale skin suggests poor perfusion caused by shock or fright, among other causes. In this situation, the patient's pale skin is most likely a result of blood loss. The body attempts to compensate for blood loss by constricting (narrowing) the vessels of the skin to shunt blood to the heart, brain, and other major organs. Hepatitis and liver disease may result in a jaundiced (yellow) appearance. High blood pressure may be associated with flushed (red) skin.

Objective: Differentiate between pale, blue, red, and yellow skin color.

14. d

The *P* in SAMPLE stands for pertinent *p*ast medical history. Examples of questions to ask include the following:

- Are you seeing a doctor for any medical or psychological condition?
- Do you have a history of heart problems, respiratory problems, high blood pressure, diabetes, epilepsy, or other ongoing medical condition?
- Have you been in the hospital recently? Have you had any recent surgery?

The other components of a SAMPLE history are *s*igns and *s*ymptoms, *a*llergies, *m*edications (currently taking), *l*ast oral intake (food or liquid), and *e*vents leading up to the problem.

Objective: Identify the components of the SAMPLE history.

15. c

Count the number of beats for 30 seconds. Then multiply the number by 2 to determine the number of beats per minute. If the pulse is irregular, count it for 1 full minute.

Objective: Describe the methods to obtain a pulse rate.

16. a

A normal pulse is easily felt and is obliterated by strong pressure, and the pressure is equal for each beat. This kind of pulse is said to be a "strong" pulse. A pulse is said to be "weak" if it is hard to feel. A pulse that is weak and fast is called a "thready" pulse. An extremely strong pulse that is difficult to obliterate with pressure is called a "bounding" pulse.

Objective: Differentiate between a strong, weak, regular and irregular pulse.

17. b

Attributes that should be assessed when evaluating a patient's pulse include the rate, rhythm, and quality (strength).

Objective: Identify the information obtained when assessing a patient's pulse.

18. d

Wheezing is the sound created by air whistling through narrowed bronchioles. Snoring occurs when the upper airway is partially obstructed by the tongue. Crowing is a long, high-pitched sound heard on inspiration. Gurgling is a sound created by air as it moves through moist respiratory secretions. (*Caution:* The absence of wheezing in a previously distressed, wheezing patient is not necessarily a good sign. Wheezing may subside if the narrowing of the airway is reversed *or* if the patient is no longer moving enough air in and out of the lungs to make the narrowed airway whistle. The absence of wheezing can, in the latter example, be an ominous sign.)

Objective: Differentiate between shallow, labored, and noisy breathing.

19. d

The brachial pulse is located on the medial aspect of the mid-upper arm. It can generally be found by palpating the "groove" between the biceps muscle and the humerus bone. The carotid pulse is found in the neck on either side of the throat. The radial pulse is located on the thumb-side of the wrist. The femoral pulse is located in the crease between the pelvis and the thigh.

Objective: Describe the methods to obtain a pulse rate.

20. c

Intercostal ("inter" = between; "costal" = pertaining to the ribs) retractions is the term for this finding. Grunting is the sound created by air forced against a closed glottis in an attempt to keep the alveoli expanded. Gastric distention occurs when air enters the stomach. Gastric distention is a concern when ventilating a patient and is the reason why ventilations should be delivered slowly in nonbreathing patients. Subcutaneous emphysema is the presence of air in the subcutaneous tissue.

Objective: Identify the attributes that should be obtained when assessing breathing.

21. c

Accessory muscle use occurs when the primary muscles of respiration, the diaphragm and intercostals, do not provide sufficient mechanical support to meet the body's oxygen demand. Additional muscles throughout the abdomen, shoulders, neck, face, and back may assist the ventilatory effort. A pneumothorax is the presence of air in the pleural space (the space created by the double-walled sac that surrounds the lungs). Gastric distention is the presence of air in the stomach. Paradoxical chest wall movement occurs when a "floating" section of broken ribs move in a direction opposite the rest of the chest wall during breathing.

Objective: Identify the attributes that should be obtained when assessing breathing.

22. a

The vital signs (pulse, blood pressure, skin condition, respiratory rate) of an unstable patient should be assessed and recorded at least every 5 minutes. Stable patients should be reevaluated every 15 minutes.

Objective: State the importance of accurately reporting and recording the baseline vital signs.

Sentence Completion

23. A **sign** is a medical or trauma condition of the patient that can be seen, heard, smelled, measured, or felt.

Objective: Differentiate between a sign and a symptom.

24. You should never check the **carotid** pulse on both sides of the body simultaneously.

Objective: Describe the methods to obtain a pulse rate.

25. A symptom is a **subjective** finding because it is dependent on (subject to) the patient's interpretation and description of his complaint.

Objective: Differentiate between a sign and a symptom.

Matching

26.	N	36.	F
27.	D	37.	M
28.	I	38.	H
29.	R	39.	O
30.	K	40.	C
31.	B	41.	A
32.	Q	42.	E
33.	G	43.	T
34.	L	44.	P
35.	S	45.	J

Short Answer

46. Possible causes of a slow heart rate include the following:

   - Coughing
   - Vomiting
   - Straining to have a bowel movement
   - Heart attack
   - Head injury
   - Very low body temperature (hypothermia)
   - Sleep apnea
   - Some medications

   Objective: Identify the information obtained when assessing a patient's pulse.

47. The strength of a pulse may be described as:

   - Strong
   - Weak
   - Thready

   Objective: Differentiate between a strong, weak, regular, and irregular pulse.

48. If your patient is complaining of pain or discomfort, OPQRST is a memory aid that may help identify the type and location of the patient's complaint:

   *O*nset
   *P*rovocation/Palliation
   *Q*uality
   *R*egion/Radiation
   *S*everity
   *T*ime

   Objective: Identify the components of the SAMPLE history.

49. Flushed (red) skin may be caused by the following:

   - Heat exposure
   - Late stages of carbon monoxide poisoning
   - Allergic reaction
   - Alcohol abuse
   - High blood pressure

   Objective: Differentiate between pale, blue, red, and yellow skin color.

50.

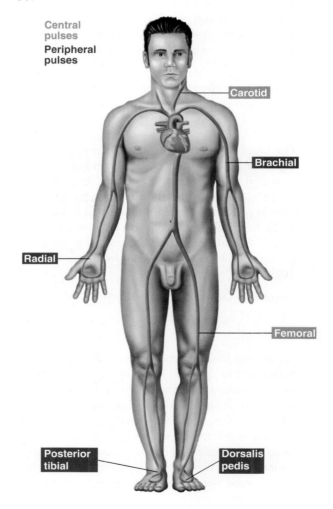

Central pulses
Peripheral pulses

Carotid
Brachial
Radial
Femoral
Posterior tibial
Dorsalis pedis

Objective: Describe the methods to obtain a pulse rate.

6 Lifting and Moving Patients

READING ASSIGNMENT ▶   Read Chapter 6, pages 119 to 145 in your textbook.

Sum It Up

- As an EMT, you will most often give initial emergency care to a patient in the position in which he is found. You will need to be able to distinguish an emergency from a non-emergency situation. Your role will also include positioning patients to prevent further injury and assisting other EMS professionals in lifting and moving patients.

- Body mechanics refers to the way we move our bodies when lifting and moving. Body mechanics includes body alignment, balance, and coordinated body movement. Good posture is key to proper body alignment.

- In order to lift safely, you should use the power grip (underhand grip). To perform this grip, you should position your hands a comfortable distance apart (about 10 inches). With your palms up, grasp the object you are preparing to lift. The power grip allows you to take full advantage of the strength of your hands, forearms, and biceps.

- Safely lifting patients requires you to use good posture and good body mechanics. You should consider the weight of the patient and call for additional help if needed. Plan how you will move the patient and where you will move him. It is also important to remember to lift with your legs and not your back. When lifting with other EMS professionals, communication and planning are key.

- An emergency move is used when there is an immediate danger to you or the patient. These dangers include scene hazards, the inability to reach patients who need lifesaving care, and a patient location or position that prevents you from giving immediate and lifesaving care.

- Safely lifting patients requires you to use good posture and good body mechanics. You should consider the weight of the patient and call for additional help if needed.

- Drags are one type of emergency move. When dragging a patient, remember to stabilize the patient's head and neck as much as possible before beginning the move. Also, always remember to pull along the length of the spine. Never pull the patient's head away from his neck and shoulders. You should also *never* drag a patient sideways. Carries are the second major type of emergency move. As an EMT, you should become familiar with the different types of carries.

- An urgent move is used to move a patient when there is an immediate threat to life, such as in the following situations: altered mental status, inadequate breathing, or shock. Rapid extrication is an example of an urgent move. It must be accomplished quickly, without compromise or injury to the spine.
- Non-urgent moves are used to move, lift, or carry patients with no known or suspected injury to the head, neck, spine, or extremities. The direct ground lift and the extremity lift are the two main types of non-urgent moves.
- The direct carry and the draw sheet method are the two primary methods used to transfer a supine patient to a bed or stretcher. In both transfer types you will be assisting hospital personnel or another EMS professional. Therefore, teamwork and coordination are essential.
- Patient positioning is an important part of the patient care you provide. In some cases, simply changing a patient's position can improve his condition. As an EMT, you should become familiar with the different types of positions and when to use them.
- Many different types of equipment are used to assist in stabilizing and moving patients. In your role as an emergency care provider, it is important to become familiar with the equipment used in your area. Commonly used equipment includes various types of stretchers and backboards as well as the stair chair.

▶ Tracking Your Progress

After reading this chapter, can you:	Page Reference	Objective Met?
• Define body mechanics?	121	☐
• Discuss the guidelines and safety precautions that need to be followed when lifting a patient?	123	☐
• Describe the safe lifting of cots and stretchers?	123	☐
• Describe the guidelines and safety precautions for carrying patients and/or equipment?	125	☐
• Discuss 1-handed carrying techniques?	125	☐
• Describe correct and safe carrying procedures on stairs?	125	☐
• State the guidelines for reaching and their application?	125	☐
• Describe correct reaching for log rolls?	125	☐
• State the guidelines for pushing and pulling?	125	☐
• Discuss the general considerations of moving patients?	121	☐
• State three situations that may require the use of an emergency move?	121	☐
• Identify the following patient carrying devices: wheeled stretcher, portable stretcher, stair chair, scoop stretcher, long spine board, basket stretcher, and flexible stretcher?	141	☐

True or False

Decide whether each statement is true or false. In the space provided, write *T* for true or *F* for false.

_____ 1. When attempting to move a patient, it is generally best to move him sideways.

_____ 2. To help maintain balance while standing, keep your feet as close together as possible.

_____ 3. Both sides of the patient must be accessible when a scoop stretcher is being used.

Multiple Choice

In the space provided, identify the letter of the choice that best completes the statement or answers each question.

_____ 4. Which of the following is an example of a situation requiring an emergency move?
  a. An 88-year-old man who is sitting in a chair in his home and is confused.
  b. A 57-year-old woman who is in a supermarket complaining of difficulty breathing.
  c. A 72-year-old woman who is sitting in a chair and is unresponsive, not breathing, and has no pulse.
  d. A 5-year-old boy who is sitting on the bench in the park complaining of stomach pain.

_____ 5. Which of the following is an example of an emergency move?
  a. Direct ground lift   **c.** Direct carry
  b. Extremity lift   **d.** Blanket drag

_____ 6. Which of the following may be used in a high-angle rescue?
  a. Wheeled stretcher, basket stretcher
  b. Basket stretcher, flexible stretcher
  c. Portable stretcher, wheeled stretcher
  d. Flexible stretcher, scoop stretcher

_____ 7. Which of the following statements is true regarding safe lifting techniques?
  a. Place your feet close together.
  b. Know your physical abilities and limitations.
  c. Use the large muscles of your back to lift.
  d. Keep the weight a minimum of 20 to 30 inches from your body.

Sentence Completion

In the blanks provided, write the words that best complete each sentence.

8. When dragging a patient, avoid reaching more than _____ in front of your body.

9. The patient move shown in this figure is called the _____ _____.

10. The patient move shown in this figure is called the _____ _____.

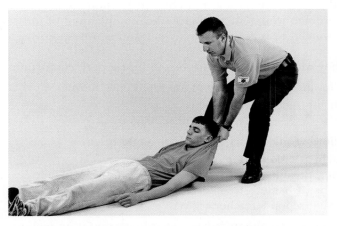

© The McGraw-Hill Companies, Inc./Rick Brady, photographer.

11. The patient move shown in this figure is called the _____ _____.

© The McGraw-Hill Companies, Inc./Rick Brady, photographer.

12. The patient move shown in this figure is called the _____ _____.

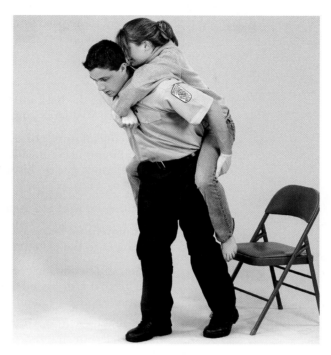

© *The McGraw-Hill Companies, Inc./Rick Brady, photographer.*

13. The patient move shown in this figure is called the _____ _____ move.

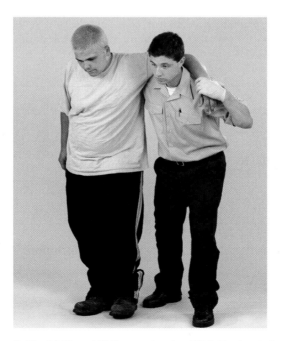

© *The McGraw-Hill Companies, Inc./Rick Brady, photographer.*

Matching

Match the key terms in the left column with the definitions in the right column by placing the letter of each correct answer in the space provided.

_____ 14. Emergency move

_____ 15. High-Fowler's position

_____ 16. Semi-Fowler's position

_____ 17. Power grip

_____ 18. Draw sheet

_____ 19. Fowler's position

_____ 20. Recovery position

_____ 21. Wheeled stretcher

_____ 22. Non-urgent move

A. Patient move used when no immediate threat to life exists and patient's safety is the primary concern

B. A narrow sheet placed crosswise on a bed under the patient

C. Lying on the back with the upper body elevated at a 45- to 60-degree angle

D. Placing an unresponsive patient who is breathing and in no need of CPR (and in whom trauma is not suspected) on his side to help keep his airway open

E. Sitting upright at a 90-degree angle

F. A move used because there is an immediate danger to the patient or rescuer

G. Method of placing your hands on an object before a lift that is designed to take full advantage of the strength of your hands and forearms

H. Sitting up with the head at a 45-degree angle and the legs out straight

I. A rolling bed commonly found in the back of an ambulance

Short Answer

Answer each question in the space provided.

24. A 62-year-old man was the unrestrained driver of a vehicle that struck a power pole at approximately 80 miles per hour. What is the greatest danger in moving this patient, if you determine that an emergency move is necessary?

25. You are preparing to transfer a patient from a stretcher to a bed by using a direct carry. Where should you place the stretcher?

26. Define a log roll and then describe the correct reaching technique for this procedure.

Answer Section

Chapter 6

True/False

1. False

Never push, pull, or drag a patient sideways. Always drag the patient in the direction of the length (the long axis) of the body. This action will provide as much protection as possible to the patient's spine.

Objective: State the guidelines for pushing and pulling.

2. False

Your feet should be separated to a comfortable distance to provide a broad base of support.

Objective: Discuss the guidelines and safety precautions that need to be followed when lifting a patient.

3. True

A scoop (orthopedic) stretcher is unique in that it is hinged and opens at the head and feet to fit around and under the patient. The scoop stretcher is also called a *split litter*. To use this device, both sides of the patient must be accessible.

Objective: Identify the following patient carrying devices: wheeled stretcher, portable stretcher, stair chair, scoop stretcher, long spine board, basket stretcher, and flexible stretcher.

Multiple Choice

4. c

An emergency move is used when there is an immediate danger to you or the patient. These dangers include scene hazards, the inability to reach patients who need lifesaving care, and a patient location or position that prevents you from giving immediate and lifesaving care.

Objective: State 3 situations that may require the use of an emergency move.

5. d

Drags are 1 type of emergency move. When dragging a patient, remember to stabilize the patient's head and neck as much as possible before beginning the move. Also, always remember to pull along the length of the spine. *Never* pull the patient's head away from his neck and shoulders. You should also never drag a patient sideways.

Carries are the second major type of emergency move. As an EMT, you should become familiar with the different types of carries.

Objective: N/A

6. b

A basket stretcher is used for moving patients over rough terrain, in water rescues, or in high-angle rescues. A flexible stretcher can be rolled up for easy storage and carrying but forms a more rigid surface that conforms to the sides of the patient when in use. Flexible stretchers are made of canvas or flexible, synthetic material and have carrying handles. Straps are used to secure the patient. This type of stretcher is particularly useful when space is limited to access the patient. It can be used in narrow hallways, stairs, cramped corners, high-angle rescues, and hazardous materials situations.

Objective: Identify the following patient carrying devices: wheeled stretcher, portable stretcher, stair chair, scoop stretcher, long spine board, basket stretcher, and flexible stretcher.

7. b

To protect yourself and the patient, you should prepare and plan *before* you actually move a patient. Important factors to consider include:

- The patient's weight
- The patient's condition
- The presence of hazards or potential hazards at the scene
- The terrain

- The distance the patient must be moved
- Your physical abilities and any limitations
- The availability of any equipment or personnel to assist with the move

Objective: Discuss the guidelines and safety precautions that need to be followed when lifting a patient.

Sentence Completion

8. When dragging a patient, avoid reaching more than **15 to 20 inches** in front of your body.

   Objective: State the guidelines for reaching and their application.

9. The patient move shown in this figure is called the **forearm drag.**

   Objective: State the guidelines for pushing and pulling.

10. The patient move shown in this figure is called the **clothes drag** (also called the clothing pull or shirt drag).

    Objective: Discuss the general considerations of moving patients.

11. The patient move shown in this figure is called the **cradle carry** (also called the one-person arm carry).

    Objective: Discuss the general considerations of moving patients.

12. The patient move shown in this figure is called the **piggyback carry.**

    Objective: Discuss the general considerations of moving patients.

13. The patient move shown in this figure is called the **human crutch** move (also called the rescuer assist or walking assist).

    Objective: Discuss the general considerations of moving patients.

Matching

14.	F	19.	C
15.	E	20.	D
16.	H	21.	I
17.	G	22.	A
18.	B		

Short Answer

24. The greatest danger to this patient is aggravating a spinal injury.

    Objective: Discuss the general considerations of moving patients.

25. The stretcher should be placed at a 90-degree angle to the bed, with the head end of the stretcher at the foot of the bed.

    Objective: Describe the guidelines and safety precautions for carrying patients and/or equipment.

26. A log roll is a technique used to move a patient from a face-down to a face-up position while keeping the head and neck in line with the rest of the body. This technique is also used to place a patient with a suspected spinal injury on a backboard. Correct reaching for log rolls includes the following guidelines:

    - Keep your back straight while leaning over the patient.
    - Lean from the hips.
    - Use your shoulder muscles to help with the roll.

    Objective: Describe correct reaching for log rolls.

Division 2

Airway

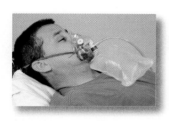

7 Airway and Breathing

READING ASSIGNMENT ▶ Read Chapter 7, pages 146 to 182 in your textbook.

Sum It Up

- As an EMT, you must maintain an open airway in order to allow a free flow of air into and out of the patient's lungs. You must be familiar with the structures of the upper and lower airways. You must also understand the mechanisms of breathing.
- One of the most important actions that you can perform is to open the airway of an unresponsive patient. You must become familiar with the two main methods of opening an airway: the head tilt–chin lift and the jaw thrust without head tilt maneuver.
  —The head tilt–chin lift maneuver is used to open the airway if trauma to the head or neck is not suspected.
  —When trauma to the head or neck of an unresponsive patient is suspected, you should use the jaw thrust without head tilt (also called the *jaw thrust without head extension maneuver*) to open the patient's airway. However, use a head tilt–chin lift maneuver if the jaw thrust does not open the airway. This method of opening the airway is effective, but it is less effective than the head tilt–chin lift and is more tiring. Because this technique requires the use of both hands, a second rescuer will be needed if the patient requires ventilation.
- If a patient's airway is obstructed, you must clear it. The three primary ways of clearing the airway of an unresponsive patient are with the recovery position, finger sweeps, and suctioning.
  —In some situations, the recovery position can be used to help maintain an open airway in an unresponsive patient. This position involves positioning a patient on his side. As an EMT, you must become familiar with placing a patient in this position. You must also remember not to place a patient with a known or suspected spinal injury in the recovery position.
  —If you see foreign material in the patient's mouth, you must remove it immediately. If foreign material is seen in an unresponsive patient's upper airway, a finger sweep may be used to remove it. A "blind" finger sweep is never performed. Performing a blind finger sweep may cause the object to become further lodged in the patient's throat.
  —You should always have suction equipment within arm's reach when you are managing a patient's airway or assisting a patient's breathing.

Suctioning is a procedure used to vacuum vomitus, saliva, blood, food particles, and other material from the patient's airway.

- After you have opened a patient's airway, you may need to use an airway adjunct to keep it open. After the airway adjunct is inserted, maintain the proper head position while the device is in place.
  - —An oral airway (also called an *oropharyngeal airway* or *OPA*) is a device that is used only in unresponsive patients without a gag reflex. An OPA is inserted into the patient's mouth and used to keep the tongue away from the back of the throat.
  - —A nasal airway (also called a *nasopharyngeal airway* or *NPA*) is a device that is placed in the patient's nose. An NPA keeps the patient's tongue from blocking the upper airway. It also allows air to flow from the hole in the NPA down into the patient's lower airway.
- After making sure that the patient's airway is open, you must check for breathing. If the patient is breathing, you must determine if the patient is breathing adequately or inadequately. You must also be able to recognize the sounds of noisy breathing, which include stridor, snoring, gurgling, and wheezing.
- If your patient's breathing is inadequate or absent, you will need to assist the patient by forcing air into the patient's lungs during inspiration. This action is called *positive-pressure ventilation* and includes the following: mouth-to-mask ventilation, mouth-to–barrier device ventilation, mouth-to-mouth ventilation, and bag-mask ventilation. As an EMT, you must be familiar with performing all of these ventilation methods. You must also learn how to remove foreign body airway obstructions in patients of every age.
- A FROPVD is used to give positive-pressure ventilation with 100% oxygen. It can be attached to a face mask, tracheal tube, or tracheostomy tube.
- You may need to give patients supplemental oxygen. Become familiar with the features and functioning of oxygen cylinders. Remember to always keep combustible materials away from oxygen equipment and never position any part of your body over the cylinder.
- The two most common oxygen delivery devices are the nonrebreather mask and the nasal cannula. In most situations, the nonrebreather mask is the preferred method of oxygen delivery. It allows the delivery of high-concentration oxygen to a breathing patient. At 15 L/min, the oxygen concentration delivered is about 90%. The nasal cannula is often used for patients who have chest pain and are breathing adequately. It is also the preferred method of oxygen delivery in some EMS systems for patients showing signs and symptoms of a possible stroke (and who are breathing adequately). A nasal cannula can deliver an oxygen concentration of 25-45% at 1-6 L/min.

▶ Tracking Your Progress

After reading this chapter, can you:	Page Reference	Objective Met?
• Name and label the major structures of the respiratory system on a diagram?	149	☐
• List the signs of adequate breathing?	160	☐
• List the signs of inadequate breathing?	162	☐
• Describe the steps in performing the head tilt–chin lift maneuver?	153	☐
• Relate mechanism of injury to opening the airway?	153	☐

After reading this chapter, can you:	Page Reference	Objective Met?
• Describe the steps in performing the jaw thrust without head tilt maneuver?	153	☐
• State the importance of having a suction unit ready for immediate use when providing emergency care?	154	☐
• Describe the techniques of suctioning?	154	☐
• Describe how to artificially ventilate a patient with a pocket mask?	164	☐
• Describe the steps in artificially ventilating a patient with a BM while using the jaw thrust without head tilt maneuver?	169	☐
• List the parts of a BM system?	167	☐
• Describe the steps in artificially ventilating a patient with a BM device for one and two rescuers?	169	☐
• Describe the signs of adequate artificial ventilation using the BM?	170	☐
• Describe the signs of inadequate artificial ventilation using the BM?	170	☐
• Describe the steps in artificially ventilating a patient with a FROPVD?	171	☐
• List the steps in performing mouth-to-barrier device and mask-to-stoma artificial ventilation?	166, 173	☐
• Describe how to measure and insert an oropharyngeal (oral) airway?	157	☐
• Describe how to measure and insert a nasopharyngeal (nasal) airway?	157	☐
• Define the components of an oxygen delivery system?	174	☐
• Identify a nonrebreather face mask and state the oxygen flow requirements needed for its use?	180	☐
• Describe the indications for using a nasal cannula versus a nonrebreather face mask?	180	☐
• Identify a nasal cannula and state the flow requirements needed for its use?	180	☐

True or False

Decide whether each statement is true or false. In the space provided, write *T* for true or *F* for false.

_____ 1. An oral airway can be used in responsive, semi-responsive, and unresponsive patients.

_____ 2. During swallowing, the cricoid cartilage covers the opening of the larynx and prevents food or liquids from entering it.

_____ 3. Air entering the alveoli from the atmosphere during inspiration is rich in oxygen and contains little carbon dioxide.

_____ 4. The thyroid cartilage is the most inferior of the cartilages in the larynx.

_____ 5. Infants and children depend more heavily on the diaphragm for breathing than adults.

_____ 6. The reservoir of a nonrebreather mask should be filled with oxygen before the mask is placed on the patient.

_____ 7. BSI precautions are unnecessary when managing a patient's airway.

_____ 8. Suctioning can cause significant changes in the patient's heart rate.

_____ 9. Room air contains 16-17% oxygen.

_____ 10. You can deliver a greater tidal volume with a pocket mask than with a BM device.

_____ 11. A nonrebreather mask is the oxygen delivery device of choice for a patient who has a poor respiratory effort.

Multiple Choice

In the space provided, identify the letter of the choice that best completes the statement or answers each question.

Questions 12–19 pertain to the following scenario.

Your rescue crew is called to the scene of an 87-year-old man in severe respiratory distress. The patient has a past medical history of emphysema and is a two-pack-a-day cigarette smoker. Because of his distress and fatigue, he has a very difficult time speaking with you.

_____ **12.** You determine this patient is breathing at a rate of 30 times per minute. This rate of breathing
    a. is normal for the patient's age.
    b. is slower than normal for the patient's age.
    c. is faster than normal for the patient's age.

_____ **13.** The patient's skin is cool, clammy, and cyanotic. Cyanotic skin is _____ in appearance.
    a. red
    b. blue
    c. pale
    d. yellow

_____ **14.** The patient's mouth is full of frothy sputum. Which of the following should be used to suction the patient's mouth?
    a. A bulb syringe or soft suction catheter
    b. A soft or rigid suction catheter
    c. A bulb syringe or tonsil tip catheter
    d. A whistle-tip catheter or bulb syringe

_____ **15.** When suctioning this patient, suction should be applied
    a. for no more than 5 seconds.
    b. for no more than 15 seconds.
    c. for a minimum of 30 seconds.
    d. for a minimum of 60 seconds.

_____ **16.** Suction should be applied
    a. only on withdrawal of the suction catheter.
    b. only during insertion of the suction catheter.
    c. on insertion and removal of the suction catheter.

_____ **17.** After suctioning the airway, you insert a nasal airway. Which of the following statements is true about this device?
    a. A nasal airway can be placed in either nostril to help maintain an open airway.
    b. A nasal airway should be used only in unresponsive patients who do not have a gag reflex.
    c. When properly positioned, the distal tip of the nasal airway rests in the patient's trachea.
    d. A correctly sized nasal airway extends from the corner of the patient's mouth to the tip of the ear lobe.

_____ **18.** You administer supplemental oxygen by means of a nonrebreather mask. Which of the following statements correctly reflects the proper oxygen liter flow and oxygen percentage delivered by this device?
    a. 2 L/min delivers about 24% oxygen
    b. 6 L/min delivers about 45% oxygen
    c. 10 L/min delivers about 65% oxygen
    d. 15 L/min delivers about 90% oxygen

19. While en route to the hospital, the patient's respiratory rate increases to 40 breaths per minute with very low tidal volume. His mental status is decreasing. You decide to assist his respiratory effort by using a BVM device with supplemental oxygen. You should deliver ventilations at a rate of

   a. 1 ventilation every 3 to 5 seconds.
   b. 1 ventilation every 5 to 6 seconds.
   c. 1 ventilation every 10 to 12 seconds.
   d. 1 ventilation every 12 to 15 seconds.

20. Oxygen regulators are designed to

   a. prevent explosion or fire.
   b. humidify the oxygen for greater patient comfort.
   c. sound an alarm when oxygen levels drop below 2000 psi.
   d. reduce the oxygen pressure to a therapeutic pressure and flow.

21. The FROPVD is also called a

   a. nasal cannula.
   b. pulse oximeter.
   c. BM device.
   d. manually triggered ventilation device.

22. The exchange of gases in the respiratory system occurs at the alveolar-capillary membrane. The primary gases exchanged during normal respiration are

   a. oxygen and plasma.
   b. oxygen and hemoglobin.
   c. oxygen and carbon dioxide.
   d. oxygen and carbon monoxide.

23. Which of the following correctly identifies a difference between the airway of an adult and the airway of a child or infant?

   a. The infant's trachea is more rigid.
   b. The adult's tongue is proportionally larger.
   c. The infant's chest wall is more unyielding to pressure.
   d. The narrowest portion of the infant's airway is the cricoid cartilage.

24. To size an oral airway correctly, you would measure from the

   a. center of the patient's mouth to the suprasternal notch.
   b. corner of the patient's mouth to the tip of the ear lobe.
   c. patient's nasal septum to the Adam's apple (thyroid cartilage).
   d. center of the patient's mouth to the Adam's apple (thyroid cartilage).

25. When delivering artificial ventilations with a BM device, adequate ventilations are achieved when

   a. the oxygen reservoir collapses.
   b. the patient slowly becomes more cyanotic.
   c. the patient's chest wall rises and falls with each ventilation.
   d. the BM device becomes progressively more difficult to compress with each ventilation.

26. An advantage of the nasal airway over the oral airway is that the nasal airway

   a. does not cause trauma during insertion.
   b. is better tolerated by semi-responsive patients.
   c. allows for delivery of greater oxygen concentrations.
   d. does not require sizing because one size fits all patients.

27. When delivering artificial ventilations by means of a BM device, rescuers can successfully deliver about _____ oxygen without the use of supplemental oxygen.

   a. 16%
   b. 21%
   c. 50%
   d. 80%

_____ **28.** Improper sizing and insertion of an oral airway may cause
  a. barotrauma.
  b. cardiac tamponade.
  c. complete airway obstruction.
  d. delivery of a higher concentration of oxygen than desired.

_____ **29.** The voice box is the
  a. larynx.
  b. pharynx.
  c. trachea.
  d. alveolus.

_____ **30.** The amount of air moved into or out of the lungs during a normal breath is called
  a. the tidal volume.
  b. the minute volume.
  c. compliance.
  d. diffusion.

_____ **31.** Which of the following statements regarding infants is correct?
  a. An infant's epiglottis is small and rigid.
  b. An infant is primarily a mouth breather.
  c. An infant's chest wall is composed mostly of cartilage.
  d. The narrowest portion of an infant's airway is at the level of the thyroid cartilage.

_____ **32.** A catheter used to clear the mouth and throat and remove secretions from an endotracheal tube in intubated patients is known as
  a. a tonsil sucker.
  b. a flexible catheter.
  c. a tonsil tip catheter.
  d. a Yankauer catheter.

_____ **33.** Which of the following is considered a portable oxygen cylinder?
  a. D
  b. G
  c. H
  d. M

_____ **34.** When an oxygen humidifier is used, it should be changed
  a. after each use.
  b. once each shift.
  c. when the water is half empty.
  d. only if it is expired.

Sentence Completion

In the blanks provided, write the words that best complete each sentence.

35. The largest cartilage of the larynx is the thyroid cartilage, also called the _____ _____.

36. OPA stands for _____ _____.

37. The most common cause of upper airway obstruction in an unresponsive patient is the _____.

38. The gases exchanged during the process of breathing are _____ and _____.

39. A _____ _____ is a permanent opening at the front of the neck that extends from the skin surface into the trachea.

40. Complete the following table, indicating the oxygen delivery percentages for a nasal cannula.

1 L/min	_____ %
2 L/min	_____ %
3 L/min	_____ %
4 L/min	_____ %
5 L/min	_____ %
6 L/min	_____ %

41. Complete the following table.

Patient	Breaths/Minute	Length of Each Breath
Adult		
Infant/Child		
Newborn		

42. The reservoir bag of the nonrebreather mask should never be less than _____ full.

Matching

Match the key terms in the left column with the definitions in the right column by placing the letter of each correct answer in the space provided.

_____ **43.** Nasal septum

_____ **44.** Blow-by oxygen

_____ **45.** Flow meter

_____ **46.** Airway adjuncts

_____ **47.** Orthopnea

_____ **48.** Diaphragm

_____ **49.** Epiglottis

_____ **50.** Minute volume

_____ **51.** Stoma

_____ **52.** Tripod position

_____ **53.** Suctioning

_____ **54.** Agonal respirations

_____ **55.** Wheezing

_____ **56.** Glottis

_____ **57.** Respiratory distress

_____ **58.** Pressure regulator

_____ **59.** Respiratory arrest

_____ **60.** Patent

_____ **61.** Aspiration

A. An absence of breathing

B. The primary muscle of respiration

C. Breathing in a foreign substance into the lungs

D. Device used to reduce pressure in an oxygen cylinder to a safe range

E. A wall of tissue that separates the right and left nostrils

F. Increased work of breathing

G. A procedure used to vacuum material from the patient's airway

H. Devices used to help keep a patient's airway open

I. Slow and shallow breathing that is sometimes seen just before the onset of respiratory failure

J. Open

K. Method of oxygen delivery in which the device used to deliver the oxygen does not make actual contact with the patient

L. The amount of air moved into or out of the lungs during a normal breath

Continued

_____ **62.** Compliance

_____ **63.** Onboard oxygen

_____ **64.** Tidal volume

M. Large oxygen cylinders carried on an ambulance

N. The ability of a patient's lung tissue to distend (inflate) with ventilation

O. An artificial opening

P. A valve that controls the liters of oxygen delivered per minute

Q. Sitting up and leaning forward with the weight of the upper body supported by the hands on the thighs or knees

R. The space between the vocal cords

S. The tidal volume multiplied by the respiratory rate

T. A piece of cartilage that closes off the trachea during swallowing

U. A whistling sound that is usually heard on exhalation

V. Breathlessness when lying flat that is relieved when the patient sits or stands

Short Answer

Answer each question in the space provided.

65. Describe how to select an oral airway of the correct size for a patient.

66. List five signs of inadequate breathing.

1.

2.

3.

4.

5.

67. List two methods that may be used to open an airway.

1.

2.

68. List three ways to deliver positive-pressure ventilation.

1.

2.

3.

69. You respond to a child choking. Upon arrival, you find a 3-year-old boy gagging and being held by his father. The father states that the child was eating grapes and started gagging. He turned blue and appeared to quit breathing. CPR was started and then stopped when the child began to gasp. You find the child alert and oriented for his age, and agitated. You note snoring respirations with gagging. Visual inspection reveals nothing in the child's oropharynx, but you can see something in the nasopharynx. What should your treatment/intervention include?

Allergies	None
Meds	None
Past Hx	Down's syndrome
Last intake	Grapes, just before you were called
Events	Choking incident

Time	Pulse	BP	Resp	Pupils	Skin	Lungs	SPO2
11:35	144 strong, regular	Not taken	36 gasping	Not assessed	Dusky, warm, dry	Clear	94
11:42	146 strong, regular	Not taken	30 gasping	Not assessed	Dusky, warm, dry	Clear	94

70. Normal breathing does not require excessive use of accessory muscles. What are accessory muscles and where are they located?

Answer Section

Chapter 7

True/False

1. False

An oral airway is inserted into the patient's mouth and used to keep the tongue away from the back of the throat. It may be used only in unresponsive patients *without* a gag reflex. If you try to use an OPA in a patient with a gag reflex, he may vomit and aspirate the vomitus into his lungs.

Objective: Describe how to measure and insert an oropharyngeal (oral) airway.

2. False

The epiglottis is a piece of cartilage that protects the lower airway from aspiration. When we swallow, the epiglottis closes off the trachea and prevents food from entering it. Choking may result if the epiglottis fails to close, allowing food or liquids to enter the airway.

Objective: Name and label the major structures of the respiratory system on a diagram.

3. True

When we breathe in, the air entering the body from the atmosphere is rich in oxygen and contains little carbon dioxide. Carbon dioxide is the waste product we rid the body of when exhaling. The oxygen-rich air enters the alveoli in the lungs and passes through the walls of capillaries into the bloodstream. Carbon dioxide passes from the blood through the capillary walls into the alveoli. It leaves the body in the air we breathe out.

Objective: N/A

4. False

The largest cartilage of the larynx is the thyroid cartilage, also called the Adam's apple. The cricoid cartilage is the most inferior (lowest) of the cartilages of the larynx.

Objective: Name and label the major structures of the respiratory system on a diagram.

5. True

Infants and children depend more heavily on the diaphragm for breathing. Gastric distention (swelling) is common when ventilating infants and children. If enough air builds up in the child's stomach to push on the lungs and diaphragm, effective breathing can be compromised. When assisting the breathing of an infant or child, avoid using too much volume. Use only enough volume to cause gentle chest rise.

Objective: Describe differences in anatomy and physiology of the infant, child, and adult patient.

6. True

The reservoir bag of a nonrebreather mask must be filled with oxygen before placing the mask on the patient. After placing the mask on the patient, adjust the flow rate so the bag does not completely deflate when the patient inhales. An oxygen flow rate of 15 L/min is usually needed to ensure proper inflation of the reservoir bag.

Objective: Describe the indications for using a nasal cannula versus a nonrebreather face mask.

7. False

Because the risk of exposure to blood, vomitus, or potentially infectious material is high, you must remember to take appropriate body substance isolation precautions when managing a patient's airway.

Objective: Describe the steps the EMT should take for personal protection from airborne and bloodborne pathogens.

8. True

Because suctioning can cause serious changes in your patient's heart rate, you must watch your patient closely when you perform this procedure. The patient's heart rate may slow or become irregular because of a lack of oxygen or stimulation of the back of the tongue or throat by the tip of the catheter.

Objective: Describe the techniques of suctioning.

9. False

Room air contains 21% oxygen. Your exhaled air contains 16-17% oxygen.

Objective: N/A

10. True

You can deliver a greater tidal volume with a pocket mask than with a BM device. There are two reasons for this. First, you can use both hands to hold a pocket mask securely in place and keep the patient's head in proper position at the same time. Second, you can adjust the depth of your breaths to make up for any leaks between the mask and the patient's face. This allows greater lung ventilation.

Objective: Describe how to artificially ventilate a patient with a pocket mask.

11. False

In most situations, a nonrebreather mask is the preferred method of oxygen delivery in the field for a patient who is breathing adequately. It is contraindicated in a patient who is not breathing or who has a poor respiratory effort.

Objective: Identify a nonrebreather face mask and state the oxygen flow requirements needed for its use.

Multiple Choice

12. c

A normal respiratory rate for an adult at rest is 12-20 respirations per minute. Tachypnea is the medical term for fast breathing. "Tachy" refers to a faster than normal pace, and "pnea" refers to breathing. Bradypnea is the medical term for a slow respiratory rate ("brady" = slow).

Objective: Describe how to measure and insert a nasopharyngeal (nasal) airway.

13. b

Cyanosis is the bluish appearance generally associated with poor oxygenation or perfusion. A red appearance may be referred to as *flushed*, and a yellowish appearance may be referred to as *jaundiced*. A flushed appearance may be associated with high blood pressure, high ambient temperature, use of certain drugs, or carbon monoxide poisoning (a late sign). A jaundiced appearance is often associated with liver disease.

Objective: List the signs of inadequate breathing.

14. b

A rigid suction catheter is also called a *hard suction catheter*, a *Yankauer catheter*, a *tonsil tip catheter*, or a *tonsil sucker*. Use a rigid suction catheter to remove secretions from a patient's mouth. Soft suction catheters are also called *flexible, whistle-tip,* or *French suction catheters*. These catheters are used to clear the mouth and throat and remove secretions from a tracheal tube in intubated patients. Bulb syringes are generally only used in infants.

Objective: Describe the techniques of suctioning.

15. b

If the patient's airway is open and a need for suction has been identified, attempt to provide 100% oxygen for 2-3 minutes before suctioning. This is called preoxygenation. Preoxygenating the patient is important because oxygen levels will drop during suctioning. The maximum length of time allowed for suctioning an adult is 15 seconds and 10 seconds in children and infants.

Objective: Describe the techniques of suctioning.

16. a

Without applying suction, place the tip of the catheter in the patient's mouth. Gently advance the catheter tip along one side of the mouth. Insert the catheter tip only as far as you can see. Do not touch the back of the airway. This can cause vomiting and/or changes in the patient's heart rate. Apply suction while moving the tip of the catheter from side to side as you withdraw it from the patient's mouth.

Objective: Describe the techniques of suctioning.

17. a

A nasal airway can be used in an unresponsive patient and may be useful in semi-responsive patients who have a gag reflex. It can be placed in either nostril to help maintain an open airway. To select an NPA of proper size, hold the NPA against the side of the patient's face. Select an airway that extends from the tip of the patient's nose to his ear lobe. When a nasal airway of the proper size is correctly positioned, the tip rests in the back of the throat.

Objective: Describe how to measure and insert a nasopharyngeal (nasal) airway.

18. d

A nonrebreather mask is a "high-concentration" oxygen delivery device. With the oxygen flow regulator set at 15 L/min, an oxygen concentration of about 90% can be delivered. A nasal cannula is a "low-concentration" oxygen delivery device. At 6 L/min, a nasal cannula can deliver an oxygen concentration of about 45%. Oxygen is stored as a compressed gas, and oxygen cylinders are pressurized to about 2000 psi.

Objective: Identify a nonrebreather face mask and state the oxygen flow requirements needed for its use.

19. b

The normal respiratory rate for an adult is 12 to 20 respirations per minute. When assisting ventilations, rescuers should deliver ventilations at a rate of delivery of 1 ventilation every 5 to 6 seconds (10 to 12 respirations per minute).

Objective: Describe the steps in artificially ventilating a patient with a BM for one and two rescuers.

20. d

Oxygen is compressed to approximately 2000 psi. A regulator is necessary to reduce this pressure to a therapeutic range. Regulators do not prevent oxygen's interaction with fire or combustibles. A separate water-filled chamber must be added to provide humidified oxygen. Humidified oxygen is generally not necessary for prehospital care.

Objective: Define the components of an oxygen delivery system.

21. d

A FROPVD is also called a *manually triggered ventilation (MTV) device*. A FROPVD is used to give positive-pressure ventilation with 100% oxygen. It can be attached to a face mask, tracheal tube, or tracheostomy tube.

Objective: Describe the steps in artificially ventilating a patient with a flow restricted, oxygen-powered ventilation device.

22. c

Oxygen and carbon dioxide are the two primary gases exchanged in the alveoli. Hemoglobin aids the transport of oxygen on the red blood cell. Carbon monoxide is an odorless, colorless, tasteless, poisonous gas that binds to hemoglobin more readily than oxygen. Plasma is the fluid in which red blood cells are suspended as they flow throughout the body.

Objective: Describe the anatomy and function of the following major body systems: respiratory, circulatory, musculoskeletal, nervous, and endocrine.

23. d

Although the narrowest portion of the adult airway is at the level of the vocal cords, the narrowest part of the young child and infant's airway is at the level of the cricoid cartilage. The infant and child's trachea and chest wall are more pliable than those of an adult. The tongue is larger in proportion to the airway in the infant and child than in the adult.

Objective: Name and label the major structures of the respiratory system on a diagram.

24. b

To select an oral airway of the correct size, hold it against the side of the patient's face. Select an oral airway that extends from the corner of the patient's mouth to the tip of the ear lobe, or from the center of the patient's mouth to the angle of the jaw. The oral airway is positioned in an adult's mouth by inserting it upside down, then rotating it right-side up as the tip of the device follows the hard palette (roof of the mouth). Improper sizing can lead to disastrous complications. An airway that is too long can press the epiglottis against the entrance of the larynx, resulting in a complete airway obstruction. An airway that is too short may come out of the mouth or it may push the tongue into the back of the throat, causing an airway obstruction.

Objective: Describe how to measure and insert an oropharyngeal (oral) airway.

25. c

The most reliable indicator of ventilation adequacy is the rise and fall of the chest wall. Remember, gas exchange does not take place until fresh air reaches the alveolar-capillary membrane. If the oxygen reservoir on the BM device collapses with each ventilation, it may indicate that the oxygen flow is too low or the ventilation rate is too rapid. If the BM device becomes progressively more difficult to squeeze when ventilating a patient, assess the need to suction, ensure that proper airway opening procedures are in use, suspect that there may be excessive air in the stomach (anticipate vomiting), and suspect a possible collapsed lung (pneumothorax).

Objective: Describe the signs of adequate artificial ventilation using the BM.

26. b

The oral airway should only be used in patients without a gag reflex; however, the nasal airway may be tolerated in semi-responsive patients. Both devices may cause minor trauma on insertion and, if properly sized, will allow for equal oxygen concentrations to be delivered. Both devices must be sized according to the patient. The nasal airway is sized by measuring from the tip of the nose to the ear lobe. Improper sizing may lead to stimulation of the gag reflex.

Objective: Describe how to measure and insert a nasopharyngeal (nasal) airway.

27. b

Unlike the pocket mask, the BM device delivers atmospheric air (not expired air). Because atmospheric air contains 21% oxygen, a BM device without supplemental oxygen will deliver 21% oxygen. With 12 to 15 L/min supplemental oxygen, the BM device can deliver about 90% oxygen.

Objective: Describe the steps in artificially ventilating a patient with a BM for one and two rescuers.

28. c

Improper sizing and insertion of the oral pharyngeal airway may cause airway obstruction. Barotrauma would not result since barotrauma occurs in the lower airway. Cardiac tamponade occurs when blood leaks into the sac surrounding the heart and is not associated with oral airway use. Because the airway is obstructed, oxygen concentrations would drop if the oral airway were inserted incorrectly.

Objective: Describe how to measure and insert an oropharyngeal (oral) airway.

29. a

The larynx contains the vocal cords. This area is the narrowest part of an adult's airway.

Objective: Name and label the major structures of the respiratory system on a diagram.

30. a

Tidal volume is the amount of air moved into or out of the lungs during a normal breath. Think of

tidal volume as the depth of a patient's breathing. Minute volume is the amount of air moved in and out of the lungs in one minute. Minute volume is determined by multiplying the tidal volume by the respiratory rate. Compliance is the ability of a patient's lung tissue to distend (inflate) with ventilation. Diffusion is the movement of gases or particles from an area of higher concentration to an area of lower concentration.

Objective: Describe the anatomy and function of the following major body systems: respiratory, circulatory, musculoskeletal, nervous, and endocrine.

31. c

The chest wall of the infant and young child is flexible because it is composed of more cartilage than bone. Because of the flexibility of the ribs, children are more resistant to rib fractures than adults. The narrowest part of an infant and young child's airway is at the level of the cricoid cartilage.

Objective: Describe differences in anatomy and physiology of the infant, child and adult patient.

32. b

A rigid suction catheter is also called a *hard suction catheter,* a *Yankauer catheter,* a *tonsil tip catheter,* or a *tonsil sucker.* Use a rigid suction catheter to remove secretions from a patient's mouth. Soft suction catheters are also called *flexible, whistle-tip,* or *French* suction catheters. These catheters are used to clear the mouth and throat and remove secretions from an endotracheal tube in intubated patients.

Objective: Describe the techniques of suctioning.

33. a

Letters are used to identify the size of an oxygen cylinder. "D" and "E" oxygen cylinders are small, portable, and often used by EMTs. Oxygen cylinders labeled "G," "H," or "M" are considered onboard cylinders.

Objective: Define the components of an oxygen delivery system.

34. a

When a humidifier is used, it should be changed after each use to prevent the growth of bacteria in the container.

Objective: Define the components of an oxygen delivery system.

Sentence Completion

35. The largest cartilage of the larynx is the thyroid cartilage, also called the **Adam's apple**.

Objective: Name and label the major structures of the respiratory system on a diagram.

36. OPA stands for **oropharyngeal airway**.

Objective: N/A

37. The most common cause of upper airway obstruction in an unresponsive patient is the **tongue**.

Objective: N/A

38. The gases that are exchanged during the process of breathing are **oxygen** and **carbon dioxide**.

Objective: N/A

39. A **tracheal stoma** is a permanent opening at the front of the neck that extends from the skin surface into the trachea. It opens the trachea to the atmosphere.

Objective: List the steps in performing the actions taken when providing mouth-to-stoma artificial ventilation.

40. Oxygen delivery percentages for nasal cannula:

1 L/min	25%
2 L/min	29%
3 L/min	33%
4 L/min	37%
5 L/min	41%
6 L/min	45%

Objective: Identify a nasal cannula and state the flow requirements needed for its use.

41.

Objective: Describe the steps in artificially ventilating a patient with a bag-mask device for one and two rescuers.

42. The reservoir bag of the nonrebreather mask should never be less than **2/3** full. This helps to make sure that there is enough supplemental oxygen available for each breath.

Objective: Identify a nonrebreather face mask and state the oxygen flow requirements needed for its use.

Matching

43. E	54. I
44. K	55. U
45. P	56. R
46. H	57. F
47. V	58. D
48. B	59. A
49. T	60. J
50. S	61. C
51. O	62. N
52. Q	63. M
53. G	64. L

Patient	Breaths/Minute	Length of Each Breath
Adult	10 to 12 (1 breath every 5 to 6 seconds)	1 second
Infant/Child	12 to 20 (1 breath every 3 to 5 seconds)	1 second
Newborn	40 to 60 (1 breath every 1 to 1.5 seconds)	1 second

Short Answer

65. Oral airways are available in a variety of sizes. To select the correct size, hold the OPA against the side of the patient's face. Select an OPA that extends from the corner of the patient's mouth to the tip of the ear lobe, or the angle of the jaw.

Objective: Describe how to measure and insert an oropharyngeal (oral) airway.

66. Signs of inadequate breathing include:

- Anxious appearance; concentration on breathing
- Confusion, restlessness
- A breathing rate that is too fast or slow for the patient's age
- An irregular breathing pattern
- A depth of breathing that is unusually deep or shallow
- Noisy breathing (stridor, snoring, gurgling, wheezing)
- Sitting upright and leaning forward to breathe
- Being unable to speak in complete sentences
- Pain with breathing
- Skin that looks flushed, pale, gray, or blue; skin that feels cold or sweaty
- Physical signs of difficulty in breathing (such as retractions, flared nostrils, or pursed lips)

Objective: List the signs of inadequate breathing.

67. 1. Head tilt–chin lift

2. Jaw thrust without head tilt

Objective: Relate mechanism of injury to opening the airway.

68. Mouth-to-mask ventilation, mouth-to–barrier device ventilation, mouth-to-mouth ventilation (not recommended), BM ventilation, and the FROPVD are methods used to deliver positive-pressure ventilation.

Objective: Describe the steps in performing the skill of artificially ventilating a patient with a BM for one and two rescuers.

69. Try to visualize the object and remove it if easily accessible. Encourage coughing, give oxygen if tolerated. Be sure to have suction equipment within arm's reach. Begin rapid transport if you are unable to clear the object.

Removal of the object will allow the patient to clear his airway. Coughing may assist in removal of the object. If the child is responsive but is not moving adequate air and the object completely obstructs the airway, perform abdominal thrusts. Monitor the patient closely.

Objective: State the importance of having a suction unit ready for immediate use when providing emergency care.

70. Accessory muscles are muscles not normally used in breathing but are used to assist respirations during respiratory distress. These muscles include muscles between the ribs, above the collarbones, or in the abdomen during inhalation or exhalation.

Objective: List the signs of inadequate breathing.

Division 3

Patient Assessment

8 Scene Size-Up

READING ASSIGNMENT ▶ Read Chapter 8, pages 184 to 198 in your textbook.

Sum It Up

- As an EMT, you must quickly look at the entire scene before approaching the patient. You must size up the scene to find out if there are any threats that may cause injury to you, other rescuers, or bystanders, or that may cause additional injury to the patient.
- Scene size-up is the first phase of patient assessment and is made up of five parts:
  1. Body substance isolation (BSI) precautions
  2. Evaluating scene safety
  3. Determining the mechanism of injury (including considerations for stabilization of the spine) or the nature of the patient's illness
  4. Determining the total number of patients
  5. Determining the need for additional resources
- You must take appropriate BSI precautions on *every* call. Consider the need for BSI precautions before you approach the patient. Put on appropriate PPE on the basis of the information the dispatcher gives you and your initial survey of the scene. This equipment includes gloves, eye protection, mask, and gown, if necessary.
- Scene safety is an assessment of the entire scene and surroundings to ensure your well-being and that of other rescuers, the patient(s), and bystanders.
- During the scene size-up, try to determine the NOI or MOI.
- A medical patient is one whose condition is caused by an illness. The NOI describes the medical condition that resulted in the patient's call to 9-1-1. Examples include fever, difficulty breathing, chest pain, headache, and vomiting. You should try to find out the nature of the illness by talking to the patient, family, coworkers, and bystanders.
- MOI refers to the way in which an injury occurs as well as the forces involved in producing the injury. Kinetic energy is the energy of motion. The amount of kinetic energy an object has depends on the mass (weight) and speed (velocity) of the object. Kinematics is the science of analyzing the mechanism of injury and predicting injury patterns. The amount of injury is determined by

the following three elements: (1) The type of energy applied, (2) How quickly the energy is applied, and (3) To what part of the body the energy is applied.

- A trauma patient is one who has experienced an injury from an external force. Traumatic situations include MVCs, motor vehicle-pedestrian crashes, falls, bicycle crashes, motorcycle crashes, and penetrating traumas.

- Blunt trauma is any mechanism of injury that occurs without actual penetration of the body. Examples of MOI causing blunt trauma include MVCs, falls, sports injuries, or assaults with a blunt object. Blunt trauma produces injury first to the body surface and then to the body's contents.

- Penetrating trauma is any MOI that causes a cut or piercing of the skin. Examples of penetrating trauma MOI include gunshot wounds, stab wounds, and blast injuries. Penetrating trauma usually affects organs and tissues in the direct path of the wounding object.

- An MVC is classified by the type of impact. The five types of impact include head on (frontal), lateral, rear end, rotational, and rollover.

- In a frontal impact, such as a head-on collision, the vehicle stops and the occupants continue to move forward by one of two pathways: down and under or up and over.
  - In the down and under pathway, the victim's knees impact the vehicle's dashboard. The down and under pathway may be seen when the occupant is not wearing a lap and shoulder restraint system, or when the occupant is wearing only the shoulder harness and not a lap belt.
  - In the up and over pathway, the victim's upper body strikes the steering wheel resulting in injuries to the head, chest, abdomen, pelvis, and/or spine. The up and over pathway may be seen when the occupant is not wearing a lap and shoulder restraint system, or when the occupant is wearing only a lap restraint (not the shoulder harness).

- Although mechanism of injury is important, it is not the only factor to consider when assessing a trauma patient and determining whether or not he is a priority patient. For some patients, the risk of significant injury is increased because of their age or a preexisting medical condition, despite what may appear to be a "minor" mechanism of injury. In some EMS systems, other factors for designating "priority" status are considered in addition to the mechanism of injury. These include anatomy, physiology, and patient factors.

- Adult pedestrians will typically turn away if they are about to be struck by an oncoming vehicle. This action results in injuries to the side or back of the body. A child will usually face an oncoming vehicle, which results in injuries to the front of the body.

- Falls are a common mechanism of injury. Factors to consider in a fall are include the height from which the patient fell, the patient's weight, the surface the patient landed on, and the part of the patient's body that struck first.

▶ Tracking Your Progress

After reading this chapter, can you:	Page Reference	Objective Met?
• Recognize hazards/potential hazards?	187	☐
• Describe common hazards found at the scene of a trauma and a medical patient?	187	☐

After reading this chapter, can you:	Page Reference	Objective Met?
• Determine if the scene is safe to enter?	187	☐
• Discuss common MOI/NOI?	190	☐
• Discuss the reason for identifying the total number of patients at the scene?	190, 196	☐
• Explain the reason for identifying the need for additional help or assistance?	196	☐

True or False

Decide whether each statement is true or false. In the space provided, write *T* for true or *F* for false.

_____ **1.** Adult pedestrians will typically turn away if they are about to be struck by an oncoming vehicle.

_____ **2.** Older children are more likely to fall from playground equipment than preschool children.

Multiple Choice

In the space provided, identify the letter of the choice that best completes the statement or answers each question.

_____ **3.** The process of sorting patients by severity of illness or injury is called
   a. triage.
   b. tagging.
   c. staging.
   d. assessment.

_____ **4.** Which of the following is a component of scene size-up and assessment?
   a. BSI precautions
   b. Containing hazardous chemical leaks
   c. Assessing baseline vital signs on all patients
   d. Opening the airway of all unresponsive patients

_____ **5.** Your crew is dispatched to the scene of a drive-by shooting. Additional information at the time of dispatch says there are multiple gunshot victims in front of the local movie theater. The suspects are believed to still be in the area. One of your patients has been reportedly shot in the chest and is not breathing. Your immediate action should be to
   a. drive into the scene and quickly remove all patients.
   b. drive into the scene and remove only the patients who are in critical condition.
   c. park a safe distance from the scene and wait for law enforcement personnel to tell you that the scene is safe.
   d. drive to the scene but do not get out of your vehicle until law enforcement personnel tell you the scene is safe.

_____ **6.** When should a scene size-up occur?
   a. As you approach the scene
   b. As you prepare to leave the scene
   c. While caring for the patient on the scene
   d. After identifying the MOI

7. Your ambulance crew is called to a wash for a child trapped on an island of debris. Your patient was rafting down the wash when he became stuck on an accumulation of tree branches. He does not appear to be in distress. Your immediate action should be to

    a. go upstream and float down to the child.

    b. wade out in the water and bring the child to shore.

    c. throw the child a rescue ring and pull him back to the shore with a rope.

    d. wait until specially trained personnel arrive on the scene to rescue the child.

8. Your rescue crew is dispatched to the scene of a collision between a car and a train. En route you are given information that a passenger van has collided with a freight train carrying unknown chemicals. Which of the following should be included in your scene size-up?

    a. Securing all derailed train cars

    b. Triaging seriously injured patients

    c. Starting CPR on all cardiac arrest victims

    d. Calling for a hazardous materials response team

9. When addressing scene safety, priority is given in which order (from highest priority to lowest)?

    a. Your safety, the patient's safety, your crew's safety, bystander safety

    b. Your safety, your crew's safety, bystander safety, the patient's safety

    c. The patient's safety, bystander safety, your safety, your crew's safety

    d. Your safety, your crew's safety, the patient's safety, bystander safety

10. Your rescue crew is called to the home of a 14-year-old female patient. Upon arrival, the patient's mother tells you that her daughter has had a headache for the past day or two and has recently begun acting in a bizarre manner. She goes on to tell you that the other five people living in the house have also "come down with a bad headache and dizziness that started when the weather turned cold." You should immediately

    a. begin treating the patients.

    b. call for additional resources.

    c. question the patient about her symptoms.

    d. request information about the patient's past medical history.

11. Countless tons of hazardous chemicals are transported across our nation's highways and streets every day. Which of the following would be the *best* indicator that hazardous materials may be involved at the scene of a MVC?

    a. The time of day

    b. The location of the crash

    c. The information provided during dispatch

    d. The presence of chemical placards on involved vehicles

12. On multiple patient incidents, after completing the scene size-up, the first responding EMTs should

    a. triage all patients.

    b. begin treating the most seriously injured patient.

    c. "scoop and run" to the hospital with the most seriously injured patient.

    d. stage away from the scene until additional rescuers arrive to assist with treatment.

13. Which of the following is an example of blunt trauma?

    a. Falls

    b. Puncture wound

    c. Stab wound

    d. Gunshot wound

Matching

Match the key terms in the left column with the definitions in the right column by placing the letter of each correct answer in the space provided.

_____ **14.** Kinetic energy

_____ **15.** NOI

_____ **16.** Blunt trauma

_____ **17.** Medical patient

_____ **18.** Trauma patient

_____ **19.** Scene size-up

_____ **20.** Kinematics

_____ **21.** Penetrating trauma

_____ **22.** MOI

A. An individual who has experienced an injury from an external force

B. The first phase of patient assessment

C. The medical condition that resulted in the patient's call to 9-1-1

D. The science of analyzing the mechanism of injury and predicting injury patterns

E. Any MOI that causes a cut or piercing of the skin

F. The energy of motion

G. An individual whose condition is caused by an illness

H. The way in which an injury occurs as well as the forces involved in producing the injury

I. Any mechanism of injury that occurs without actual penetration of the body

Short Answer

Answer each question in the space provided.

23. You are called to respond to a single vehicle rollover. The bystander who called 9-1-1 said the vehicle rolled twice, hit a power pole, and is resting on its side. Once on the scene, you find a vehicle on its side next to a damaged power pole with power lines resting on the vehicle and the ground nearby. There is heavy damage to the vehicle.

1. Is it safe to approach the vehicle?

2. What hazards or potential hazards in this scenario have the potential to cause harm to rescue crews?

24. List the five components of a scene size-up.

1.

2.

3.

4.

5.

25. Why is determining the MOI an important part of scene size-up?

26. What is meant by the term *medical patient*?

27. What is kinetic energy?

28. List the five types of impacts that can occur in a MVC.

1.

2.

3.

4.

5.

Answer Section

Chapter 8

True/False

1. True

   Adult pedestrians will typically turn away if they are about to be struck by an oncoming vehicle. This action results in injuries to the side or back of the body. A child will usually face an oncoming vehicle, which results in injuries to the front of the body.

   Objective: Discuss common MOI/NOI.

2. True

   Infants are more likely to fall from changing tables, countertops, and beds. Preschool children usually fall from windows. Older children fall more often from playground equipment.

   Objective: Discuss common MOI/NOI.

Multiple Choice

3. a

   The process of sorting patients by the severity of their illness or injury is called *triage*. This will help determine which patients need to be treated first.

   Objective: Discuss the reason for identifying the total number of patients at the scene.

4. a

   Proper personal protective measures (BSI) must be addressed in the scene size-up. Further, your level of protection must be in response to each individual scenario. Err in favor of over protecting yourself. Containing hazardous chemical leaks is not a size-up task and is not generally the responsibility of EMTs. However, calling for the resources necessary to deal with a hazardous leak would be appropriate during your scene size-up. Assessing vital signs would come after the size-up and after triage. Opening the airway of all unresponsive patients may be a task performed during triage (or according to your local protocol).

   Objective: Recognize hazards/potential hazards.

5. c

   Rescue personnel should not enter a potentially violent scene until law enforcement personnel ensure that the scene is safe. While the temptation is present to rescue the injured patients, rescue personnel who rush into hazardous situations often become part of the problem rather than part of the solution. Parking a safe distance away allows you to be out of harm's way. Additionally, rescuers should park far enough away that they are not motioned into an unsecured scene by bystanders.

   Objective: Determine if the scene is safe to enter.

6. a

   Scene size-up should begin before you enter the scene. It should begin with the analysis of the information provided at time of dispatch, knowledge about the local area and its hazards, and information you observe as you approach the scene.

   Objective: Recognize hazards/potential hazards.

7. d

   Remember that you need to be a part of the solution, not a part of the problem. There are many hazards associated with water rescues, hence the development of specially trained swift-water rescue teams. A rescue ring or other flotation device would place the patient back in the running water and may rapidly worsen the scenario. With this patient in no apparent distress, your efforts should be limited to calling for the additional resources needed for rescue, establishing an area in which to evaluate and treat the patient after the rescue is performed, and reassuring the patient that the appropriate help is on the way.

Objective: Explain the reason for identifying the need for additional help or assistance.

8. d

Calling any additional resources necessary to secure the hazard, treat, and transport the injured is a critical component of the scene size-up. The other tasks listed are performed by appropriate personnel after the scene size-up.

Objective: Explain the reason for identifying the need for additional help or assistance.

9. d

Your safety and the safety of your crew must come first. You can address your safety (and crew safety) before entering the scene by taking appropriate anticipated BSI and scene safety precautions (e.g., traffic vests). Next, protect the patient from further harm. Protection of patients can generally be accomplished through appropriate emergency vehicle positioning and removal of unnecessary personnel from the hazard scene. Finally, bystander safety must be addressed by moving all unnecessary personnel away from hazards at scene.

Objective: Determine if the scene is safe to enter.

10. b

Your on-scene resources were immediately depleted when the number of patients increased from one to six. You should immediately call for the necessary resources to deal with this scene. This particular scenario illustrates the classic presentation of carbon monoxide poisoning: multiple patients in the same house (building) complaining of neurological problems (headache, dizziness, confusion, and bizarre behavior). The onset of the symptoms when the "weather turned cold" should alert you that the heating system in the residence is not adequately vented, which can create high levels of carbon monoxide inside. These patients should be immediately removed from the building. High-flow oxygen should be administered during transport to an appropriate receiving facility.

Objective: Discuss the reason for identifying the total number of patients at the scene.

11. d

This question is designed to illustrate that hazardous materials can complicate a scene regardless of time of day, day of week, location, or information given by dispatchers. Some areas

(such as heavy industrial complexes) may be more prone to hazardous materials incidents (also known as *HazMat incidents*). However, rescuers are generally more alert for the presence of hazardous materials in an industrial setting. At incidents in rural areas, on side roads, or in residential areas, rescuers may fail to recognize the hazardous materials component until it is too late.

Objective: Recognize hazards/potential hazards.

12. a

Triage, sorting the patients according to injury, should follow scene size-up in multiple patient incidents. This allows the initial crew to prioritize treatment and make meaningful, organized assignments to the additional responding units. Treating the most seriously injured patient may end up costing the lives of several lesser injured patients. Follow your local triage protocols. Scooping up the most seriously injured patient for rapid transport not only leaves the other patients without treatment but also neglects the needed scene structure and direction for additional responding units.

Objective: Discuss the reason for identifying the total number of patients at the scene.

13. a

MVCs, falls, sports injuries, or assaults with blunt objects are considered blunt trauma. Penetrating trauma is any mechanism of injury that causes a cut or piercing of the skin. A penetration or puncture wound results when the skin is pierced with a sharp, pointed object. Examples of MOI involving penetrating trauma include gunshot wounds, stab wounds, and blast injuries.

Objective: Discuss common MOI/NOI.

Matching

14.	F	**19.**	B
15.	C	**20.**	D
16.	I	**21.**	E
17.	G	**22.**	H
18.	A		

Short Answer

23. 1. No, it is not safe to approach the vehicle.

Objective: Determine if the scene is safe to enter.

2. Hazards or potential hazards that have the potential to cause harm to rescue crews include an unstable vehicle, uncontrolled traffic, and downed power lines.

Objective: Determine if the scene is safe to enter.

24. Scene size-up is the first phase of patient assessment and is made up of five parts:

1. BSI precautions
2. Evaluating scene safety
3. Determining the MOI (including considerations for stabilization of the spine) or the nature of the patient's illness
4. Determining the total number of patients
5. Determining the need for additional resources.

Objective: N/A

25. Identifying the MOI, the manner in which an injury occurs and the forces involved in the injury, is an important part of scene size-up. By evaluating the mechanism of injury, rescuers can begin to understand the required resources needed on scene and anticipate the types of injuries they may encounter.

Objective: Discuss common MOI/NOI.

26. A medical patient is one whose condition is caused by an illness. In medical situations, try to determine the nature of the patient's illness.

Objective: N/A

27. Kinetic energy is the energy of motion. The amount of kinetic energy an object has depends on the mass (weight) and speed (velocity) of the object. Kinematics is the science of analyzing the mechanism of injury and predicting injury patterns.

Objective: Discuss common MOI/NOI.

28. An MVC is classified by the type of impact. The five types of impact include head on (frontal), lateral, rear end, rotational, and rollover. The injuries that result depend on the type of collision, the position of the occupant inside the vehicle, and the use or nonuse of active or passive restraint systems.

Objective: Discuss common MOI/NOI.

9 Patient Assessment

READING ASSIGNMENT ▶ Read Chapter 9, pages 199 to 238 in your textbook.

Sum It Up

- The ability to properly assess a patient is one of the most important skills you can master. As an EMT, you must learn to work quickly and efficiently in all types of situations. To work efficiently, you must approach patient assessment systematically. The emergency care you provide to your patient will be based on your assessment findings.

- While assessing your patient, you will discover his signs and symptoms. You must provide emergency medical care based on those signs and symptoms. Discovering the patient's signs and symptoms requires you to use your senses of sight (look), sound (listen), touch (feel), and smell.

- Patient assessment consists of the following components:
  —Initial assessment
   • Scene size-up
      —Take BSI precautions
      —Evaluate scene safety
      —Determine the MOI or the nature of the patient's illness
      —Determine the total number of patients
      —Determine the need for additional resources
   • Primary survey
      —General impression
         • Appearance
         • (Work of) Breathing
         • Circulation
      —*A*irway, level of responsiveness, cervical spine protection
      —*B*reathing (ventilation)
      —*C*irculation (perfusion)
      —*D*isability (mini-neurological exam)
      —*E*xpose
      —*I*dentify priority patients
   • Secondary survey
      —Vital signs, pulse oximetry
      —Focused SAMPLE history, OPQRST
      —Head-to-toe or focused physical examination

—Ongoing assessment
  • Repeat the primary survey
  • Reassess vital signs
  • Repeat the focused assessment regarding patient complaint or injuries
  • Reevaluate emergency care

• The primary survey is a rapid assessment to find and treat all immediate life-threatening conditions. It begins after the scene or situation has been found safe or made safe and you have gained access to the patient. During this phase of patient assessment, you will look for and treat life-threatening conditions as you discover them ("find and fix"; "treat as you go") and decide if the patient needs immediate transport or additional on scene assessment and treatment. You must perform a primary survey on *every* patient.

• The secondary survey is a physical examination performed to discover medical conditions and/or injuries that were not identified in the primary survey. During this phase of the patient assessment, you will also obtain vital signs, reassess changes in the patient's condition, and determine the patient's chief complaint, history of present illness, and significant past medical history. The secondary survey does not begin until the primary survey has been completed and treatment of life-threatening conditions has begun.

• A general impression (also called a *first impression*) is an "across-the-room" assessment. As you approach him, you will form a general impression without the patient telling you what his complaint is. You can complete it in 60 seconds or less. The purpose of forming a general impression is to decide if the patient looks "sick" or "not sick." If the patient looks sick, you must act quickly. As you gain experience, you will develop an instinct for quickly recognizing when a patient is sick and when you need to act quickly. You will base your general impression of a patient on three main areas: (1) appearance, (2) breathing, and (3) circulation.

• After forming a general impression, begin the primary survey by assessing the patient's airway and level of responsiveness. Assessment of a patient's airway and level of responsiveness occur at the same time. Level of responsiveness is also called *level of consciousness* or *mental status*. These terms refer to a patient's level of awareness. A patient's mental status is "graded" by using a scale called the *AVPU scale* as follows.
  —A = **A**lert
  —V = Responds to **V**erbal stimuli
  —P = Responds to **P**ainful stimuli
  —U = **U**nresponsive

• A patient who is oriented to person, place, time, and event is said to be "alert and oriented x ('times') 4" or "A and O × 4." Assessing the mental status of a child older than 3 years of age is the same as that of an adult.

• For trauma patients or unresponsive patients with an unknown nature of illness, take spinal precautions. Spinal precautions are used to stabilize the head, neck, and back in a neutral position. This stabilization is done to minimize movement that could cause injury to the spinal cord.

• After making sure that the patient's airway is open, assess the patient's breathing to determine if breathing is adequate or inadequate. If the patient is unresponsive and breathing is inadequate or if the patient is not breathing, begin positive-pressure ventilation using a pocket mask, mouth-to-barrier device, or BM device.

• Assessment of circulation involves evaluating for signs of obvious bleeding, central and peripheral pulses; skin color, temperature, and condition; and capillary refill (in children less than 6 years of age). Look from the patient's head to toes for signs of significant external bleeding. Control major bleeding, if present.

- Altered mental status means a change in a patient's level of awareness. Altered mental status is also called an *altered level of consciousness* (ALOC). A patient who has an altered mental status is at risk of an airway obstruction. Most EMS systems use the GCS during the disability phase of the primary survey to obtain a more detailed assessment of the patient's neurological status. This mini-neurological examination is used to establish a baseline level of responsiveness and note any obvious problem with central nervous system (brain and spinal cord) function. Three categories are assessed with the GCS: (1) eye opening, (2) verbal response, and (3) motor response.

- Expose pertinent areas of the patient's body for examination. Factors that you must consider when exposing the patient include protecting the patient's modesty, the presence of bystanders, and environment/weather conditions.

- Determine if the patient requires on-scene stabilization or immediate transport ("load-and-go" situations) with additional emergency care en route to a hospital.

- The secondary survey is patient, situation, and time dependent. For instance, a patient with an isolated injury, such as a painful ankle, would typically not require a head-to-toe physical examination. However, a secondary survey should be performed in the following situations:
  —Trauma patients with a significant MOI
  —Trauma patients with an unknown or unclear MOI
  —Trauma patients with an injury to more than one area of the body
  —All unresponsive patients
  —All patients with an altered mental status
  —Some responsive medical patients, as indicated by history and focused physical examination findings

- A quick secondary survey (head-to-toe assessment) of a trauma patient with a significant mechanism of injury is called a *rapid trauma assessment*. A significant mechanism of injury is one that is likely to produce serious injury. A quick secondary survey of a medical patient who is unresponsive or has an altered mental status is called a *rapid medical assessment*. The phrase *focused physical examination* is used to describe an assessment of specific body areas that relate to the patient's illness or injury. The procedure for performing a secondary survey is the same for trauma and medical patients. However, the physical findings that you are looking for and discover may have a different meaning depending on whether the patient is a trauma or medical patient.

- When examining your patient, first look (inspect), listen (auscultate), and then feel (palpate) body areas to identify potential injuries.

- DCAP-BTLS is a helpful memory aid to remember what to look and feel for during the physical exam:
  —*D*eformities
  —*C*ontusions (bruises)
  —*A*brasions (scrapes)
  —*P*unctures/penetrations
  —*B*urns
  —*T*enderness
  —*L*acerations (cuts)
  —*S*welling

- Remember to take two or more sets of vital signs. Doing so will allow you to note changes (trends) in the patient's condition and response to treatment. Reassess and record vital signs at least every 5 minutes in an unstable patient, and at least every 15 minutes in a stable patient.

- The conclusion you reach about what is wrong with your patient is called a *field impression*.

- The history of the present illness is a chronological record of the reason a patient is seeking medical assistance. It includes the patient's chief complaint and the patient's answers to questions about the circumstances that led up to the request for medical help. The chief complaint is the reason the patient called for assistance.

- When asking questions to find out the patient's medical history, use open-ended questions when possible. Open-ended questions require the patient to answer with more than a "yes" or "no." Questions that require a yes or no answer are called direct questions.

- It is important to obtain a SAMPLE history from all responsive patients. Using the SAMPLE history format provides an organized approach to gathering important patient information. OPQRST is a great tool to use when you have a patient who is complaining of pain or discomfort.

- At a scene that involves trauma, perform a scene size-up and primary survey and then reconsider the MOI. MOI is the way in which an injury occurs, as well as the forces involved in producing the injury. By evaluating the MOI, you can often predict the types of injuries the patient is most likely to experience.

- If the MOI is significant, time is of the essence. The goal for prehospital trauma care is to limit scene time to 10 minutes. If the MOI is significant, you need to perform a rapid trauma assessment. This means that you must move quickly and efficiently, examining the patient from head-to-toe for obvious and potential injuries. You will also need to determine the need for ALS personnel and immediate transport. If you determine the MOI is not significant, you will perform a focused physical exam. This means that you will begin the secondary survey with an assessment of the injured body part. Other areas of the body would be examined as needed.

- If a patient has experienced a significant MOI, follow the primary survey with a rapid trauma assessment. Begin the rapid trauma assessment by reassessing the patient's mental status and then checking the patient's head. Then examine the neck, chest, abdomen, pelvis, lower extremities, upper extremities, and the back. Compare one side of the body to the other. For example, if an injury involves one side of the body, use the uninjured side as the normal finding for comparison.

- If a trauma patient has no significant mechanism of injury, perform a focused physical examination. The focused physical exam concentrates on the specific injury site (and related structures) based on what the patient states is wrong and your suspicions based on the MOI and initial assessment findings.

- For the medical patient, the patient's level of responsiveness is the first important factor in determining the type of physical examination you need to perform. If your primary survey reveals that the patient is unresponsive or has an altered mental status, a rapid secondary survey (head-to-toe assessment) needs to be done to find out what is wrong. A quick secondary survey of a medical patient who is unresponsive or has an altered mental status is called a rapid medical assessment. A focused physical exam is usually performed for a responsive medical patient because he or she can usually tell you what is wrong that prompted a call for medical help.

- An ongoing assessment consists of four main areas:
  —Repeating the primary survey
  —Reassessing vital signs
  —Repeating the focused assessment
  —Reevaluating emergency care
- An ongoing assessment should be performed on every patient. It is performed after the secondary survey, if one is performed. In some situations, the patient's condition may prevent performance of a secondary survey. An ongoing assessment is usually performed en route to the receiving facility. However, if transport is delayed, the ongoing assessment should be performed on the scene.
- Repeat the ongoing assessment at least every 15 minutes for a stable patient and every 5 minutes for an unstable patient. Continue to calm and reassure the patient throughout the ongoing assessment.

▶ Tracking Your Progress

After reading this chapter, can you:	Page Reference	Objective Met?
• Summarize the reasons for forming a general impression of the patient?	203	☐
• Discuss methods of assessing altered mental status?	205	☐
• Differentiate between assessing the altered mental status in the adult, child, and infant patient?	206	☐
• Discuss methods of assessing the airway in the adult, child, and infant patient?	205	☐
• State reasons for management of the cervical spine once the patient has been determined to be a trauma patient?	207	☐
• Describe methods used for assessing if a patient is breathing?	208	☐
• State what care should be provided to the adult, child and infant patient with adequate breathing?	208	☐
• State what care should be provided to the adult, child and infant patient without adequate breathing?	209	☐
• Differentiate between a patient with adequate and inadequate breathing?	208	☐
• Distinguish between methods of assessing breathing in the adult, child, and infant patient?	208	☐
• Compare the methods of providing airway care to the adult, child, and infant patient?	205	☐
• Describe the methods used to obtain a pulse?	209	☐
• Differentiate between obtaining a pulse in an adult, child, and infant patient?	209	☐
• Discuss the need for assessing the patient for external bleeding?	209	☐
• Describe normal and abnormal findings when assessing skin color?	210	☐
• Describe normal and abnormal findings when assessing skin temperature?	210	☐
• Describe normal and abnormal findings when assessing skin condition?	210	☐
• Describe normal and abnormal findings when assessing skin capillary refill in the infant and child patient?	210	☐

True or False

Decide whether each statement is true or false. In the space provided, write *T* for true or *F* for false.

_____ **1.** A patient who refuses to talk to you should be graded as "U" (unresponsive) when the AVPU scale is used.

_____ **2.** One of the first signs of cyanosis may be noticed in the fingertips or around the mouth.

_____ **3.** A patient who has a sinus infection may complain of pain or tenderness when you feel the areas just above or below the eyes.

_____ **4.** A patient who suffers from peritonitis is often restless and moves in an attempt to find a comfortable position.

_____ **5.** The procedure for performing a head-to-toe physical examination is the same for trauma and medical patients.

_____ 6. You are caring for a stable patient involved in a motor vehicle collision. Initially, the patient complains of low back pain. During transport, the patient begins to complain of right lower leg pain. Your best course of action regarding this new complaint is to advise the patient that you will make a note of it in your report and wait for the physician at the receiving facility to examine the affected leg.

_____ 7. When preparing to transfer patient care, document and communicate any changes in the patient's condition.

_____ 8. Paradoxical movement refers to shifting of the trachea from its normal midline position.

_____ 9. You can often predict the types of injuries the patient is most likely to experience by evaluating the MOI.

Multiple Choice

In the space provided, identify the letter of the choice that best completes the statement or answers each question.

_____ 10. Forming a general impression is a critical component of the initial assessment. The general impression helps to determine the priority of care and is based on an assessment of
   a. a predetermined set of guidelines.
   b. the information given at the time of dispatch.
   c. the environment and the patient's appearance, work of breathing, and skin color.
   d. the information gathered during the head-to-toe physical examination.

_____ 11. While forming a general impression of a patient, which of the following should you consider a life-threatening condition?
   a. Difficulty breathing   **c.** Abdominal pain
   b. Lower back pain   **d.** Swollen ankles

_____ 12. After forming a general impression of a patient and evaluating mental status, you should turn your attention to
   a. splinting and bandaging.   **c.** evaluating breathing status.
   b. evaluating airway status.   **d.** evaluating circulation and perfusion.

_____ 13. When a patient's mental status is being charted, the term *alert and oriented + 4* refers to assessing the patient's ability to recall which 4 parameters?
   a. Person, place, time, and event
   b. Month, year, day of week, and time of day
   c. History, medications, allergies, and personal physician
   d. Address, phone number, social security number, and birth date

_____ 14. While assessing a patient's mental status, you observe that the patient is not alert, will not respond to verbal commands, and opens his eyes when a painful stimulus is applied. Which of the following would be the *most appropriate* way of recording this finding?
   a. The patient is not alert.
   b. The patient is semi-responsive.
   c. The patient responds to painful stimuli.
   d. The patient responds to painful stimuli by opening his eyes.

_____ 15. To evaluate the level of mental status of patients younger than 3 years of age, rescuers should assess the patient's
   a. speech.   **c.** coordination.
   b. vital signs.   **d.** interaction with parent.

_____ 16. After completing the primary survey, you should
   a. evaluate the patient's airway status.
   b. evaluate the patient's circulatory status.
   c. evaluate the patient's mental status and breathing.
   d. decide whether to begin on-scene stabilization or transport immediately.

_____ 17. If a life-threatening condition is discovered during the primary survey, you should immediately
   a. treat the condition.
   b. repeat the primary survey.
   c. assess the patient's baseline vital signs.
   d. perform a head-to-toe physical examination.

_____ 18. Which of the following actions should be performed first during the primary survey?
   a. Splinting a fractured arm
   b. Assessing the patient's circulatory status
   c. Asking the patient, "Why did you call for help?"
   d. Addressing BSI precautions

_____ 19. Which of the following should be evaluated during the respiratory assessment?
   a. Respiratory rate and lung sounds
   b. Respiratory rate, depth, rhythm, and lung sounds
   c. Respiratory rate, capillary refill, and lung sounds
   d. Respiratory rate, pulse rate, capillary refill, and lung sounds

_____ 20. Perfusion is the flow of blood to the tissues of the body. Which of the following is a reliable indicator of perfusion in children and infants, but _not_ adults?
   a. Skin color   c. Skin temperature
   b. Capillary refill   d. Skin condition (moisture)

_____ 21. Your rescue crew is called to a local park for a 34-year-old man complaining of ankle pain. Upon arrival, you find your patient sitting on a bench seat with a shoe off and ice on his foot. He states he was playing tennis with his wife when he twisted his ankle. He did not fall to the ground. He denies any other complaint. The secondary survey
   a. should be performed immediately.
   b. should be performed after the scene size-up.
   c. should be performed at the same time as the primary survey.
   d. may be replaced with a focused assessment because of the nature and extent of this patient's injury.

_____ 22. You are attempting to use spinal precautions on a patient involved in a motorcycle accident. When you begin to move his head and neck to a neutral position, the patient screams in pain. What should you do next?
   a. Continue to move the patient's head and neck until the neutral position is reached.
   b. Stop and stabilize the head and neck at the point just before resistance was met.
   c. Have the patient lie still and instruct him not to move his head until he has been completely immobilized to a long backboard.
   d. Place a pad under the patient's neck and head so he feels more comfortable.

_____ 23. Which of the following is a sign of inadequate breathing?
   a. The patient is restless and confused.
   b. The effort is quiet and effortless.
   c. Both sides of the patient's chest rise and fall equally.
   d. The patient's skin is warm and dry to the touch.

_____ 24. Your ambulance crew is dispatched to the scene of a high-speed motor vehicle collision. You are assigned responsibility for a patient who was ejected from one of the vehicles. Your initial assessment reveals that he has experienced head and chest trauma. He is not breathing and does not have a pulse. The secondary survey
   a. should be performed before starting CPR.
   b. should be performed quickly while stopping CPR.
   c. should be performed before leaving the scene of the collision.
   d. may not be performed because of the extent of this patient's injuries.

_____ 25. You are caring for a 32-year-old man who has suffered a stab wound to the abdomen. The knife is still in place. You should

    a. cover the area with a saline-soaked gauze dressing.

    b. leave the object as you found it to preserve evidence.

    c. remove the object immediately to prevent further trauma.

    d. leave the object in place and stabilize it in place with bulky dressings.

_____ 26. Your rescue crew is called to the scene of a motor vehicle collision. Your patient is a 27-year-old woman complaining of neck and lower back pain. As part of the ongoing assessment of this patient, you reassess the patient's airway. She is alert and speaking clearly. You should

    a. assume that the airway is open.

    b. immediately begin suctioning the airway.

    c. open the airway with the head tilt–chin lift technique.

    d. open the airway with a jaw thrust without head tilt maneuver.

Questions 27–30 pertain to the following scenario.

Your ambulance is dispatched to a long-term care facility for a 76-year-old woman in severe respiratory distress. The patient is cool and pale, with a respiratory rate of 28 breaths per minute. She speaks in short, choppy sentences and is coughing up white, foamy sputum.

_____ 27. For this patient, the ongoing assessment should be repeated and the findings documented at least every

    a. 5 minutes.   **c.** 15 minutes.

    b. 10 minutes.   **d.** 30 minutes.

_____ 28. This patient is given oxygen by nonrebreather mask at 15 L/min. While reevaluating your emergency care interventions for this patient, you should

    a. ensure an oral airway is in place.

    b. ensure the mask's reservoir is inflated.

    c. ensure suction is turned on and left in the patient's mouth.

    d. ensure the mask's reservoir deflates completely with each inspiration.

_____ 29. This patient's mental status decreases until she is completely unresponsive. A carotid pulse is present at a rate of 120 beats per minute. Respirations are shallow at 30 breaths per minute. When reassessing the patient's airway, you should consider

    a. changing the patient's airway delivery device to a nasal cannula.

    b. inserting an oral airway and assisting ventilations with a BM device.

    c. discontinuing the use of the nonrebreather mask for better breath sound auscultation.

    d. not changing any of your emergency care procedures until a physician can evaluate the patient.

_____ 30. At what point in the emergency care of this patient should the ongoing assessment be performed?

    a. As part of the scene size-up

    b. During the initial assessment

    c. Just before assessing baseline vital signs

    d. After the primary and secondary surveys and emergency care interventions

_____ 31. The rapid trauma assessment

    a. is necessary only for adult patients.

    b. is performed immediately following scene size-up.

    c. involves assessing the body to identify potential injuries.

    d. is performed only if life-threatening injuries are reported.

_____ 32. Your ambulance crew is treating a 45-year-old woman who fell while skating. Initially, your patient is in mild distress and complains of left hip pain and a slight headache. During your focused trauma assessment, the patient complains of "lightheadedness and weakness." You should

    a. reconsider your transportation priority.

    b. reassure the patient that nothing is wrong.

    c. put smelling salts (ammonia capsules) under the patient's nose.

    d. instruct the patient to put her head between her knees and breathe deeply.

_____ 33. MOI is not the only factor to consider when assessing a trauma patient and determining whether or not he is a priority patient. Each of the responses below represents additional categories of factors to be considered. An altered mental status belongs in which category?

      a. Anatomy   **b.** Physiology   **c.** Patient factors

_____ 34. The *P* in the SAMPLE history memory aid stands for

      a. Pain   **c.** Patient's name, gender, and age

      b. Perfusion   **d.** Pertinent past medical history

_____ 35. When evaluating the MOI, rescuers must recognize that certain circumstances pose a severe threat of significant bodily harm. For an adult patient, falls from greater than _____ are considered significant.

      a. 3 feet or equal to 3 times the patient's height

      b. 6 feet or equal to twice the patient's height

      c. 10 feet or equal to twice the patient's height

      d. 15 feet or equal to 3 times the patient's height

Questions 36–41 pertain to the following scenario.

Your rescue crew is dispatched to the scene of a motor vehicle collision. You find a 34-year-old man supine on the pavement. Bystanders state he was struck by a vehicle that has fled the scene. During your initial assessment, you identify that the patient is in moderate distress, complaining of right leg pain. His airway, breathing, and circulatory status seem within acceptable range. He is alert and answers questions appropriately.

_____ 36. The MOI in this patient suggests

      a. the need for ALS personnel.

      b. that you should take down the names of all witnesses on the scene.

      c. that you should concern yourself with getting a vehicle description from the bystanders.

      d. that you should allow law enforcement personnel to speak with the patient before transporting him to the appropriate receiving facility.

_____ 37. While stabilizing this patient, your crew takes measures to immobilize this patient's spine. Your partner begins manual in-line stabilization of the patient's head and neck. When may your partner release manual stabilization?

      a. After application of the cervical collar

      b. Upon arrival at the appropriate receiving facility

      c. After the patient is completely immobilized on a long backboard

      d. After you determine that the patient does not have head or neck pain

_____ 38. In this situation, the secondary survey should address

      a. the patient's entire body.   **c.** only the lower half of the body.

      b. only the patient's right leg.   **d.** only those areas where the patient complains of pain.

_____ 39. Which of the following memory aids would assist you in performing a rapid trauma assessment on this patient?

      a. ABC   **c.** DOT

      b. ALS   **d.** DCAP-BTLS

_____ 40. During your rapid assessment of this patient, you note that he has a 1-inch laceration to the chin. Appropriate emergency care for this finding would be to

      a. apply a first aid cream.

      b. dress the wound with dry, sterile gauze.

      c. attempt to close the wound with a "butterfly" bandage.

      d. leave the wound alone so it can be properly evaluated in the Emergency Department.

_____ 41. While assessing the patient's right leg, you find the thigh is twisted at an unusual angle, suggesting a probable femur injury. This finding

      a. is common and not overly alarming.

      b. does not require any emergency care.

      c. is frequently associated with significant blood loss.

      d. can be corrected in the field without the need for hospital intervention.

Questions 42–44 pertain to the following scenario.

Your rescue crew is called to the scene of a "motorcyclist down." Upon arrival, you find a 32-year-old male patient lying supine (on his back) in the middle of a parking lot. He informs you that his motorcycle slid on a patch of ice while he was turning at approximately 20 miles per hour. He is complaining of head, neck, and left hip pain.

_____ 42. To facilitate the assessment of his head for the presence of blood, you should
    a. have the patient sit up.
    b. turn the patient's head from side to side to visualize the entire scalp.
    c. palpate the entire skull and periodically check your gloves for blood.
    d. wrap the patient's head with gauze and check for spots of blood leaking through.

_____ 43. At what point should a cervical collar be applied to this patient?
    a. After inspecting and palpating the neck
    b. Immediately, based on the MOI
    c. After wrapping his neck with an airtight dressing
    d. After fully securing the patient to a long backboard

_____ 44. How would you address the assessment of this patient's posterior body (back side)?
    a. Stand him up before taking full spinal precautions.
    b. Logroll the patient while manually maintaining in-line spinal stabilization.
    c. Apply a long backboard to the patient, then roll the patient into the prone position on a second backboard and remove the first backboard to expose his back.
    d. An assessment cannot be accomplished because of the patient's position.

Questions 45–48 pertain to the following scenario.

Your crew is called by concerned neighbors to check the welfare of a 64-year-old woman who has not been seen for several days. Upon arrival, you find the patient moaning unintelligibly in her bed. A shoebox full of medication bottles is on her nightstand. She does not respond to you or your crew. The scene is safe. The primary survey reveals that the patient has a clear airway, is breathing adequately, has a weak radial pulse, and responds to painful stimuli by moaning more loudly.

_____ 45. Your next step should be to
    a. begin a rapid medical assessment.
    b. attempt to contact the patient's next of kin.
    c. examine and record the medications in the shoebox.
    d. attempt to obtain information from the concerned neighbors about the patient's past medical history.

_____ 46. While examining this patient, you attempt to check the symmetry of her face. Facial symmetry refers to
    a. the condition of the fontanelles.
    b. the condition of the mucous membranes.
    c. the presence of drainage from the nose or mouth.
    d. comparing the muscle tone of one side of the face to the other.

_____ 47. While assessing this patient's neck, you check for JVD. JVD is assessed by looking for distention of the neck veins with the patient in a _____ position.
    a. prone
    b. supine
    c. semi-Fowler's (sitting up at a 45-degree angle)
    d. Trendelenburg (head lower than the feet)

_____ 48. Which of the following regarding the evaluation of this patient's abdomen is correct?
    a. Evaluation of the abdomen is unnecessary because the patient is unresponsive.
    b. Evaluation of the abdomen is useful because this patient may react if palpation of the abdomen elicits pain.
    c. Evaluation of the abdomen is useful only if the patient has a past medical history of abdominal or pelvic problems.
    d. Evaluation of the abdomen does not reveal anything about the medical patient and is valuable only in the trauma patient.

Questions 49–53 pertain to the following scenario.

Your crew has been called to a restaurant for a 54-year-old woman complaining of chest pain. On arrival, you note the patient is awake, alert, and speaking in full sentences without obvious difficulty.

_____ **49.** The first step in this patient's secondary survey should be
   a. obtaining a history of present illness.
   b. performing a rapid trauma assessment.
   c. laying the patient supine on the ambulance stretcher.
   d. opening the patient's airway with a jaw thrust without head tilt.

_____ **50.** Which of the following memory aids would assist you in questioning the patient about her past medical history?
   a. NREMT   **c.** SAMPLE
   b. OPQRST   **d.** DCAP-BTLS

_____ **51.** Which of the following questions should you use when asking the patient about her discomfort?
   a. "Are you having chest pain?"
   b. "Have you had pain like this before?"
   c. "Are you having difficulty breathing?"
   d. "Would you describe how you are feeling?"

_____ **52.** Which of the following memory aids would assist you in questioning the patient about the history of this present illness?
   a. NREMT   **c.** SAMPLE
   b. OPQRST   **d.** DCAP-BTLS

_____ **53.** When asked to describe her chest pain, the patient states, "I was sitting here having dinner when all of a sudden I got this chest pain. It's been going on for about the past 20 minutes. It feels very sharp on my left side and hurts more when I take a deep breath. It makes my shoulder ache, too." To complete your history of present illness questioning using the OPQRST memory aid, what would be an appropriate question to ask this patient?
   a. "What medications are you allergic to?"
   b. "What medications are you currently taking?"
   c. "When is the last time you were seen by a physician?"
   d. "On a scale of 0 to 10 with 10 being the worst pain you have felt, how would you rate this pain?"

Questions 54–58 pertain to the following scenario.

Your ambulance is called to the scene of a 47-year-old woman who was found unresponsive in her yard by neighbors.

_____ **54.** As you approach the patient, you notice that she is unaware of your approach. She appears to be breathing normally and her skin is pink. Based on this information, which of the following reflects your best course of action?
   a. Perform an initial assessment and then a rapid medical assessment.
   b. Obtain a SAMPLE history and then conduct a focused physical exam.
   c. Obtain a baseline set of vital signs and then a history of the present illness.
   d. Obtain a history of present illness by conducting the OPQRST examination.

_____ **55.** Vital signs should be reassessed and recorded at least every _____ for this patient.
   a. 2 minutes   **c.** 15 minutes
   b. 5 minutes   **d.** 30 minutes

_____ **56.** When assessing the patient's pulse, you should address both the pulse rate and pulse quality. A "normal" pulse quality (felt at the radial artery of a healthy adult) should be
   a. bounding.   **c.** weak, but regular.
   b. strong and full.   **d.** bounding and slightly irregular.

_____ 57. While physically assessing this patient, you observe that her capillary refill time is slightly more than the "normal" 2 seconds. This finding
   a. is a clear indicator that this patient is in shock.
   b. should immediately change your first impression about this patient's condition.
   c. requires you to immediately contact medical direction for further orders regarding the treatment of this patient.
   d. may not be significant because capillary refill is an unreliable indicator of perfusion in patients older than 6 years of age.

_____ 58. During the physical examination, the assessment of the abdomen should be performed with the patient in which position?
   a. Prone   **c.** Standing
   b. Supine   **d.** Lying on her left side

_____ 59. Your ambulance crew responds to the home of a 65-year-old man complaining of severe shortness of breath. Upon arrival, you find the patient sitting upright in a chair. He is conscious and in severe respiratory distress, speaking in one- to two-word sentences. During your physical examination, you note that this patient has a "barrel chest." This finding may indicate a past medical history of
   a. stroke.   **c.** gallstones.
   b. diabetes.   **d.** chronic lung disease.

Questions 60–61 pertain to the following scenario.

Your rescue crew is called to the scene of a 13-year-old boy who fell from a tree. Upon arrival, this patient is complaining of right-sided chest pain and left shoulder pain.

_____ 60. Upon visualization of the chest wall, you note a small puncture wound on the right upper chest. It appears a tree limb caused the wound. Appropriate emergency care for this injury should include application of
   a. a dry, sterile dressing.   **c.** a butterfly-type bandage.
   b. an airtight dressing.   **d.** a moistened sterile dressing.

_____ 61. While assessing the left shoulder, you note deformity and swelling are present. Proper evaluation of the patient's distal motor function would include
   a. manually taking the left arm through rotation.
   b. asking the patient if he can wiggle all his fingers.
   c. asking the patient to lift both arms over his head.
   d. pulling on the left arm to assess resistance and strength.

_____ 62. Your ambulance is called to the home of a 23-year-old woman who has cut her finger on a knife. Upon your arrival, the patient is up and walking in no apparent distress. She informs you that while opening a package, she cut her finger. She has a 1/2-inch partial-thickness laceration to her index finger, and bleeding is controlled. Which of the following reflects your *best* course of action in this situation?
   a. You should perform a head-to-toe physical examination.
   b. You should perform a focused physical examination on the area of injury.
   c. You should perform a focused physical examination on the area of injury, baseline vital signs, and SAMPLE history.
   d. You should perform a head-to-toe physical examination, baseline vital signs, and SAMPLE history.

_____ 63. While assessing pupil response in an unresponsive patient, particular attention should be paid to
   a. pupil size, equality, and reactivity.
   b. pupil reactivity, equality, and tracking.
   c. iris color, size, equality, and reactivity.
   d. pupil size, equality, and response to pain.

_____ 64. Swelling of the lips can be an indication of
   a. dehydration.   **c.** dry environment.
   b. sun exposure.   **d.** medication allergy.

_____ 65. In which of the following situations are you most likely to conduct a head-to-toe physical examination?

    a. A 57-year-old woman complaining of left knee pain

    b. A 6-year-old boy who slammed his finger in a car door

    c. A 3-year-old boy who has inserted a grape into his nose

    d. A 33-year-old woman who has been drinking alcohol and fell down a flight of stairs

_____ 66. One purpose of the ongoing assessment is to

    a. evaluate the effectiveness of the emergency care provided.

    b. assist in forming an initial general impression about the patient's condition.

    c. ensure that BSI precautions have been addressed.

    d. ensure that the patient or the patient's guardian has granted the appropriate consent for treatment.

_____ 67. The ongoing assessment should be performed

    a. only during transport.

    b. immediately after the initial assessment.

    c. only if you think the patient's condition has changed.

    d. after the detailed physical exam and pertinent emergency care.

Matching

Match the key terms in the left column with the definitions in the right column by placing the letter of each correct answer in the space provided.

_____ 68. Contusion

_____ 69. Crepitus

_____ 70. Abrasion

_____ 71. Raccoon eyes

_____ 72. Index of suspicion

_____ 73. Occlusive

_____ 74. Pneumothorax

_____ 75. Ecchymosis

_____ 76. Pulmonary contusion

_____ 77. Edema

_____ 78. Subcutaneous emphysema

_____ 79. Hyphema

_____ 80. Tracheal deviation

_____ 81. Laceration

_____ 82. Rapid trauma assessment

_____ 83. Paradoxical

_____ 84. History of the present illness

_____ 85. Open-ended question

_____ 86. Jugular venous distention

_____ 87. Direct question

_____ 88. Chief complaint

_____ 89. Tracheal stoma

A. Anticipating potential injuries or complications of an illness

B. Opposing, moving in opposite directions

C. A scrape

D. Shifting of the trachea from a midline position

E. A quick head-to-toe assessment of a trauma patient with a significant MOI

F. Blood in the anterior chamber of the eye

G. Airtight

H. A crackling sensation heard and felt beneath the skin caused by bone ends grating against each other

I. A crackling sensation under the fingers that suggests laceration of a lung and the leakage of air into the pleural space

J. Bluish discoloration caused by leakage of blood into the skin or mucous membrane

K. Bruise

L. Swelling

M. A buildup of air between the outer lining of the lung and the chest wall, causing collapse of the lung

N. Knife wound

O. Bruising of the lung

P. Bilateral bluish discoloration around the eyes

Q. "How can I help you?"

Continued

R. "Have you had this discomfort before?"

S. Surgical opening in the neck

T. The reason why a patient called for medical assistance

U. Engorgement of the neck veins when the patient is placed in a sitting position at a 45-degree angle

V. A chronological record of the reason a patient is seeking medical assistance

Short Answer

Answer each question in the space provided.

90. Explain what is meant by the phrase *spinal precautions*.

91. Describe the mental status changes that you should anticipate in a child whose mental status is decreasing (in order of decreasing status).

92. Healthcare professionals often ask if a patient's airway is "patent." What does this term mean?

93. Describe how you would reevaluate the effectiveness of oxygen delivery (by nonrebreather mask and nasal cannula) to a patient.

94. Explain what each of the letters in the DCAP-BTLS memory aid stands for.

    D =

    C =

    A =

    P =

    B =

    T =

    L =

    S =

95. A 40-year-old man is complaining of abdominal pain after a motorcycle crash. Describe how you will examine this patient's abdomen.

96. List five findings that you should look for when assessing the abdomen of a trauma patient.
1.
2.
3.
4.
5.

97. List six factors to consider in an MVC.
1.
2.
3.
4.
5.
6.

98. The memory aid PMS is used when assessing the extremities. What does each letter stand for?
P =
M =
S =

99. Describe how to assess PMS in the extremities.

100. List four situations in which a head-to-toe physical examination should be performed.
1.
2.
3.
4.

Answer Section

Chapter 9

True/False

1. False

An unresponsive patient does not respond to a verbal or painful stimulus and does not have an intact gag reflex. Unresponsive should not be confused with uncooperative.

Objective: Discuss methods of assessing altered mental status.

2. True

Cyanotic (blue-gray) skin suggests inadequate oxygenation or poor perfusion. It often appears first in the fingertips or around the mouth (circumoral cyanosis).

Objective: Describe normal and abnormal findings when assessing skin color.

3. True

Objective: State the areas of the body that are evaluated during the detailed physical exam.

4. False

The patient with inflammation of the abdominal lining (peritonitis) usually prefers to lie absolutely still. The patient with a bowel obstruction is often restless and often moves in an attempt to find a position of comfort.

Objective: N/A

5. True

The procedure for performing a head-to-toe physical examination is the same for trauma and medical patients. However, the physical findings that you are looking for and discover may have a different meaning depending on whether the patient is a trauma or medical patient.

Objective: Distinguish between the detailed physical exam that is performed on a trauma patient and that of the medical patient.

6. False

If the patient develops a new complaint or if a previously identified sign or symptom changes, perform a focused assessment on the area of complaint.

Objective: Discuss the reason for performing a focused history and physical exam.

7. True

Document any changes or trends in the patient's condition in your prehospital care report. Be sure to accurately record all times associated with the care given. When transferring patient care, provide the healthcare professional assuming patient care with a report (written and verbal) that addresses the patient's progress while under your care.

Objective: Describe the components of the ongoing assessment.

8. False

Paradoxical movement usually refers to uneven chest movement. When paradoxical movement is present, a part of the chest wall moves in an opposite direction from the rest of the chest wall during breathing. This finding is a sign of a flail segment. Shifting of the trachea (tracheal deviation) from a midline position suggests a collapsed lung (pneumothorax).

Objective: Describe the areas included in the rapid trauma assessment and discuss what should be evaluated.

9. True

By evaluating the MOI, you can often predict the types of injuries the patient is most likely to experience.

Objective: Discuss the reasons for reconsideration concerning the mechanism of injury.

Multiple Choice

10. c

Form a general impression to determine the priority of care. The general impression is based on your immediate assessment of the environment and the patient's appearance, work of breathing, and skin color. A predetermined set of guidelines should not dictate your care priorities because each patient situation is different. Whereas the information given at time of dispatch is helpful, this information must be confirmed at the scene with the patient. Your physical impression may be much different from the "phone" impression the dispatcher may have formed. Information gathered during the detailed physical examination may greatly influence your care priorities; however, the general impression is formed during the primary survey, which precedes the head-to-toe physical exam.

Objective: Summarize the reasons for forming a general impression of the patient.

11. a

Suspect a life-threatening condition in any patient who presents with any of the following:

- Patients who give a poor general impression
- Unresponsive patients
- Responsive patients who cannot follow commands
- Patients who have difficulty breathing
- Patients who are in shock
- Women who are undergoing a complicated childbirth
- Patients with chest pain and a systolic blood pressure less than 100 mm Hg
- Patients with uncontrolled bleeding
- Patients with severe pain anywhere

Objective: Summarize the reasons for forming a general impression of the patient.

12. b

Forming a general impression is part of the initial assessment. The next step in the initial assessment is to perform a primary survey. Primary survey priorities include assessing the patient's level of responsiveness and airway, noting the need for spinal precautions. Assessing the status of breathing and circulation/perfusion follow. Splinting and bandaging should be incorporated into the secondary survey that follows the primary survey, unless control of life-threatening hemorrhage is necessary.

Objective: Discuss methods of assessing the airway in the adult, child, and infant patient.

13. a

The standard parameters for "alert and oriented × 4" (A & O × 4) are the patient's ability to recall his full name, where he is, the time of day or day of week, and the events leading up to your arrival at the scene. An example of a patient that is A & O × 4 is one who can tell you, "My name is Josh Brown. It is noon on Friday. I am at the intersection of Center Street and Main, and I was rear-ended in my car while I was waiting at a red light." If a patient cannot recall any one of these factors, you may document that he or she is A & O × 3, and you must identify the parameter that the patient cannot recall. For example, "Patient is A & O × 3. He cannot recall the events leading up to this incident."

Objective: Discuss methods of assessing altered mental status.

14. d

When documenting or communicating a patient's mental status, you should be as descriptive as necessary to convey the patient's actual presentation. The other responses, while not completely false, do not paint as accurate a picture.

Objective: Discuss methods of assessing altered mental status.

15. d

Perhaps the best indicator of a young child's mental status is the interaction (or lack of) between the child and a familiar face, especially the parent. It is important to document and treat accordingly when a parent tells you, "He is just not acting right." Because children go through such drastic developmental changes during their early years, assessing a child solely on the basis of age is difficult for rescuers.

Objective: Differentiate between assessing the altered mental status in the adult, child, and infant patient.

16. d

After completing the primary survey, you should have sufficient information to decide whether to stabilize your patient on-scene or begin immediate transport and stabilize en route to the receiving facility. Evaluating the patient's mental status, airway, breathing, and circulatory status should be done during the primary survey.

Objective: Explain the reason for prioritizing a patient for care and transport.

17. a

The purpose of the primary survey is to identify life-threatening problems, begin treatment, and initiate rapid transport for critical patients. If a life-threatening condition is found, begin immediate emergency care and transportation. Some patients will be so seriously ill or injured that you may never fully perform a head-to-toe physical examination, and obtaining a medical history or complete set of baseline vital signs may not be possible until the patient can be stabilized (or more resources become available).

Objective: Explain the reason for prioritizing a patient for care and transport.

18. c

The first step in the primary survey is to assess the patient's level of responsiveness and airway while considering the need for cervical spine protection. Approaching the patient and asking him to tell you in his own words what the problem is will quickly provide this information. Splinting fractures should be addressed during the secondary survey that follows the primary survey. The patient's circulatory status is evaluated during the primary survey after assessing airway and breathing. BSI precautions should be addressed before any contact with the patient (during the scene size-up).

Objective: N/A

19. b

When evaluating respiratory status for baseline vital signs, it is important to note the rate of respirations, the depth (amount of air moved or tidal volume), the rhythm of respirations, and lung sounds. Capillary refill is assessed during assessment of skin condition. Pulse rate is also assessed during assessment of vital signs but not as a component of the patient's respiratory status. An abnormal finding in one area may influence the response in another.

Objective: Identify the attributes that should be obtained when assessing breathing.

20. b

Capillary refill evaluates the time required for the return of a normal, pink appearance in the capillary beds after blanching (pinching). Normal refill time is less than 2 seconds. In adults, this technique is not completely reliable because capillary refill is easily affected by medications, chronic medical conditions, cold weather, and smoking.

Objective: Describe normal and abnormal findings when assessing skin capillary refill in the infant and child patient.

21. d

Because this is an isolated, minor injury without complications, a complete head-to-toe secondary survey is not necessary. Instead, a focused exam of the injured area should be performed. If the patient suffered a fall or appeared to have other injuries, a head-to-toe exam would be performed after the focused physical exam.

Objective: Discuss the reason for performing a focused history and physical exam.

22. b

If the patient complains of pain or you meet resistance when moving his head and neck to a neutral position, stop and stabilize the head and neck at the point just before resistance was met. Once begun, manual stabilization of the patient's head and neck must be continued without interruption until the patient is properly secured to a backboard with the head and neck stabilized.

Objective: State reasons for management of the cervical spine once the patient has been determined to be a trauma patient.

23. a

A patient who is confused or restless may be experiencing a decreased supply of oxygen. The other signs listed are signs of adequate breathing.

Objective: Differentiate between a patient with adequate and inadequate breathing.

24. d

The secondary survey is performed only after all critical interventions have been performed. Do not delay life-saving care such as CPR or rapid transportation to perform a secondary survey.

Objective: Explain what additional care should be provided while performing the detailed physical exam.

25. d

If you see an object impaled in the abdomen, leave the object in place and stabilize it in place with bulky dressings. You should not remove the object because of risk of bleeding.

Objective: Describe the emergency medical care of a patient with an impaled object.

26. a

Because the patient is conscious and speaking without difficulty, you may assume that the airway is open. This assumption should not preclude you from questioning the patient further about her airway status or from suctioning if necessary. However, routine suctioning or maneuvers to open the airway would not be appropriate. If this patient did require airway positioning, the jaw thrust without head tilt maneuver is preferred rather than the head tilt–chin lift maneuver because of the patient's MOI and chief complaint.

Objective: Relate mechanism of injury to opening the airway.

27. a

Unstable patients should be reassessed *at least* every 5 minutes. However, you may have to reassess this patient sooner if the situation calls for it. By reassessing every 5 minutes, you can closely monitor the patient's progress and adapt your treatment and transportation decision accordingly.

Objective: Describe trending of assessment components.

28. b

To evaluate the effectiveness of the set flow rate when using a device with a reservoir, ensure that the reservoir remains at least partially inflated during inspiration. If the reservoir completely collapses during inspiration, the oxygen flow rate should be increased. Inserting an oral airway would not be appropriate because this patient is conscious. Although suctioning may be necessary, leaving the suction device on and in the patient's mouth would greatly reduce oxygen delivery concentrations and cause harm to the patient.

Objective: Identify a nonrebreather face mask and state the oxygen flow requirements needed for its use.

29. b

Because the patient is now unconscious, you will need to assist in the maintenance of an open airway. If a gag reflex is absent, an oral airway may be used. If a gag reflex is still present, a nasal airway may be better tolerated. If the respiratory rate is still rapid and shallow, assist ventilations by delivering ventilations every

5 to 6 seconds with a BM device connected to 100% oxygen. Decreasing or stopping the flow of oxygen is inappropriate and may cause the patient to deteriorate further. The ongoing assessment is conducted so that you may adapt your treatment to changes in the patient's condition. Failure to adapt to the patient's changes negates the benefit of conducting the ongoing assessment.

Objective: Discuss the reasons for repeating the initial assessment as part of the ongoing assessment.

30. d

The ongoing assessment is the last phase of your interaction with a patient before transferring care. The ongoing assessment involves patient reevaluation and appropriate management of findings.

Objective: Describe the components of the ongoing assessment.

31. c

A rapid trauma assessment should be conducted on all patients who have a significant MOI, regardless of whether the injuries appear initially to be life threatening. The assessment should be performed on children and infants as well as adults. It is performed after the initial assessment (not immediately following the scene size-up).

Objective: State the reasons for performing a rapid trauma assessment.

32. a

If your patient becomes unstable during assessment, you should immediately reconsider your transportation priority. Do not falsely assure a patient that nothing is wrong. Putting smelling salts under the nose of an injured patient is inappropriate. Having the patient put her head between her knees does not address the problem and complicates the situation because you cannot provide spinal immobilization with the patient in this position.

Objective: Differentiate when the rapid assessment may be altered in order to provide patient care.

33. b

Although MOI is important, it is not the only factor to consider when assessing a trauma patient and determining whether or not he is a priority patient. In some EMS systems, other factors for designating "priority" status are considered in addition to the MOI. These include anatomy, physiology, and patient factors. Altered mental status is an example of a physiological factor that affects trauma patient prioritizing.

Objective: Discuss the reasons for reconsideration concerning the MOI.

34. d

SAMPLE is a memory aid used for history gathering. The *P* stands for pertinent past medical history. Information may be obtained from the patient, family or friends, medical records found on the patient or at the facility, and/or medical identification bracelet, or by obtaining a list of medications the patient takes. For example, insulin would indicate a patient with a diabetic history.

Objective: Discuss the reason for performing a focused history and physical exam.

35. d

Falls more than 15 feet (or 3 times the patient's height) for adults is the general rule of thumb (falls greater than 10 feet if the patient is less than 14 years of age or older than 55). However, falls from a lesser height can also be significant. Many factors must be evaluated: the surface the patient landed on, the body position upon impact, the patient's presentation during the initial assessment and physical examination, and the patient's past medical history.

Objective: Discuss the reasons for reconsideration concerning the MOI.

36. a

A vehicle-pedestrian collision is a significant MOI. Although this collision certainly has legal ramifications, your attention should be on providing the appropriate level of stabilization for this patient. Given the MOI, ALS personnel should be called to the scene.

Objective: Discuss the reasons for reconsideration concerning the mechanism of injury.

37. c

Not until the patient is completely immobilized can you release manual stabilization, regardless of the patient's denial of head or neck pain. The MOI suggests that this patient may have spinal compromise, regardless of current physical status. The cervical collar by itself does not provide sufficient support to maintain spinal alignment.

Objective: Describe how to stabilize the cervical spine.

38. a

Although the patient's complaint was initially limited to the right leg, the MOI (vehicle striking a pedestrian) suggests that other injuries may be present. Therefore, the entire body should be rapidly inspected (looked at), auscultated (listened to), and palpated (felt).

Objective: Recite examples and explain why patients should receive a rapid trauma assessment.

39. d

DCAP-BTLS is a mnemonic designed to assist rescuers in remembering what signs to look for on a trauma patient. It stands for *d*eformities, *c*ontusions (bruises), *a*brasions (scrapes), *p*unctures or *p*enetrating wounds, *b*urns, *t*enderness to palpation, *l*acerations (cuts), and *s*welling. ABC is a memory aid for the initial assessment: *a*irway, *b*reathing, and *c*irculation. ALS refers to Advanced Life Support (AEMTs and Paramedics). DOT stands for the Department of Transportation.

Objective: Describe the areas included in the rapid trauma assessment and discuss what should be evaluated.

40. b

Dressing the wound is the appropriate action. Use a dry, sterile dressing. Creams should be avoided because the patient may have an adverse reaction to such products. Do not attempt to close open wounds unless it is necessary to control bleeding. Closing the wound before it is disinfected may increase the risk of infection.

Objective: Describe the emergency medical care of the patient with an open soft-tissue injury.

41. c

A significant amount of blood can be lost as a result of a femur fracture. Emergency care should include a full assessment of the extremity and application of the appropriate splint. This condition may be aided by on-scene stabilization; however, it is important that this patient be transported to an appropriate medical facility.

Objective: Discuss the reasons for reconsideration concerning the mechanism of injury.

42. c

The best way to check for bleeding without manipulating the patient's spine is to periodically inspect your gloves while palpating the patient's head. Standing the patient or turning the patient's head are unacceptable techniques because they jeopardize the integrity of full spinal immobilization. Wrapping the patient's head in gauze dressing is not a practical alternative.

Objective: Establish the relationship between body substance isolation and bleeding.

43. a

Although spinal stabilization is a high priority, you should assess the patient's neck before application of the cervical collar. Manual stabilization should begin immediately, as indicated by the MOI. Covering the neck with an airtight dressing is only necessary if soft-tissue injury is present.

Objective: Discuss indications for sizing and using a cervical spine immobilization device.

44. b

The best method for assessing the patient's posterior body is the logroll method. When performing this maneuver, one rescuer is positioned at the head for manual stabilization of the patient's head and neck. Additional rescuers are positioned at the patient's side, and an assistant prepares the backboard for positioning. The rescuer at the patient's head is in charge of all patient movement and coordinates the log roll. Another rescuer is necessary to assess the patient's back once he is rolled onto his side. The backboard is then put in place, and the patient is rolled back onto the backboard and secured.

Objective: Describe the areas included in the rapid trauma assessment and discuss what should be evaluated.

45. a

Because this patient is unresponsive, you should *immediately* attempt to identify the factors influencing her condition through a rapid medical assessment. If you have sufficient personnel, you may want to send a crew member to find a neighbor knowledgeable about the patient's present illness and past medical history. If the information is readily available, notifying relatives (next of kin) may also assist in gaining insight into the patient's presentation. The types of medications in the shoe box may

also assist you in gathering more information about the patient. Many receiving facilities prefer that these medications be brought with the patient.

Objective: Differentiate between the assessment that is performed for a patient who is unresponsive or has an altered mental status and other medical patients requiring assessment.

46. d

Evaluating facial symmetry refers to checking for a difference in muscle tone on one side of the face compared with the other. A lack of symmetry is often referred to as *facial droop* and may be indicative of a stroke. A stroke is also called a *CVA* or *brain attack*. Checking for symmetry in a completely unresponsive patient may be impossible; however, because this patient is moaning, you may note a lack of symmetry about the mouth. Fontanelles are soft spots in an infant's skull and are not present in adults (the bones fuse together at about 18 months of age). The condition of the mucous membranes of the mouth and eyes, whether moist or dry, may give you a good indication of how long the patient has been ill.

Objective: Describe the unique needs for assessing an individual who is unresponsive or has an altered mental status.

47. c

JVD is assessed with the patient's body at a 45-degree angle. When the patient is prone, supine, or in a Trendelenburg position, JVD may be present merely as a result of gravity's effect on blood flow.

Objective: N/A

48. b

Because this patient has an altered mental status, a rapid physical examination should be performed that includes an evaluation of all body regions and systems. When palpating the abdomen of a patient with an altered mental status, you should note the position the patient is in (fetal position may indicate abdominal pain). Inspect the abdomen for color, scars (indicating past abdominal surgery), or other abnormalities. Finally, palpate the abdomen while paying close attention to any response the patient may exhibit (tightening of the muscles, grimacing, or increased moaning).

Objective: Describe the unique needs for assessing an individual who is unresponsive or has an altered mental status.

49. a

The first step in the secondary survey for a responsive patient is to obtain a history of the present illness and the patient's chief complaint. The information gathered during the history taking will help guide and prioritize the actions that follow. A rapid trauma assessment would not be appropriate unless this patient's complaint was the result of a traumatic event (such as a vehicle collision). Putting the patient in a supine position may be appropriate; however, it is not a priority unless the patient shows signs that she may pass out and fall to the ground. Finally, the jaw thrust without head tilt maneuver is used to open the airway of an unresponsive patient with a potential spinal injury. This patient does not have a potential spinal injury and is not in need of assistance in keeping her airway open.

Objective: Describe the unique needs for assessing an individual with a specific chief complaint with no known prior history.

50. c

The SAMPLE acronym assists in obtaining information about the patient's past medical history. SAMPLE stands for *s*igns and *s*ymptoms, *a*llergies, *m*edications, *p*ertinent *p*ast medical history, *l*ast oral intake, and *e*vents leading up to this illness.

Objective: Describe the unique needs for assessing an individual with a specific chief complaint with no known prior history.

51. d

While questioning the patient about her pain and breathing status is appropriate, it is best to use open-ended questions. Open-ended questions are those that cannot be answered with a "yes" or "no." By using open-ended questions, you are assured that you will not be putting words or thoughts in the patient's mouth. You may still direct the patient's responses (many times patients will wander from pertinent information), but it is best to do so by allowing the patient to tell you her "story" about what is happening.

Objective: Describe the unique needs for assessing an individual with a specific chief complaint with no known prior history.

52. b

OPQRST is the correct response. Each letter of the OPQRST acronym represents a line of questioning about a different facet of this complaint. NREMT stands for National Registry of Emergency Medical Technicians, the agency that provides national EMT certification. SAMPLE is a memory aid used to obtain information about the patient's past medical history (as opposed to the current complaint). DCAP-BTLS is the memory aid used to recall the injuries to look for during a physical assessment of a trauma patient.

Objective: Describe the unique needs for assessing an individual with a specific chief complaint with no known prior history.

53. d

In response to an initial open-ended question, this patient gave all the OPQRST information with the exception of *S*, severity. The other questions listed are appropriate to ask. However, organizing the questions so that you deal with the current complaint followed by the patient's history is much less confusing to the patient. It is helpful to have one person asking questions of the patient, rather than having the patient answer questions from everyone on the scene. This allows a logical progression of questioning and also allows the patient to develop a rapport with the rescuer asking the questions.

Objective: Differentiate between the history and physical exam that is performed for responsive patients with no known prior history and patients responsive with a known prior history.

54. a

Unlike the responsive medical patient whose history of present illness is examined first, the unresponsive medical patient or patient who has an altered mental status is first assessed with an initial assessment and then a rapid head-to-toe physical examination (rapid medical assessment). Next, baseline vital signs should be assessed, followed by a history of present illness that may be obtained from family members, friends, or bystanders.

Objective: Differentiate between the assessment that is performed for a patient who is unresponsive or has an altered mental status and other medical patients requiring assessment.

55. b

For unresponsive patients, vital signs should be assessed at least every 5 minutes or as the patient's condition changes. If an adequate number of rescuers are present, assign one person the responsibility of repeating and recording vital signs every 5 minutes. This ensures that vital signs will be assessed without interrupting your care or train of thought.

Objective: State the importance of accurately reporting and recording the baseline vital signs.

56. b

A normal pulse quality should have a regular rhythm and should be easily palpated at the radial artery of an adult. Aerobically fit adults and young children often have a slightly irregular pulse (called a "sinus arrhythmia"). In this condition, the pulse rate may change speed slightly with respirations. It typically increases on inspiration and decreases on expiration.

Objective: Identify the information obtained when assessing a patient's pulse.

57. d

In young patients, capillary refill is a more reliable indicator of poor perfusion. It is not uncommon for the initial signs of hypoperfusion (shock) in a pediatric patient to be delayed capillary refill, a slightly faster than anticipated pulse rate, and subtle changes in the child's level of activity (slightly more or less active according to the parent or guardian). Children compensate well during illness or injury up until the point at which they "crash" (suddenly, rapidly decompensate).

In patients older than 6 years of age, capillary refill is not a reliable indicator of perfusion because it may be influenced by many factors, including weather and medications. If other signs of shock (hypoperfusion) are present in addition to delayed capillary refill, you should note these findings. However, if capillary refill is the only sign that this patient may be in shock, the indication is probably not reliable. Document your findings, whatever they are.

Objective: Describe the methods to assess the skin color, temperature, condition (capillary refill) in infants and children.

58. b

The most thorough way to assess the abdomen is to position the patient on her back (supine).

Before repositioning the patient, observe her current position because it may give you insight into the location and extent of her discomfort. Sometimes a responsive patient will be in such severe pain that she is unable to lie supine. Be thorough in your examination, but gentle.

Objective: N/A

59. d

A barrel chest is common in patients with a past medical history of chronic lung disease such as emphysema and bronchitis. Because of the chronic (long-term) nature of these diseases and the increased effort involved with breathing, it is not uncommon for the chest wall of these patients to change dimensions over time. A patient with a past medical history of diabetes may appear very thin and may be a partial amputee because of the destructive effect diabetes can have on the peripheral blood vessels. A patient with a history of gallstones may present with a surgical scar over the right upper quadrant of the abdomen. Finally, a patient with a past medical history of a stroke (CVA) may present with neuromuscular deficits (such as partial paralysis, impaired speech, personality changes, and facial droop).

Objective: Differentiate between the history and physical exam that is performed for responsive patients with no known prior history and responsive patients with a known prior history.

60. b

Injuries to the anterior and posterior chest wall and the neck should be sealed with an airtight dressing to ensure that air does not leak through the wound into the surrounding tissues. The dressing should be secured to the patient on three of four sides with the fourth side left free to act as a flutter valve for the escape of trapped air.

Objective: Differentiate the care of an open wound to the chest from an open wound to the abdomen.

61. b

Do not cause further damage in your attempts to assess or treat patients. Manipulating this obviously injured joint may cause further damage. Asking the patient to wiggle his fingers is an adequate test for the assessment of distal motor function.

Objective: N/A

62. c

Because no significant MOI exists, this patient should receive an appropriate focused history and physical examination that includes a full assessment of the injury site, baseline vital signs, and a SAMPLE history.

Objective: Discuss the reason for performing a focused history and physical exam.

63. a

Proper pupil assessment should include the pupil size, equality, and reactivity. Some healthcare professionals refer to the pupil as the "window to the brain." The nerve that controls pupil response comes directly from the brain; therefore, abnormal pupil response (unequal or nonreactive pupils) is indicative of changes in the condition of the central nervous system.

Objective: Identify normal and abnormal pupil size.

64. d

Swelling of the lips may be due to trauma or to an allergic reaction to medications, foods, or other allergens. Lips that are dry and cracked may be due to exposure to the sun, wind, or a dry environment, or to dehydration.

Objective: State the areas of the body that are evaluated during the detailed physical exam.

65. d

This patient most closely fits the criteria for needing a head-to-toe physical examination. She possibly has an alerted mental status (history of alcohol ingestion) and does have a significant MOI (falling down a flight of stairs). To be thorough, it would be appropriate to perform a head-to-toe physical examination on all of these patients—provided that your doing so does not unnecessarily delay treatment or transportation.

Objective: Discuss the components of the detailed physical exam.

66. a

A main reason for performing the ongoing assessment is to reevaluate the emergency care you have provided. For example, did a bandage help control a bleeding wound? Did a splint properly support a limb without further compromising distal functions such as movement, sensation, and circulation? BSI precautions should begin before patient contact and should not be discontinued until patient care has been transferred and your equipment is decontaminated. The general impression should be formed early in your interaction with the patient. Consent, too, should be addressed much earlier in the incident.

Objective: Describe the components of the ongoing assessment.

67. d

The ongoing assessment should follow all initial assessments, examinations, and treatments. If transport is delayed, use that extra time to reevaluate the patient's status. Do not wait to perform an ongoing assessment until you suspect the patient's status has changed. If you are waiting for the obvious signs of change rather than evaluating for the presence of subtle changes, your emergency care interventions will be delayed. Subtle changes to watch for include any changes in mental status, vital signs, and level of distress.

Objective: Describe the components of the ongoing assessment.

Matching

68.	K	**79.**	F
69.	H	**80.**	D
70.	C	**81.**	N
71.	P	**82.**	E
72.	A	**83.**	B
73.	G	**84.**	V
74.	M	**85.**	Q
75.	J	**86.**	U
76.	O	**87.**	R
77.	L	**88.**	T
78.	I	**89.**	S

Short Answer

90. Spinal precautions are measures used to stabilize the head, neck, and back in a neutral position. This stabilization is done to minimize movement that could cause injury to the spinal cord.

Objective: State reasons for management of the cervical spine once the patient has been determined to be a trauma patient.

91. The usual progression in deteriorating mental status for a child is: the child cries but can be comforted; the child cries despite attempts to be comforted; the child becomes irritable, agitated, and restless; and finally, the child does not react at all to his surroundings. Often, rescuers confuse a child with an altered mental status with a child who is simply "being good." For example, it is not normal for a 2-year-old child to allow a stranger (the rescuer) to take him away from mom or dad. If the rescuer can take the child, ask the parent if the child normally allows strangers to hold him.

Objective: Differentiate between assessing the altered mental status in the adult, child, and infant patient.

92. A patent airway is an open airway.

Objective: N/A

93. 1. If oxygen is being delivered by nonrebreather mask:

    a. Ensure the mask is connected to oxygen at 15 L/min.

    b. Ensure the reservoir bag is not pinched off and remains inflated.

    c. Ensure the inhalation valve is not obstructed.

  2. If oxygen is being delivered by nasal cannula:

    a. Ensure the oxygen flow rate is set at no more than 6 L/min.

    b. Ensure the prongs are properly placed in the patient's nose.

    c. Evaluate the patient's respiratory effort (tidal volume and respiratory rate).

    d. Assess the patient's skin color.

    e. Attach a pulse oximeter and evaluate the patient's SpO2.

Objective: Discuss the reasons for repeating the initial assessment as part of the ongoing assessment.

94. *D*eformities
*C*ontusions (bruises)
*A*brasions (scrapes)
*P*unctures/penetrations
*B*urns
*T*enderness
*L*acerations (cuts)
*S*welling

Objective: Describe the areas included in the rapid trauma assessment and discuss what should be evaluated.

95. The abdomen is normally soft and is not painful or tender to touch. To examine the abdomen, first inspect it for any contusions, discolorations, abrasions, cuts, or swelling. Then palpate the abdomen by placing one hand on top of the other. Use the pads of the fingers of the lower hand and gently feel the upper and lower areas of the abdomen for injuries or tenderness. If the patient is responsive, ask him to point to the area that hurts (point tenderness). Assess the area that hurts last. Determine if the abdomen feels soft or firm. During your examination, watch the patient's facial expression for signs of tenderness.

Objective: Describe the areas included in the rapid trauma assessment and discuss what should be evaluated.

96. Assess the abdomen for DCAP-BTLS and look for the following:

- Surgical scars
- Bruising
- Open wounds
- Protruding abdominal organs
- An impaled object
- Distention
- Signs of obvious pregnancy

Objective: Describe the areas included in the rapid trauma assessment and discuss what should be evaluated.

97. Factors to consider in a MVC include the following:

- Rate of speed
- Seatbelt use
- Impact site
- Amount of intrusion
- Airbag deployment
- Vehicle size
- Condition of steering wheel
- Condition of windshield

Objective: Discuss reasons for reconsidering the mechanism of injury.

98. PMS = *p*ulse, *m*ovement, and *s*ensation. Compare each extremity to the opposite extremity.

    Objective: Describe the areas included in the rapid trauma assessment and discuss what should be evaluated.

99. PMS = *p*ulse, *m*ovement, and *s*ensation. Assess the dorsalis pedis pulse (on the top of the foot) in each lower extremity. Assess the radial pulse in each upper extremity. Assess movement and sensation in each extremity. If the patient is awake, assess movement of the lower extremities by asking if he can push both of his feet into your hands at the same time. Assess movement of the upper extremities by asking the patient to squeeze your fingers, using both of his hands at the same time. Compare the strength of his grips and note if they are equal or if one side appears weaker. If the patient is awake, assess sensation by touching the hands and toes of each extremity and asking him to tell you where you are touching. If the patient is unresponsive, assess movement and sensation by applying a pinch to each foot and hand. See if the patient responds to pain with facial movements or movement of the extremity.

    Objective: Describe the areas included in the rapid trauma assessment and discuss what should be evaluated.

100. A head-to-toe physical examination should be performed in the following situations:

     • Trauma patients with a significant mechanism of injury
     • Trauma patients with an unknown or unclear mechanism of injury
     • Trauma patients with an injury to more than 1 area of the body
     • All unresponsive patients
     • All patients with an altered mental status
     • Some responsive medical patients, on the basis of history and focused physical examination findings

     Objective: Distinguish between the detailed physical exam that is performed on a trauma patient and that of the medical patient.

10 Communications

READING ASSIGNMENT ▶ Read Chapter 10, pages 239 to 254 in your textbook.

Sum It Up

- Communication is the process of sending and receiving information. As an EMT, you must be able to communicate effectively with crewmembers, emergency dispatchers, medical direction, and other healthcare professionals; law enforcement personnel and other public safety workers; the patient; and the patient's family.

- The Federal Communications Commission (FCC) is the U.S. government agency responsible for the development and enforcement of rules and regulations pertaining to radio transmissions.

- VHF radio frequencies can be subdivided into low-band and high-band. Low-band frequencies generally have a greater range than high-band VHF frequencies. Radio waves in the low-band frequency range bend and follow the curvature of the Earth, allowing radio transmission over long distances. Radio waves in the high-band frequency range travel in a straight line. This straight-line quality means that the radio wave is easily blocked by topography such as a hill, mountain, or large building.

- UHF radio waves travel in a straight line but do have an ability to reflect or bounce around buildings. 800-megahertz frequencies are UHF radio signals that use computer technology to make transmissions more secure than the other types of radio transmission.

- A base station is a transmitter/receiver at a stationary site such as a hospital, mountaintop, or public safety agency. A radio signal generated by the base station may be sent directly to a receiving unit or to a repeater as needed. A mobile two-way radio is a vehicular-mounted communication device. A portable radio is a handheld communication device. A repeater is a device that receives a transmission from a low-power portable or mobile radio on one frequency and then retransmits it at a higher power on another frequency so it can be received at a distant location.

- MDCs (also called *MDTs*) are computers mounted in emergency vehicles that display information pertaining to the calls for which EMS personnel are dispatched. The computer is also used to send and receive text messages between the EMS crew and the dispatch center.

- An EMS communications network must provide a means by which a citizen can reliably access the EMS system (usually by dialing 9-1-1). To ensure adequate EMS system response and coordination, there must also be a means for dispatch to emergency vehicle communication, communication between emergency vehicles, communication from the emergency vehicle to the hospital, hospital-to-hospital communication, and communication between agencies, such as between EMS and law enforcement personnel.

- 9-1-1 is the official national emergency number in the United States and Canada. When the numbers 9-1-1 are dialed, the caller is quickly connected to a single location called a PSAP. Although EMS is usually activated by dialing 9-1-1, other methods of activating an emergency response include emergency alarm boxes, citizen band radios, and wireless telephones. Enhanced 9-1-1, or E9-1-1, is a system that routes an emergency call to the 9-1-1 center closest to the caller, and automatically displays the caller's phone number and address. VoIP (also known as *Internet Voice*) is technology that allows users to make telephone calls by means of a broadband Internet connection instead of using a regular telephone line.

- EMDs are trained professionals who are responsible for verifying the address of the incident, asking questions of the caller, assigning responders to the incident, alerting/activating responders to the incident, providing prearrival instructions to the caller, communicating with responders, and recording incident times.

- Dispatch should be notified when receiving the call, responding to the call, arriving at the scene, leaving the scene for the receiving facility, arriving at the receiving facility, leaving the hospital for the station, returning to service, and arriving at the station.

- When communicating with a patient, identify yourself and explain that you are there to provide assistance. Recognize the patient's need for privacy, preserve the patient's dignity, and treat the patient with respect.

- When talking with family members and bystanders, avoid interrupting when they are talking. Speak clearly and use common words (avoid using medical terms). Speak at an appropriate speed or pace, not too rapidly and not too slowly. When communicating with individuals from other agencies, be organized, concise, thorough, and accurate.

- It may be necessary to contact medical direction for advice, obtain orders to give medications, or receive other orders. The information given to the physician must be accurate because the physician will use this information to determine whether to order medications and procedures. Repeat orders back to the physician, word for word.

- Use a standardized reporting format when relaying a verbal report to medical direction or to the staff of the receiving facility.

- HIPAA limits the medical information that may be shared about an individual.

▶ Tracking Your Progress

After reading this chapter, can you:	Page Reference	Objective Met?
• List the proper methods of initiating and terminating a radio call?	245, 246	☐
• State the proper sequence for delivery of patient information?	252	☐
• Explain the importance of effective communication of patient information in the verbal report?	252	☐
• Identify the essential components of the verbal report?	252	☐
• Describe the attributes for increasing effectiveness and efficiency of verbal communication?	247	☐

After reading this chapter, can you:	Page Reference	Objective Met?
• State legal aspects to consider in verbal communication?	253	☐
• Discuss the communication skills that should be used to interact with the patient?	247	☐
• Discuss the communication skills that should be used to interact with the family, bystanders, and individuals from other agencies while providing patient care and the difference between skills used to interact with the patient and those used to interact with others?	247, 250, 251, 252	☐
• List the correct radio procedures in the following phases of a typical call:	246, 251, 252, 253	☐

—To the scene?

—At the scene?

—To the facility?

—At the facility?

—To the station?

—At the station?

Multiple Choice

In the space provided, identify the letter of the choice that best completes the statement or answers each question.

_____ 1. Which of the following radio transmission frequencies has the clearest reception ability combined with the shortest range?
   a. UHF frequencies
   b. 800-MHz frequencies
   c. VHF low-band frequencies
   d. VHF high-band frequencies

_____ 2. When transmitting patient information, it is important to be an advocate for patient privacy and confidentiality. Which of the following devices provides protection against eavesdropping by persons with scanners?
   a. Cellular telephone technology
   b. VHF low-band radio transmission
   c. VHF high-band radio transmission
   d. None of the above

_____ 3. Which of the following radio communications devices typically has a range of 10-15 miles and operates at 20-50 watts?
   a. Portable radio
   b. Handheld radio
   c. Base station transmitter/receiver
   d. Vehicle-mounted mobile two-way radio

Questions 4–6 pertain to the following scenario.

Your rescue crew has been called to the home of a 74-year-old man who is "acting inappropriately," according to his son. During your assessment of this patient, you note the following: His name is Geoff Gregory, he has a history of diabetes and tuberculosis, he has had five beers in the past four hours, and he is unable to recall the date or time of day.

_____ 4. During your communication with medical direction by radio, which of the following information is not necessary to relay?
   a. "This patient is 74 years old."
   b. "His name is Geoff Gregory."
   c. "He has a history of diabetes."
   d. "He has had five beers in the past four hours and cannot recall the date or time of day."

_____ **5.** The medical direction physician, Dr. Gary, instructs you to give one tube of oral glucose to the patient. Your reply to these instructions should be,

    a. "Copy, Doctor."
    b. "10-4. Over and out."
    c. "Copy. We will give the oral glucose."
    d. "Copy, Dr. Gary, we will give this patient one tube of oral glucose."

_____ **6.** When communicating with this elderly patient, you should

    a. stand off to one side of the patient.
    b. speak more slowly than usual in short, simple sentences.
    c. ask a string of questions, then allow the patient to answer you.
    d. begin speaking in a louder-than-normal tone to compensate for the patient's possible hearing loss.

_____ **7.** Which of the following devices is typically mounted on a stationary site, such as a hospital or mountaintop, and is capable of transmitting and receiving radio communications?

    a. A base station
    b. A cellular phone
    c. A mobile two-way radio
    d. A multiple-channel portable radio

_____ **8.** Which of the following receives transmissions on one frequency and then retransmits the transmission on a different frequency so that it will travel farther?

    a. A repeater
    b. A base station
    c. A multi-channel portable radio
    d. A VHF low-band radio frequency

_____ **9.** Which of the following lists the proper procedure to follow when transmitting radio communications?

    a. Depress the PTT button and immediately begin speaking with the microphone 1-2 feet from your mouth.
    b. Depress the PTT button and immediately begin speaking with the microphone 10-12 inches from your mouth.
    c. Depress the PTT button, wait 1 second, and then begin talking with the microphone 2-3 inches from your mouth.
    d. Depress the PTT button, wait 4 seconds, and then begin talking with the microphone 10-12 inches from your mouth.

_____ **10.** Which of the following is an advantage of a PSAP?

    a. It allows a longer range of radio transmission.
    b. It allows security from eavesdropping via scanner.
    c. It allows rapid access to fire, police, and EMS agencies.
    d. It allows the maximum amount of radio frequencies from which to choose.

_____ **11.** The process of sending and receiving information is called

    a. feedback.
    b. interference.
    c. transmission.
    d. communication.

_____ **12.** The primary advantage of enhanced 9-1-1 (E9-1-1) over standard 9-1-1 is that E9-1-1

    a. routes the call directly to the closest responding rescue unit.
    b. displays the caller's telephone number and address for the call-taker.
    c. can be used effectively from hotel rooms and other buildings with switchboards.
    d. does not require the caller to state the problem in order to get an appropriate response.

_____ **13.** When communicating via radio, you should

    a. keep your transmissions to 1-minute bursts of information.
    b. be courteous, and say "please" and "thank you" when appropriate.
    c. use as many codes as possible to speed transmission of information.
    d. use the terms "affirmative" and "negative" in place of "yes" and "no."

_____ 14. You are assigned to work on an ambulance designated as EMS-1. Which of the following responses would be the appropriate method to make contact with EMT James McCoy on another ambulance, EMS-5?

    a. "EMS-1 to Jim, come in Jim."

    b. "Come in Jim, are you out there?"

    c. "EMS-5 to EMS-1, do you copy?"

    d. "EMS-1 to EMS-5, do you copy?"

_____ 15. What radio transmission band would be ideal for use in metropolitan areas where building penetration is needed?

    a. UHF

    b. VHF low band

    c. VHF high band

    d. VHF medium band

_____ 16. Which of the following characteristics is true regarding low-band VHF frequencies?

    a. They are very effective in metropolitan areas.

    b. They require the use of a repeater because of their short range.

    c. They have an ability to reflect or bounce around buildings.

    d. Radio waves bend and follow the curvature of the earth.

_____ 17. When communicating with a patient,

    a. avoid eye contact with the patient.

    b. treat all patients abruptly to maintain control.

    c. do not tell the patient your name for legal reasons.

    d. position yourself at, or slightly lower, than the patient's line of vision.

_____ 18. When dealing with hearing-impaired patients who are able to read lips, you should

    a. speak more loudly.

    b. avoid using facial expressions.

    c. speak clearly and directly at the patient.

    d. pay particular attention to pronouncing every syllable slowly and concisely.

_____ 19. When treating a visually-impaired patient, pay particular attention to make sure that you

    a. speak to the patient from a distance.

    b. avoid such terms as "blind" and "sees."

    c. lead the patient around by grasping the patient's arm.

    d. speak to the patient before handling, touching, and treating him.

_____ 20. You are questioning an 83-year-old man about his past medical history. Which of the following is correct regarding special communications needs with this patient?

    a. You should communicate with the patient in written form.

    b. You should speak in a normal tone until you discover the need to do otherwise.

    c. You should assume that the patient is hearing impaired and speak more loudly.

    d. You should speak loudly but refer to the patient as "honey" or "dear" to avoid having the patient mistake your loud tone for yelling at them.

Answer Section

Chapter 10

Multiple Choice

1. b

800-MHz technology allows high clarity of transmission; however, this technology is dependent upon repeaters to ensure that messages meet their intended recipient.

Objective: N/A

2. d

Any nonencrypted radio device is subject to eavesdropping via scanner. A general rule of message transmission is do not transmit something you, your agency, or your patient wouldn't want printed in the local newspaper.

Objective: State legal aspects to consider in verbal communication.

3. d

The mobile two-way radio operates at 20-50 watts and generally has a transmission range of 10-15 miles. The local terrain can influence the range of transmission. Handheld portable radios operate at a much lower power (1-5 watts) and have a lower transmission range. Base station radio transmissions are much more powerful and have a farther range.

Objective: N/A

4. b

It is not necessary to include the patient's name in your transmission to medical direction. Remember that your transmission may be monitored and recorded by anyone with access to simple scanning equipment.

Objective: Identify the essential components of the verbal report.

5. d

When transmitting messages, you should use plain English rather than codes (such as 10-codes). When given orders, you should clarify the order by repeating it back to the sender. If the order calls for administration of a medication, repeat back (echo) the ordered drug, dosage, and route of administration.

Objective: N/A

6. b

Patients more easily understand short, simple questions. However, be careful not to "talk down" to your patient, who may interpret this as disrespectful. Stand directly in the patient's line of vision at the same level with or slightly below the patient. Do not string your questions together, which may confuse the patient regardless of his age. Finally, do not assume any impairment on the part of the patient. If you are unsure about an impairment, ask the patient—for example, "Can you hear me well enough, Mr. Gregory?"

Objective: Discuss the communication skills that should be used to interact with the patient.

7. a

Base station devices are typically mounted at the highest local elevation, such as a tall building or a close mountain peak. Cellular phones are mobile devices that depend on local networks (cells) to route their transmissions. As their names imply, mobile two-way radios and multiple-channel portable radios are not stationary devices.

Objective: N/A

8. a

Repeaters greatly enhance the performance of portable radios. Most portable radios operate at low wattage and hence have limited transmission range. Repeaters are located throughout the transmission area (county boundaries, for example) and receive the transmissions from low wattage devices. The repeater then retransmits the intended message with greater power and range on a different frequency.

Objective: N/A

9. c

The proper procedure for radio transmission is to first depress the PTT button and wait a second or two. This "opens" the transmission at the repeater (if one is present in your system), thus decreasing the chance that your first words will be lost. You should then speak clearly in a normal tone and volume with the microphone held about 2-3 inches from your mouth.

Objective: List the proper methods of initiating and terminating a radio call.

10. c

The PSAP system allows rapid access to emergency agencies because it centralizes emergency calls for assistance. Calls may in turn be routed to different agencies depending on the origin and type of call.

Objective: N/A

11. d

Communication is the process of sending and receiving information.

Objective: Describe the attributes for increasing effectiveness and efficiency of verbal communications.

12. b

Enhanced 9-1-1 uses telephone company records to provide additional information to the call processing agency. If the 9-1-1 call goes through a switchboard, the ability to pinpoint the origin of the call is lost. With E9-1-1, callers must still state the problem (medical emergency, fire, police situation). The ability to route a call to the closest appropriate response unit is a separate system, sometimes referred to as AVL. AVL uses satellite technology to select response units on the basis of geography.

Objective: N/A

13. d

The words "yes" and "no" are often difficult to understand in radio transmissions. Transmissions should be kept to 30 seconds or less to allow

the listener an opportunity to interact in the transmission (such as, "We didn't copy the pulse rate, Rescue 204, could you repeat"). Courtesy is assumed in radio transmissions. "Please," "thank you," and "you're welcome" are generally implied. Finally, use plain English in your transmissions (unless local protocol dictates otherwise). Codes may be misunderstood by the person on the other end of the radio transmission.

Objective: List the correct radio procedures in the following phases of a typical call: to the scene, at the scene, to the facility, at the facility, to the station, and at the station.

14. d

When attempting to contact another field unit, identify yourself and the unit you are seeking. Avoid using personal names.

Objective: N/A

15. a

UHF band transmissions offer strong penetrating power into densely populated areas. Like the 800-MHz systems, UHF systems necessitate the use of repeaters because of short transmission distances.

Objective: N/A

16. d

Radio waves in the low-band frequency range bend and follow the curvature of the Earth, allowing radio transmission over long distances. These radio waves are subject to interference by atmospheric conditions, including weather disturbances and electrical equipment. These waves do not penetrate solid structures (such as buildings) well, making VHF low band less effective for use in metropolitan areas.

Objective: N/A

17. d

To facilitate a nonthreatening, comfortable exchange of information, position yourself where the patient can easily see you, if possible. Making eye contact with the patient is important for building trust. Do not assume that your patient will be "challenging" to deal with. Sometimes this assumption may cause an otherwise amicable (friendly) patient to assume a negative attitude.

Objective: Discuss the communication skills that should be used to interact with the patient.

18. c

Sometimes our ability to communicate with hearing-impaired patients is hindered by the knowledge that the patient is impaired. If a patient can read lips, speak in a normal tone, look at the patient when speaking, make sure you have the patient's attention before speaking, and avoid over pronunciation. Mild facial expression may assist in conveying your meaning.

Objective: Discuss the communication skills that should be used to interact with the patient.

19. d

Because the patient cannot visualize your actions, it is imperative that you describe what you are doing. Something as simple as obtaining a blood pressure should be clearly communicated with the patient. Avoid speaking from a great distance to the patient or moving around too much while communicating. These patients are aware of their impairment and generally will not be insulted if you tactfully question them about their degree of impairment. It is not necessary to avoid the words "blind" or "I see." When leading the patient, allow the patient to grasp your arm. Then communicate with the patient to help them understand your directions and any obstacles.

Objective: Discuss the communication skills that should be used to interact with the patient.

20. b

Do not assume older adults are impaired. Do not assume your patient cannot hear, see, or understand you. If, however, you find you are having difficulty communicating with a patient, take whatever steps necessary to facilitate your communications.

Objective: Discuss the communication skills that should be used to interact with the patient.

READING ASSIGNMENT ▶   Read Chapter 11, pages 255 to 273 in your textbook.

Sum It Up

- Good documentation is complete, clear, concise, objective, timely, accurate, and legible.
- A PCR has many important functions.
  - *Continuity of care.* The PCR may be used by receiving facility staff to help determine the direction of treatment following the EMS treatments given.
  - *Legal document.* Good documentation reflects the emergency medical care provided, status of the patient on arrival at the scene, and any changes upon arrival at the receiving facility.
  - *Education and research.* The PCR can be used to show proper documentation and how to handle unusual or uncommon situations, as well as identify training needs for the EMS providers.
  - *Administrative.* The PCR is used for billing and EMS service statistics.
  - *Quality management.* Completed reports are typically evaluated for adequacy of documentation, compliance with local rules and regulations, compliance with agency documentation standards, and appropriateness of medical care.
- A PCR generally consists of an administrative section, patient and scene information section, and patient assessment (narrative) section.
  - The administrative section includes data pertaining to the EMS call, such as the date, times, service, unit, and crew information.
  - The patient and scene information section includes data such as the patient's name, age, gender, weight, address, date of birth, and insurance information.
  - The patient assessment section includes the patient's chief complaint, MOI/NOI, location of the patient, treatment given before arrival of EMS, patient signs and symptoms, care given, vital signs, SAMPLE history, and changes in condition.
- The PCR form and the information on it are considered confidential. Local and state protocols and procedures determine where the different copies of the PCR should be distributed.
- Mentally competent adults have the right to refuse care and transport. You must make sure that the patient fully understands your explanation and the consequences of refusing treatment or transport. Call advanced medical

personnel to the scene as soon as possible to evaluate the patient or contact medical direction.

- Falsification of information on the PCR may lead not only to suspension or revocation of the EMT's certification/license but also to poor patient care because other healthcare professionals have a false impression of which assessment findings were discovered or what treatment was given.
- When a documentation error occurs, do not try to cover it up. Instead, document what did or did not happen, and time, date, and initial your entry.

▶ Tracking Your Progress

After reading this chapter, can you:	Page Reference	Objective Met?
• Explain the components of the written report and list the information that should be included on the written report?	260	☐
• Identify the various sections of the written report?	260	☐
• Describe what information is required in each section of the PCR and how it should be entered?	260	☐
• Define the special considerations concerning patient refusal?	264	☐
• Describe the legal implications associated with the written report?	264	☐
• Discuss all state and/or local record and reporting requirements?	269	☐

Multiple Choice

In the space provided, identify the letter of the choice that best completes the statement or answers each question.

_____ 1. A PCR may be called many names, including a patient care report, incident report, run report, or trip sheet. After the patient encounter, this document
  a. is intended to stay with the EMT.
  b. is used solely for billing purposes.
  c. is intended to become part of the patient's receiving facility medical record.
  d. is intended to stay with the EMS agency (ambulance service, fire department, etc.).

_____ 2. The PCR helps ensure the continuity of patient care. This document may be the only source for important information that hospital personnel need to appropriately assess and treat the patient. An example of such information is
  a. the patient's past medical history.
  b. the patient's condition at the scene.
  c. the patient's condition at time of transfer of care at the receiving facility.
  d. the patient's current prescription medications and any allergies to medications.

_____ 3. From a legal standpoint, the PCR is
  a. the sole property of its author and may be released only with his consent.
  b. confidential and may be reviewed only by the agency providing EMS services
  c. an official record of the care rendered and may be used in court proceedings.
  d. an official record of the care rendered, although review of the form may be denied by the agency providing EMS services.

_____ **4.** The PCR should indicate
   a. the name and certification of the document author only.
   b. the name and certification of the personnel performing assessment and interventions only.
   c. the name and certification of the document author and all personnel assisting in patient care.
   d. no names, for legal reasons.

_____ **5.** The PCR and the information contained in it are
   a. public record and may be freely discussed.
   b. considered confidential and should not be discussed with unauthorized persons.
   c. considered confidential and should not be shown to unauthorized persons, but may be discussed freely.
   d. considered confidential and should not be discussed with persons other than the patient, the patient's family and friends, or the patient's employer.

_____ **6.** Falsification of the information on the PCR may harm the patient. Falsification may also lead to
   a. suspension of duties.
   b. termination with present employer only.
   c. suspension or revocation of certification and other legal action.
   d. suspension or revocation of certification but not any other legal action.

_____ **7.** Your ambulance crew is called to the scene of a motor vehicle collision. While documenting, you accidentally record, "Patient was a front seat passenger without a seat belt on." After writing this, the patient informs you that he was the driver of the vehicle and was wearing his seat belt. You should
   a. scribble the error out completely and continue with the form.
   b. start the entire form over since mistakes are not acceptable on PCRs.
   c. draw a line through the error, date and initial it, and continue with the form.
   d. leave the wrong information as is, but make another note on the form that the patient was the driver and was wearing his seat belt.

_____ **8.** Your rescue crew is called to the scene of an explosion at a large apartment complex. There are three obviously dead victims and at least 25 other residents seriously injured. For documentation purposes
   a. you need not fill out a PCR for the deceased victims.
   b. no patient may be transported before having a comprehensive PCR completed.
   c. a comprehensive PCR may have to wait until after the casualties are triaged and transported.
   d. you must triage and treat the patients only; documentation is not needed for MCIs.

_____ **9.** You are returning to your quarters after transporting a 29-year-old woman who accidentally cut herself with scissors. While in the back of the ambulance, this patient told you she was feeling dizzy and short of breath. While reviewing your documentation, you notice that you did not document this information. You should
   a. write the information at the bottom of the original PCR.
   b. erase the misinformation on the original form and correct it.
   c. write the information on a supplement (addendum) form and sign and date it.
   d. ignore it since patient care has already been transferred to the hospital staff.

Questions 10–13 pertain to the following scenario.

Your rescue crew is called to the home of a 54-year-old man complaining of difficulty breathing. You arrive to find the patient sitting up in bed and very anxious. You are responsible for documentation of this patient encounter.

_____ 10. Your partner gives the patient supplemental oxygen by nonrebreather mask. For documentation purposes, you should
   a. document that the patient was given oxygen.
   b. document that the patient was given oxygen and include the flow rate, delivery device, and time.
   c. document that the patient was given oxygen and include the flow rate, delivery device, time, and your partner's certification number.
   d. document that the patient was given oxygen and include the flow rate, delivery device, time, and your certification number since you are responsible for the documentation.

_____ 11. After several minutes of oxygen therapy, you should
   a. document the patient's response to the intervention.
   b. document the patient's response to the intervention only if his condition has changed.
   c. document the patient's response to the intervention only if his condition has improved.
   d. document the patient's response to the intervention only if his condition has deteriorated.

_____ 12. Which of the following statements would be considered a "pertinent negative" for this patient's complaint?
   a. "Patient has a history of asthma."
   b. "Patient speaks in complete sentences without difficulty."
   c. "Lungs have wheezes throughout with diminished tidal volume."
   d. "Patient states that his difficulty breathing began 4 hours ago while working in the yard."

_____ 13. Which of the following statements would be considered a pertinent positive for this patient's complaint?
   a. "Patient denies chest pain."
   b. "Patient's skin is dry, warm, and pink."
   c. "Patient has not had any recent trauma or surgeries."
   d. "Patient uses accessory muscles throughout the chest and abdomen to assist respirations."

Questions 14–16 pertain to the following scenario.

Your ambulance crew is called to the home of a 34-year-old woman complaining of finger pain. She states that she accidentally slammed her index finger in a car door. Her finger shows gross deformity but no bleeding. She denies any other injury. You are responsible for documentation of this patient encounter.

_____ 14. Because of the minor, isolated nature of this patient's complaint and her denial of other injuries, you decide a detailed physical examination is not necessary. Which of the following responses should you document on the PCR regarding the patient's posterior body?
   a. "N/A"
   b. "Pain only in the finger."
   c. "No trauma, pain, or deformity to palpation."
   d. "The patient's back was not assessed because of the minor nature of the complaint."

_____ 15. This patient requests transportation to the closest emergency department. While preparing to transport, the patient's husband informs you that she is HIV positive. For documentation purposes, you should
   a. leave this information out since the patient is not bleeding.
   b. document, "Patient has a communicable disease."
   c. document, "Patient has past medical history of AIDS."
   d. document, "Patient's husband states the patient is HIV positive."

_____ 16. After transferring care of this patient in the Emergency Department, you notice that you only assessed and documented one set of vital signs. You should
   a. leave the document with only one set of vital signs recorded.
   b. document that you did not want to take a second set of vital signs.
   c. document that a second set of vital signs was taken 5 minutes after the first set.
   d. document that a second set of vital signs was taken 15 minutes after the first set.

Questions 17–20 pertain to the following scenario.

Your rescue crew is dispatched to a motor vehicle collision. Your patient is a 24-year-old man complaining of neck pain. When you arrive on scene, the patient is out of his vehicle and standing on the sidewalk. You are responsible for documenting this patient encounter.

_____ 17. As you approach this patient, he tells you that he does not want any help. You notice he is massaging his neck and wincing in pain. Which of the following is correct regarding refusing care?
   a. Any patient may refuse care.
   b. Patients with obvious injuries cannot refuse care.
   c. Once the patient states he does not want care, you are not allowed to speak with him.
   d. Competent, informed adults may refuse care for themselves or for a minor of their responsibility.

_____ 18. Before acknowledging the patient's refusal, you must be certain the patient understands that care is being offered and that you believe care is needed. You must also
   a. have a legal guardian assume responsibility for the patient.
   b. make sure that you document at least 1 set of vital signs.
   c. express the possible complications of refusing care, including potential death.
   d. express the possible complications of refusing care but do not mention death as the patient may mistake it for a threat.

_____ 19. The patient fits the criteria for refusing treatment. He agrees to sign the refusal form. To witness this form, which of the following persons should ideally sign the form?
   a. Yourself
   b. A third party
   c. Your supervisor
   d. Another EMT on your crew

_____ 20. Before leaving the scene, you should say to the patient,
   a. "This is your last chance for help."
   b. "You are probably going to die."
   c. "Feel free to call us back if you change your mind."
   d. "You are probably going to be pretty sore from the collision. Take some aspirin when you get home."

Short Answer

Answer each question in the space provided.

Use the following information in answering questions 21-23.

Pelvis—DCAP-BTLS negative, femoral pulses strong and equal. Bystanders state pt was hit by vehicle and then "flew through the air." Per bystanders, + loss of consciousness. Chest—DCAP-BTLS negative, breath sounds clear/equal bilaterally. Rx: Oxygen by nonrebreather mask at 15 L/min. Full spinal stabilization (cervical collar, spider straps, head blocks, backboard). Transported code 3 by ground ambulance to XYZ pediatric trauma center. Found in street, right lat recumbent position with altered LOC. Patient: 10-year-old female who weighs 90 pounds. Facial bruising, left side. Blood from mouth. Loose teeth. PERL. No drainage from ears or nose. Pt responds to pain with periods of combative behavior and crying. Does not follow verbal commands. Abdomen—bruising LUQ. Significant damage to front of vehicle on hood and windshield. Per father on the scene: Allergies: none. Takes no medications, no pertinent PMH. Dinner at 1800. Back—bruising, left flank. Respond to motor vehicle crash—car versus pedestrian. Estimated speed: 50 miles per hour. Neck—DCAP-BTLS negative, trachea midline. Extremities—Left elbow laceration; equal pulses, movement.

Vital signs:

2215	P 120 strong/regular	BP 110/74	R 32
2219	P 110 strong/regular	BP 112/80	R 30
2226	P 97 strong/regular	BP 97/64	R 24
2235	P 94 strong/regular	BP 94/58	R 18

21. Using the preceding EMS call information, rewrite the information in the SOAP documentation format.

22. Using the preceding EMS call information, rewrite the information in the CHART documentation format.

23. Using the preceding EMS call information, rewrite the information in a narrative documentation format.

Answer Section

Chapter 11

Multiple Choice

1. c

The PCR helps ensure the continuity of care and must be included in the patient's receiving facility medical record. Generally, PCRs are printed on carbonless-copy paper, which allows multiple forms to be generated at once. The original generally goes with the patient's records, and the remaining copies may be filed with billing, a quality control officer, the EMS agency, or other agency. When writing a PCR, be aware that many people may ultimately read your report.

Objective: Describe the legal implications associated with the written report.

2. b

The hospital staff cannot be present at the scene. By painting a clear picture in the PCR, you help ensure that proper assessment and treatment are carried out. Some agencies, in fact, require a photograph of the scene in certain circumstances. For example, when transporting a motor vehicle collision victim, being able to show the hospital staff the MOI and the damage to the vehicles is sometimes helpful. Information about the patient's past medical history, current medications, and condition upon transfer of care can all be collected at the hospital. These things are important and should be included on the PCR; however, you must appreciate the hospital's need for scene-specific information.

Objective: Explain the components of the written report and list the information that should be included on the written report.

3. c

The PCR is the official document recording prehospital care. It may be subpoenaed and used in court. Therefore, it is important to take documentation seriously. Remember that the general rules are, "If it is not written down, it was not done," and "If it was not done, do not write it down."

Objective: Describe the legal implications associated with the written report.

4. c

List all persons involved with the patient encounter. Protect yourself from punitive action by treating patients appropriately and documenting your encounter completely, honestly, and neatly. Including the names of all the personnel involved in the encounter may be life-saving. For example, your crew responds on a 12-year-old male patient complaining of a headache. You transport the patient to the hospital and think nothing of the brief encounter. However, if this patient tests positive for a certain type of meningitis, your crew can be at risk of developing the disease. Without complete documentation, notification of your exposure may be greatly delayed or absent.

Objective: Explain the components of the written report and list the information that should be included on the written report.

5. b

Different agencies and different states regulate the confidentiality of the PCR differently. You should attempt to maintain the confidentiality of the report for your protection and for the protection of the patient's privacy. You will often be approached by concerned friends and coworkers who want to know how the patient is doing. Be tactful, compassionate, and nonspecific in your response (e.g., "I appreciate your concern. We are doing everything we can for Mr. Smith"). Do not discuss the patient's medical history, current medications, insurance status, your impression regarding the legitimacy of the complaint, or any similar topics.

Objective: Describe the legal implications associated with the written report.

6. c

The PCR is a legal document. Falsification of this document may result in punitive measures by your employer, medical direction, your local regulatory agency, and any local, state, or federal law that applies.

Objective: Describe the legal implications associated with the written report.

7. c

Because the PCR is a legal document, use the standard method of correcting mistakes for such documents. Draw a single line through the error, initial and date the line, and write the correct information. It is not appropriate to scribble or erase mistakes, nor is it appropriate to leave a mistake in the document with a reference to the correct information somewhere else on the form. Both of these approaches could be confusing to anyone reading the document.

Objective: Describe the legal implications associated with the written report.

8. c

Preservation of life is the most important duty with which you may be charged. Documentation, however critical, takes a back seat to prompt and appropriate stabilization, interventions, and transportation. Sometimes the PCR has to wait. All victims must have some form of documentation, even morbidly injured ones.

Objective: N/A

9. c

This information is pertinent and should be documented. Because you already transferred care of the patient to the receiving facility (and gave the facility its copy of the PCR), putting the information at the bottom of the original form fails to ensure continuity of patient care. A separate form will need to be submitted. Use whatever form your agency deems appropriate and document the date and time of the supplement information, include the information you omitted, and sign the form. If you failed to verbally express the information to the receiving facility, you may need to contact them with the "new" information.

Objective: N/A

10. c

Be complete. When skills are performed, note the time, equipment used, and the person performing the skill. Do not give yourself credit for performing the skill simply because you are documenting completion of the skill.

Objective: Describe what information is required in each section of the PCR and how it should be entered.

11. a

With all interventions, you should record the patient's response regardless of whether the patient's condition has changed. If there was no change according to the patient, simply document, "No change." When documenting the patient's response to an intervention such as splinting or full spinal immobilization, it is important to list the condition of the body area treated before and after your intervention. For example, if a splint is applied to a possibly broken arm, it would be appropriate to document, "Motor, sensory, and circulation intact before and after splint application."

Objective: Describe what information is required in each section of the PCR and how it should be entered.

12. b

A pertinent negative is a finding contrary to what you may typically associate with the patient's chief complaint. It would be a significant pertinent negative that this patient, complaining of difficulty breathing, can speak in complete sentences without difficulty. The history of asthma and wheezes are pertinent positives (what you may expect from this patient based on his complaint). The time of onset is not a pertinent negative but does help to complete the picture for this patient's condition.

Objective: Describe what information is required in each section of the PCR and how it should be entered.

13. d

A pertinent positive is a finding that is consistent with the patient's chief complaint. The use of accessory muscles to assist respirations is significant and pertinent to the complaint. The denial of chest pain or recent trauma help to narrow the origin of the complaint, and the skin condition (warm, dry, and pink) is a pertinent negative. Patients in respiratory distress often have cool, wet, pale, or cyanotic skin.

Objective: Describe what information is required in each section of the PCR and how it should be entered.

14. a

Be honest but not wordy. N/A for "not applicable" is widely understood and accepted. It is also a good idea to document that the patient denies any other injuries. "Pain only in the finger" and "The patient's back was not assessed because of the minor nature of the complaint" are wordy. "No trauma, pain, or deformity to palpation" implies that you actually evaluated the patient's back.

Objective: Describe the legal implications associated with the written report.

15. d

Document your observations, not your conclusions. Observations are medically pertinent and should be included on the form regardless of whether the patient is bleeding. A person who is HIV positive (infected with the human immunodeficiency virus) may not necessarily have AIDS. If your information comes from someone other than the patient (and is not confirmed by the patient), include the source of the information. It may be appropriate to confirm this information with the patient tactfully and privately.

Objective: Explain the components of the written report and list the information that should be included on the written report.

16. a

Be honest! If only one set of vital signs were assessed, then only one set should be recorded. Because this patient seems stable, a set of vital signs is recommended at least every 15 minutes (every 5 minutes for unstable patients). Do not falsify documents.

Objective: Describe the legal implications associated with the written report.

17. d

For a valid refusal of care, the patient must be informed that care is offered and recommended. Furthermore, you must indicate to the patient the possible complications of refusing care.

Objective: Define the special considerations concerning patient refusal.

18. c

If you think a possible complication of this patient's refusal of care may be death, you have the responsibility to inform the patient. Be professional, not melodramatic. Seeking assistance from family or friends when encouraging a patient to accept care is often helpful. If an ill or injured patient is adamant about refusing care, you should contact medical direction, according to local protocol.

Objective: Define the special considerations concerning patient refusal.

19. b

Having a third party sign the refusal form is best. It is beneficial to illustrate your efforts to care for the patient by having an outside party witness the patient's refusal.

Objective: Define the special considerations concerning patient refusal.

20. c

While it is preferred that patient's receive care initially, always give your patients the option of contacting EMS again for assistance. Do not take the patient's refusal of care as a personal issue. Be professional. If the patient does not want your assistance, direct the patient to contact his personal physician for follow-up care rather than instructing the patient to take aspirin or any other medication. Leave with the understanding that the patient may change his mind later and request your assistance.

Objective: N/A

Short Answer

21. S: Chief complaint: MVC—car vs. ped. 10 y/o, 90 lb., female

SAMPLE—Per father on scene: Allergies: none. Takes no medications, no pertinent PMH. Dinner at 1800.

O: Car vs. pedestrian. Pt found in street, right lat recumbent position with altered LOC. Bystanders state pt was hit by vehicle and then "flew through the air." Est speed 50 mph. Significant damage to front of vehicle on hood and windshield.

Head/face/airway—Per bystanders, + loss of consciousness. Pt responds to pain with periods of combative behavior and crying. Does not follow verbal commands. Facial bruising, left side. Blood from mouth. Loose teeth. PERL. No drainage from ears or nose.

Neck—DCAP-BTLS negative, trachea midline

Chest—DCAP-BTLS negative, breath sounds clear/equal bilaterally

Abdomen—bruising LUQ

Pelvis—DCAP-BTLS negative, femoral pulses strong and equal

Back—bruising left flank

Extremities—Left elbow lac; equal pulses, movement

A: Fall injury with hip and lower back trauma

P: Oxygen by nonrebreather mask at 15 L/min. Full spinal stabilization (cervical collar, spider straps, head blocks, backboard). Transported code 3 by ground ambulance to XYZ pediatric trauma center.

Vital signs:

2215	P 120 S/R	BP 110/74	R 32
2219	P 110 S/R	BP 112/80	R 30
2226	P 97 S/R	BP 97/64	R 24
2235	P 94 S/R	BP 94/58	R 18

Objective: Explain the components of the written report and list the information that should be included on the written report.

22. Chief complaint: MVC—car vs. ped. 10 y/o, 90 lb., female

History: Car vs. ped. Pt found in street, right lat recumbent position with altered LOC. Bystanders state pt was hit by vehicle and then "flew through the air." Est speed 50 mph. Significant damage to front of vehicle on hood and windshield. Per father on scene: Allergies: none. Takes no medications, no pertinent PMH. Dinner at 1800.

Assessment:

Head/face/airway—Per bystanders, + loss of consciousness. Pt responds to pain with periods of combative behavior and crying. Does not follow verbal commands. Facial bruising, left side. Blood from mouth. Loose teeth. PERL. No drainage from ears or nose.

Neck—DCAP-BTLS negative, trachea midline

Chest—DCAP-BTLS negative, breath sounds clear/equal bilaterally

Abdomen—bruising LUQ

Pelvis—DCAP-BTLS negative, femoral pulses strong and equal

Back—bruising left flank

Extremities—Left elbow lac; equal pulses, movement

Rx: Oxygen by nonrebreather mask at 15 L/min. Full spinal stabilization (cervical collar, spider straps, head blocks, backboard).

Transport: Transported code 3 by ground ambulance to XYZ pediatric trauma center.

Vital signs:

2215	P 120 S/R	BP 110/74	R 32
2219	P 110 S/R	BP 112/80	R 30
2226	P 97 S/R	BP 97/64	R 24
2235	P 94 S/R	BP 94/58	R 18

Objective: Explain the components of the written report and list the information that should be included on the written report.

23. R/T MVC—car vs. ped. 10 y/o, 90 lb., female found in street, right lat recumbent position with altered LOC. Bystanders state pt was hit by vehicle and then "flew through the air." Est speed 50 mph. Significant damage to front of vehicle on hood and windshield. Per father on scene: Allergies: none. Takes no medications, no pertinent PMH. Dinner at 1800.

Head/face/airway: Per bystanders, + loss of consciousness. Pt responds to pain with periods of combative behavior and crying. Does not follow verbal commands. Facial bruising, left side. Blood from mouth. Loose teeth. PERL. No drainage from ears or nose.

Neck: DCAP-BTLS negative, trachea midline

Chest: DCAP-BTLS negative, breath sounds clear/equal bilaterally

Abdomen: bruising LUQ

Pelvis: DCAP-BTLS negative, femoral pulses strong and equal

Back: bruising left flank

Extremities: Left elbow lac; equal pulses, movement

Rx: Oxygen by nonrebreather mask at 15 L/min. Full spinal stabilization (cervical collar, spider straps, head blocks, backboard). Transported code 3 by ground ambulance to XYZ pediatric trauma center.

Vital signs:

2215	P 120 S/R	BP 110/74	R 32
2219	P 110 S/R	BP 112/80	R 30
2226	P 97 S/R	BP 97/64	R 24
2235	P 94 S/R	BP 94/58	R 18

Objective: Explain the components of the written report and list the information that should be included on the written report.

Division 4

4

Medical-Behavioral Emergencies and Obstetrics and Gynecology

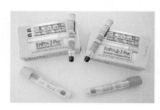

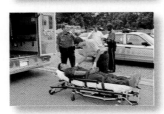

12 Pharmacology

Sum It Up

- A drug's chemical name is a description of its composition and molecular structure. The generic name (also called the *nonproprietary name*) is the name given to a drug by the company that first manufactures it. A drug's trade name is its *brand name* or *proprietary name*.

- A local effect of a drug usually occurs only in a limited part of the body (usually at the site of drug application). Drugs with systemic effects are absorbed into the bloodstream and distributed throughout the body.

- Each drug is in a specific medication form to allow properly controlled concentrations of the drug to enter the bloodstream where the drug has an effect on the target body system.

- Before giving a drug, an EMT must know the following:
  —The drug's mechanism of action: the desired effects the drug should have on the patient
  —Indications for the drug's use, including the most common uses of the drug in treating a specific illness
  —Contraindications: situations in which the drug should not be used because it may cause harm to the patient or offer no possibility of improving the patient's condition or illness
  —Correct dose (amount) of the drug to be given
  —The proper route by which the drug is given
  —Side effects: the actions of a drug other than those desired. Some side effects may be predictable.

- Medications that are typically carried on the EMS unit and may be given by EMTs include activated charcoal, oral glucose, and oxygen. Some EMS systems also include aspirin.

- Medications an EMT can assist a patient in taking with approval by medical direction include a prescribed inhaler, NTG, and an epinephrine auto-injector.

- Before giving a drug, use the five rights of drug administration: right drug, right patient, right dose, right route, and right time (frequency).

- After giving a drug, document the time you gave the drug, document the patient's response to the drug, monitor the patient for possible adverse (harmful) effects, and reassess and record the patient's vital signs.

► Tracking Your Progress

After reading this chapter, can you:	Page Reference	Objective Met?
• Identify which medications will be carried on the unit?	284	☐
• State the medications carried on the unit by the generic name?	284	☐
• Identify the medications with which the EMT may assist the patient with administering?	287	☐
• State the medications the EMT can assist the patient with by the generic name?	287	☐
• Discuss the forms in which the medications may be found?	281	☐

Multiple Choice

In the space provided, identify the letter of the choice that best completes the statement or answers each question.

_____ 1. Before administering any medication, you should
   a. assess the patient's physical status.
   b. obtain a medication history from the patient.
   c. obtain permission to administer the medication from medical direction.
   d. all of the above.

_____ 2. A drug's effect that occurs in a limited part of the body is known as a(n)
   a. side effect.   c. adverse effect.
   b. local effect.   d. systemic effect.

_____ 3. Which of the following medications is considered a Schedule IV controlled substance?
   a. Xanax   c. Tylenol #3
   b. Robitussin AC   d. Oxycontin

_____ 4. Oxygen is an example of which type of drug form?
   a. Liquid   c. Gas
   b. Solid   d. Suspension

_____ 5. You assisted a patient in taking prescribed NTG for chest discomfort. Which of the following is the most important action that you should take at this time?
   a. Assess the patient's mental status.
   b. Assess the patient's breath sounds.
   c. Assess the patient for changes in pain level after taking the medication.
   d. Assess the patient's distal pulses, motor function, and sensation.

_____ 6. Oxygen is a drug carried by EMTs. Which of the following best defines its indication for use?
   a. Cardiac arrest   c. Respiratory distress
   b. Massive bleeding   d. Hypoxia from any cause

_____ 7. When taken, NTG generally lowers the blood pressure. This effect is
   a. local.   c. a sign of hypersensitivity.
   b. systemic.   d. an idiosyncrasy.

_____ 8. A tablet that has a special coating so that it breaks down in the intestines instead of the stomach is known as
   a. a capsule.   c. a suppository.
   b. a gelcap.   d. an enteric-coated tablet.

_____ 9. A drug's mechanism of action refers to
   a. the route by which a drug is administered.
   b. an exaggerated response to a drug by an individual.
   c. how a drug exerts its effect on body cells and tissues.
   d. the condition(s) for which a specific drug has documented usefulness.

_____ 10. Your rescue crew is treating a 54-year-old man complaining of severe chest pain. After consulting with medical direction, you are given orders to assist this patient with taking his prescribed NTG tablets. The medical direction physician tells you that the patient can take up to three tablets sublingually at 5-minute intervals, provided that his systolic blood pressure remains greater than 100 mm Hg. While you are preparing to administer the second NTG tablet, the patient stops breathing. Assessment reveals he has no pulse. You should immediately
   a. reestablish contact with medical direction.
   b. begin CPR and rapid transport.
   c. put the tablet under the patient's tongue and reestablish contact with medical direction.
   d. put the remaining two NTG tablets under the patient's tongue and begin CPR.

_____ 11. Which of the following patient statements illustrates a pharmacological side effect?
   a. "I am allergic to aspirin."
   b. "My albuterol inhaler makes me feel jittery."
   c. "The nitroglycerin spray has completely relieved my chest pain."
   d. "The oxygen has not helped decrease my difficulty breathing."

_____ 12. Glucose is an example of which type of liquid drug form?
   a. Gel   c. Elixir
   b. Syrup   d. Tincture

_____ 13. Which of the following medications may an EMT assist a patient in taking (provided the patient has a current prescription for the medication)?
   a. Lasix
   b. Insulin
   c. Albuterol
   d. Any prescription medication as long as the patient's name appears on the medication container

_____ 14. In some states, EMTs are permitted to give _____ in cases of narcotic overdose.
   a. aspirin   c. naloxone
   b. ibuprofen   d. Lasix

_____ 15. Sublingual medications
   a. should be chewed.   c. should be swallowed.
   b. are rapidly absorbed. d. include albuterol.

_____ 16. Your rescue crew is called to a local law office for a 74-year-old woman complaining of severe chest pain located in the center of her chest. She states the pain is a "9" on a 0 to 10 scale (with "10" being the most severe). Her skin is cool, clammy, and ashen. A radial pulse cannot be felt, but a carotid pulse is weak and irregular at 154 beats per minute. You are unable to obtain a blood pressure. After consulting medical direction, you are given orders to assist this patient in taking her NTG tablets. You are concerned that this treatment may be harmful to the patient and should
   a. give the medication as ordered.
   b. give the medication and begin rapid transport to the receiving facility.
   c. ask the physician to repeat the order, then give the medication as ordered.
   d. ask the physician to repeat the order but do not give the medication as ordered if you feel it may harm the patient.

_____ 17. You are treating a 74-year-old man for difficulty breathing. He informs you that he was seen in the Emergency Department yesterday for the same complaint and diagnosed with a respiratory infection. The Emergency Department physician gave him a prescription for Augmentin. The medication container states the patient is to take one pill twice daily for 10 days. These instructions refer to the drug's

    a. dosage.
    b. indication.
    c. distribution.
    d. mechanism of action.

_____ 18. Your rescue crew is called to the home of a 3-year-old male patient who may have ingested a handful of his grandmother's "heart pills" about 15 minutes ago. Which medication would you anticipate administering to this patient?

    a. Epinephrine
    b. Oral glucose
    c. Albuterol
    d. Activated charcoal

_____ 19. Your ambulance is dispatched to the nurse's office of a local high school. A 15-year-old female patient is experiencing an "asthma attack." Which medication would you anticipate assisting this patient in taking?

    a. Oral glucose
    b. Albuterol
    c. Activated charcoal
    d. NTG

Questions 20–21 pertain to the following scenario.

Your rescue crew is called to the home of a 24-year-old man who has been stung by a bee for the first time in his life. He informs you that his wife is allergic to bee stings and almost died when she was stung. He is complaining of pain at the site of the sting (on his upper arm), and a welt is beginning to form at the site. He has his wife's prescribed epinephrine auto-injector and called you for assistance with administering the medication.

_____ 20. Administration of this type epinephrine is given by what route?

    a. Oral
    b. Buccal
    c. Sublingual
    d. Intramuscular

_____ 21. Which of the following is true regarding administration of epinephrine to this patient?

    a. This patient fits the criteria for medication administration.
    b. You may not give this patient epinephrine, but his wife can (and should) because it is her medication.
    c. You may not give this patient epinephrine but should encourage him to self-administer the medication.
    d. You may not give this patient epinephrine and should encourage him to wait until further evaluation at the hospital before taking any action.

Questions 22–24 pertain to the following scenario.

Your ambulance crew is called to the apartment of a 19-year-old woman. Her friend called you for assistance because "she is just not acting right." The patient has a history of diabetes. She is conscious but answers questions inappropriately with slurred speech.

_____ 22. Which medication should you consider giving this patient?

    a. Insulin
    b. NTG
    c. Oral glucose
    d. Activated charcoal

_____ 23. You contact your medical direction physician to get approval to administer this medication. After the physician tells you what medication to use, the dose of the medication, and its route into the body, you should

    a. immediately give the medication.
    b. reply "10-4, copy" and give the medication.
    c. repeat the orders back to the physician.
    d. begin transporting the patient to the receiving facility before giving the medication.

_____ **24.** While you are getting the medication out of the drug box, the patient becomes unconscious. Medical direction instructed you to give the medication buccally. You should

    a. give the medication sublingually and prepare to suction.

    b. Begin rapid transport and reestablish contact with medical direction.

    c. mix the medication with water and have the patient drink the mixture.

    d. quickly proceed to give the medication according to the physician's instructions.

Short Answer

Answer the question in the space provided.

_____ **25.** List the five rights of medication administration.

    1.

    2.

    3.

    4.

    5.

Answer Section

Chapter 12

Multiple Choice

1. d

Assessing the patient's physical status is essential to ensuring that a correct treatment plan is developed. You must be knowledgeable about each drug you may administer. The medication history you obtain from the patient should include prescription medications, over-the-counter medications, and medication allergies. Finally, as an EMT, you must gain approval from medical direction before administering a medication. Approval may be in the form of on-line medical direction (speaking with the physician via phone or radio) or off-line medical direction (through standing orders).

Objective: N/A

2. b

A drug's effects may be local or systemic. A local effect of a drug means that the drug's effects occur only in a limited part of the body (usually at the site of drug application). For instance, if you apply calamine lotion to a rash on your arm or leg, the effects of the drug are limited to the extremity where the drug was applied.

Objective: N/A

3. a

A Schedule IV controlled substance includes alprazolam (Xanax), diazepam (Valium), lorazepam (Ativan), midazolam (Versed), and phenobarbital. Robitussin AC is considered a Schedule V drug. Tylenol # 3 is a schedule III drug. Oxycontin is considered a schedule II drug.

Objective: N/A

4. c

Drugs that are in a gas form are breathed in and absorbed through the respiratory tract. Oxygen is an example of a drug that is given in gas form.

Objective: Discuss the forms in which the medications may be found.

5. c

Reassess the patient's response to any medications you may have given or assisted the patient in taking. For example, if you assisted the patient in taking prescribed NTG for chest discomfort, assess the patient's response, including vital signs and degree of discomfort after taking the medication. If glucose was given to a patient experiencing a diabetic emergency, reassess the patient's mental status and vital signs. If you assisted a patient with asthma in taking a prescribed MDI, reassess the patient's breath sounds, degree of breathing difficulty, and vital signs.

Objective: Identify the medications with which the EMT may assist the patient with administering.

6. d

Any condition that results in hypoxia should be treated with oxygen therapy. Cardiac arrest, massive blood loss, and respiratory distress are all examples of conditions that result in hypoxia. Oxygen therapy should begin early. Do not wait until the patient becomes cyanotic (blue) or complains of respiratory difficulty before administering oxygen.

Objective: Identify which medications will be carried on the unit.

7. b

Lowering blood pressure is a systemic effect of NTG. Systemic effects are those that can be observed throughout the body, whereas local effects are those that can be observed in a specific area. Burning under the tongue is a common and acceptable localized side effect of NTG administration. An example of a hypersensitive response would be an undetectable blood pressure after administration of one NTG tablet. Before administering NTG, the patient's systolic blood pressure should be above 100 mm Hg. An example of an idiosyncratic response would be an increase in the patient's blood pressure because of NTG therapy.

Objective: State the contraindications and side effects for the use of NTG.

8. d

Enteric-coated tablets have a special coating so that they break down in the intestines instead of the stomach.

Objective: Discuss the forms in which the medications may be found.

9. c

The mechanism of action is the method by which a medication acts on the body. For example, albuterol is a bronchodilator used to relieve difficulty breathing. The mechanism of action for albuterol is relaxation of the smooth muscles of the respiratory tree, thus allowing a freer flow of air.

Objective: N/A

10. b

If your patient's condition changes between the time you are given an order by medical direction and the time you prepare to carry out the order, reassess the patient. In this scenario, you should *immediately* begin CPR and rapid transportation. If possible (or per local protocol), recontact medical direction to inform the physician and receiving facility of the change in the patient's condition.

Objective: Recognize the need for medical direction of protocols to assist in the emergency medical care of the patient with chest pain.

11. b

A side effect is an expected and usually unavoidable effect of a drug that generally has no consequence on the drug's intended use. A side effect of albuterol administration may be "jitters" and agitation. It is important to know and understand the side effects of the medications you may be asked to administer. For example, headache is a common side effect of taking NTG.

Objective: N/A

12. a

Glucose is an example of a gel. A gel is a clear or transparent semisolid substance that liquefies when applied to the skin or a mucous membrane. An elixir is a clear liquid made with alcohol and water and sweetened with flavors or sweeteners. A syrup is a drug suspended in sugar and water. A tincture is an alcohol solution prepared from an animal or vegetable drug or chemical substance.

Objective: Discuss the forms in which the medications may be found.

13. c

EMTs may assist in the administration of albuterol for patients experiencing difficulty breathing. Other medications that EMTs may assist patients in taking include NTG and epinephrine by epinephrine auto-injector. These medications must be prescriptions belonging to the patient. In some states, EMTs may also assist patients in taking aspirin. Unless specified differently by state law, an EMT is not authorized to administer (or assist the patient in taking) other prescription medications, even if the patient's name appears on the medication container.

Objective: Identify the medications with which the EMT may assist the patient with administering.

14. c

In some states, EMTs are permitted to give naloxone in cases of narcotic overdose. With an order from medical direction, the EMT gives naloxone to the patient by means of an atomizer that is connected to a syringe. The atomizer is placed a short distance (about 1.5 cm) into the patient's nose. When the EMT pushes the plunger on the syringe, the atomizer disperses a mist-like spray onto the inner surface of the patient's nostril, where the drug is quickly absorbed.

Objective: N/A

15. b

Sublingual medications, such as NTG, are administered under the tongue and are designed to be absorbed into the capillary beds of the mouth. These medications are rapidly absorbed within 1 to 2 minutes and should not be chewed or swallowed. Bronchodilators such as albuterol are inhaled medications.

Objective: N/A

16. d

Shock is a possible adverse effect of NTG administration. Therefore, it is important to assess a patient's blood pressure before each dose of NTG. NTG should not be given if the patient's systolic blood pressure is less than 100 mm Hg. Although the medical direction physician has a high level of training, education, and responsibility, you should never blindly follow any order. Tactfully help the medical direction physician understand your thoughts and concerns about the intervention. If you fail to come to a mutual conclusion and you are concerned about possible adverse effects of the ordered intervention for the patient, inform the medical direction physician that you will begin rapid transportation of the patient without starting the intervention until the physician has the opportunity to evaluate the patient firsthand. Be sure to follow up with medical direction and your EMS Coordinator.

Objective: State the contraindications and side effects for the use of NTG.

17. a

Dosage refers to the frequency, size, and number of doses for prescription and non-prescription medications. A drug's indication is the condition or conditions for which the drug has a documented usefulness. Distribution is the means by which the drug is transported throughout the body. The mechanism of action refers to how the drug works in the body.

Objective: N/A

18. d

Activated charcoal is indicated for poisonings or overdoses by ingestion. Activated charcoal is an "adsorbent." Its microscopic pores adsorb many poisons and medications. The poisons or medications then pass through the GI tract bound to the activated charcoal.

Objective: Identify which medications will be carried on the unit.

19. b

Ventolin and Proventil are trade names for albuterol. Albuterol is a bronchodilator. Bronchodilators are inhaled and absorbed deep in the respiratory tree where they "relax" constricted airway passages. EMTs may assist in the administration of albuterol and similar medications to ease difficulty breathing associated with asthma or COPD. Patients must be instructed to inhale the atomized medication as deeply as possible for maximum benefit. If the patient's tidal volume (amount of air moved in and out of the lungs) is severely low, he may not benefit from inhaling a bronchodilator because the drug will not reach the terminal air sacs (alveoli) where it is absorbed.

Objective: Identify the medications with which the EMT may assist the patient with administering.

20. d

Epinephrine is a medication that is used frequently in emergency care. It can be given by many routes; however, when it is given by means of an auto-injector it is given via the intramuscular route.

Objective: Identify the medications with which the EMT may assist the patient with administering.

21. d

Do not give a patient a medication that was not prescribed for him and do not encourage a patient to take a medication that was not prescribed for him. Unless specified otherwise by state law, the only medications that you may administer without a previous prescription are oral glucose, activated charcoal, and oxygen. This patient is not experiencing the signs and symptoms associated with a severe allergic reaction. If he were, it would be up to medical direction and local protocol to decide what to do for this patient.

Objective: Identify the medications with which the EMT may assist the patient with administering.

22. c

Oral glucose is indicated for patients showing signs of altered mental status with a history of diabetes. If possible, you should attempt to obtain a blood glucose reading to make sure that the patient is "sugar deficient" rather than "insulin deficient." A low blood sugar reading would suggest the need for oral glucose administration. Be very careful when giving an oral medication to a patient with an altered mental status. If the patient becomes unconscious with the medication in her mouth, the patient will require aggressive airway maintenance. EMTs are not authorized to assist patients with insulin administration.

Objective: State the medications carried on the unit by the generic name.

23. c

Always echo (repeat back) the orders you are given. Echoing ensures that you received the instructions correctly. Additionally, echoing allows medical direction the opportunity to hear his orders a second time, thus ensuring the orders are correct.

Objective: Discuss the forms in which the medications may be found.

24. b

As a rule of thumb, if the patient's condition drastically changes, contact medical direction. In this case, medical direction instructed you to give an oral medication to a conscious patient; however, by the time you were prepared to give it, the patient became unconscious. The circumstances under which the physician ordered the medication to be given have changed. Because the patient's presentation is worsening, begin immediate and rapid transport and reestablish contact with medical direction.

Objective: Discuss the forms in which the medications may be found.

Short Answer

25. Always ask yourself these five questions before you give a patient a medication:

1. Do I have the right patient?
2. Is this the right medication?
3. Is this the right dose?
4. Is this the right route?
5. Is this the right time?

Note: Some EMS instructors have added a sixth right of medication administration. The sixth R is right documentation.

Objective: Demonstrate general steps for assisting a patient with self-administration of medications.

13 Respiratory Emergencies

READING ASSIGNMENT ▶ Read Chapter 13, pages 292 to 314 in your textbook.

Sum It Up

- Signs of adequate breathing include a breathing rate within normal limits for the patient's age. The rhythm of breathing should be regular, breath sounds should be present and equal, chest expansion should be adequate and equal, and the depth of respirations (tidal volume) should be adequate.

- Signs of inadequate breathing include a rate outside the normal range for the patient's age, an irregular rhythm of breathing, diminished or absent breath sounds, and chest expansion that is unequal or inadequate. The patient shows signs of an increased effort of breathing through the use of accessory muscles. His depth of respirations (tidal volume) may be inadequate. His skin may be pale or cyanotic (blue) and cool and clammy. There may be retractions above the clavicles, between the ribs, and below the rib cage, especially in children. Nasal flaring may be present, especially in children. Seesaw breathing may be seen in infants. Agonal breathing (occasional gasping breaths) may be seen just before death.

- Signs of adequate artificial ventilation include:
  —The chest rises and falls with each artificial ventilation
  —The rate is sufficient, about 10 to 12 times per minute for adults and 12 to 20 times per minute for children and infants
  —Heart rate improves with successful artificial ventilation

- Artificial ventilation is inadequate when:
  —The chest does not rise and fall with artificial ventilation
  —The rate is too slow or too fast
  —Heart rate does not improve with artificial ventilation

- Signs and symptoms of breathing difficulty include shortness of breath, restlessness, increased pulse rate, increased or decreased breathing rate, skin color changes, noisy breathing, inability to speak caused by breathing efforts, retractions, use of accessory muscles, altered mental status, abdominal breathing, coughing, irregular breathing rhythm, tripod position, and unusual anatomy (barrel chest).

- An MDI is used to deliver inhaled respiratory medications. A patient who has a prescribed MDI typically has reversible constriction of his airways. An MDI is small and consists of two parts, the medication canister and a plastic dispenser with a mouthpiece. A physician will often prescribe a "spacer" to be used with the MDI. The spacer increases the amount of medication delivered into the respiratory tract. The patient squeezes the MDI into a plastic holding chamber, then inhales the medication from the chamber. The use of spacers is very common in children and older adults. The spacer can also be attached to a resuscitation mask to aid medication delivery for a young child.

- As an EMT, you can assist a patient in taking a prescribed inhaler if all of the following criteria are met:
  —The patient has signs and symptoms of a respiratory emergency.
  —The patient has a physician-prescribed handheld inhaler.
  —There are no contraindications to giving the medication.
  —You have specific authorization by medical direction.
- Assisting a patient with the use of an MDI is contraindicated if any of the following conditions exists:
  —The patient is unable to use the device. (This may be caused by the level of the patient's respiratory distress.)
  —The inhaler is not prescribed for the patient.
  —Permission is not received from medical direction.
  —The patient has already met the maximum prescribed dose before your arrival.

▶ Tracking Your Progress

After reading this chapter, can you:	Page Reference	Objective Met?
• List the structure and function of the respiratory system?	293	☐
• State the signs and symptoms of a patient with breathing difficulty?	300, 301, 302, 303	☐
• Describe the emergency medical care of the patient with breathing difficulty?	301, 302, 303	☐
• Recognize the need for medical direction to assist in the emergency medical care of the patient with breathing difficulty?	307, 309	☐
• Describe the emergency medical care of the patient with breathing distress?	301, 302, 303	☐
• Establish the relationship between airway management and the patient with breathing difficulty?	303	☐
• List signs of adequate air exchange?	301	☐
• State the generic name, medication forms, dose, administration, action, indications, and contraindications for the prescribed inhaler?	310	☐
• Distinguish between the emergency medical care of the infant, child, and adult patient with breathing difficulty?	297	☐
• Differentiate between upper airway obstruction and lower airway disease in the infant and child patient?	303, 304, 305	☐

Multiple Choice

In the space provided, identify the letter of the choice that best completes the statement or answers each question.

_____ 1. Inhalation is an active process involving muscular contraction of the primary breathing muscles. Exhalation is normally
   a. an active process involving contraction of the abdominal muscles.
   b. a passive process involving contraction of the abdominal muscles.
   c. an active process involving contraction of the accessory muscles.
   d. a passive process involving relaxation of the primary breathing muscles.

_____ 2. The exchange of cellular gases occurs in the capillary beds. In the lungs, _____ is absorbed across the lung tissue into the bloodstream of the capillary beds, and _____ is allowed to leave the bloodstream and enter the air space of the lungs.
   a. oxygen, hemoglobin
   b. oxygen, carbon dioxide
   c. oxygen, carbon monoxide
   d. hemoglobin, carbon monoxide

_____ 3. For most patients, the main stimulus for breathing is derived from the level of _____ in the bloodstream. However, chronic respiratory disease may change the stimulus for breathing to the level of _____ in the bloodstream.
   a. carbon dioxide, oxygen
   b. oxygen, carbon dioxide
   c. oxygen, carbon monoxide
   d. carbon dioxide, hemoglobin

_____ 4. "Difficulty breathing" is often called
   a. dyspnea.   **c.** tachycardia.
   b. diaphoresis.   **d.** minute volume.

_____ 5. Which of the following is *not* a sign that is typically associated with breathing difficulty?
   a. Nasal flaring   **c.** Decreased pulse rate
   b. Use of accessory muscles   **d.** Retractions

_____ 6. During your assessment of a patient complaining of difficulty breathing, you should note the position the patient assumed before your arrival. Often this position indicates the level of the patient's distress. Conscious, alert patients in severe distress will often be found
   a. lying in a fetal position.
   b. sitting or standing bolt upright.
   c. lying flat on their back (supine).
   d. lying flat on their stomach (prone).

_____ 7. Apnea means
   a. difficulty breathing.
   b. absent breathing.
   c. breathlessness when lying flat.
   d. difficulty breathing that occurs at night.

_____ 8. An early sign of nontraumatic respiratory distress is
   a. facial droop.   **c.** agonal respirations.
   b. unconsciousness.   **d.** increased respiratory rate.

_____ 9. Asthma causes difficulty breathing because of
   a. dilation of the bronchioles, which causes wheezing.
   b. constriction of the bronchioles, which causes wheezing.
   c. collapse of the alveoli, which causes diminished tidal volume.
   d. infection of the lower respiratory tract, which causes rhonchi.

_____ **10.** Your ambulance is called to an adult-care facility for a 78-year-old woman complaining of difficulty breathing that has worsened over the past two days. Which of the following comments by the patient would *not* be consistent with the typical signs and symptoms of pneumonia?

   a. "My chest hurts when I take a deep breath."
   b. "My feet are much more swollen than normal."
   c. "I have had a fever and the chills for the past week."
   d. "I keep coughing up yellow stuff from my lungs."

_____ **11.** Your ambulance responds to the home of a 34-year-old man complaining of difficulty breathing and chest pain. He states that his chest pain worsens with deep inspiration and coughing. He denies any recent trauma and denies any past medical history. The term given this complaint is

   a. hemothorax.
   b. flail segment.
   c. tracheal deviation.
   d. pleuritic chest pain.

_____ **12.** Many patients diagnosed with respiratory complications will be prescribed MDIs. These medications attempt to decrease difficulty breathing by dilating the smooth muscles of the respiratory tract, thus decreasing airway resistance. Which of the following is *not* a bronchodilator that EMTs may assist in administering?

   a. Lasix   **c.** Proventil
   b. Alupent   **d.** Bronkosol

_____ **13.** Before assisting a patient with the administration of an MDI, you must ensure that

   a. the patient is apneic and has a history of chronic bronchitis.
   b. the patient is unconscious, has a history of asthma, and has a prescribed inhaler.
   c. the patient is having difficulty breathing and has access to his brother's MDI.
   d. the patient is having difficulty breathing and has a prescribed inhaler and you have authorization from medical direction.

_____ **14.** Your ambulance is called to the home of a 7-year-old male patient complaining of difficulty breathing. His mother tells you he has been having a hard time breathing for the last 5 hours. The child appears very tired, and he is using accessory muscles to assist with breathing. The child has asthma and has a prescription for metered-dose albuterol. Medical direction authorizes you to assist the patient with his albuterol. Which of the following indicates that the patient is responding well to this intervention?

   a. The patient's tidal volume decreases.
   b. The patient appears to have fallen asleep.
   c. The patient's wheezing stops, and his agitation increases.
   d. The patient's level of consciousness and activity improves.

_____ **15.** A pulmonary embolus is a clot in the bloodstream that travels to the lungs where it becomes lodged. The lung sounds of a patient with a pulmonary embolus are

   a. absent in all lobes of the lung.
   b. absent in the lobes affected by the clot.
   c. absent in the lobes not affected by the clot.
   d. clear throughout but with a possibly diminished tidal volume because of an increased respiratory rate.

_____ **16.** Which of the following would be proper instructions for informing a patient how to use an MDI?

   a. "Point the inhaler under your tongue and depress the button one time."
   b. "Spray the medication into a plastic bag several times, then breathe from the bag until you feel relief."
   c. "Exhale deeply, put the inhaler in your mouth, and depress the button several successive times while panting rapidly."
   d. "Exhale deeply, put the inhaler in your mouth, and depress the button while inhaling. Then attempt to hold your breath as long as you comfortably can."

_____ **17.** Your ambulance has been called to the home of a 47-year-old man complaining of chest pain. He has a history of angina and emphysema and takes a shoebox full of medications. He tells you that for the past four days he has been experiencing chest pain, and he feels slightly warm to the touch. Which one question may best help you decide if this patient's chest pain is cardiac or respiratory in nature?

   a. "Are you nauseated?"
   b. "Do you have a headache?"
   c. "Have you taken all your prescribed medications?"
   d. "Does the pain in your chest change when you take a deep breath?"

_____ **18.** Your rescue crew is called to the home of a 5-year-old female patient. Her parents tell you that she started developing a high fever several hours ago and now is acting "funny." The patient is found sitting up in bed. She is drooling and does not answer your questions although she appears to be responsive. When treating this patient,

   a. you should attempt to visualize the back of her throat for an obstruction.
   b. you should allow the patient to sit up and administer oxygen by blow-by mask.
   c. you should insist on laying the patient down to increase perfusion to the brain.
   d. you should lay the patient down gently, insert an oral airway, and begin positive-pressure ventilations with a BM device.

_____ **19.** Your rescue crew responds to the home of a 22-month-old male patient with difficulty breathing and a nonproductive cough. His father tells you that he has had a fever for the last several days. While assessing the patient, you observe a harsh, bark-like cough and stridor. He is conscious and responds appropriately for his age. These findings are consistent with _____. Appropriate emergency care for this patient should consist of _____.

   a. croup; blow-by oxygen therapy, position of comfort, and transport to the hospital for further evaluation
   b. croup; blow-by oxygen therapy, insertion of a nasal airway, and transport in the recovery position to the hospital for further evaluation
   c. epiglottitis; blow-by oxygen therapy, close inspection of the mouth and throat, and transport to hospital for further evaluation
   d. epiglottitis; oxygen by nonrebreather mask, position of comfort, and transport to the hospital for further evaluation

Questions 20–25 pertain to the following scenario.

Your rescue crew is called to the home of a 76-year-old man complaining of difficulty breathing. It is 4:00 a.m. The patient is conscious and appears to be in severe respiratory distress.

_____ **20.** While observing this patient, you note the skin above his collarbones (clavicles) is sucked in with each breath. This finding is called

   a. stridor.
   b. tenting.
   c. supraclavicular retractions.
   d. subcutaneous emphysema.

_____ **21.** Upon completing the scene size-up, general impression, and primary survey, you determine that this patient is a priority patient. You should immediately

   a. insert an oral airway.
   b. give the patient a bronchodilator.
   c. call for ALS assistance.
   d. give the patient a sublingual NTG tablet.

_____ **22.** The patient states he has awakened the last several nights because of an increase in his level of distress. He tells you, "Last night it was so bad that I had to sleep sitting up so I could breathe." The medical term for this specific condition is

   a. hypoxia.   **c.** pedal edema.
   b. retractions.   **d.** paroxysmal nocturnal dyspnea.

_____ 23. The patient says he has had a productive cough for the last three days. Which of the following sputum characteristics would indicate that this patient may have pulmonary edema (fluid in the lungs)?

    a. Thick, green sputum   **c.** Brownish-yellow sputum

    b. Frothy, pink-tinged sputum   **d.** A significant amount of bright red blood in the sputum

_____ 24. When listening to this patient's breath sounds, you detect a high-pitched "popping" sound in the lower lobes of his lungs. The sound is similar to the sound of Velcro tearing apart. The correct term for this abnormal breath sound is

    a. stridor.   **c.** wheezes.

    b. grunting.   **d.** crackles (rales).

_____ 25. The patient's skin condition is cool, moist, and pale. He is breathing at a rate of 20 respirations per minute. His tidal volume is adequate. Appropriate oxygen therapy for this patient would be

    a. nasal cannula at 2 L/min.   **c.** nonrebreather mask at 15 L/min.

    b. nasal cannula at 15 L/min.   **d.** BM-assisted ventilations at 30 respirations per minute.

Matching

Match the key terms in the left column with the definitions in the right column by placing the letter of each correct answer in the space provided.

_____ **26.** Sternum

_____ **27.** Tidal volume

_____ **28.** Seesaw breathing

_____ **29.** Pulmonary edema

_____ **30.** Bradypnea

_____ **31.** Hypoxia

_____ **32.** Croup

_____ **33.** Subcostal retractions

_____ **34.** Trachea

_____ **35.** Nasal flaring

_____ **36.** Supraclavicular retractions

_____ **37.** Pulmonary embolus

_____ **38.** Orthopnea

_____ **39.** Head bobbing

_____ **40.** Tripod position

_____ **41.** Non-allergic asthma

_____ **42.** Hypoxic drive

_____ **43.** Respiration

_____ **44.** Tachypnea

_____ **45.** Pneumonia

_____ **46.** Paroxysmal nocturnal dyspnea

_____ **47.** Intercostal retractions

A. A clot that travels through the circulatory system, eventually becoming trapped in the smaller branches of the pulmonary arteries, causing partial or complete blood flow obstruction

B. Windpipe

C. Indentations of the skin above the collarbones (clavicles)

D. A respiratory infection that may involve the lower airways and alveoli, part of a lobe, or an entire lobe of the lung

E. Sitting up and leaning forward with the weight of the upper body supported by the hands on the thighs or knees

F. Asthma that is triggered by factors not related to allergies

G. Low levels of oxygen in the blood that stimulate breathing instead of an increase in carbon dioxide levels

H. Breastbone

I. Indentations of the skin between the ribs

J. The exchange of gases between a living organism and its environment

K. A faster than normal respiratory rate for age

L. A buildup of fluid in the alveoli, most commonly caused by failure of the left ventricle of the heart

M. A sudden onset of difficulty breathing that occurs at night because of a buildup of fluid in the alveoli or pooling of secretions during sleep

Continued

N. A lack of oxygen

O. The amount of air moved into or out of the lungs during a normal breath

P. Abnormal breathing in which the abdominal muscles move in a direction opposite the chest wall

Q. Widening of the nostrils when a patient breathes in

R. Indentations of the skin below the rib cage

S. Breathlessness when lying flat that is relieved or lessened when the patient sits or stands

T. A slower-than-normal respiratory rate for age

U. An infection that affects the larynx and the area just below it

V. An indicator of increased work of breathing in infants; when the baby breathes out, the head falls forward, and when the baby breathes in and its chest expands, the head comes up

Short Answer

Answer each question in the space provided.

48. List the two primary muscles involved with normal breathing.
1.
2.

49. List five signs or symptoms of acute pulmonary edema.
1.
2.
3.
4.
5.

50. A patient was recently diagnosed with asthma and has been prescribed a MDI of albuterol to be used with a spacer. What is the purpose of the spacer?

51. List the criteria that must be met for you to assist a patient in taking a prescribed inhaler.

52. When is assisting a patient with the use of a MDI contraindicated?

Answer Section

Chapter 13

Multiple Choice

1. d

   Normal exhalation is a passive event (it does not require muscle force). When the diaphragm and intercostal muscles relax, the chest returns to its resting position. The area of the chest decreases, causing the pressure of the air in the lungs to increase. This increase in pressure pushes the air out.

   Objective: List the structures and functions of the respiratory system.

2. b

   The two main gases exchanged during respiration are oxygen and carbon dioxide. Oxygen, required by all living cells, is absorbed from atmospheric air. Carbon dioxide, a cellular waste product, returns to the lungs by means of the blood and is exhaled. Hemoglobin allows oxygen to bind to the red blood cells for transport throughout the body. Carbon monoxide is an odorless, colorless, tasteless, toxic gas.

   Objective: List the structures and functions of the respiratory system.

3. a

   The main stimulus for breathing is the level of carbon dioxide in the blood. A buildup of carbon dioxide in the blood causes an increase in the rate and depth of ventilation. An unusually low level of carbon dioxide in the blood results in a decrease in the rate and depth of ventilation.

   Chronic respiratory diseases may alter the normal respiratory drive over time because of the prolonged high levels of carbon dioxide. Instead of an increase in carbon dioxide levels stimulating breathing, low levels of oxygen in the blood become the breathing stimulus. This kind of breathing stimulus is called *hypoxic drive.* In these patients, giving high concentration oxygen

for prolonged periods may depress respirations and result in respiratory arrest.

   Objective: List the structures and functions of the respiratory system.

4. a

   Dyspnea is difficulty breathing (dys- = difficulty; -pnea = breathing). Diaphoresis is another term for a moist or sweaty condition of the skin. Tachycardia means fast heart rate. Minute volume is the volume of air moved in and out of the lungs during 1 minute of breathing.

   Objective: State the signs and symptoms of a patient with breathing difficulty.

5. c

   Patients in respiratory distress will most likely exhibit a rapid pulse rate. The pulse rate increases to compensate for the insult to the respiratory system. Imagine that red blood cells are the boxcars of a train. They carry oxygen to all cells of the body and return with the by-products of cell life (i.e., carbon dioxide). The heart is the steam engine that pulls (pushes) the boxcars. If the boxcars are capable of delivering only 1/2 of their normal oxygen load (either because of a problem with the engine [heart], a problem or decrease in the number of the available boxcars [red blood cells], or a problem with the availability of the oxygen [respiratory compromise]), the engineer of the train (the brain) will attempt to run the train at twice its normal speed to please its customers (the cells of the body). When you provide oxygen therapy to a patient, you are, in essence, increasing the amount of oxygen each boxcar (red blood cell) carries.

   Objective: State the signs and symptoms of a patient with breathing difficulty.

6. b

   Conscious patients in respiratory distress are generally found sitting upright. This position is sometimes called the *tripod position* if the patient is sitting upright and leaning forward onto outstretched arms. Patients assume this position to allow for maximum chest wall and diaphragm expansion.

Objective: State the signs and symptoms of a patient with breathing difficulty.

7. b

Apnea means an absence of breathing (a- = without, -pnea = breathing). Dyspnea is difficulty breathing. Orthopnea is breathlessness when lying flat that is relieved or lessened when the patient sits or stands. Paroxysmal nocturnal dyspnea is a sudden onset of difficulty breathing that occurs at night. It occurs because of a buildup of fluid in the alveoli or pooling of secretions during sleep.

Objective: State the signs and symptoms of a patient with breathing difficulty.

8. d

When in distress (respiratory or otherwise), one of the body's first lines of defense is to increase the respiratory rate to increase oxygen content in the blood. A facial droop is most commonly associated with a patient who has experienced a cerebrovascular accident (stroke). Unconsciousness, if caused by respiratory distress, is a very late sign of disease progression. Patients in respiratory distress generally progress from anxious and agitated, to confused, to a sleepy or tired appearance, to unconsciousness. Agonal respirations are slow, gasping respirations associated with a critical patient who is about to become completely apneic. These patients must be quickly and aggressively managed with a BM device and supplemental oxygen.

Objective: State the signs and symptoms of a patient with breathing difficulty.

9. b

Constriction of the bronchioles and an increased production of mucus associated with asthma leads to wheezing. Wheezing occurs as air is forced out of the alveoli through the narrowed air passages. The air whistles, and the accumulation of thousands of tiny whistles produces the wheeze. Remember that it takes a certain amount of air going through a whistle to create sound. The absence of wheezing in an unstable asthmatic patient may indicate that the patient is not moving sufficient air to wheeze, which is a worrying sign.

Objective: State the signs and symptoms of a patient with breathing difficulty.

10. b

Pedal edema (pooling of fluid in the lower extremities) is not commonly associated with pneumonia; it is more commonly associated with congestive heart failure. Pleuritic chest pain, fever and chills, and a productive cough with yellow or green sputum are commonly associated with pneumonia. Other signs and symptoms may include an increased respiratory rate, an increased heart rate, and abnormal lung sounds in the area of the lung affected by the infection.

Objective: State the signs and symptoms of a patient with breathing difficulty.

11. d

Chest pain may be described as "pleuritic" if the pain increases with movement, palpation, or deep inspiration. True pleuritic chest pain is caused by an infection of the pleura (the double-walled sac that surrounds the lungs). Hemothorax (blood in the pleural space) and a flail segment (multiple rib fractures creating a free-floating section of the chest wall) may also present with this type of chest pain. Tracheal deviation, discovered on palpation of the trachea, is a late sign of a tension pneumothorax.

Objective: State the signs and symptoms of a patient with breathing difficulty.

12. a

Lasix is a medication that helps eliminate excess fluid from the body. Patients taking Lasix will generally have this medication in tablet form. The bronchodilators you may assist in administering (if the correct criteria have been met) are albuterol (Proventil, Ventolin); isoetharine (Bronkosol, Bronkometer); and metaproterenol (Metaprel, Alupent).

Objective: State the generic name, medication forms, dose, administration, action, indications, and contraindications for the prescribed inhaler.

13. d

The following criteria must be met in order to assist a patient with an MDI: The patient exhibits the signs and symptoms of breathing difficulty, the patient has a prescribed handheld inhaler (prescribed for this patient), and medical direction has authorized assisting the patient.

Objective: Describe the emergency medical care of the patient with breathing distress.

14. d

As this patient's hypoxia (lack of oxygen in the blood) decreases, you should note changes (possibly slight) in the patient's interaction with his surroundings. These changes are due to increased oxygen delivery to the brain and muscle groups. If the patient's wheezing subsides but his distress is the same or worse, the patient's condition may be worsening. Be prepared to provide assisted ventilations. Ideally, the patient's tidal volume (amount of air moved in and out of the lungs with each breath) would increase as a result of dilation of the bronchioles. This patient's mother tells you that her son has been distressed for several hours. If this patient appears to have fallen asleep, this, too, could be a worrying sign that the patient's condition is worsening. He may need ventilatory support with supplemental oxygen provided via a BM device.

Objective: Distinguish between the emergency medical care of the infant, child, and adult patient with breathing difficulty. Differentiate between upper airway obstruction and lower airway disease in the infant and child patient.

15. d

Pulmonary emboli affect the flow of blood to the lungs, not the flow of air through the lungs. Air will still be drawn into the affected area, but without perfused alveoli, gas exchange will not take place.

Objective: State the signs and symptoms of a patient with breathing difficulty.

16. d

These medications are absorbed in the alveoli; therefore, for maximum benefit from inhaled medications, most of the medication must reach the alveoli. The key is to have the patient inhale the medication as deeply as possible and momentarily hold the breath to allow the medication to settle in the alveoli. Any other method would be less effective. The plastic bag option may harm the patient and should *not* be used.

Objective: Describe the emergency medical care of the patient with breathing difficulty. Recognize the need for medical direction to assist in the emergency medical care of the patient with breathing difficulty.

17. d

Pleuritic chest pain can be differentiated from cardiac chest pain by assessing the change in the intensity of pain during deep inhalation. Pleuritic chest pain will increase during inhalation because the pleura (the double-walled membrane that surrounds the lungs) is inflamed. Cardiac chest pain typically will not change dramatically during inhalation. Also, the presence of a fever suggests that the nature of the discomfort is an infection of the pleura. How does this change how you will treat this patient? You should still provide this patient with supplemental oxygen. If he is prescribed NTG and you are considering contacting medical direction for an order to assist the patient with this medication, you must make sure that you paint an accurate picture for the medical direction physician. NTG will not relieve pain associated with pleurisy.

Objective: State the signs and symptoms of a patient with breathing difficulty.

18. b

This patient is exhibiting signs and symptoms of epiglottitis. Do not attempt to visualize the airway, and do not upset the patient. Allow the patient to assume a position of comfort, allow the parent to stay with the patient if removal makes the patient agitated, maximize oxygen delivery without upsetting the patient, and provide prompt transport to an appropriate facility. You may not be able to perform a physical examination on this patient if your efforts upset her.

Objective: Describe the emergency medical care of the patient with breathing distress.

19. a

The gradual onset, the age of the patient, the presence of stridor, and the harsh barking cough are signs and symptoms suggestive of croup. Your treatment should focus on keeping the patient calm and providing supplemental oxygen. Epiglottitis generally has a more rapid onset, affects older children (age 3 to 7 years), and presents with difficulty swallowing, talking, and breathing. Epiglottitis may progress to complete blockage of the airway by the swollen epiglottis. Patients with croup should be treated carefully and rapidly. Make sure the patient is comfortable (generally sitting up and next to a parent), give high-flow oxygen (blow-by if a nonrebreather mask agitates the child), and transport as quickly and safely as possible to the closest appropriate medical facility.

Objective: Distinguish between the emergency medical care of the infant, child, and adult patient with breathing difficulty. Differentiate between upper airway obstruction and lower airway disease in the infant and child patient.

20. c

Retractions are evident when the skin above and between accessory muscles and other structures (e.g., bones) is drawn in during the work of inspiration. Retractions are generally most notable at the clavicles, the notch above the sternum, and at the bottom of the rib cage. Stridor is a harsh high-pitched sound made during inspiration. It is caused by upper airway obstruction. Tenting of the skin generally occurs because of dehydration. To evaluate tenting, pinch the skin to see how long it takes for it to assume its original position. Subcutaneous emphysema is the presence of air in the tissues outside the respiratory system. Found most commonly in the tissues of the chest, neck, and face, subcutaneous emphysema suggests a break in the integrity of the respiratory tree (usually following a traumatic event).

Objective: State the signs and symptoms of a patient with breathing difficulty.

21. c

In systems where ALS-level care is available, ALS assistance should be called to assist with all unstable patients. Inserting an oral airway would cause this conscious patient to vomit. Administering a bronchodilator may be appropriate; however, there are strict criteria you must follow first. NTG is indicated for patients experiencing chest pain of suspected cardiac origin.

Objective: Describe the emergency medical care of the patient with breathing distress.

22. d

Paroxysmal nocturnal dyspnea occurs because of the pooling of fluid in the lungs. By sitting or standing up, gravity helps in moving the excess fluid down, thus increasing tidal volume. Hypoxia is the term for low oxygen content in the blood. Patients experiencing paroxysmal nocturnal dyspnea may also be hypoxic because of impaired gas exchange. Pedal edema is the pooling of fluid in the lower extremities (legs) as a result of impaired pumping ability of the heart.

Objective: State the signs and symptoms of a patient with breathing difficulty.

23. b

The sputum associated with this patient's condition (pulmonary edema) would be frothy and possibly blood-tinged. The sputum is frothy from being forced through the small air passages and is pink from a small amount of blood leaking into the lungs with the fluid. Thick green or brownish yellow sputum is generally associated with a respiratory infection. Copious bright red blood is indicative of hemorrhage rather than pulmonary edema.

Objective: State the signs and symptoms of a patient with breathing difficulty.

24. d

Crackles (rales) are an abnormal lung sound created by fluid in the alveoli and bronchioles. The sound has been compared with the sound of opening a Velcro fastener or gentle rolling of the hair back and forth between the fingers. Grunting, most commonly associated with respiratory distress in infants, is a noise (a grunt) heard during exhalation. This grunt forms a small amount of back pressure in the lungs to help keep the alveoli from collapsing during exhalation. Stridor is a harsh, high-pitched sound associated with upper airway obstruction. Wheezes occur because of air whistling through narrowed bronchioles (as with asthma).

Objective: State the signs and symptoms of a patient with breathing difficulty.

25. c

High-flow oxygen is important for this patient. The correct device for high-flow oxygen administration is the nonrebreather mask. The nasal cannula becomes very uncomfortable at flow rates greater than 6 L/min. Because this patient is breathing at an acceptable rate with good tidal volume, assisting ventilations with a BM device is not yet necessary. However, anticipate that this patient's condition may worsen. Have a BM device, suction equipment, oral airways, nasal airways, and an AED readily available.

Objective: Describe the emergency medical care of the patient with breathing distress.

Matching

26. H	37. A
27. O	38. S
28. P	39. V
29. L	40. E
30. T	41. F
31. N	42. G
32. U	43. J
33. R	44. K
34. B	45. D
35. Q	46. M
36. C	47. I

Short Answer

48. Normal breathing involves two primary muscles: the diaphragm and the external intercostal muscles between the ribs.

    Objective: List the structures and functions of the respiratory system.

49. Signs and symptoms of acute pulmonary edema include the following:

    - Restlessness, anxiety
    - Dyspnea on exertion
    - Orthopnea
    - Paroxysmal nocturnal dyspnea
    - Frothy, blood-tinged sputum
    - Cool, moist skin
    - Use of accessory muscles
    - Jugular venous distention
    - Wheezing
    - Crackles
    - Rapid, labored breathing
    - Increased heart rate
    - Increased or decreased blood pressure (depending on severity of edema)

    Objective: N/A

50. An MDI is small and consists of two parts, the medication canister and a plastic dispenser with a mouth piece. A physician will often prescribe a spacer to be used with the MDI.

The spacer increases the amount of medication delivered into the respiratory tract. The patient squeezes the MDI into a plastic holding chamber, and then inhales the medication from the chamber. The use of spacers is very common in children and older adults. The spacer can also be attached to a resuscitation mask to aid medication delivery for a young child.

Objective: State the generic name, medication forms, dose, administration, action, indications, and contraindications for the prescribed inhaler.

51. As an EMT, you can assist a patient in taking a prescribed inhaler if all of the following criteria are met:

    - The patient has signs and symptoms of a respiratory emergency.
    - The patient has a physician-prescribed handheld inhaler.
    - There are no contraindications to giving the medication.
    - You have specific authorization by medical direction.

    Objective: Describe the emergency medical care of the patient with breathing difficulty. Recognize the need for medical direction to assist in the emergency medical care of the patient with breathing difficulty.

52. Assisting a patient with the use of an MDI is contraindicated if any of the following conditions exists:

    - The patient is unable to use the device. (This may be due to the level of the patient's respiratory distress.)
    - The inhaler is not prescribed for the patient.
    - Permission is not received from medical direction.
    - The patient has already met the maximum prescribed dose before your arrival.

    Objective: Describe the emergency medical care of the patient with breathing difficulty. Recognize the need for medical direction to assist in the emergency medical care of the patient with breathing difficulty.

14 Cardiovascular Emergencies

READING ASSIGNMENT ▶ Read Chapter 14, pages 315 to 347 in your textbook.

Sum It Up

- The circulatory system consists of the cardiovascular and lymphatic systems. The cardiovascular system is made up of the heart, blood, and blood vessels. The lymphatic system consists of lymph, lymph nodes, lymph vessels, the tonsils, the spleen, and the thymus gland. The circulatory system is responsible for transporting oxygen, water, and nutrients (such as sugar and vitamins) throughout the body. It also carries away wastes produced by body cells (such as carbon dioxide) to the lungs, kidneys, or skin for removal from the body.

- The heart is divided into four chambers. The two upper chambers are the right and left atria. The atria receive blood from the body and lungs. The right atrium receives blood that is low in oxygen from the body. The left atrium receives blood rich in oxygen from the lungs. The two lower chambers of the heart are the right and left ventricles. The ventricles are larger and have thicker walls than the atria because their function is to pump blood to the lungs and body. The right ventricle pumps blood to the lungs. The left ventricle pumps blood to the body.

- Four heart valves prevent the backflow of blood and keep blood moving in one direction. The tricuspid and mitral valves are called *AV valves* because they lie between the atria and ventricles. The aortic and pulmonic valves are called *semilunar valves* because they are shaped like half-moons.

- The liquid portion of the blood is called *plasma*. Plasma carries blood cells throughout the body. The formed elements of the blood include red blood cells, white blood cells, and platelets.

- Blood vessels that carry blood away from the heart to the rest of the body are called arteries. Arteries have thick walls because they transport blood under high pressure. Vessels that return blood to the heart are called *veins*. The walls of veins are thinner than arteries. Capillaries are the smallest and most numerous of the blood vessels.

- ACSs are conditions caused by temporary or permanent blockage of a coronary artery as a result of CAD. ACSs include unstable angina pectoris and myocardial infarction.

- Arteriosclerosis means hardening (-sclerosis) of the walls of the arteries (arterio-). As the walls of the arteries become hardened, they lose their elasticity. In atherosclerosis, the inner lining (endothelium) of the walls of large and medium-sized arteries become narrowed and thicken.

- Conditions that may increase a person's chance of developing a disease are called *risk factors*. While some risk factors can be changed, others cannot. Risk factors that can be changed are called *modifiable risk factors*. Risk factors that cannot be changed are called *non-modifiable risk factors*. Factors that can be part of the cause of a person's risk of heart disease are called *contributing risk factors.*

- Ischemia is decreased blood flow to an organ or tissue. Ischemia can result from narrowing or blockage of an artery or spasm of an artery. Atherosclerosis is a common reason for narrowing of a coronary artery.

- Angina pectoris (literally, "choking in the chest") is a symptom of CAD that occurs when the heart's need for oxygen exceeds its supply. A person is said to have stable angina pectoris when his symptoms are relatively constant and predictable in terms of severity, signs and symptoms, precipitating events, and response to therapy. A person who has unstable angina *pectoris* has angina that is progressively worsening, occurs at rest, or is brought on by minimal physical exertion.

- An acute MI (*heart attack*) occurs when a coronary artery becomes severely narrowed or is completely blocked, usually by a blood clot (thrombus). When the affected portion of the heart muscle (myocardium) is deprived of oxygen long enough, the area dies (infarcts). If too much of the heart muscle dies, shock (hypoperfusion) and cardiac arrest will result.

- The risk of death from a heart attack is related to the time elapsed between the onset of symptoms and start of treatment. The earlier the patient can receive emergency care, the greater the chances of preventing ischemic heart tissue from becoming dead heart tissue.

- When a person has CHF, one or both sides of the heart fail to pump efficiently. When the left ventricle fails as a pump, blood backs up into the lungs. When the right ventricle fails, blood returning to the heart backs up and causes congestion in the organs and tissues of the body.

- Signs and symptoms of a heart attack vary. Although chest discomfort is the most common symptom of a heart attack, some patients never have chest pain. Older adults, diabetic individuals, and women who have a heart attack are more likely to present with signs and symptoms that differ from those of a "typical" patient. This is called an *atypical presentation* or *atypical signs and symptoms*.

- Many states have passed legislation to include aspirin as a medication that can be carried on an EMS unit and given by EMTs. Check your state and local protocols for the appropriate use of this drug.

- As an EMT, you can assist a patient in taking prescribed NTG if the patient has signs and symptoms of chest pain or discomfort, the patient has physician-prescribed NTG, there are no contraindications to giving the medication, and you have specific authorization by medical direction (off-line or on-line).

- If the heart stops beating, no blood will flow. If no blood flows, oxygen cannot be delivered to the body's cells. When the heart stops, the patient is said to be in cardiac arrest. The signs of cardiac arrest include sudden unresponsiveness, absent breathing, and no signs of circulation. Brain damage begins 4 to 6 minutes after the patient suffers a cardiac arrest. Brain damage becomes irreversible in 8 to 10 minutes. Chest compressions are used to circulate blood any time that the heart is not beating. Chest compressions are combined with rescue breathing to oxygenate the blood. The combination of rescue breathing and external chest compressions is called *CPR*.

- SCD is the unexpected death from cardiac causes early after symptom onset (immediately or within one hour) or without the onset of symptoms. Survival of cardiac arrest depends on a series of critical actions called the *Chain of Survival*. The Chain of Survival is the ideal series of events that should take place immediately after recognizing an injury or the onset of sudden illness. The chain consists of four steps:
  1. Early access
  2. Early CPR
  3. Early defibrillation
  4. Early advanced cardiac life support

- An AED contains a computer programmed to recognize heart rhythms that should be shocked (defibrillated), such as VF (or Vfib). A standard AED is used for a patient who is unresponsive, not breathing, pulseless, and greater than or equal to 8 years of age (about 55 pounds or more than 25 kg). A special key or pad-cable system is available for some AEDs so that the machine can be used on children between 1 and 8 years of age. The key or pad-cable system decreases the amount of energy delivered to a dose appropriate for a child. If a child is in cardiac arrest and a key or pad-cable system is not available, use a standard AED.

- When an adult experiences a cardiac arrest as a result of VF, prompt defibrillation is the most important treatment you can provide from the time of the arrest to about 5 minutes following the arrest. If you witness a cardiac arrest, assess the patient's airway, breathing, and circulation, and then quickly apply an AED. Perform CPR until the AED is ready.

- To ensure delivery of the best-quality patient care possible, the medical director (or designated representative) carefully reviews every call in which an AED is used. Each call is reviewed to determine if the patient was treated according to professional standards and local standing orders.

- If the patient has a pacemaker or ICD in place, place the AED pads at least one inch from the device.

- Before using an AED, familiarize yourself with the manufacturer's recommendations regarding the use of the device around water. If a medication patch is present on the patient's chest, make sure you are wearing gloves and then remove the patch.

- To operate an AED, place the AED next to the rescuer who will be operating it. Turn on the power. Connect the AED pads to the AED cables (if not preconnected). Then apply the pads to the patient's bare chest in the locations indicated on the pads. Connect the cable to the AED. Analyze the patient's heart rhythm. If the AED advises that a shock is indicated, check the patient from head to toe to make sure no one is touching the patient (including you) before pressing the shock control. Make sure oxygen is not flowing over the patient's chest. Shout, "Stand clear!" Press the shock control once it is illuminated and the machine indicates it is ready to deliver the shock. Resume CPR, beginning with chest compressions, immediately after delivery of the shock.

- If you are transporting a patient who stops breathing and becomes pulseless, stop the vehicle. Start CPR and apply the AED. Analyze the rhythm as soon as the AED is ready. Deliver a shock, if indicated. Immediately resume CPR. Continue resuscitation (and transport) according to your local protocol.

- Maintenance procedures for an AED should be performed according to the manufacturer's recommendations. Failure of an AED is most often related to improper device maintenance, commonly battery failure.
- Many organizations publish materials about CPR and automated external defibrillation, including the American Heart Association, American Safety and Health Institute, American Red Cross, and National Safety Council.

► Tracking Your Progress

After reading this chapter, can you:	Page Reference	Objective Met?
Describe the structure and function of the cardiovascular system?	317	☐
Describe the emergency medical care of the patient experiencing chest pain/discomfort?	328	☐
List the indications for automated external defibrillation?	341	☐
List the contraindications for automated external defibrillation?	341	☐
Define the EMT's role in the emergency cardiac care system?	336	☐
Explain the impact of age and weight on defibrillation?	340	☐
Discuss the position of comfort for patients with various cardiac emergencies?	328	☐
Establish the relationship between airway management and the patient with cardiovascular compromise?	341	☐
Predict the relationship between the patient experiencing cardiovascular compromise and Basic Life Support?	341	☐
Discuss the fundamentals of early defibrillation?	335	☐
Explain the rationale for early defibrillation?	335	☐
Explain that not all patients with chest pain will experience cardiac arrest, nor do all patients with chest pain need to be attached to an AED?	341	☐
Explain the importance of prehospital ACLS intervention if it is available?	327	☐
Explain the importance of urgent transport to a facility with ACLS if it is not available in the prehospital setting?	327	☐
Discuss the various types of AEDs?	339	☐
Differentiate between the fully automated and the semi-automated defibrillator?	339	☐
Discuss the procedures that must be taken into consideration for standard operations of the various types of AEDs?	339	☐
State the reasons for ensuring that the patient is pulseless and apneic when using the AED?	343	☐
Discuss the circumstances that may result in inappropriate shocks?	343	☐
Explain the considerations for interruption of CPR when using an AED?	343	☐
Discuss the advantages of AEDs?	341	☐
Summarize the speed of operation of automated external defibrillation?	341	☐
Discuss the use of remote defibrillation through adhesive pads?	341	☐

After reading this chapter, can you:	Page Reference	Objective Met?
• Discuss the special considerations for rhythm monitoring?	341	☐
• List the steps in the operation of the AED?	342	☐
• Discuss the standard of care that should be used to provide care to a patient with persistent ventricular fibrillation and no available ACLS?	342	☐
• Discuss the standard of care that should be used to provide care to a patient with recurrent ventricular fibrillation and no available ACLS?	343	☐
• Differentiate between the single rescuer and multi-rescuer care with an AED?	342	☐
• Explain the reason for pulses not being checked between shocks with an AED?	342	☐
• Discuss the importance of coordinating ACLS trained providers with personnel using AEDs?	343	☐
• Discuss the importance of postresuscitation care?	343	☐
• List the components of postresuscitation care?	343	☐
• Explain the importance of frequent practice with the AED?	345	☐
• Discuss the need to complete the Automated Defibrillator: Operator's Shift Checklist?	345	☐
• Discuss the role of national organizations such as the American Heart Association, American Safety and Health Institute, and others in the use of automated external defibrillation?	345	☐
• Explain the role medical direction plays in the use of automated external defibrillation?	341	☐
• State the reasons why a case review should be completed following the use of the AED?	341	☐
• Discuss the components that should be included in a case review?	341	☐
• Discuss the goal of quality improvement in automated external defibrillation?	341	☐
• Recognize the need for medical direction of protocols to assist in the emergency medical care of the patient with chest pain?	329, 330	☐
• List the indications for the use of NTG?	330	☐
• State the contraindications and side effects for the use of NTG?	330	☐
• Define the function of all controls on an AED, and describe event documentation and defibrillator battery maintenance?	342	☐

True or False

Decide whether each statement is true or false. In the space provided, write *T* for true or *F* for false.

_____ 1. All veins carry deoxygenated blood through the body.

_____ 2. The heart contains cells that are capable of producing an electrical impulse without being stimulated by another source.

Multiple Choice

In the space provided, identify the letter of the choice that best completes the statement or answers each question.

_____ 3. Which of the following correctly reflects the main components of the cardiovascular system?

    a. The lung and the alveoli

    b. Lymph and the lymph system

    c. The lungs, the heart, and the capillaries

    d. The heart, blood, and the blood vessels

_____ 4. Blood pressure is best defined as
   a. adequate circulation of blood through an organ or part of the body.
   b. the force exerted by the blood on the inner walls of the heart and blood vessels.
   c. the pressure exerted against the walls of the arteries when the left ventricle contracts.
   d. the pressure exerted against the walls of the arteries when the left ventricle is relaxed.

_____ 5. The largest artery of the body is the
   a. aorta.   c. femoral artery.
   b. carotid artery.   d. pulmonary artery.

_____ 6. Which of the following is the liquid part of blood?
   a. Plasma   c. Leukocytes
   b. Platelets   d. Erythrocytes

_____ 7. Platelets are essential for
   a. defending the body from microorganisms.
   b. transporting carbon dioxide away from body cells.
   c. stopping bleeding and repairing ruptured blood vessels.
   d. carrying nutrients to the cells and waste products from the cells.

_____ 8. The human heart is divided into chambers. By pumping blood out of these chambers in one direction, the heart effectively perfuses the body with an adequate blood supply. The upper chambers of the heart are called
   a. atria.   c. valves.
   b. septa.   d. ventricles.

_____ 9. The tricuspid valve
   a. is located between the left atrium and left ventricle.
   b. is located between the right atrium and right ventricle.
   c. is located at the junction of the left ventricle and aorta.
   d. is called a semilunar valve because it is shaped like a half-moon.

_____ 10. To assist in lowering body temperature, blood vessels may
   a. dilate, thus giving the patient a red or flushed appearance.
   b. dilate, thus giving the patient a pale or cyanotic appearance.
   c. constrict, thus giving the patient a red or flushed appearance.
   d. constrict, thus giving the patient a pale or cyanotic appearance.

_____ 11. The lower chambers of the heart are larger than the upper chambers because they do the bulk of the work of pumping blood. These chambers are called the
   a. atria.   c. valves.
   b. septa.   d. ventricles.

_____ 12. Which chamber of the heart is responsible for pumping blood to the lungs?
   a. Left atrium   c. Left ventricle
   b. Right atrium   d. Right ventricle

_____ 13. Blood is carried back to the heart in vessels of relative low pressure. Many of these vessels contain valves to prevent the backflow of blood as it returns to the heart. These vessels are called
   a. aortas.   c. veins.
   b. arteries.   d. capillaries.

_____ 14. The heart muscle (myocardium) requires a constant supply of fresh blood for proper functioning. The arteries that supply the heart with blood are the
   a. carotid arteries.   c. coronary arteries.
   b. femoral arteries.   d. pulmonary arteries.

_____ **15.** Signs and symptoms of shock include

    a. rapid pulse, warm skin, and intense thirst.
    b. rapid pulse, shallow breathing, and anxiety or restlessness.
    c. slow pulse, high blood pressure, and rapid, deep respirations.
    d. rapid pulse, dry skin, and rapid, deep respirations with a fruity breath odor.

_____ **16.** The term given to the death (necrosis) of heart cells is

    a. angina pectoris.   **c.** acute MI.
    b. cardiac tamponade.   **d.** CHF.

_____ **17.** The most common symptom associated with cardiac compromise and the lack of oxygenation of the heart is

    a. nausea.   **c.** chest pain or discomfort.
    b. pulmonary edema.   **d.** swelling of the feet or lower back.

_____ **18.** When performing a focused history and physical examination on a patient with chest pain, your physical examination

    a. should precede the primary survey.
    b. should be limited to a rapid assessment of the chest.
    c. should be limited to a thorough assessment of the upper torso.
    d. should evaluate all areas of the body that may be affected by cardiac compromise.

_____ **19.** With approval from medical direction, EMTs may assist a patient in taking NTG tablets or spray. This medication is to be

    a. swallowed with water.   **c.** given only after a full meal.
    b. chewed and swallowed.   **d.** placed and dissolved under the tongue.

_____ **20.** NTG may relieve chest pain associated with CAD. It does so by

    a. numbing the heart muscle.
    b. dilating the coronary arteries, thus increasing blood flow to the heart.
    c. constricting the coronary arteries, thus increasing blood pressure and perfusion.
    d. constricting the veins of the body, thus increasing blood pressure and blood flow to the heart.

_____ **21.** Which of the following is a contraindication for NTG?

    a. Nausea
    b. Hypotension (low blood pressure)
    c. Hypertension (high blood pressure)
    d. Severe chest pain accompanied by a heart rate greater than 80 beats/min

_____ **22.** Your rescue crew is at the home of a 58-year-old woman complaining of chest pain. After evaluation of the patient, medical direction instructs you to assist the patient in taking her NTG, up to a maximum of three sublingual tablets. It is absolutely essential to reassess which of the following before giving the patient a NTG tablet?

    a. Pulse rate   **c.** Blood pressure
    b. Capillary refill   **d.** Respiratory rate

_____ **23.** Common side effects of NTG administration include

    a. tremors or seizures.
    b. slurred speech and partial paralysis.
    c. headache, dizziness, and hypotension.
    d. increase in the intensity of the chest pain and difficulty breathing.

Matching

Match the key terms in the left column with the definitions in the right column by placing the letter of each correct answer in the space provided.

_____ 24. Peripheral artery disease

_____ 25. Acute myocardial infarction

_____ 26. Pulmonic valve

_____ 27. Ventricular fibrillation

_____ 28. Coronary artery bypass graft

_____ 29. Manual defibrillator

_____ 30. Congestive heart failure

_____ 31. Systolic blood pressure

_____ 32. Fainting

_____ 33. Coronary artery disease

_____ 34. Implantable cardioverter-defibrillator

_____ 35. Acute coronary syndromes

_____ 36. Stent

_____ 37. Coronary heart disease

_____ 38. Sudden cardiac death

_____ 39. Angioplasty

_____ 40. Atherosclerosis

_____ 41. Defibrillation

_____ 42. Tricuspid valve

_____ 43. Diastolic blood pressure

_____ 44. Chain of Survival

_____ 45. Ischemia

_____ 46. Mitral valve

_____ 47. Palpitations

A. Disease of the coronary arteries and the complications that result, such as angina pectoris or a heart attack

B. Unexpected death from cardiac causes early after symptom onset (immediately or within one hour) or without the onset of symptoms

C. Decreased blood flow to an organ or tissue

D. The delivery of an electrical shock to a patient's heart to end an abnormal heart rhythm

E. An abnormal awareness of one's heartbeat

F. Narrowing and thickening of the inner lining (endothelium) of the walls of large and medium-sized arteries because of a buildup of plaque

G. Death of heart tissue that occurs when a coronary artery becomes severely narrowed or is completely blocked, usually by a blood clot (thrombus)

H. An atrioventricular valve located between the left atrium and left ventricle

I. A term used for diseases that slow or stop blood flow through the arteries that supply the heart muscle with blood

J. A semilunar valve located at the junction of the right ventricle and pulmonary artery

K. A surgical procedure in which a graft is created from a healthy blood vessel from another part of the patient's body to reroute blood flow around a diseased coronary artery

L. The pressure exerted against the walls of the arteries when the left ventricle is at rest

M. Atherosclerosis that affects the arteries that supply the arms, legs, and feet

N. An atrioventricular valve located between the right atrium and right ventricle

O. The pressure exerted against the walls of the arteries when the left ventricle contracts

P. A surgically implanted device placed in the chest or upper abdomen and programmed to recognize heart rhythms that are too fast or life-threatening and deliver a shock to reset the rhythm

Q. A small plastic or metal tube that is inserted into a vessel or duct to help keep it open and maintain fluid flow through it

R. A sudden, temporary loss of consciousness

Continued

S. A machine that requires the rescuer to analyze and interpret the patient's cardiac rhythm

T. An abnormal heart rhythm in which the heart's electrical impulses are completely disorganized and the heart cannot pump blood effectively

U. A condition in which one or both sides of the heart fail to pump efficiently

V. The ideal series of events that should take place immediately after recognizing an injury or the onset of sudden illness

W. A procedure in which a balloon-tipped catheter is inserted into a partially blocked coronary artery; when the balloon is inflated, plaque is pressed against the walls of the artery, improving blood flow to the heart muscle

X. Conditions caused by temporary or permanent blockage of a coronary artery due to coronary artery disease

Short Answer

Answer each question in the space provided.

48. In the following illustration, label these structures of the cardiovascular system: aorta, aortic semilunar valve, inferior vena cava, left atrium, left pulmonary artery, left pulmonary veins, left ventricle, mitral valve, right atrium, right pulmonary artery, right pulmonary veins, pulmonary semilunar valve, right ventricle, superior vena cava, tricuspid valve.

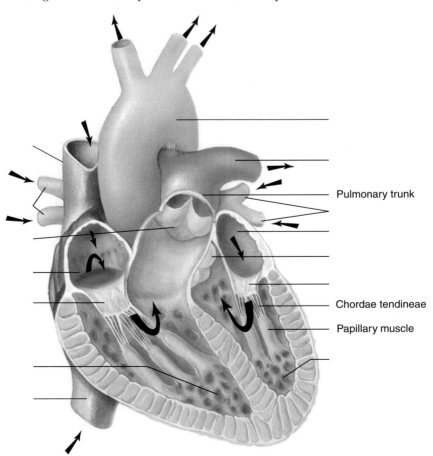

Pulmonary trunk

Chordae tendineae

Papillary muscle

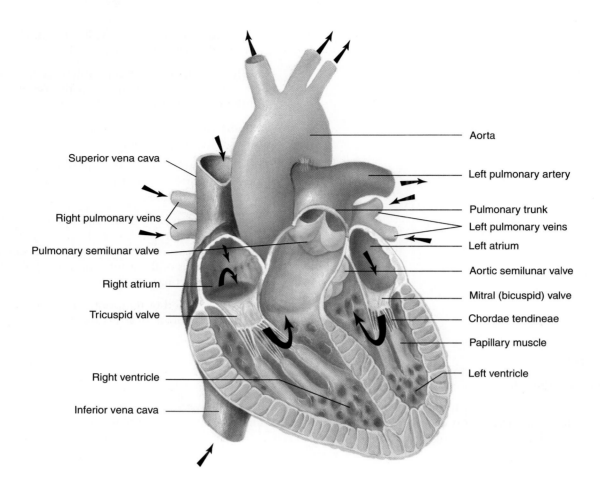

Aorta

Superior vena cava

Left pulmonary artery

Right pulmonary veins

Pulmonary trunk

Left pulmonary veins

Pulmonary semilunar valve

Left atrium

Right atrium

Aortic semilunar valve

Tricuspid valve

Mitral (bicuspid) valve

Chordae tendineae

Papillary muscle

Right ventricle

Left ventricle

Inferior vena cava

49. Using the right atrium as a starting point, describe the pathway of blood through the body. Include the heart's valves and the body's major blood vessels in your description.

50. What is sudden cardiac death?

51. List three signs of obvious death.

1.

2.

3.

52. List and describe each of the four steps in the Chain of Survival.

1.

2.

3.

4.

53. List seven "typical" signs and symptoms of a heart attack.

1.

2.

3.

4.

5.

6.

7.

54. List three groups of patients who are more likely to have a heart attack and present with signs and symptoms that differ from a "typical" patient.

1.

2.

3.

55. Explain why a patient with a heart or breathing-related complaint should not be permitted to walk to the stretcher.

56. MONA is a memory aid used to recall the initial treatments often used by healthcare professionals when caring for patients experiencing an acute coronary syndrome. What does MONA stand for?

M =

O =

N =

A =

57. Before you assist a patient in taking his prescribed NTG, why is it important to ask if he has taken any medications for erectile problems?

58. List five possible causes of cardiac arrest.

1.

2.

3.

4.

5.

59. Complete the following table.

	Adult	Child	Infant
Rescue Breaths			
Location of Pulse Check			
Depth of Chest Compressions			
Rate of Chest Compressions			
Ratio of Chest Compressions to Rescue Breaths (One Cycle)	1 rescuer: 2 rescuers:	1 rescuer: 2 rescuers:	1 rescuer: 2 rescuers:

60. When should an AED be applied to a patient and put in the "analyze" mode?

61. Explain the difference between a fully automated external defibrillator and a semi-automated external defibrillator.

62. When should a pediatric-capable AED be used?

63. You are on the scene of a cardiac arrest. As you prepare to apply the AED pads, you note the patient has an excessive amount of chest hair. Describe the appropriate actions that should be taken in this situation.

64. Explain why it is important to make sure that oxygen is not flowing over the patient's chest before delivering a shock with an AED.

65. Explain why a case review should be completed following the use of an AED, and list the components that should be included in the case review.

Answer Section

Chapter 14

True/False

1. False

All veins, except the pulmonary veins, carry deoxygenated (oxygen-poor) blood. The pulmonary veins deliver blood rich in oxygen from the lungs to the left atrium of the heart.

Objective: Describe the structure and function of the cardiovascular system.

2. True

The heart is more than a muscle. It contains specialized contractile and conductive tissue that allows the generation of electrical impulses. Unlike other cells of the body, specialized electrical (pacemaker) cells in the heart can produce an electrical impulse without being stimulated by another source, such as a nerve. This property is called *automaticity*. The electrical (pacemaker) cells in the heart are arranged in a system of pathways called the *conduction system*.

Objective: Describe the structure and function of the cardiovascular system.

Multiple Choice

3. d

The circulatory system is made up of the cardiovascular and lymphatic systems. The cardiovascular system is made up of three main parts: a pump (the heart), fluid (blood), and a container (the blood vessels).

Objective: Describe the structure and function of the cardiovascular system.

4. b

Blood pressure takes into account the pressure during contraction and relaxation of the heart muscle. A reading of 120/80, for example, indicates that during contraction of the heart a force of 120 mm Hg is exerted on the walls of the arteries while during relaxation this force drops to 80 mm Hg. A blood pressure taken by palpation (i.e., 120/P) is an approximation of the systolic blood pressure. Adequate circulation of blood through an organ or the body refers to perfusion. Adequate blood pressure supports perfusion.

Objective: Describe the structure and function of the cardiovascular system.

5. a

The aorta is the largest artery of the body and is the major artery originating from the heart.

Objective: Describe the structure and function of the cardiovascular system.

6. a

Formed elements of the blood include red blood cells (erythrocytes), white blood cells (leukocytes), and platelets (thrombocytes). Plasma is the liquid part of blood.

Objective: Describe the structure and function of the cardiovascular system.

7. c

Red blood cells have two functions. They also transport carbon dioxide away from body cells. White blood cells defend the body from microorganisms, such as bacteria and viruses that have invaded the bloodstream or tissues of the body. Platelets are essential for the formation of blood clots. They function to stop bleeding and repair ruptured blood vessels. Plasma carries nutrients to the cells and waste products from the cells.

Objective: Describe the structure and function of the cardiovascular system.

8. a

The atria (left and right) are the upper chambers of the heart. The right atrium receives deoxygenated blood from the vena cavae. The left atrium receives freshly reoxygenated blood from the pulmonary veins as it returns from the lungs.

Objective: Describe the structure and function of the cardiovascular system.

9. b

The tricuspid valve is an AV valve located between the right atrium and right ventricle. The mitral (bicuspid) valve is located between the left atrium and left ventricle. The pulmonic valve is located at the junction of the right ventricle and pulmonary artery. The aortic valve is located at the junction of the left ventricle and aorta.

Objective: Describe the structure and function of the cardiovascular system.

10. a

By dilating the peripheral vessels, the circulatory system sends more blood to the surface of the body. This blood is cooled and returns to the body's core. Imagine yourself playing basketball on a hot day. Your skin may become red or flushed because of increased blood flow to the skin. Sweating allows the skin to cool down. This cooler temperature is transmitted to the blood supply. Some medications may interfere with this process.

Objective: Describe the structure and function of the cardiovascular system.

11. d

The lower chambers of the heart are the right and left ventricles. The ventricles receive blood from the atria. The left ventricle pumps reoxygenated blood through the aorta to the cells of the body. The right ventricle pumps deoxygenated blood through the pulmonary artery to the lungs for reoxygenation.

Objective: Describe the structure and function of the cardiovascular system.

12. d

The right ventricle pumps blood to the lungs. The left ventricle pumps blood to the body. The atria are thin-walled chambers that receive blood from the systemic circulation and lungs.

Objective: Describe the structure and function of the cardiovascular system.

13. b

Veins always carry blood toward the heart. Deoxygenated blood returns from the capillary beds of the body through veins to the heart. Rexoygenated blood returns from the capillary beds within the lungs through the two pulmonary veins to the left atrium.

Objective: Describe the structure and function of the cardiovascular system.

14. c

The right and left coronary arteries are the first arteries that branch off the aorta as blood flows from the left ventricle. The carotid arteries are located in the neck just lateral to the trachea (windpipe). The femoral arteries are located in the crease between the abdomen and the thigh. The pulmonary arteries are responsible for delivering deoxygenated blood from the right ventricle to the lungs.

Objective: Describe the structure and function of the cardiovascular system.

15. b

Perfusion is the circulation of blood through an organ or a part of the body. Perfusion is necessary for the proper functioning of all body systems. Hypoperfusion, also called *shock*, occurs when organs are not provided with an adequate blood supply. Other common signs and symptoms of shock include a rapid, weak pulse; rapid, shallow breathing; altered mental status; cool, pale, moist skin; nausea; and a low or falling blood pressure (a late sign). A rapid pulse with warm skin and intense thirst may be associated with hyperglycemia (a diabetic emergency). A slow pulse accompanied by high blood pressure and rapid, deep respirations may suggest a head injury with increased intracranial pressure. A rapid pulse with dry skin and rapid, deep respirations (Kussmaul respirations) with a fruity breath odor is also associated with hyperglycemia.

Objective: List signs and symptoms of shock (hypoperfusion).

16. c

CAD results in the reduced flow of blood through the coronary arteries. If the flow of blood to the heart is reduced too much, heart muscle cells will die. Infarction refers to death. Myocardium is the medical term for the heart muscle; therefore, acute MI is a heart attack. Although a heart attack and angina pectoris both present in much the same way and both may be attributed to CAD, a heart attack differs from angina pectoris. In angina, death of heart cells does not occur. Because EMTs are not physicians, patients presenting with cardiac-type chest pain should be assumed to be having an acute MI. Cardiac tamponade is a traumatic injury to the heart in which blood leaks into the sac surrounding the heart (pericardium), and the accumulating blood impedes the heart's ability to pump blood. CHF is a condition most commonly associated with patients who have suffered a heart attack. Because of decreased pumping ability of the damaged heart, blood begins to back up in the vessels. Common findings in CHF include difficulty breathing, pulmonary edema (fluid buildup in the lungs), JVD, and swelling in the extremities or lower back.

Objective: Describe the emergency medical care of the patient experiencing chest pain/discomfort.

17. c

When the heart is deprived of oxygen, the result is chest pain or discomfort. Any patient complaining of chest pain or discomfort should be immediately treated with high-flow oxygen by nonrebreather mask. The pain associated with cardiac compromise may be described in many ways: a dull ache, indigestion, a heavy weight on the chest, or a sharp pain that radiates to another body area. Pulmonary edema, nausea, and pedal or sacral edema (swelling of the feet or lower back) may accompany chest pain; however, chest pain is the most common complaint.

Objective: Predict the relationship between the patient experiencing cardiovascular compromise and Basic Life Support.

18. d

Do not be confused by the word *focused* in the term "focused history and physical examination." The emphasis of the physical examination is determined by the conscious patient's chief complaint. However, the physical findings for a particular complaint may be seen in body regions away from the area of distress. For example, a patient complaining of chest pain may have swelling of the feet (pedal edema) from failure of the right ventricle. This sign is an important and pertinent finding. Do not merely examine the area of discomfort, or you may miss additional signs relevant to the patient's distress.

Objective: Describe the emergency medical care of the patient experiencing chest pain/discomfort.

19. d

NTG, whether in the tablet or spray form, is administered sublingually (absorbed under the tongue). Make sure you have on a clean pair of medical gloves before administering NTG as you may absorb the medication through your skin.

Objective: List the indications for the use of NTG.

20. b

NTG causes relaxation (dilation) of the smooth muscle of blood vessel walls. Relaxation of the veins results in pooling of blood in the dependent portions of the body as a result of gravity. This effect reduces the amount of blood returning to the heart, decreasing the heart's workload. NTG causes some relaxation of the walls of arteries, including the coronary arteries. This helps reduce the resistance the heart must overcome to pump blood out to the body, thus decreasing the heart's workload. NTG relaxes normal and atherosclerotic coronary arteries on the outer surface of the heart. This helps to improve blood flow and the delivery of oxygen to the heart, thus improving blood flow to the heart muscle that was previously deprived of oxygen (ischemia). Relief of ischemia reduces chest pain and discomfort.

Objective: List the indications for the use of NTG.

21. b

Assisting a patient in taking prescribed NTG is contraindicated if any of the following conditions exists:

- No permission from medical direction
- Medication not prescribed for the patient
- Patient who has already taken the maximum prescribed dose before EMT's arrival
- Hypotension or blood pressure below 100 mm Hg systolic
- Heart rate <50 beats/min or >100 beats/min
- Head injury (recent) or stroke (recent)
- Infants and children
- Patient who has taken a medication for erectile dysfunction within the last 24 to 48 hours

Objective: State the contraindications and side effects for the use of NTG.

22. c

Remember that NTG is a potent blood pressure–lowering agent. The interval for repeating doses of NTG is 5 minutes, with a maximum total dose of three tablets. The blood pressure changes from NTG can generally be seen after about 2 minutes. Although reassessment of the patient's pulse rate and respiratory rate is important, reassessing the patient's blood pressure before giving the first and subsequent tablets is absolutely essential. Capillary refill findings are unreliable in patients older than 6 years of age.

Objective: State the contraindications and side effects for the use of nitroglycerin.

23. c

NTG also dilates the vessels in the brain and can thus cause headache and possible dizziness. A lower blood pressure is commonly observed after NTG administration. Tremors, seizures, slurred speech, and partial paralysis are not common side effects. If these events occur, it is more likely that the patient has suffered a cerebrovascular accident (stroke) than a reaction to the NTG.

Objective: State the contraindications and side effects for the use of NTG.

Matching

24.	M	36.	Q
25.	G	37.	A
26.	J	38.	B
27.	T	39.	W
28.	K	40.	F
29.	S	41.	D
30.	U	42.	N
31.	O	43.	L
32.	R	44.	V
33.	I	45.	C
34.	P	46.	H
35.	X	47.	E

Short Answer

48.

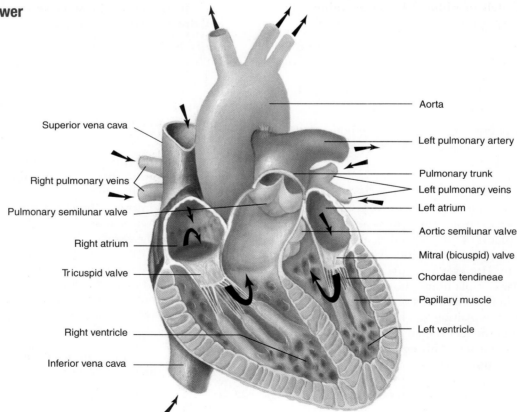

Superior vena cava

Right pulmonary veins

Pulmonary semilunar valve

Right atrium

Tricuspid valve

Right ventricle

Inferior vena cava

Aorta

Left pulmonary artery

Pulmonary trunk

Left pulmonary veins

Left atrium

Aortic semilunar valve

Mitral (bicuspid) valve

Chordae tendineae

Papillary muscle

Left ventricle

Objective: Describe the structure and function of the cardiovascular system.

49. Blood low in oxygen enters the right atrium and flows through the tricuspid valve and into the right ventricle. From the right ventricle, blood is pumped through the pulmonic valve into the pulmonary arteries (pulmonary circuit) and then to the lungs, where red blood cells are oxygenated. From the lungs, oxygen-rich blood flows through the pulmonary veins and into the left atrium. From the left atrium, blood flows through the mitral (also called the *bicuspid*) valve and into the left ventricle. From the left ventricle, blood is pumped through the aortic valve and into the aorta (systemic circuit). From the aorta, blood flows to the rest of the body through arteries, arterioles, capillaries, venules, and veins. Cells use the oxygen, along with nutrients from food, to make energy. Then, veins carry the blood (now low in oxygen) from the body cells back to the right heart. The superior and inferior vena cavae deliver oxygen-poor blood from the body to the right atrium.

Objective: Describe the structure and function of the cardiovascular system.

50. Sudden cardiac death is the unexpected death from cardiac causes early after symptom onset (immediately or within 1 hour) or without the onset of symptoms. About 2/3 of sudden cardiac deaths take place outside the hospital, usually in a private or residential setting.

Objective: List the indications for AED.

51. Signs of obvious death:

- Decapitation or other obvious mortal injury
- Putrefaction (decomposition)
- Extreme dependent lividity
- Rigor mortis

Objective: N/A

52. The Chain of Survival is the ideal series of events that should take place immediately after recognizing an injury or the onset of sudden illness (Figure 14-11). The chain consists of four crucial steps:

1. *Early access* (recognition of an emergency and calling 9-1-1). The public must be educated to recognize the early warning signs of a heart attack. Many patients do nothing and hope their symptoms will go away. The average time between the onset of symptoms and admission to a medical facility is about 3 hours. Some patients may delay seeking help for more than 24 hours. A patient's collapse must be identified by a person who can activate the EMS system. CPR training teaches citizens how to contact the EMS

system, decreasing the time to defibrillation. EMS personnel must arrive rapidly at the scene with all necessary equipment.

2. *Early CPR.* Bystander CPR is the best treatment the patient can receive until arrival of a defibrillator and ACLS personnel.

3. *Early defibrillation.* Defibrillation is the delivery of an electrical shock to a patient's heart to end an abnormal heart rhythm, such as VF.

4. *Early ACLS.* Early advanced care provided by Paramedics at the scene is a critical link in the treatment of cardiac arrest. Paramedics combine rapid defibrillation by first responding units with airway management and IV medications by the ALS units. If ACLS units are not available, the patient should be transported rapidly to a facility for definitive ACLS care.

Objective: Discuss the fundamentals of early defibrillation.

53. Typical heart attack signs and symptoms:

- Uncomfortable squeezing, ache, dull pressure, or pain in the center of the chest lasting more than a few minutes
- Discomfort in one or both arms, the back, the neck, the jaw, or the stomach
- Anxiety, dizziness, irritability
- Abnormal pulse rate (may be irregular)
- Abnormal blood pressure
- Nausea, vomiting
- Lightheadedness
- Fainting or near-fainting
- Breaking out in a cold sweat
- Weakness
- Shortness of breath
- Difficulty breathing (dyspnea)
- Palpitations
- Feeling of impending doom

Objective: Describe the emergency medical care of the patient experiencing chest paindiscomfort.

54. (1) Older adults, (2) diabetic individuals, and (3) women are more likely to have a heart attack and present with signs and symptoms that differ from a "typical" patient. This is called *an atypical presentation* or *atypical signs and symptoms.*

Objective: Describe the emergency medical care of the patient experiencing chest pain/discomfort.

55. Do not allow any patient who has a heart or breathing-related complaint to perform activities that require exertion, such as walking to the stretcher. Asking the patient to walk to a stretcher or ambulance *increases* the heart's need for oxygen. When providing emergency care to these patients, your goal is to *decrease* oxygen demand. Bring the stretcher to the patient—not the patient to the stretcher.

Objective: Describe the emergency medical care of the patient experiencing chest pain/discomfort.

56. MONA is a memory aid used to recall the initial treatments often used by healthcare professionals when caring for patients experiencing an acute coronary syndrome. MONA stands for:

M = *M*orphine

O = *O*xygen

N = *N*itroglycerin

A = *A*spirin

Although morphine is given only by ALS personnel in the field, EMTs can begin treating the patient with the remaining three drugs (in most EMS systems).

Objective: Describe the emergency medical care of the patient experiencing chest pain/discomfort.

57. Before giving NTG, it is very important to ask the patient if he has taken any medications for erectile problems. Examples of oral medications that are used for this purpose include sildenafil (Viagra), tadalafil (Cialis), and vardenafil (Levitra). Giving NTG to a patient who has taken any of these drugs within 24 to 48 hours may lead to irreversible hypotension and death.

Objective: State the contraindications and side effects for the use of NTG.

58. Possible causes of cardiac arrest:

- Heart and blood vessel diseases, such as heart attack and stroke
- Choking or respiratory arrest
- Seizures
- Diabetic emergency
- Severe allergic reaction
- Severe electrical shock
- Poisoning or drug overdose
- Drowning
- Suffocation
- Trauma
- Severe bleeding
- Abnormalities present at birth

Objective: Predict the relationship between the patient experiencing cardiovascular compromise and Basic Life Support.

59. See table below.

	Adult	Child	Infant
Rescue Breaths	About 10-12 breaths/min 1 breath every 5-6 sec	About 12-20 breaths/min 1 breath every 3-5 sec	About 12-20 breaths/min 1 breath every 3-5 sec
Location of Pulse Check	Carotid	Carotid	Brachial
Depth of Chest Compressions	1 1/2 to 2 inches	1/3 to 1/2 the chest depth	1/3 to 1/2 the chest depth
Rate of Chest Compressions		About 100/min	
Ratio of Chest Compressions to Rescue Breaths (One Cycle)	1 or 2 rescuers: 30 compressions to 2 breaths (30:2)	1 rescuer: 30 compressions to 2 breaths (30:2) 2 rescuers: 15 compressions to 2 breaths (15:2)	1 rescuer: 30 compressions to 2 breaths (30:2) 2 rescuers: 15 compressions to 2 breaths (15:2)

Objective: N/A

60. An AED should be applied to patients older than 1 year of age in cardiac arrest. Before analyzing the rhythm, ensure all movement around the patient stops, all radio communications halt, transportation is stopped, and the area is safe.

Check the AED manufacturer's instructions for information about the use of the device around metal or water.

Objective: State the reasons for assuring that the patient is pulseless and apneic when you are using the AED.

61. You must know the difference between a fully automated external defibrillator and a SAED. When a fully automated external defibrillator is used, the pads are attached to the patient and the power turned on. The AED then performs all of the necessary steps to defibrillate the patient. A fully automated machine analyzes the patient's heart rhythm, warns everyone to stand clear of the patient if it recognizes a shockable rhythm, and then delivers a shock through the pads that have been applied to the patient's chest.

An SAED is also called a *shock-advisory defibrillator*. When an SAED is used, the adhesive pads are attached to the patient and the power turned on. Some AEDs require the rescuer to press an "analyze" control to begin analyzing the patient's cardiac rhythm while others automatically begin analyzing the patient's cardiac rhythm when the adhesive pads are attached to the patient's chest. The SAED "advises" the rescuer of the steps to take based on its analysis of the patient's heart rhythm by means of a voice or visual message. For example, if an SAED detects a shockable rhythm, it will advise the rescuer to press the shock control to deliver a shock.

Objective: Differentiate between the fully automated and the semi-automated defibrillator.

62. A standard AED is used for a patient who is unresponsive, not breathing, pulseless, and older than or equal to 8 years of age (about 55 pounds or >25 kg). A special key or pad-cable system is available for some AEDs so that the machine can be used on children between 1 and 8 years of age. The key or pad-cable system decreases the amount of energy delivered to a dose appropriate for a child. If a child is in cardiac arrest and a key or pad-cable system is not available, use a standard AED.

Objective: Explain the impact of age and weight on defibrillation.

63. If the patient has a hairy chest, the AED pads may not stick to the patient's chest. The AED will be unable to analyze the patient's heart rhythm and will give a "check electrodes" message. Try pressing down firmly on each AED pad and see if that corrects the problem. If the "check electrodes" message from the AED persists (and you have a second set of AED pads available), quickly remove the AED pads. This will remove some of the patient's chest hair. Quickly look at the patient's chest. If a lot of chest hair remains, quickly shave the areas of the chest where the AED pads will be placed. Put on a second set of AED pads. Follow the prompts by the AED.

Objective: Discuss the use of remote defibrillation through adhesive pads.

64. Before delivering a shock with an AED, make sure that oxygen is not flowing over the patient's chest. Fire can be ignited by sparks from poorly applied AED pads in an oxygen-enriched atmosphere.

Objective: List the steps in the operation of the AED.

65. To ensure delivery of the best-quality patient care possible, the medical director (or designated representative) carefully reviews every call in which an AED is used. Quality management involves evaluating the performance of individuals using AEDs, the effectiveness of the EMS system in which AEDs are used, and data collection and review.

AEDs are equipped with memory modules that record important information for later review by medical direction. The data from the AED can be downloaded to a computer or Pocket PC. Examples of information recorded by an AED include the patient's heart rhythm, number of shocks delivered, time of each shock delivered, and the energy level used for each shock. Some AEDs also document CPR compression data. Some AEDs have an audio recording feature that is voice activated so that conversation during the call is recorded.

In addition to the data from the AED, the medical director will also review the PCR pertaining to the call, voice recordings (if the AED is so equipped), and magnetic tape recordings stored in the AED (if so equipped). Each call is reviewed to determine if the patient was treated according to professional standards and local standing orders. Other areas that may be evaluated include:

- Scene command
- Safety
- Efficiency
- Speed
- Professionalism
- Ability to troubleshoot
- Completeness of patient care
- Interactions with other professionals and bystanders

By reviewing each call in which an AED is used, problems within the EMS system can be identified, each link in the Chain of Survival can be evaluated, and EMS personnel can learn from their successes and mistakes.

Objective: State the reasons why a case review should be completed following the use of the AED. Discuss the components that should be included in a case review.

15 Diabetes and Altered Mental Status

READING ASSIGNMENT ▷ Read Chapter 15, pages 348 to 369 in your textbook.

Sum It Up

- As an EMT, you should assess every patient and determine his chief complaint as well as his signs and symptoms. Give emergency medical care based on the patient's signs and symptoms. Keep in mind that some patient complaints may apply to more than one illness.

- An altered mental status refers to a change in a patient's level of awareness. It is also called an *ALOC*. A change in the patient's mental status may occur gradually or suddenly. It may last briefly or it may be prolonged. A patient with an altered mental status may appear confused, agitated, combative, sleepy, difficult to awaken, or unresponsive. An altered mental status should be treated as a medical emergency. Regardless of the cause, emergency care of the patient with an altered mental status focuses on his airway, breathing, and circulation.

- A seizure is a temporary change in behavior or consciousness caused by abnormal electrical activity within one or more groups of brain cells. A seizure is a symptom of an underlying problem within the CNS. The most common cause of adult seizures in patients with a known seizure history is the failure to take anti-seizure medication. The most common cause of seizures in infants and young children is a high fever. Epilepsy is a condition of recurring seizures; the cause is usually irreversible.

- The type of seizure that involves stiffening and jerking of the patient's body is called a *tonic-clonic seizure* (formerly called a *grand mal seizure*). This type of seizure typically has four phases:
  Aura—A peculiar sensation that comes before a seizure
  Tonic phase—The body's muscles stiffen, the patient's breathing may be noisy, and the patient may turn blue
  Clonic phase—Alternating jerking and relaxation of the body occurs
  Postictal phase—The period of recovery that follows a seizure; the patient often appears limp, has shallow breathing, and has an altered mental status

- Status epilepticus is recurring seizures without an intervening period of consciousness. Status epilepticus is a medical emergency. It can cause brain damage or death if it is not treated.

- A stroke is caused by the blockage or rupture of an artery supplying the brain. There are two main forms of stroke: ischemic and hemorrhagic.

- Ischemic strokes are caused by a blood clot that decreases blood flow to the brain. Ischemic strokes can be further classified as either thrombotic or embolic. In a thrombotic stroke, a blood clot (thrombus) forms in a blood vessel of, or leading to, the brain. In an embolic stroke, a blood clot breaks up and travels through the circulatory system, where it lodges in a vessel within or leading to the brain.
- Hemorrhagic strokes (also called *cerebral hemorrhage*) are caused by bleeding into the brain. Subarachnoid hemorrhage is caused by a ruptured blood vessel in the subarachnoid space, usually a result of an aneurysm (an abnormal bulging of a blood vessel). Intracerebral hemorrhage is caused by a ruptured blood vessel within the brain itself (usually a result of chronic high blood pressure).

- A TIA is a temporary interruption of the blood supply to the brain. Signs and symptoms completely resolve within 24 hours with no permanent damage.
- The Cincinnati Prehospital Stroke Scale is a useful tool that can be used to find out if a person who has an altered mental status might be having a stroke. The scale assesses three main areas:
  1. Ask the patient to smile. Both sides of the face should move equally. If one side droops, does not move at all, or does not move as well as the other side, request ALS personnel right away or begin transport to the closest appropriate facility.
  2. Ask the patient to close his eyes and raise his arms out in front of him. Both arms should move the same or both arms should not move at all. If one arm either does not move or one arm drifts down compared with the other, request ALS personnel right away or begin transport to the closest appropriate facility.
  3. Ask the patient to say a simple sentence. The patient should be able to say the right words without slurring or forgetting or substituting words. Request ALS personnel right away or begin transport to the closest appropriate facility if the patient is unable to speak, slurs words, or uses the wrong words.

▶ Tracking Your Progress

After reading this chapter, can you:	Page Reference	Objective Met?
• Identify the patient taking diabetic medications with altered mental status and the implications of a diabetes history?	354	☐
• State the steps in the emergency medical care of the patient taking diabetic medicine with an altered mental status and a history of diabetes?	354	☐
• Establish the relationship between airway management and the patient with altered mental status?	349, 354	☐
• State the generic and trade names, medication forms, dose, administration, action, and contraindications for oral glucose?	356	☐
• Evaluate the need for medical direction in the emergency medical care of the diabetic patient?	356	☐

Multiple Choice

In the space provided, identify the letter of the choice that best completes the statement or answers each question.

_____ 1. All the cells of the body require a constant supply of fuel and oxygen for normal functioning. The basic fuel for the body is
   a. insulin.
   b. glucose.
   c. glucagon.
   d. cholesterol.

_____ 2. What role does insulin play in the delivery of sugar to the cells of the body?
   a. It helps sugar cross the cell membrane.
   b. It helps the kidneys remove excess sugar.
   c. It breaks down food into sugars that the body can use.
   d. It rids the body of the waste products produced when sugar is "burned" in the cells for energy.

_____ 3. In adults, the normal blood glucose range is from
   a. 30 to 80 mg/dL.
   b. 40 to 90 mg/dL.
   c. 70 to 120 mg/dL.
   d. 100 to 150 mg/dL.

_____ 4. A lack of glucose can cause irreversible brain damage. Therefore, any diabetic patient with an altered mental status should be considered to have
   a. hypoglycemia and should be treated with insulin therapy as per medical direction.
   b. hyperglycemia and should be treated with insulin therapy as per medical direction.
   c. hypoglycemia and should be treated with oral glucose therapy as per medical direction.
   d. hyperglycemia and should be treated with oral glucose therapy as per medical direction.

_____ 5. Which of the following scenarios would be consistent with hypoglycemia in a patient with a history of diabetes?
   a. The patient ran out of insulin three days ago.
   b. The patient has a bad stomach flu and threw up all morning.
   c. The patient cut her insulin dose in half to make it last longer.
   d. The patient had a huge breakfast, then ate some cake and ice cream.

_____ 6. The onset of hyperglycemia
   a. is rapid (minutes).
   b. is slow (hours to days).
   c. is chronic (weeks to years).
   d. follows no consistent time frame.

_____ 7. The most common diabetic emergency is
   a. bradycardia.
   b. hypoglycemia.
   c. hyperglycemia.
   d. hyperventilation.

Questions 8–11 pertain to the following scenario.

Your ambulance crew is called to an adult care facility for a 76-year-old man with an altered mental status. The healthcare worker at the facility states the patient was found supine in bed shortly after she came on duty. She has never seen this patient before and leaves the room to retrieve his medical record.

_____ 8. You should first
   a. form a general impression as you approach the patient.
   b. begin CPR.
   c. radio dispatch immediately for ALS assistance.
   d. immediately begin looking for the facility healthcare worker.

_____ 9. While examining the patient, you find that his mouth is dry and he has a faint odor, somewhat like alcohol, on his breath. His vital signs are as follows: pulse 120 beats/min (weak and regular), BP 96/64, and respirations 24/min. His skin is warm, dry, and pink. His pupils are unequal and nonreactive (apparently from past eye surgeries). He complains of nausea. There are no signs of trauma. These findings are consistent with

    a. hypoglycemia.   **c.** epileptic seizure.

    b. hyperglycemia.   **d.** status epilepticus.

_____ 10. The patient is wearing medical identification indicating he is a diabetic and has high blood pressure. You have a glucometer and determine that it is appropriate to assess this patient's blood sugar level. Which of the following sites is preferred when obtaining a blood sample for this purpose?

    a. Fingertip   **c.** Back of the calf

    b. Upper arm   **d.** Fleshy part of the hand

_____ 11. The patient's blood glucose level is 370 mg/dL. Your best course of action will be to

    a. place the patient in the recovery position, give oxygen, and transport.

    b. immobilize the patient on a long backboard, give oxygen, and transport.

    c. contact medical direction and request an order to administer oral glucose.

    d. place the patient in the recovery position, give oxygen, and then contact medical direction and request an order to administer oral glucose.

Questions 12–15 pertain to the following scenario.

Your rescue crew is called to a local grocery store for a 27-year-old man experiencing a seizure. You arrive to find the patient on the ground at the checkout counter having an active, full-body seizure.

_____ 12. Which of the following would be an appropriate action?

    a. Move objects away from the patient to prevent injury.

    b. Lie on top of the patient to control his body movements.

    c. Restrain the patient by strapping him to a long backboard.

    d. Keep your distance from the patient until the seizure stops.

_____ 13. During the seizure, the patient repeatedly strikes his head on the tile floor. After the seizure is over, which of the following is indicated?

    a. Give oral glucose.

    b. Fully immobilize the patient's spine.

    c. Begin cooling the patient's body with ice water.

    d. Place the patient in the recovery position to help clear his airway.

_____ 14. For about 2 minutes following the active seizure, this patient is slow to respond and confused. Suddenly, he begins seizing again. This condition is called

    a. a febrile seizure.   **c.** severe head trauma.

    b. status epilepticus.   **d.** a cerebrovascular accident.

_____ 15. Following the second seizure, the patient is not alert but moans when you call him by name. His vital signs are: pulse 112 beats/min, BP 118/90, and respirations 6/min with decreased tidal volume. His skin is warm, moist, and pale. To manage this patient's airway and breathing, you should

    a. insert an oral airway and deliver oxygen by nasal cannula at 10 to 15 L/min.

    b. insert an oral airway and deliver oxygen by nonrebreather mask at 15 L/min.

    c. provide continuous suctioning and give oxygen by nasal cannula at 4 to 6 L/min.

    d. insert a nasal airway and assist ventilations with a BM device connected to oxygen at 15 L/min.

Questions 16–19 pertain to the following scenario.

Your rescue crew is called to the home of a 54-year-old woman. A neighbor called 9-1-1 when he found the patient wandering around the neighborhood confused and disoriented.

_____ 16. Upon arrival, you find the patient standing on the sidewalk about two blocks from her home. She looks dazed and weak. You find no evidence of trauma. You should

    a. leave the patient in a standing position.
    b. have the patient lean against a tree if necessary.
    c. instruct the patient to walk home and lie on the couch.
    d. assist the patient to the ground or stretcher to assume the recovery position.

_____ 17. During the focused history and physical examination, you note the patient is confused, complains of weakness and hunger, and has cool, clammy skin. These finding are consistent with

    a. hypoglycemia.
    b. hyperglycemia.
    c. epilepsy.
    d. diabetic ketoacidosis.

_____ 18. During questioning, the patient informs you she is an insulin-dependent diabetic. Which of the following statements by the patient would be consistent with your findings?

    a. "I ate too much food today."
    b. "I have exercised too much today."
    c. "I have not taken my insulin in two days."
    d. "I have a history of lower back problems."

_____ 19. Insulin-dependent diabetes is another name for

    a. adult-onset diabetes.
    b. type 1 diabetes.
    c. type 2 diabetes.
    d. gestational diabetes.

Matching

Match the key terms in the left column with the definitions in the right column by placing the letter of each correct answer in the space provided.

_____ **20.** Insulin

_____ **21.** Lancet

_____ **22.** Partial seizure

_____ **23.** Aneurysm

_____ **24.** Diabetic ketoacidosis

_____ **25.** Syncope

_____ **26.** Complex partial seizure

_____ **27.** Automatisms

_____ **28.** Somatostatin

_____ **29.** Glucometer

_____ **30.** Insulin resistance

_____ **31.** Simple partial seizure

_____ **32.** Embolus

_____ **33.** Tonic-clonic seizure

_____ **34.** Near syncope

_____ **35.** Postictal phase

A. Purposeless repetitive behavior such as lip smacking, eye blinking, or chewing or swallowing movements

B. A device used to measure the amount of glucose in a blood sample

C. A clot that travels through the circulatory system

D. The period of recovery that follows a seizure

E. A type of partial seizure that involves motor or sensory symptoms with no change in mental status

F. Warning symptoms of an impending loss of consciousness

G. An abnormal bulging of a blood vessel

H. A condition in which the cells of the body fail to respond to the presence of insulin, thus not allowing glucose to enter the cells

I. A device used to prick a patient's skin to obtain a blood sample

J. A hormone released by delta cells in the pancreas that inhibits the release of insulin and glucagon

K. Formerly called a grand mal seizure

L. Severe, uncontrolled hyperglycemia

M. A brief loss of responsiveness caused by a temporary decrease in blood flow to the brain

N. A hormone released from beta cells in the pancreas that helps glucose enter the body's cells to be used for energy

O. A type of partial seizure in which the patient's consciousness, responsiveness, or memory is impaired

P. A category of seizures in which nerve cells fire abnormally in one hemisphere of the brain

Short Answer

Answer each question in the space provided.

36. List common causes of altered mental status using the memory aid A-E-I-O-U TIPPS.

37. Why is aggressive airway management critical for a patient with an altered level of consciousness?

38. What is the most common type of diabetes?

39. List the four phases of a tonic-clonic seizure.
1.
2.
3.
4.

40. List the two types of stroke and give two examples of each.
1.
2.

41. What is a seizure?

42. Is status epilepticus a medical emergency? Why or why not?

43. Explain the difference between a thrombotic stroke and an embolic stroke.

44. Explain the differences between the tonic and clonic phases of a generalized seizure.

Answer Section

Chapter 15

Multiple Choice

1. b

   Glucose is the form of sugar that the body burns for energy. Insulin is a hormone produced in the pancreas that helps move sugar into the cells. Glucagon is also a hormone produced in the pancreas. It stimulates the liver to release stored sugar. Cholesterol is a by-product of ingesting animal products.

   Objective: Describe the anatomy and function of the following major body systems: respiratory, circulatory, musculoskeletal, nervous, and endocrine.

2. a

   Sugar is a very large molecule, and without insulin, it would not be able to enter the cells of the body. Insulin helps move sugar across the cell membrane.

   Objective: Describe the anatomy and function of the following major body systems: respiratory, circulatory, musculoskeletal, nervous, and endocrine.

3. c

   The values used for a normal blood glucose level vary. Some references state the normal range is from 70 to 120 mg/dL. Others state that the normal range is from 80 to 120 mg/dL. Although both are acceptable, be aware that these norms may vary. In addition, it is important to note that when these tests are performed in a laboratory, the norms may vary by lab.

   Objective: Identify the patient taking diabetic medications with altered mental status and the implications of a diabetes history.

4. c

   Diabetic patients with an altered mental status should be considered hypoglycemic. If you give oral glucose and the patient is ultimately diagnosed as hyperglycemic rather than hypoglycemic, the extra sugar given will not adversely affect the patient. EMTs are not authorized to assist in the administration of insulin.

   Objective: Evaluate the need for medical direction in the emergency medical care of the diabetic patient.

5. b

   The blood sugar level may become too low if the diabetic patient:

   - Has taken too much insulin
   - Has not eaten enough food
   - Has overexercised and burned off sugar faster than normal
   - Experiences significant physical (such as an infection) or emotional stress

   Remember that the brain cannot store glucose. If hypoglycemia is not corrected, signs and symptoms reflecting the brain's lack of an adequate glucose supply will quickly follow. These signs and symptoms may include tiredness, irritability, visual disturbances, difficulty concentrating, confusion, combativeness, fainting, seizures, and loss of consciousness. Prolonged hypoglycemia can lead to irreversible brain damage. Taking too little insulin or eating too much would lead to the reverse disorder, hyperglycemia.

   Objective: Identify the patient taking diabetic medications with altered mental status and the implications of a diabetes history.

6. b

   While hyperglycemia may take hours or days to develop, hypoglycemia has a rapid onset. For this reason, it is important to be thorough when obtaining information pertaining to the history surrounding the patient's present illness.

Objective: Identify the patient taking diabetic medications with altered mental status and the implications of a diabetes history.

7. b

Hypoglycemia is the most common diabetic emergency.

Objective: Identify the patient taking diabetic medications with altered mental status and the implications of a diabetes history.

8. a

Your first action should be to form a general impression as you approach the patient and then perform a primary survey. At this point, you do not have enough information to know if CPR or ALS assistance is necessary.

Objective: Summarize the reasons for forming a general impression of the patient.

9. b

This patient's rapid pulse and respirations; unusual breath odor; warm, dry skin; nausea; and altered mental status are consistent with hyperglycemia. Because of the unusual odor on the breath, hyperglycemic patients may be mistaken for being under the influence of alcohol. Other signs and symptoms of hyperglycemia include loss of appetite, vomiting, and weakness.

Objective: Identify the patient taking diabetic medications with altered mental status and the implications of a diabetes history.

10. a

Use the fingertip for glucose testing. If you use a site other than the fingertip to test a patient's blood glucose level, keep in mind that alternate sites will not show changes in blood glucose levels as quickly as the fingertips.

Objective: State the steps in the emergency medical care of the patient taking diabetic medicine with an altered mental status and a history of diabetes.

11. a

Because the patient's blood sugar level is higher than normal (he is hyperglycemic), he does not require oral glucose. The patient does not require immobilization on a long backboard because he was found lying in a bed and there are no signs of trauma. Place the patient in the recovery position, give oxygen, and transport the patient for evaluation by a physician.

Objective: State the steps in the emergency medical care of the patient taking diabetic medicine with an altered mental status and a history of diabetes.

12. a

While a patient is experiencing a seizure, attempt to limit the amount of harm the patient may do to himself. Move objects out of the patient's path and put padding between the patient's head and the ground. Do not attempt to physically restrain the patient; restraining the patient may cause harm to you or the patient.

Objective: Discuss the roles and responsibilities of the EMT toward the safety of the crew, the patient, and bystanders.

13. b

This medical condition (a tonic-clonic seizure) now has a trauma element to it. Because the patient struck his head, protect his spine from further injury. Patients with an altered mental status should be placed in the recovery position only if trauma is not suspected.

Objective: State reasons for management of the cervical spine once the patient has been determined to be a trauma patient.

14. b

Status epilepticus is recurring seizures without an intervening period of consciousness. It is a medical emergency and can cause brain damage or death if it is not treated. Febrile seizures are due to a rapid rise in body temperature. Severe head trauma is also a cause of seizures. A cerebrovascular accident is another name for a stroke.

Objective: N/A

15. d

This patient is breathing well below the normal range for his age (12 to 20 breaths/min), and, with the patient's decreased tidal volume (the amount of air moved in and out of the lungs with each breath) and pale skin condition, aggressive airway support is needed. A nasal airway may be tolerated by this patient. An oral airway would not be tolerated and may induce vomiting. The patient's ventilations should be assisted with a BM device until his respiratory rate and tidal volume return to a normal range.

Objective: Establish the relationship between airway management and the patient with altered mental status.

16. d

Assist the patient to the ground or stretcher and place her in the recovery position. Do not allow a patient with an altered mental status to remain standing, walk unassisted, or sit on an object from which she may fall.

Objective: State the steps in the emergency medical care of the patient taking diabetic medicine with an altered mental status and a history of diabetes.

17. a

Early signs and symptoms of hypoglycemia (low blood sugar level) include headache, hunger, nausea, and weakness. As this condition progresses, the patient may experience tremors and tachycardia (increased heart rate), and the skin will be cool and pale. Epilepsy is a disease associated with seizures. Diabetic ketoacidosis is severe, uncontrolled hyperglycemia (usually over 300 mg/dL).

Objective: Identify the patient taking diabetic medications with altered mental status and the implications of a diabetes history.

18. b

This patient has signs and symptoms of hypoglycemia. A patient response consistent with hypoglycemia would be "I have exercised too much today." By overexerting herself, the patient burned off most of her sugar, resulting in hypoglycemia. Overeating and a failure to take prescribed insulin would lead to hyperglycemia. Lower back pain would not be a factor.

Objective: Identify the patient taking diabetic medications with altered mental status and the implications of a diabetes history.

19. b

Insulin-dependent diabetes is also called *type 1 diabetes*. Although it may occur at any age, type 1 diabetes usually begins during childhood or young adulthood. Type 2 diabetes is also called *noninsulin-dependent diabetes mellitus* or *adult-onset diabetes*. Gestational diabetes is diabetes during pregnancy.

Objective: Identify the patient taking diabetic medications with altered mental status and the implications of a diabetes history.

Matching

20.	N	**28.**	J
21.	I	**29.**	B
22.	P	**30.**	H
23.	G	**31.**	E
24.	L	**32.**	C
25.	M	**33.**	K
26.	O	**34.**	F
27.	A	**35.**	D

Short Answer

36.
- *A*lcohol, Abuse
- *E*pilepsy (seizures)
- *I*nsulin (diabetic emergency)
- *O*verdose, (lack of) oxygen (hypoxia)
- *U*remia (kidney failure)
- *T*rauma (head injury), Temperature (fever, heat- or cold-related emergency)
- *I*nfection
- *P*sychiatric conditions
- *P*oisoning (including drugs and alcohol)
- *S*hock, Stroke

Objective: N/A

37. Any patient who has an altered mental status is at risk of not being able to manage his own airway. It is critical for you to aggressively assess the need for an oral or nasal airway and to continuously monitor and reassess the patient's airway. Suction as necessary.

Objective: Establish the relationship between airway management and the patient with altered mental status.

38. Type 2 diabetes mellitus is the most common type of diabetes. It usually affects people older than 40 years of age, especially those who are overweight.

Objective: Identify the patient taking diabetic medications with altered mental status and the implications of a diabetes history.

39. A tonic-clonic seizure usually has four phases:

1. Aura
2. Tonic phase
3. Clonic phase
4. Postictal phase

Objective: N/A

40. There are two main forms of stroke: ischemic and hemorrhagic. Ischemic strokes can be further classified as either thrombotic or embolic. Subarachnoid hemorrhage and intracerebral hemorrhage are two types of hemorrhagic stroke.

Objective: N/A

41. A seizure is a temporary change in behavior or consciousness caused by abnormal electrical activity within one or more groups of brain cells. A seizure is a symptom (not a disease) of an underlying problem within the CNS.

Objective: N/A

42. Status epilepticus is recurring seizures without an intervening period of consciousness. Status epilepticus is a medical emergency because brain damage (caused by a lack of oxygen or a depletion of glucose) can occur in as little as 5 minutes of sustained seizure activity.

Objective: N/A

43. Ischemic strokes are classified as either thrombotic or embolic. In a thrombotic stroke, a blood clot (thrombus) forms in a blood vessel of, or leading to, the brain. The blood vessel may be partially or completely blocked by the blood clot.

In an embolic stroke, a blood clot breaks up and travels through the circulatory system. The blood clot is now called an *embolus*. A cerebral embolus results from blockage of a vessel within the brain by a fragment of a foreign substance originating from outside the CNS, usually the heart or a carotid artery.

Objective: N/A

44. During the tonic phase of a generalized seizure, the body's muscles stiffen. The patient's breathing may be noisy and he may turn blue. This phase usually lasts 15 to 20 seconds. During the clonic phase, alternating jerking and relaxation of the body occurs. The jerking movements during the clonic phase are often called *convulsions*. This is the longest phase of the seizure. It may last several minutes. The patient's heart rate and blood pressure are increased. His skin is usually warm, flushed, and moist. He may lose control of his bowels and bladder. Bleeding may occur if the patient bites his tongue or cheek.

Objective: N/A

16 Allergic Reactions

READING ASSIGNMENT ▶ Read Chapter 16, pages 370 to 382 in your textbook.

Sum It Up

- An allergic reaction is an exaggerated immune response to any substance. The substance that causes an allergic reaction can enter the body in four ways: ingestion, injection, inhalation, or absorption through the skin or mucous membranes. Possible causes include insect bites or stings, food, plants, and medications, among others.

- An antigen is any substance that is foreign to an individual and causes antibody production. An antibody is a substance produced by white blood cells to defend the body against bacteria, viruses, or other antigens. The antibodies attach to mast cells, which are found in connective tissue. This process, called *sensitization*, occurs with the body's first exposure to the antigen. When an antigen causes signs and symptoms of an allergic reaction, the antigen is called an *allergen*. When an allergic reaction is severe and affects multiple body systems, it is called *anaphylaxis*. Anaphylaxis is a life-threatening emergency.

- Assessment findings pertaining to the respiratory system may include tightness in the throat ("lump in the throat") or chest, coughing, rapid breathing, labored breathing, noisy breathing, hoarseness, stridor, difficulty talking, and wheezing. Assessment findings pertaining to the cardiovascular system may include an increased heart rate, lightheadedness, fainting, weakness, irregular heart rhythm, decreased blood pressure, and circulatory collapse. Assessment findings pertaining to the nervous system may include restlessness, fear, panic or a feeling of impending doom, headache, an altered mental status or unresponsiveness, and seizures. Assessment findings pertaining to the skin may include itching (pruritus), hives (urticaria), red skin (flushing), and swelling of the face, neck, hands, feet, and/or tongue. The patient may state he has a warm tingling feeling in the face, mouth, chest, feet, and hands. Assessment findings pertaining to the GI system may include nausea, vomiting, abdominal cramps/pain, an urgency to urinate, and diarrhea. Generalized findings may include itchy, watery eyes and a runny nose.

- Assessment findings that reveal shock (hypoperfusion) or respiratory distress indicate the presence of a severe allergic reaction.

- If the patient has come in contact with a substance that caused past allergic reaction and complains of respiratory distress or shows signs and symptoms of shock, form a general impression, perform a primary survey, and perform a focused history and physical exam. Assess the patient's baseline vital signs and SAMPLE history. Give oxygen if not already done. Find out if the patient has a prescribed epinephrine auto-injector available. With approval from medical direction, help the patient with administration of the epinephrine auto-injector. Reassess in 2 minutes. Record reassessment findings. If the patient does not have an epinephrine auto-injector available, transport immediately.

- If the patient has contact with a substance that causes an allergic reaction without signs of respiratory distress or shock, continue with a focused assessment. A patient who is not wheezing or without signs of respiratory compromise or hypotension should not receive epinephrine.

- A patient experiencing an allergic reaction may initially present with airway/respiratory compromise, or airway/respiratory compromise may develop as the allergic reaction progresses.

- If the patient's condition improves, provide supportive care. Continue to give oxygen and treat for shock. If the patient's condition worsens, contact medical direction for orders to give an additional dose of epinephrine, if available. Signs that indicate the patient's condition is worsening include decreasing mental status, increasing breathing difficulty, and decreasing blood pressure. Treat for shock. Be prepared to begin CPR and use the AED, if necessary.

▶ Tracking Your Progress

After reading this chapter, can you:	Page Reference	Objective Met?
• Recognize the patient experiencing an allergic reaction?	374	☐
• Describe the emergency medical care of the patient with an allergic reaction?	377	☐
• Establish the relationship between the patient with an allergic reaction and, airway management?	375	☐
• Describe the mechanisms of allergic response and the implications for airway management?	377	☐
• State the generic and trade names, medication forms, dose, administration, action, and contraindications for the epinephrine auto-injector?	378	☐
• Evaluate the need for medical direction in the emergency medical care of the patient with an allergic reaction?	377	☐
• Differentiate between the general category of those patients having an allergic reaction and those patients having an allergic reaction and requiring immediate medical care, including immediate use of epinephrine auto-injector?	377	☐

Multiple Choice

In the space provided, identify the letter of the choice that best completes the statement or answers each question.

_____ 1. Any substance that is foreign to an individual and causes antibody production is known as an
   a. antigen.
   b. antibody.
   c. allergen.
   d. antihistamine.

_____ 2. Which of the following are considered signs or symptoms of a moderate or severe allergic reaction?
   a. Anxiety, runny nose
   b. Stridor, wheezing
   c. Rash, itching
   d. Coughing, tingling of the hands and/or feet

_____ 3. Which of the following foods have a high association with latex allergy?
   a. Hazelnut and mango
   b. Fig and walnut
   c. Kiwi and papaya
   d. Avocado and banana

_____ 4. What is the appropriate site for administration of the epinephrine auto-injector?
   a. The back of the hand
   b. Under the tongue (sublingual)
   c. The center of a buttock
   d. The lateral aspect of the mid-thigh

_____ 5. When administering an epinephrine auto-injector, it is important to
   a. hold the applicator at a 45- to 60-degree angle to the skin.
   b. hold the injector in place until all the medication has been delivered.
   c. remove the injector from the skin immediately after the needle springs forward.
   d. make the needle spring forward before applying the device to the patient's skin.

_____ 6. The generic name for the drug administered by an epinephrine auto-injector is epinephrine. A trade name for this drug is
   a. Albuterol.
   b. Adrenalin.
   c. Bronkosol.
   d. Solu-Medrol.

_____ 7. Which of the following regarding the use of an epinephrine auto-injector for an infant or child is correct?
   a. An epinephrine auto-injector should not be used on patients younger than 12 years of age.
   b. Epinephrine auto-injectors are prescribed for children, but generally at one-half the adult dose.
   c. Children do not have severe allergic reactions and would derive no benefit from epinephrine auto-injector administration.
   d. An epinephrine auto-injector can be used, but administration of the medication is at a different site than for adult patients.

Questions 8–13 pertain to the following scenario.

Your ambulance crew is called to the scene of a one-car vehicle collision. You arrive at the scene to find a pick-up truck has hit a tree. There is only one occupant in the vehicle, and his seat belt is still on. The damage to the vehicle is minimal. Your scene size-up indicates that the patient's car is not leaking any fluids, and there do not appear to be any hazards other than oncoming traffic. Local law enforcement has diverted traffic away from the scene. You are wearing a reflective traffic vest and appropriate PPE.

_____ 8. Following the scene size-up, you should immediately
  a. remove the patient from the vehicle.
  b. form a general impression and begin the primary survey.
  c. attempt to pry the vehicle away from the tree.
  d. provide supplemental oxygen by nonrebreather mask at 15 L/min.

_____ 9. The patient is unconscious. His respiratory rate is 30 breaths/min. His pulse rate is 96 beats/min with moderate strength at the radial artery. Which of the following signs would lead you to believe that this patient may be experiencing an anaphylactic reaction?
  a. The patient's abdomen is rigid to palpation.
  b. The patient's face is swollen and blotchy red.
  c. The patient's blood pressure is 150/84 and rising.
  d. The patient's pupils are unequal and do not react to light.

_____ 10. During the rapid head-to-toe physical exam, you find the patient has a stinger embedded in his neck. The area around the sting is swollen and white and is surrounded by a red, rash-like appearance. The patient is wearing a bracelet that indicates he is allergic to bee stings. While the police are attempting to gather information about the patient, they find several epinephrine auto-injectors in the vehicle's glove compartment. Use of an epinephrine auto-injector
  a. is contraindicated because the patient is unconscious.
  b. is contraindicated because the patient has suffered trauma.
  c. is appropriate if authorization is given by medical direction.
  d. is appropriate regardless of authorization from medical direction because this patient is near death.

_____ 11. Assuming you administer the epinephrine auto-injector, which of the following is true regarding the administration of subsequent (additional) epinephrine auto-injectors?
  a. Only one dose may be given.
  b. Subsequent administrations may be given if approved by medical direction.
  c. Subsequent administrations may be given only if the patient stops breathing.
  d. A second dose may be given without consulting medical direction, if medical direction authorized the first dose.

_____ 12. If the patient's breathing is adequate, which of the following regarding airway and breathing support for this patient is correct?
  a. The patient's airway should be maintained with an OPA and oxygen should be given by nonrebreather mask at 15 L/min.
  b. The patient's airway should be maintained with the head tilt–chin lift maneuver. Oxygen therapy should be delivered by nonrebreather mask at 15 L/min.
  c. The patient's airway should be maintained with the head tilt–chin lift maneuver and an oral airway. Oxygen should be delivered by nasal cannula at 4 to 6 L/min.
  d. The patient's airway should be maintained with a jaw thrust without head tilt maneuver and an oral airway. Oxygen should be administered by nonrebreather mask at 15 L/min.

_____ 13. While en route to the hospital, you reassess the patient and find that he is breathing at a rate of 40 breaths/min with a greatly decreased tidal volume. He is also becoming increasingly cyanotic, and his pulse is now 150 beats/min at the brachial artery (you cannot feel the radial pulse). Which of the following would be an appropriate intervention?
  a. Begin CPR.
  b. Increase the oxygen flow to 20 L/min by nonrebreather mask.
  c. Begin assisting the patient's ventilations with a BM device and supplemental oxygen at a rate of 1 breath every 3 seconds.
  d. Begin assisting the patient's ventilations with a BM device and supplemental oxygen at a rate of 1 breath every 5 to 6 seconds.

Matching

Match the key terms in the left column with the definitions in the right column by placing the letter of each correct answer in the space provided.

_____ 14. Pruritus

_____ 15. Anaphylaxis

_____ 16. Sensitization

_____ 17. Allergen

_____ 18. Antibody

_____ 19. Urticaria

_____ 20. Allergic reaction

_____ 21. Antigen

A. Hives

B. Any substance that is foreign to an individual and causes antibody production

C. An exaggerated response by the body's immune system to a substance

D. An antigen that causes signs and symptoms of an allergic reaction

E. A severe allergic reaction; a life-threatening emergency

F. A substance produced by white blood cells to defend the body against bacteria, viruses, or other antigens

G. Itching

H. The production of antibodies in response to the body's first exposure to an antigen

Short Answer

Answer each question in the space provided.

22. Explain the difference between an antigen and an antibody.

23. The substance that causes an allergic reaction can enter the body in four ways. List the four routes of entry.

1.

2.

3.

4.

24. Explain the actions of epinephrine that are beneficial for a patient experiencing a moderate-to-severe allergic reaction.

Answer Section

Chapter 16

Multiple Choice

1. a

An antigen is any substance that is foreign to an individual and causes antibody production. When the body's immune system detects an antigen, white blood cells respond by producing antibodies specific to that antigen. An antibody is a substance produced by white blood cells to defend the body against bacteria, viruses, or other antigens. When an antigen causes signs and symptoms of an allergic reaction, the antigen is called an *allergen*. An antihistamine is a substance (such as Benadryl) that is used to counteract the effects of histamine in the body and treat allergic reactions.

Objective: N/A

2. b

Hoarseness, difficulty swallowing or talking, stridor, difficulty breathing, coughing, and wheezing are all examples of moderate-to-severe allergic reaction signs and symptoms.

Objective: Differentiate between the general category of those patients having an allergic reaction and those patients having an allergic reaction and requiring immediate medical care, including immediate use of an epinephrine auto-injector.

3. d

Association with Latex Allergy	Food
High	Banana, avocado, chestnut
Moderate	Apple, celery, kiwi, papaya, potato, tomato
Low or uncertain	Cherry, fig, hazelnut, mango, nectarine, peach, peanut, pear, pineapple, walnut

Objective: N/A

4. d

Epinephrine is injected into the large muscle of the thigh. The correct placement of the auto-injector is the lateral (outside) aspect of the thigh, midway between the waist and the knee.

Objective: State the generic and trade names, medication forms, dose, administration, action, and contraindications for the epinephrine auto-injector.

5. b

When the auto-injector is pressed flush against the skin, the spring-loaded needle is released to pierce the skin. The medication is then injected. You must keep the device flush with the skin until all of the medication is delivered. If the needle is not flush (at a 90-degree angle) with the skin, the medication may not be delivered deeply enough for proper absorption. Do not release the spring-loaded needle before applying the device to the skin. These devices are designed for use by nonmedical personnel and should be complete with instructions. When in doubt, read the instructions and consult medical direction.

Objective: State the generic and trade names, medication forms, dose, administration, action, and contraindications for the epinephrine auto-injector.

6. b

Adrenalin is a trade name for epinephrine. Albuterol (generic name) and Bronkosol (trade name) are metered dose bronchodilators. Solu-Medrol is a trade name for a steroid medication that may be given to the patient by ALS or hospital personnel. Solu-Medrol helps to decrease inflammation and can be useful in treating patients with allergic reactions.

Objective: State the generic and trade names, medication forms, dose, administration, action, and contraindications for the epinephrine auto-injector.

7. b

Children are susceptible to anaphylactic reactions just like adults. The dose of the injector is generally one-half the adult dose.

Objective: State the generic and trade names, medication forms, dose, administration, action, and contraindications for the epinephrine auto-injector.

8. b

The scene size-up indicates the patient is in no danger in his current position; therefore, you should turn your attention to forming a general impression and then performing a primary survey to determine the presence of any life-threatening conditions. Freeing the vehicle from the tree does not appear to be at all necessary and may only result in disturbing the patient's spinal alignment. Any such actions should be carried out only by properly trained personnel when access to the patient is denied because of obstruction. The method of maintaining the patient's airway and delivering oxygen should be decided upon after evaluating the MOI, the patient's presentation, status, and past medical history.

Objective: Explain the value of performing an initial assessment.

9. b

Red, swollen skin with hives suggests an allergic reaction. A rigid abdomen should lead you to suspect that the patient has damaged an abdominal organ and may be bleeding internally. Generally, in anaphylactic reactions, the patient's blood pressure will decrease. An increasing blood pressure in a trauma patient may indicate closed head trauma. Deviation from a normal pupil response may also suggest closed head injury.

Objective: Recognize the patient experiencing an allergic reaction.

10. c

As with all medications that EMTs are trained to assist in administering, specific criteria must be met before administration of the drug. First, the patient must be showing the signs and symptoms associated with the indication for giving the medication. Second, the patient must have been prescribed the medication or the EMT is authorized to carry and administer the drug.

Finally, the EMT must have specific authorization from medical direction to administer the medication (either on-line or off-line medical direction).

Objective: Differentiate between the general category of those patients having an allergic reaction and those patients having an allergic reaction and requiring immediate medical care, including immediate use of epinephrine auto-injector.

11. b

In severe allergic reactions, more than one dose of epinephrine may be necessary to resolve the patient's signs and symptoms. If several epinephrine auto-injectors are available, when you consult with medical direction for permission to use the device, you may ask about the possibility and time frame for repeat doses. Asking up front may save you time if the patient fails to improve after the first dose and subsequent doses are needed.

Objective: State the generic and trade names, medication forms, dose, administration, action, and contraindications for the epinephrine auto-injector.

12. d

You are dealing with a patient with two main problems. First, he has been involved in a vehicle collision, and second, he is possibly having a severe allergic reaction. Both problems must be addressed. Opening and maintaining the patient's airway must be accomplished with the jaw thrust without head tilt maneuver, and the patient's spine must be fully immobilized. If the patient has no gag reflex, either an oral or nasal airway may be used. However, if the patient is semi-responsive, a nasal airway may be tolerated whereas an oral airway will not be tolerated. High-flow oxygen should be administered by nonrebreather mask because the patient's breathing is adequate but his condition is unstable.

Objective: Relate mechanism of injury to opening the airway.

13. d

The patient's breathing is now inadequate as evidenced by the increased respiratory rate (twice the normal adult rate of 12 to 20 breaths/min), increased cyanosis, and decreased peripheral perfusion (lack of a radial pulse). Assisting ventilations in an apneic adult is accomplished at a rate of 1 breath every 5 to 6 seconds (10 to 12 breaths/min) with high-flow oxygen connected to the BM device. CPR should be started for a nonbreathing patient with no palpable pulse. This patient has a brachial (upper arm) pulse.

Objective: Describe the steps in performing the skill of artificially ventilating a patient with a BVM device while using the jaw thrust without head tilt maneuver.

Matching

14.	G	**18.**	F
15.	E	**19.**	A
16.	H	**20.**	C
17.	D	**21.**	B

Short Answer

22. An antigen is any substance that is foreign to an individual and causes antibody production. When the body's immune system detects an antigen, white blood cells respond by producing antibodies specific to that antigen. An antibody is a substance produced by white blood cells to defend the body against bacteria, viruses, or other antigens.

Objective: N/A

23. The substance that causes an allergic reaction can enter the body in four ways:

1. Ingestion
2. Injection
3. Inhalation
4. Absorption through the skin or mucous membranes

Objective: N/A

24. Epinephrine works by relaxing the bronchial passages of the airway and constricting the blood vessels. The opening of the airway allows the patient to move more air into and out of the lungs, which will increase the amount of oxygen in the bloodstream. Constriction of the blood vessels slows the leakage of fluid from the blood vessels into the space around the cells of the body.

Objective: State the generic and trade names, medication forms, dose, administration, action, and contraindications for the epinephrine auto-injector.

17 Poisoning and Overdose

READING ASSIGNMENT ▶ Read Chapter 17, pages 383 to 398 in your textbook.

Sum It Up

- A poison is any substance taken into the body that interferes with normal body function. Poisoning is exposure to a substance that is harmful in any dosage. A toxin is a poisonous substance. An antidote is a substance that neutralizes a poison.

- A PCC is a medical facility that provides free telephone advice to the public and medical professionals in case of exposure to poisonous substances. Medical professionals at a PCC can help determine the toxicity of a substance and give advice about the emergency care the patient should receive.

- A poison may be a solid, liquid, spray, or gas. Toxins enter the body in four ways: ingestion, inhalation, injection, or absorption. Exposure to a toxin may be accidental or intentional.

- Signs and symptoms of a toxic exposure can vary depending on the substance involved; route of entry; the amount ingested, inhaled, injected, or absorbed; and the length of the exposure.

- Signs, symptoms, and characteristics that often occur together in toxic exposures are called *toxidromes*. When the cause of a toxic exposure is unknown, knowing the "typical" signs and symptoms of certain toxic exposures can help you to identify the poison and give appropriate care. Toxic exposures that involve more than one substance (such as alcohol and recreational drugs) are often difficult to recognize and treat. In these situations, the patient will most likely not have signs and symptoms specific to only one toxidrome.

- A thorough scene size-up on arrival at the scene of a toxic exposure is essential. Resist the temptation to immediately enter the scene and begin patient care. Without some knowledge of the substance involved, you could place yourself and your crew at an unnecessary risk for exposure. Assess the situation for potential or actual danger. Contact dispatch for additional resources as necessary.

- Finding out as much information as you can about the circumstances surrounding a toxic exposure is important. In cases involving an intentional exposure, keep in mind that the history obtained from the patient may or may not be reliable. Relay all information you obtained when transferring care to ALS personnel or the staff at the receiving facility.

• When caring for a patient exposed to a toxin, try to find out (and document) the exact name of the substance. If applicable, bring all containers, bottles, labels, and other evidence of poison agents to the receiving facility.

▶ Tracking Your Progress

After reading this chapter, can you:	Page Reference	Objective Met?
• List various ways that poisons enter the body?	384	☐
• List signs and symptoms associated with poisoning?	391	☐
• Discuss the emergency medical care for the patient with possible overdose?	389	☐
• Describe the steps in the emergency medical care for the patient with suspected poisoning?	389	☐
• Establish the relationship between the patient suffering from poisoning or overdose and airway management?	389	☐
• State the generic and trade names, indications, contraindications, medication form, dose, administration, actions, side effects, and reassessment strategies for activated charcoal?	393	☐
• Recognize the need for medical direction in caring for the patient with poisoning or overdose?	391	☐

Multiple Choice

In the space provided, identify the letter of the choice that best completes the statement or answers each question.

_____ 1. Alcohol withdrawal syndrome occurs after a decline in or cessation of alcohol consumption. The signs and symptoms associated with this syndrome include tremors, anxiety, GI distress, hallucinations, disorientation, and seizures. These signs and symptoms generally appear within ___ after the last ingestion of alcohol.

    a. 30 to 60 minutes   **c.** 6 to 48 hours
    b. 1 to 2 hours   **d.** 1 to 2 weeks

_____ 2. The most serious potential side effect from the ingestion of large quantities of alcohol is

    a. death.   **c.** impaired judgment.
    b. loss of brain cells.   **d.** damage to the liver.

_____ 3. Your rescue crew is called to the scene of a 2-year-old female patient who has ingested about 5 to 10 "heart pills" prescribed for her grandfather. After determining that the patient meets the appropriate criteria and obtaining permission from medical direction, you prepare to administer activated charcoal. Which of the following would be the best way to get this patient to take this medication?

    a. Mix the medication with chocolate milk or ice cream.
    b. Shake it vigorously, put it in an opaque container with a lid, and have the patient drink it through a straw.
    c. Do not shake the medication and have the patient drink the more liquefied solution at the top of the bottle.
    d. Pour the entire solution into a clear glass, mix with chocolate milk, and have the patient drink the solution with a straw.

4. Which of the following are common side effects of activated charcoal ingestion?

a. Difficulty breathing and chest pain
b. Abdominal cramping and constipation
c. Unconsciousness and rapid pulse rate
d. Altered mental status and difficulty breathing

5. Activated charcoal may assist in limiting the effects of ingested poisons by

a. adsorbing the poison.
b. neutralizing the poison.
c. causing the patient to throw up (vomit) the poison.
d. lining the stomach, thus not allowing the poison to be absorbed.

6. Which of the following is true regarding medical direction and activated charcoal?

a. Activated charcoal can be given without approval from medical direction because it is "charcoal."
b. Authorization must be given by medical direction for the administration of activated charcoal.
c. Activated charcoal can be given only if the patient has already been prescribed activated charcoal, has a bottle(s) of activated charcoal, and medical direction approval has been obtained.
d. Activated charcoal can be given before approval by medical direction, but the physician must be contacted after administration.

7. The correct dose of activated charcoal is

a. 1 g of activated charcoal per kilogram of body weight.
b. 1 g of activated charcoal per pound of body weight.
c. 1 g of activated charcoal per 10 pounds of body weight.
d. 25 g of activated charcoal per pound of body weight.

8. Which of the following patients would *not* be a candidate for activated charcoal administration?

a. A patient who has ingested "rock" cocaine and is complaining of chest pain.
b. A patient who has ingested an overdose of Valium and is unconscious.
c. A patient who has ingested approximately 150 Tylenol and has no complaint of illness or injury.
d. A patient who has ingested an overdose of aspirin combined with alcohol and is complaining of cramping.

Questions 9–15 pertain to the following scenario.

Your rescue crew responds for an "unknown" medical problem at a local apartment complex. Your scene size-up reveals a woman found lying in bed. There are pill and alcohol bottles on the nightstand. There do not appear to be any weapons in the immediate area.

9. Before making contact with this patient you should

a. look for a suicide note.
b. inspect the labels of the pill bottles.
c. check the fluid level in the alcohol bottles.
d. ensure that BSI precautions have been taken.

10. Which of the following should be performed first?

a. SAMPLE history
b. Primary survey
c. Baseline vital signs
d. Head-to-toe physical examination

11. The patient is conscious and crying. She will not answer any of your questions but appears to be alert. While assessing her airway, you note there are pill fragments in her mouth. You should

a. instruct the patient to spit out all the fragments.
b. give the patient a glass of water to wash down the fragments.
c. probe the patient's mouth with your finger to get all the fragments.
d. leave the fragments in place for further examination at the receiving facility.

_____ 12. You are successful in gaining the patient's trust, and she ultimately confides in you that she has ingested an unknown amount of the pills on the nightstand. Administration of which of the following (trade name) medications may be appropriate for this patient's condition?

  a. Alupent
  b. LiquiChar
  c. Adrenalin
  d. Bronkosol

_____ 13. To administer the correct dose of this medication, you must determine the

  a. patient's weight.
  b. number of pills ingested.
  c. presence of alcohol in the patient's stomach.
  d. patient's past medical history, including past suicide attempts.

_____ 14. You are preparing to transport this patient. What should you do with the pill bottles?

  a. Bring them in a bag to the hospital for further examination.
  b. Throw them away in an approved biohazard waste container.
  c. Leave them where found for a subsequent police investigation.
  d. Leave them on the nightstand but write down the names of the medications for further examination at the hospital.

_____ 15. Which of the following is true about the presence of alcohol at this scene?

  a. It is not important because alcohol is a legal substance.
  b. It is important only if the patient is under legal drinking age.
  c. It is only important if the substance is distilled spirits rather than beer or wine.
  d. It is important because alcohol may enhance, hasten, or otherwise change the nature of the drug overdose.

Questions 16–18 pertain to the following scenario.

Your ambulance is called to a local park for a 24-year-old man with an altered mental status. You arrive to find your patient standing on a park bench yelling gibberish and laughing hysterically. His face is flushed and red. As you approach, he begins crying uncontrollably. He attempts to get away from you by digging a hole in the cement.

_____ 16. Which of the following substances would most commonly be associated with this reaction?

  a. Alcohol   c. Hallucinogens
  b. Barbiturates   d. Benzodiazepines

_____ 17. When treating this patient, you should anticipate what type of behavior?

  a. Joyful and funny
  b. Slow to respond and sleepy
  c. Calm and thoughtful
  d. Disruptive, possibly violent, and dangerous

_____ 18. Your physical examination of this patient fails to reveal any findings other than his altered mental status. If physically possible, this patient should be transported in what position?

  a. Fully immobilized and restrained if appropriate (according to local protocol and patient's signs and symptoms)
  b. Recovery position (lateral recumbent) and restrained if appropriate (according to local protocol and patient's signs and symptoms)
  c. Prone with a backboard secured over the patient to prevent any patient movement
  d. Supine between two secured backboards (one on top and one on the bottom) to prevent any patient movement

Matching

Match the key terms in the left column with the definitions in the right column by placing the letter of each correct answer in the space provided.

_____ 19. Toxin

_____ 20. Poisoning

_____ 21. Substance abuse

_____ 22. Poison Control Center

_____ 23. Withdrawal

_____ 24. Sudden sniffing death syndrome

_____ 25. Antidote

_____ 26. Addiction

_____ 27. Overdose

_____ 28. Toxidrome

_____ 29. Substance misuse

_____ 30. Poison

_____ 31. Delirium tremens

_____ 32. Tolerance

_____ 33. Alcohol withdrawal syndrome

_____ 34. Inhalants

A. Any substance taken into the body that interferes with normal body function

B. An intentional or unintentional overmedication or ingestion of a toxic substance

C. Signs, symptoms, and characteristics that often occur together in toxic exposures

D. The self-administration of a substance for unintended purposes, or for appropriate purposes but in improper amounts or doses, or without a prescription for the person receiving the medication

E. Exposure to a substance that is harmful in any dosage

F. A series of signs and symptoms that occur 6 to 48 hours after a chronic alcoholic reduces his or her intake or stops consuming alcohol

G. Requiring progressively larger doses of a drug to achieve the desired effect

H. A psychological and physical dependence on a substance that has gone beyond voluntary control

I. Household and commercial products that can be abused by intentionally breathing the product's gas or vapors for its mind-altering effects

J. A poisonous substance

K. The deliberate, persistent, and excessive self-administration of a substance in a way that is not medically or socially approved

L. A substance that neutralizes a poison

M. Signs and symptoms associated with alcohol withdrawal that have progressed beyond the usual symptoms of withdrawal and are potentially fatal

N. A medical facility that provides free telephone advice to the public and medical professionals in case of exposure to poisonous substances

O. A condition that can occur when a person sniffs highly concentrated amounts of the chemicals in solvents or aerosol sprays

P. The condition produced when an individual stops using or abusing a drug to which he is physically or psychologically addicted

Short Answer

Answer each question in the space provided.

35. List five signs or symptoms of alcohol withdrawal syndrome.

1.
2.
3.
4.
5.

36. List three examples of medical conditions that can mimic signs and symptoms of alcohol misuse or abuse.

1.
2.
3.

37. What is sudden sniffing death syndrome?

38. List five examples of narcotics.

1.
2.
3.
4.
5.

39. What are "designer drugs"? Why is it important to be aware of these substances?

40. List five common signs or symptoms of poisoning.

1.
2.
3.
4.
5.

Answer Section

Chapter 17

Multiple Choice

1. c

Typically, the signs and symptoms associated with alcohol withdrawal syndrome will occur within 6 to 48 hours after the last ingestion of alcohol. The onset of these symptoms does not necessarily mean that the all the alcohol has left the patient's body. Rather, it means that the blood alcohol level has fallen below the patient's physical dependency level. In other words, a patient may begin to exhibit the signs and symptoms of withdrawal while still legally intoxicated. These patients should be considered unstable, and ALS care should be requested immediately.

Objective: Establish the relationship between the patient suffering from poisoning or overdose and airway management.

2. a

Alcohol is a poison. In large amounts, the concentration of this poison can be potentially fatal. The root word of the term *intoxicated* is "toxin." A toxin is a poisonous substance. Chronic alcohol use may also contribute to or worsen conditions (such as diabetes, liver disease).

Objective: List signs and symptoms associated with poisoning.

3. b

Activated charcoal is a thick, chalky, black substance. It is generally tasteless, but its appearance is less than appetizing. The best method to administer the medication is to shake it vigorously (because the charcoal tends to settle rapidly), keep it in its container (they are generally white and not transparent), and have the patient drink it with a straw. Mixing the charcoal with milk products reduces its effectiveness.

Objective: State the generic and trade names, indications, contraindications, medication form, dose, administration, actions, side effects, and reassessment strategies for activated charcoal.

4. b

Common side effects of activated charcoal administration are constipation, black stools, abdominal cramping, and possibly vomiting. Because activated charcoal is not absorbed into the bloodstream, any other complications should be attributed to the poison or the patient's underlying medical history.

Objective: State the generic and trade names, indications, contraindications, medication form, dose, administration, actions, side effects, and reassessment strategies for activated charcoal.

5. a

Activated charcoal is a very porous substance. It acts by adsorbing and binding to the ingested poison. The charcoal then moves through the GI tract without being absorbed. The poison and charcoal are then eliminated as a bowel movement.

Objective: State the generic and trade names, indications, contraindications, medication form, dose, administration, actions, side effects, and reassessment strategies for activated charcoal.

6. b

The criteria for administration of activated charcoal are the same as for other EMT-assisted medications: the patient must be showing signs and symptoms of the illness for which the medication is indicated (in this case, an ingested poison), and medical direction authority must be given (either on line or off line). Activated charcoal is a medication that EMTs may supply for the patient (oral glucose and oxygen are examples of others). MDIs, NTG, and (in some EMS systems) epinephrine auto-injectors must be prescribed for the specific patient.

Objective: Recognize the need for medical direction in caring for the patient with poisoning or overdose.

7. a

Activated charcoal is given in doses according to the patient's body weight. The exact dose is 1 g of activated charcoal per kilogram of the patient's body weight. To calculate the patient's weight in kg, divide the patient's weight in pounds by 2.2. For example, a 200-pound patient weighs 90.9 kg and would receive 91 g of activated charcoal. When obtaining authorization to administer the medication from medical direction, request a dose from the physician (be prepared to give the patient's weight).

Objective: State the generic and trade names, indications, contraindications, medication form, dose, administration, actions, side effects, and reassessment strategies for activated charcoal.

8. b

Because activated charcoal is given orally and must be swallowed by the patient, its use is limited to patients with an intact gag reflex and alert mental status. Its effectiveness is limited or absent in patients who have ingested acids, alkalis, iron products, arsenic, or lithium.

Objective: State the generic and trade names, indications, contraindications, medication form, dose, administration, actions, side effects, and reassessment strategies for activated charcoal.

9. d

After a rapid scene size-up, you need to turn your attention to assessing the patient. There will be adequate time later to gather specific information about the medications and the alcohol; they are potentially important "pieces of the puzzle." The most important piece is your patient's condition. You cannot (should not) address the patient's condition before taking proper BSI precautions.

Objective: Determine if the scene is safe to enter.

10. b

Performing a primary survey to assess the patient's mental status, airway, breathing, circulation status, and potentially life-threatening conditions must take precedence over any other activity. If the patient is conscious, a focused history and physical exam should follow the primary survey. If the patient is unconscious, a

rapid head-to-toe physical examination should follow.

Objective: Explain the value of performing an initial assessment.

11. a

Do not stick your fingers in the mouth of a conscious patient with a possible altered mental status. The patient may follow your instructions and spit the pill fragments out. If not, you may attempt to remove the fragments with a suction catheter or other appropriate device. Do not have the patient wash the fragments down or leave the fragments in the patient's mouth. Swallowing the fragments may further complicate the incident and the patient's outcome. If the fragments are left in the patient's mouth, they will dissolve in the mouth and be ingested.

Objective: Establish the relationship between the patient suffering from poisoning or overdose and airway management.

12. b

LiquiChar is a trade name for a type of activated charcoal. Activated charcoal is indicated for ingestion poisonings. Alupent and Bronkosol are trade names for bronchodilator medications, and Adrenalin is a trade name of epinephrine (given for severe allergic reactions).

Objective: State the generic and trade names, indications, contraindications, medication form, dose, administration, actions, side effects, and reassessment strategies for activated charcoal.

13. a

Activated charcoal is given according to patient body weight. The number of pills ingested, the presence of alcohol, and the patient's past medical history are all important; however, these factors do not typically change the dose of the medication.

Objective: State the generic and trade names, indications, contraindications, medication form, dose, administration, actions, side effects, and reassessment strategies for activated charcoal.

14. a

Whenever possible, bring the medication bottles to the hospital. The name of the medication is important but is only one part of the total picture. Bringing the bottles allows the hospital the opportunity to compare the date of purchase of the medication to the daily dose prescribed and the amount of medications in the bottle. This comparison allows the facility to better appreciate the total ingestion dose. The pill bottle labels may also contain other information valuable to the receiving facility staff.

Objective: Discuss the emergency medical care for the patient with possible overdose.

15. d

Alcohol is a "drug" and a "toxin" (a poisonous substance). Alcohol may affect the reaction to the pill overdose. This information is important and should be passed on to the receiving facility.

Objective: Discuss the emergency medical care for the patient with possible overdose.

16. c

Whereas alcohol can cause erratic behavior, the presence of the irrational behavior and quick mood swings are suggestive of hallucinogens. The other choices (alcohol, barbiturates, and benzodiazepines) are depressants and are not typically associated with the behavior described in this scenario.

Objective: List signs and symptoms associated with poisoning.

17. d

Use extreme caution when handling this patient. He may go from being calm to violent very quickly. Make sure that local law enforcement personnel are available to help you control this patient.

Objective: List signs and symptoms associated with poisoning.

18. b

The ideal position would be the recovery position because no factors are present that indicate the need for spinal immobilization. Do *not* "sandwich" the patient between backboards or between a backboard and the stretcher. Continuous assessments and treatment are hampered by this unnecessary and unprofessional technique of controlling the patient. Patients placed in these positions have died from unwitnessed aspiration of vomitus. Contact medical direction and follow local protocol if restraints are necessary to protect you and the patient from harm.

Objective: Demonstrate various techniques to safely restrain a patient with a behavioral problem.

Matching

19.	J	27.	B
20.	E	28.	C
21.	K	29.	D
22.	N	30.	A
23.	P	31.	M
24.	O	32.	G
25.	L	33.	F
26.	H	34.	I

Short Answer

35. Alcohol withdrawal syndrome occurs 6 to 48 hours after a chronic alcoholic reduces or stops his alcohol consumption. Signs and symptoms of alcohol withdrawal include tremors ("the shakes"), anxiety, irritability, inability to sleep, sweating, nausea, and vomiting.

Objective: N/A

36. Signs and symptoms of alcohol misuse or abuse can mimic those of other medical conditions (such as a diabetic emergency, head injury, epilepsy, drug reaction, or CNS infection).

Objective: List signs and symptoms associated with poisoning.

37. According to the NIDA, sudden sniffing death syndrome can occur when a person sniffs highly concentrated amounts of the chemicals in solvents or aerosol sprays. Death occurs within minutes because of heart failure. This syndrome is particularly associated with the abuse of butane, propane, and chemicals in aerosols.

Objective: N/A

38. Narcotic examples:
- Morphine
- Fentanyl (Sublimaze)
- Codeine
- Paregoric
- Diphenoxylate (Lomotil)
- Hydrocodone (Codone)
- Acetaminophen and hydrocodone (Vicodin)
- Hydromorphone (Dilaudid)
- Meperidine (Demerol)
- Methadone (Dolophine)
- Acetaminophen and oxycodone (Percocet)
- Aspirin and oxycodone (Percodan)

- Propoxyphene (Darvon)
- Butorphanol (Stadol)
- Nalbuphine (Nubain)
- Pentazocine (Talwin)

Objective: List signs and symptoms associated with poisoning.

39. Designer drugs are variations of federally controlled substances that have high abuse potential (such as narcotics and amphetamines). These drugs are produced by persons ranging from amateurs to highly skilled chemists (called *cookers*) and sold on the street. Designer drugs can be injected, smoked, snorted, or ingested. Signs and symptoms of designer drug misuse and abuse are unpredictable and depend on the drug that is being chemically altered. Because designer drugs are often much stronger than the original form of the drug, overdose occurs frequently.

Objective: Discuss the emergency medical care for the patient with possible overdose.

40. Common signs and symptoms of poisoning:

- Altered mental status
- Difficulty breathing
- Headache
- Nausea
- Vomiting
- Diarrhea
- Chest or abdominal pain
- Sweating
- Seizures
- Burns around the mouth
- Burns on the skin

Objective: List signs and symptoms associated with poisoning.

18 Environmental Emergencies

READING ASSIGNMENT ▶ Read Chapter 18, pages 399 to 428 in your textbook.

Sum It Up

- The skin plays a very important role in temperature regulation. Cold and warmth sensors (receptors) in the skin detect changes in temperature. These receptors relay the information to the hypothalamus. The hypothalamus (located in the brain) functions as the body's thermostat. It coordinates the body's response to temperature.

- The body loses heat to the environment in five ways:
  1. Radiation
     —Radiation is the transfer of heat from the surface of one object to the surface of another without contact between the two objects. When the temperature of the body is more than the temperature of the surroundings, the body will lose heat.
  2. Convection
     —Convection is the transfer of heat by the movement of air current. Wind speed affects heat loss by convection (wind-chill factor).
  3. Conduction
     —Conduction is the transfer of heat between objects that are in direct contact. Heat flows from warmer areas to cooler ones.
  4. Evaporation
     —Evaporation is a loss of heat by vaporization of moisture on the body surface. The body will lose heat by evaporation if the skin temperature is higher than the temperature of the surroundings.
  5. Breathing
     —The body loses heat through breathing. With normal breathing, the body continuously loses a relatively small amount of heat through the evaporation of moisture.

- Hypothermia is a core body temperature of less than 95°F (35°C). This condition results when the body loses more heat than it gains or produces.
  —A rectal temperature gives the most accurate measure of core temperature. However, obtaining a rectal temperature in the field often raises issues of patient sensitivity and welfare, such as exposure to cold by removal of clothing.
  —Your main concern in providing care should be to remove the patient from the environment. Use trained rescuers for this purpose when necessary.

Perform a primary survey, keeping in mind that you need to move the patient to a warm location as quickly and as safely as possible. Remove any cold or wet clothing. Protect the patient from the environment. Assess the patient's mental status, airway, breathing, and circulation. Keep in mind that mental status decreases as the patient's body temperature drops.

— You may need to rewarm the patient. The two main types of rewarming are passive and active.

  • Passive rewarming is the warming of a patient with minimal or no use of heat sources other than the patient's own heat production. Passive rewarming methods include placing the patient in a warm environment, applying warm clothing and blankets, and preventing drafts.

  • Active rewarming should be used only if sustained warmth can be ensured. Active rewarming involves adding heat directly to the surface of the patient's body. Warm blankets, heat packs, and/or hot water bottles may be used, depending on how severe the hypothermia is.

• Local cold injury (also called *frostbite*) involves tissue damage to a specific area of the body. It occurs when a body part, such as the nose, ears, cheeks, chin, hands, or feet, is exposed to prolonged or intense cold. When the body is exposed to cold, blood is forced away from the extremities to the body's core. A local cold injury may be early (superficial frostbite) or late (deep frostbite).

• When the body gains or produces more heat than it loses, hyperthermia (a high core body temperature) results. The three main types of heat emergencies are heat cramps, heat exhaustion, and heat stroke.

  1. Heat cramps usually affect people who sweat a lot during strenuous activity in a warm environment. Water and electrolytes are lost from the body during sweating. This loss leads to dehydration and causes painful muscle spasms.

  2. Heat exhaustion is also a result of too much heat and dehydration. A patient with heat exhaustion usually sweats heavily. His body temperature is usually normal or slightly elevated. Severe heat exhaustion often requires IV fluids. Heat exhaustion may progress to heat stroke if it is not treated.

  3. Heat stroke is the most severe form of heat-related illness. It occurs when the body can no longer regulate its temperature. Most patients have hot, flushed skin and do not sweat. Individuals who wear heavy uniforms and perform strenuous activity for long periods in a hot environment are at risk for heat stroke.

• The first step in the emergency care of a patient suffering from a heat-related illness is to remove him from the hot environment. Move the patient to a cool (air-conditioned) location and follow treatment guidelines recommended for the patient's degree of heat-related illness.

• When providing emergency care for a drowning victim, ensure the safety of the rescue personnel. Suspect a possible spine injury if a diving accident is involved or unknown.

• Any breathless, pulseless patient who has been submerged in cold water should be resuscitated.

• Signs and symptoms of bites and stings typically include a history of a bite (spider, snake) or sting (insect, scorpion, marine animal), pain, redness, swelling, weakness, dizziness, chills, fever, nausea, and vomiting. Bite marks may be present.

• If a stinger is present, remove it by scraping the stinger out with the edge of a card. Avoid using tweezers or forceps as these can squeeze venom from the venom sac into the wound.

• When caring for a victim of a bite or sting, watch closely for development of signs and symptoms of an allergic reaction; treat as needed.

► Tracking Your Progress

After reading this chapter, can you:	Page Reference	Objective Met?
• Describe the various ways that the body loses heat?	401	☐
• List the signs and symptoms of exposure to cold?	403	☐
• Explain the steps in providing emergency medical care to a patient exposed to cold?	405	☐
• List the signs and symptoms of exposure to heat?	408	☐
• Explain the steps in providing emergency care to a patient exposed to heat?	409	☐
• Recognize the signs and symptoms of water-related emergencies?	412	☐
• Describe the complications of drowning?	412	☐
• Discuss the emergency medical care of bites and stings?	419, 422	☐

Multiple Choice

In the space provided, identify the letter of the choice that best completes the statement or answers each question.

_____ 1. Your ambulance crew is called to a local park for a 9-year-old male patient who has been stung by a bee. When you arrive, the stinger is still imbedded in his forearm. Treatment for this patient should include

  a. applying cold packs around the site of the sting, leaving the stinger in, and transporting.
  b. scraping the stinger off with a card and thoroughly washing the area with soap and water.
  c. removing the stinger with tweezers, saving it in a bag for inspection at the receiving facility, and elevating the arm.
  d. encouraging the patient to remove the stinger with his fingers, applying ice packs to the area, and elevating the arm.

Questions 2–4 pertain to the following scenario.

Your rescue crew has been called to a local park for a 65-year-old woman complaining of weakness and dizziness. It is a hot, humid summer day. You arrive to find the patient sitting in the sun on a park bench. Her skin condition is cool, pale, and moist. She greets you as you approach and is in a moderate level of distress.

_____ 2. Which of the following should you do first?

  a. Assess baseline vital signs.
  b. Perform a rapid trauma assessment.
  c. Begin cooling the patient with ice packs to the groin, armpits, and neck area.
  d. Perform a primary survey and then move the patient to the back of your air-conditioned ambulance.

_____ 3. This patient is responsive and does not complain of nausea. Which of the following regarding oral intake is correct?

  a. You may allow the patient to drink water.
  b. You may allow the patient to drink iced tea.
  c. You may allow the patient to eat but not drink.
  d. You may allow the patient to drink a cold beer.

_____ **4.** The preferred position in which to transport this patient is

    a. supine.

    b. prone on the stretcher.

    c. sitting upright at a 90-degree angle.

    d. fully immobilized to a long backboard.

Questions 5–6 pertain to the following scenario.

You have been called to the home of a 24-year-old woman complaining of weakness, nausea, and joint pain. She informs you she just returned from a scuba diving excursion. She tells you, "I think it is just the flu, but my boyfriend made me call." She denies any past medical history.

_____ **5.** This patient should be transported in what position?

    a. Prone, with her head slightly elevated

    b. Fully immobilized on a long backboard

    c. On her left side with the head and chest tilted downward

    d. Sitting upright at a 90-degree angle with her legs dangling over the edge of the stretcher

_____ **6.** En route, the patient suffers a full-body seizure and does not regain consciousness. On the basis of history of present illness, you suspect

    a. barotrauma and treat with low-flow oxygen by nasal cannula and continuous reassessment.

    b. epilepsy and treat with high-flow oxygen by nonrebreather mask and continuous reassessment.

    c. hypoglycemia and treat with oral glucose, low-flow oxygen by nasal cannula, and continuous reassessment.

    d. decompression sickness (the "bends") and treat with high-flow oxygen by nonrebreather mask and continuous reassessment en route to the hospital.

_____ **7.** Your ambulance crew is called to treat a 34-year-old man complaining of severe abdominal cramping and difficulty breathing. He states that he was cleaning the garage about 10 hours ago when something pricked his thigh. The site is red and tender but has no discolored "rings" surrounding it. You suspect a

    a. coral snake bite and treat by cleaning the site and administering high-flow oxygen.

    b. black widow spider bite and treat by removing all distal jewelry, cleaning the site, and administering high-flow oxygen.

    c. scorpion sting and treat by cleaning the site, applying a tourniquet, and suctioning the area en route to the hospital.

    d. brown recluse spider bite and treat by making a small incision over the site and suctioning.

_____ **8.** Your ambulance crew has been called to a local mountain range to assist in the treatment of a 34-year-old man who got lost while hunting. He was out overnight in freezing temperatures and was unable to get a fire started. While examining the patient, you discover that both feet appear to have suffered a deep cold injury. After consulting medical direction, you are instructed to begin active rewarming of the affected areas. This may be accomplished by

    a. massaging the affected areas with warm compresses.

    b. covering the bare feet with sterile gauze and a blanket.

    c. submersing the patient's feet in circulating, warm water.

    d. starting a fire and putting the patient's bare feet near the fire.

_____ **9.** Your rescue crew is called to a construction site for a 29-year-old woman who has suffered a snakebite. She is complaining of weakness and nausea from a bite to the left hand that occurred about 1 hour ago. You should

    a. apply a tourniquet to the affected limb.

    b. apply cold packs to slow the absorption of the venom.

    c. provide oxygen by nonrebreather mask at 15 L/min.

    d. make an incision at the site of the bite and withdraw the venom by using a syringe.

Questions 10–11 pertain to the following scenario.

Your ambulance crew is called to an industrial plant for a 32-year-old man who was exposed to a cryogenic (extremely cold) liquid. Upon arrival, your patient informs you that he was closing a valve when the system discharged a cold vapor on his right hand.

_____ **10.** Which of the following signs is exclusively indicative of deep injury to the hand?
   a. Red, inflamed fingers
   b. A white, waxy appearance of the skin
   c. Loss of sensation in the affected area
   d. The failure of normal skin color to immediately return when the nail beds are blanched (pressed)

_____ **11.** After contacting medical direction, you are instructed to actively rewarm the hand in warm water. After rewarming, you should dress the hand by
   a. placing the hand in a sock.
   b. wrapping the hand with an elastic bandage.
   c. applying salve to the fingers, then wrapping the hand with an elastic bandage.
   d. placing sterile dressings between the fingers, then wrapping loosely with cotton gauze.

_____ **12.** When treating a heat exposure patient with hot, dry skin and an altered mental status, your treatment should be geared toward
   a. decreasing the patient's body temperature slowly and methodically.
   b. rapidly decreasing the patient's body temperature to induce shivering.
   c. rapidly decreasing the patient's body temperature without inducing shivering.
   d. maintaining the patient's current temperature until arrival at the emergency department.

Matching

Match the key terms in the left column with the definitions in the right column by placing the letter of each correct answer in the space provided.

_____ **13.** Hypoxia

_____ **14.** Passive rewarming

_____ **15.** Immersion

_____ **16.** Wet drowning

_____ **17.** Decompression sickness

_____ **18.** Hyperthermia

_____ **19.** Convection

_____ **20.** Clenched fist injury

_____ **21.** Body temperature

_____ **22.** Evaporation

_____ **23.** Submersion

_____ **24.** Drowning

_____ **25.** Conduction

_____ **26.** Barotrauma

_____ **27.** Active rewarming

_____ **28.** Laryngospasm

_____ **29.** Hypothermia

_____ **30.** Radiation

_____ **31.** Dry drowning

_____ **32.** Air embolism

A. A loss of heat by vaporization of moisture on the body surface

B. Closing of the larynx to prevent the passage of water into the lungs

C. The presence of air bubbles in the circulatory system

D. The transfer of heat, as infrared heat rays, from the surface of one object to the surface of another without contact between the two objects

E. A core body temperature of less than 95°F (35°C)

F. The transfer of heat by the movement of air current

G. Injury caused by pressure

H. Contraction of the sensitive tissue near the vocal cords

I. A diving-related injury that results from dissolved nitrogen in the blood and tissues

J. Adding heat directly to the surface of the patient's body

K. Warming of a patient with minimal or no use of heat sources other than the patient's own heat production

Continued

L. A "fight bite"

M. A process that results in harm to the respiratory system from submersion or immersion in a liquid

N. The entry of water into the trachea and lungs

O. The balance between the heat produced by the body and the heat lost from the body

P. High core body temperature

Q. Covering of the face and airway in water or other fluid

R. The transfer of heat between objects that are in direct contact

S. A decreased supply of oxygen to the body's tissues

T. An incident in which the victim's entire body, including his airway, is under water or other fluid

Short Answer

Answer each question in the space provided.

33. Name the structure that functions as the body's thermostat.

34. List five mechanisms by which the body loses heat to the environment.
1.
2.
3.
4.
5.

35. List five signs or symptoms of a scorpion sting.
1.
2.
3.
4.
5.

36. List seven factors that contribute to hypothermia.
1.
2.
3.
4.
5.
6.
7.

37. List five factors that influence a drowning victim's chances for survival.

1.

2.

3.

4.

5.

38. Briefly explain the difference between an immersion incident and a submersion incident.

39. Explain the significance of the mammalian diving reflex.

40. You are at the scene of a drowning incident. If observed, what circumstances would lead you to suspect a neck injury and the need for spinal stabilization?

Answer Section

Chapter 18

Multiple Choice

1. b

   Tweezers or fingers should not be used to remove a stinger since the venom sac may still be full of venom. Squeezing this sac would force the contents of the sac though the stinger and into the patient.

   Objective: Discuss the emergency medical care of bites and stings.

2. d

   Before obtaining your SAMPLE history and focused physical exam, you must prevent further injury to the patient. All other assessments and interventions should be conducted in an air-conditioned environment.

   Objective: Explain the steps in providing emergency care to a patient exposed to heat.

3. a

   If allowed by local protocol and medical direction, this patient may take sips of water. If, however, the patient complains of nausea or has an altered mental status, you should not allow any oral intake. Do not allow a heat (or cold) emergency patient to drink any caffeinated or alcoholic beverage.

   Objective: Explain the steps in providing emergency care to a patient exposed to heat.

4. a

   The preferred position for this patient is a supine position. This position may assist in maintaining an acceptable blood pressure. Sitting at a 90-degree angle would have the opposite effect. There are no indications that spinal immobilization is necessary. Positioning the patient prone (on her stomach) complicates your ability to monitor the patient's airway.

   Objective: Demonstrate the assessment and emergency medical care of a patient with exposure to heat.

5. c

   If this patient has a diving-related injury, the possibility exists that small bubbles of gas are floating around in her body. The best way to remember the proper positioning of such a patient is to remember that the brain and the heart are important organs, and gases tend to rise. Therefore, lower the brain and lower the heart.

   Objective: Recognize the signs and symptoms of water-related emergencies.

6. d

   Decompression sickness, also known as the *bends*, occurs when divers ascend (come up) too quickly. Gases in their body expand too rapidly and bubbles are formed. The signs and symptoms associated with this are fatigue, weakness, shortness of breath, skin rash, itch, joint pain, dizziness, headache, paralysis, seizures, and unconsciousness. If the possibility exists that you will treat a diving-related injury, you should be aware of the nearest decompression chamber. When patients are put in this device, the pressure is increased so that the air bubbles "dissolve," and then the pressure is brought down in a controlled manner so that bubbles do not form. Barotrauma is also an ascent injury. It occurs when divers surface too quickly. The change in atmospheric pressure changes too rapidly for the air-filled chambers of the body (such as the sinus cavities, abdomen, lungs, and ears). These cavities become damaged or rupture. The signs and symptoms are associated with the rupture of these chambers.

   Objective: Recognize the signs and symptoms of water-related emergencies.

7. b

The location, sensation, and side effects of the bite suggest a black widow spider bite. A coral snakebite would not, in an awake and conscious patient, go unnoticed (especially on the thigh). While a scorpion sting may produce similar complaints, treatment with a tourniquet is inappropriate. Brown recluse spider bites will usually present with a "target" mark within 8 hours. A "target" mark is a bluish ring surrounding the bite area and a blister at the bite. The treatment for these bites and stings is basically the same: continue to monitor closely to ensure that the patient is not having an allergic (anaphylactic) reaction to the bite, obtain SAMPLE information, perform a focused history and physical examination, clean the site, remove distal jewelry, provide oxygen therapy, and transport.

Objective: Discuss the emergency medical care of bites and stings.

8. c

The best method for warming an affected extremity is to submerse the extremity in warm water because the temperature of water can be closely monitored. The water temperature should be consistent and uniform. Make sure that the water is not allowed to cool. Anticipate that this patient will experience extreme pain as the area warms. As with all unstable heat and cold emergency patients, ALS-level care should be requested early. Covering the patient's feet with gauze and a blanket is an example of passive warming measures. Massaging is contraindicated. Finally, the use of an open fire is not a good idea for several reasons. This patient needs to be transported to a medical facility. The heat from a fire cannot be adequately measured. You may burn the patient, causing more harm. If you are unable to begin transport and are considering starting a fire, do not attempt to warm or thaw a frostbitten area if the danger of refreezing exists. The damage will be worse than if the area were initially allowed to stay cold.

Objective: Explain the steps in providing emergency medical care to a patient exposed to cold.

9. c

Supportive care such as oxygen therapy is best for managing this patient. Be prepared for nausea and vomiting. Do not apply a constricting band or tourniquet. A constricting band is not the same as a tourniquet. A tourniquet completely stops the flow of blood (arterial and venous) to and from extremity. A constricting band slows the return of blood from an extremity (venous blood) but permits arterial blood flow. If a tourniquet or constricting band was applied to the affected arm or leg before your arrival, and pulses are present in the extremity, leave it in place until the victim is evaluated at the hospital. If a tourniquet or constricting band was applied and pulses are absent in the extremity, consult medical direction for instructions. Cold packs should not be applied to the skin of snakebite victims. Do not incise and suck at the bite site.

Objective: Discuss the emergency medical care of bites and stings.

10. b

A severe local cold injury may be characterized by a white, waxy appearance of the skin, stiff tissues, swelling, blisters, or discoloration of the local tissues (purple, mottled, pale, or cyanotic).

Objective: List the signs and symptoms of exposure to cold.

11. d

Appropriate management would call for separating the fingers before dressing the entire hand. Never apply salves in a prehospital setting. An elastic bandage should be avoided. Loose cotton dressings are preferred because they facilitate warming of the area.

Objective: Explain the steps in providing emergency medical care to a patient exposed to cold.

12. c

Core body temperatures can soar above 105°F. The brain and internal organs can take this type of punishment only for a short period before irreversible damage takes place. Your efforts should be directed at cooling the body as quickly as possible without activating the body's heat-generating mechanisms (e.g., shivering). Move the patient to a cool area; remove clothing; moisten the skin with cool water; and apply padded cool compresses to the armpits, back of the neck, and the groin. Never apply ice directly to the skin as you may cause a local cold emergency (frostbite), which can also result in shivering.

Objective: Explain the steps in providing emergency care to a patient exposed to heat.

Matching

13.	S	23.	T
14.	K	24.	M
15.	Q	25.	R
16.	N	26.	G
17.	I	27.	J
18.	P	28.	B
19.	F	29.	E
20.	L	30.	D
21.	O	31.	H
22.	A	32.	C

Short Answer

33. The hypothalamus (located in the brain) functions as the body's thermostat. It coordinates the body's response to temperature.

    Objective: Describe the anatomy and function of the following major body systems: respiratory, circulatory, musculoskeletal, nervous, and endocrine.

34. The body loses heat to the environment in five ways:

    1. Radiation
    2. Convection
    3. Conduction
    4. Evaporation
    5. Breathing

    Objective: Describe the various ways that the body loses heat.

35. Signs and symptoms of a scorpion sting include the following:

    - Local pain, numbness or tingling, swelling, and redness at the sting site
    - SLUDGEM (*s*alivation, *l*acrimation [tearing], *u*rination, *d*iarrhea, *g*astric cramping, *e*mesis [vomiting], *m*iosis [pupil constriction])
    - Slurred speech
    - Blurred vision
    - Restlessness, jerking, and involuntary shaking
    - Wandering eye movements
    - Difficulty breathing
    - Trouble swallowing
    - Increased heart rate
    - Seizures

    Objective: N/A

36. Factors that contribute to hypothermia include the following:

    - Cold, windy weather conditions
    - Prolonged exposure to a cool environment
    - Immersion in water
    - Improper, inadequate, or wet clothing
    - Low body weight
    - Poor physical condition
    - Low blood sugar
    - Recent trauma or burn injury
    - Drug or alcohol intake
    - Extremes in age (very young children, the elderly)
    - Impaired judgment resulting from mental illness or Alzheimer's disease
    - Preexisting medical conditions
    - Previous cold exposure

    Objective: N/A

37. Factors that influence a drowning victim's chances for survival:

    - Length of immersion or submersion
    - Duration of hypoxia
    - Ability to swim
    - Age of victim
    - Cleanliness of the water
    - Temperature of the water
    - Victim signs and symptoms
    - Preexisting medical conditions
    - Presence of drugs and/or alcohol
    - Presence of associated injuries (especially cervical spine and head)
    - Response to initial resuscitation efforts

    Objective: Describe the complications of near drowning.

38. Immersion refers to covering of the face and airway in water or other fluid. In a submersion incident, the victim's entire body, including his airway, is under the water or other fluid.

    Objective: Describe the complications of near drowning.

39. In some individuals, cold water stimulation of the temperature receptors in the skin triggers the mammalian diving reflex. This reflex is present in seals and other diving mammals. In humans, the diving reflex is strongest in infants less than 6 months old, and the effects decrease with age. The diving reflex triggers the shunting of blood to the brain and heart from the skin, GI tract, and extremities. The victim's heart rate slows in response to the increased volume of blood in the body's core. These actions help the body conserve oxygen and may help the victim survive.

Objective: Recognize the signs and symptoms of water-related emergencies.

40. When you are at the scene of a drowning incident, you should suspect a neck injury (and begin appropriate spinal stabilization procedures):

- When the MOI is unknown
- When signs of facial trauma are present
- When signs of drug or alcohol use are present
- In incidents involving use of a water slide and swimming, boating, water-skiing, or diving accidents

Objective: Recognize the signs and symptoms of water-related emergencies.

19 Behavioral Emergencies

READING ASSIGNMENT ▶ Read Chapter 19, pages 429 to 439 in your textbook.

Sum It Up

- As an EMT, you will likely encounter various behavioral emergencies. A behavioral emergency is a situation in which a patient displays abnormal behavior that is unacceptable to the patient, family members, or community. A behavioral emergency can be caused by extremes of emotion or by psychological or physical conditions. A number of factors can result in these emergencies, including mental illness, a lack of oxygen, low blood sugar, alcohol or drugs, situational stressors, medical illnesses, or psychiatric illnesses or crises.

- Anxiety is a state of worry and agitation that is usually triggered by a real or imagined situation. An anxiety disorder is more intense than normal anxiety.

- A panic attack is an intense fear that occurs for no apparent reason.

- OCD is a type of anxiety disorder. Obsessions are recurring thoughts, impulses, or images that cause the person anxiety. Compulsions are recurring behaviors or rituals that are performed with the hope of preventing obsessive thoughts or making them go away.

- A phobia is an irrational and constant fear of a specific activity, object, or situation (other than a social situation). A social phobia is an extreme anxiety response in situations in which the individual may be seen by others. A phobic reaction resembles a panic attack.

- Depression is a state of mind characterized by feelings of sadness, worthlessness, and discouragement. It often occurs in response to a loss. The loss may be losing a job, the death of a loved one, or the end of a relationship.

- Bipolar disorder is a brain disorder that causes unusual shifts in a person's mood, energy, and ability to function. A person with bipolar disorder has alternating episodes of mood elevation (mania) and depression. The person's mood is often normal between the periods of mania and depression.

- Paranoia is a mental disorder characterized by excessive suspiciousness or delusions. Paranoid patients are suspicious, distrustful, and prone to argument. They are excitable and unpredictable, with outbursts of bizarre or aggressive behavior.
  —Delusions are false beliefs that the patient believes are true, despite facts to the contrary.
  —Hallucinations are false sensory perceptions. The patient sees, hears, or feels things that others cannot.

- Schizophrenia is a group of mental disorders. Symptoms include hallucinations, delusions, disordered thinking, rambling speech, and bizarre or disorganized behavior. These patients can become combative and are at high risk for suicidal and homicidal behavior.

- A suicide gesture is self-destructive behavior that is unlikely to have any possibility of being fatal. A suicide attempt is self-destructive behavior for the purpose of ending one's life that, for unanticipated reasons, fails. A completed suicide is death by a self-inflicted, consciously intended action.

- Most people who commit suicide express their intentions beforehand. You should take every suicide action seriously and arrange for patient transport for evaluation.

- When called to a scene that involves a behavioral emergency, remember that the scene may be unpredictable. Take steps to ensure your safety and that of other healthcare professionals responding to the scene. Complete a scene size-up before beginning emergency medical care. Carefully assess the scene for possible dangers. Start by visually locating the patient. Visually scan the area for possible weapons. Be prepared to spend time at the scene. Limit the number of people around the patient. Take time to calm the patient.

- Avoid restraining a patient unless the patient is a danger to you, himself, or others. When using restraints, have police present, if possible, and get approval from medical direction. If you must use restraints, apply them with the help of law enforcement and other EMS personnel.

▶ Tracking Your Progress

After reading this chapter, can you:	Page Reference	Objective Met?
• Define behavioral emergencies?	430	☐
• Discuss the general factors that may cause an alteration in a patient's behavior?	430	☐
• State the various reasons for psychological crises?	430	☐
• Discuss the characteristics of an individual's behavior that suggest that the patient is at risk for suicide?	434	☐
• Discuss special medical and legal considerations for managing behavioral emergencies?	438	☐
• Discuss the special considerations for assessing a patient with behavioral problems?	435	☐
• Discuss the general principles of an individual's behavior that suggest that he is at risk for violence?	435	☐
• Discuss methods to calm behavioral emergency patients?	436	☐

True or False

Decide whether each statement is true or false. In the space provided, write *T* for true or *F* for false.

_____ 1. You should assume that a patient has a psychiatric illness if he shows signs of panic, agitation, or self-destructive behavior or acts in a threatening manner.

_____ 2. A behavioral emergency is a situation in which a patient displays abnormal behavior that is unacceptable to the patient, family members, or community.

Multiple Choice

In the space provided, identify the letter of the choice that best completes the statement or answers each question.

_____ 3. You are treating a 17-year-old female patient who tells you that Abraham Lincoln is in her room and is speaking to her. You should

   a. ask her to recite the Gettysburg Address.
   b. play along with the scenario to win the patient's trust.
   c. ignore the patient's comments regarding imagined persons or noises.
   d. tell her that you cannot see him but would like to know what President Lincoln is saying.

_____ 4. Your rescue crew is called to a local shopping mall for a 43-year-old woman who is acting erratically. Bystanders tell you that before you arrived the patient was dancing around the mall telling people that she could see the future. You find her sitting on a bench crying inconsolably. She is most likely suffering from

   a. paranoia.   **c.** bipolar disorder.
   b. a panic attack.   **d.** severe depression.

_____ 5. Your ambulance crew is called to the home of a 13-year-old male patient for a "welfare check." His mother called 9-1-1 because he hasn't been acting normally since his parents divorced. She tells you her son hasn't been eating much for the past month, keeps to himself, and complains of constant mild headaches. This patient is exhibiting signs and symptoms of

   a. a panic attack.   **c.** bipolar disorder.
   b. normal puberty.   **d.** severe depression.

_____ 6. The legal considerations for patients experiencing a behavioral emergency who refuse treatment can be confusing. Field healthcare professionals are often put in the middle, with the patient adamantly denying treatment on one side and a medical facility requesting transport on the other. To provide care against a patient's will, you must be able to show a reasonable belief that the patient may harm himself or others. When operating in such a situation, your best resource for advice is

   a. the patient.
   b. the patient's family.
   c. local law enforcement.
   d. your medical direction physician.

_____ 7. An intense fear that occurs for no apparent reason is known as

   a. a panic attack.   **c.** anxiety.
   b. a phobia.   **d.** an anxiety disorder.

_____ 8. If a restrained patient is spitting, it is acceptable to cover the patient's mouth with

   a. duct tape.   **c.** a disposable surgical mask.
   b. medical tape.   **d.** a nonrebreather mask that is not connected to oxygen.

_____ 9. Which of the following is correct regarding the use of physical restraints?

   a. The use of handcuffs, rather than Velcro or nylon straps, is preferred.
   b. Once the decision to restrain a patient is made, you must act quickly and decisively.
   c. Physical restraints should be the first measure taken when attempting to control a patient.
   d. The use of BSI precautions is not practical or recommended when physically restraining a patient.

___ **10.** Which of the following regarding depression and patient age is correct?

    a. Children younger than 13 years old never have true depression.

    b. Depression is often first observed after a suicide attempt.

    c. The signs and symptoms of depression differ according to the age of the patient.

    d. Depressed patients generally have the same signs and symptoms, regardless of age.

___ **11.** Which of the following scenarios suggests a phobia?

    a. Being chronically sad and feeling worthless

    b. Being afraid of large open spaces like stores and theaters

    c. Attempting to commit suicide by ingesting an overdose of pills and alcohol

    d. Suddenly being overcome with an intense state of fear that passes with time

Matching

Match the key terms in the left column with the definitions in the right column by placing the letter of each correct answer in the space provided.

___ **12.** Obsessions

___ **13.** Completed suicide

___ **14.** Abnormal behavior

___ **15.** Hallucinations

___ **16.** Bipolar disorder

___ **17.** Compulsions

___ **18.** Panic attack

___ **19.** Phobia

___ **20.** Suicide attempt

___ **21.** Anxiety disorder

___ **22.** Suicide gesture

___ **23.** Delusions

___ **24.** Behavior

___ **25.** Obsessive-compulsive disorder

___ **26.** Reasonable force

___ **27.** Anxiety

___ **28.** Depression

___ **29.** Schizophrenia

___ **30.** Behavioral emergency

___ **31.** Social phobia

___ **32.** Paranoia

A. The amount of force necessary to keep a patient from injuring you, himself, or others

B. A situation in which a patient displays abnormal behavior that is unacceptable to the patient, family members, or community

C. False sensory perceptions seen, heard, or felt by a person that others cannot

D. A state of worry and agitation that is usually triggered by a real or imagined situation

E. Recurring thoughts, impulses, or images that cause the person anxiety

F. A state of mind characterized by feelings of sadness, worthlessness, and discouragement

G. Self-destructive behavior that is unlikely to have any possibility of being fatal

H. Conditions that involve excessive anxiety ranging from uneasiness to terror

I. A type of anxiety disorder in which the individual performs recurring behaviors or rituals with the hope of preventing obsessive thoughts or making them go away

J. Recurring behaviors or rituals performed with the hope of preventing obsessive thoughts or making them go away

K. An extreme anxiety response in situations in which the individual may be seen by others and fears that he will act in an embarrassing or shameful manner

L. A group of mental disorders characterized by hallucinations, delusions, disordered thinking, and bizarre or disorganized behavior

M. A brain disorder that causes alternating episodes of mood elevation (mania) and depression

Continued

N. False beliefs that the patient believes are true, despite facts to the contrary

O. Death by a self-inflicted, consciously intended action

P. A mental disorder characterized by excessive suspiciousness or delusions

Q. Self-destructive behavior for the purpose of ending one's life that, for unanticipated reasons, fails

R. A way of acting or conducting one's self that is not consistent with society's norms and expectations

S. An irrational and constant fear of a specific activity, object, or situation (other than a social situation)

T. The way in which a person acts or performs

U. An intense fear that occurs for no apparent reason

Short Answer

Answer each question in the space provided.

33. List five examples of medical conditions that may cause changes in behavior.
   1.
   2.
   3.
   4.
   5.

34. List two examples of common obsessions.
   1.
   2.

35. List five signs or symptoms of an anxiety disorder.
   1.
   2.
   3.
   4.
   5.

36. List seven risk factors for suicide.
   1.
   2.
   3.
   4.
   5.
   6.
   7.

Answer Section

Chapter 19

True/False

1. False

   Do not assume that a patient has a psychiatric illness until you have ruled out possible physical causes for his behavior. Psychological crises include panic, agitation, bizarre thinking and behavior, and destructive behavior. The patient who experiences a psychological crisis may be a danger to himself. He may show self-destructive behavior, such as suicide. He may also be a danger to others, acting in a threatening manner or even committing violence.

   Objective: Define behavioral emergencies.

2. True

   A behavioral emergency is a situation in which a patient displays abnormal behavior that is unacceptable to the patient, family members, or community. A behavioral emergency can be due to extremes of emotion that lead to violence or other inappropriate behavior. A behavioral emergency can also be due to a psychological or physical condition such as mental illness, lack of oxygen, or low blood sugar.

   Objective: Define behavioral emergencies.

Multiple Choice

3. d

   Always be honest with your patients. Although you should not be critical of this patient's belief, you should let her know that you do not hear or see the same things. Sometimes patients may use "voices" to tell you things they wouldn't otherwise tell you about their situation. In this case, by asking the patient what she hears, you may get valuable information about the source of the patient's problem.

   Objective: Discuss the special considerations for assessing a patient with behavioral problems.

4. c

   Bipolar disorder is characterized by major swings in mood. One day the bipolar patient is full of energy and believes she has special powers; the next day the same patient may be severely depressed.

   Objective: Discuss the special considerations for assessing a patient with behavioral problems.

5. d

   This patient is exhibiting the classic signs of severe adolescent depression. Signs of depression vary with age but commonly include feelings of worthlessness, discouragement, and sadness. Depression often occurs in response to an emotional event, such as divorce or death of a loved one.

   Objective: Discuss the special considerations for assessing a patient with behavioral problems.

6. d

   When in doubt, contact medical direction. Medical direction is your ultimate authority in treating patients and will often shed light into your gray area. Get to know your medical direction physician(s) so that when problems or gray areas arise, open lines of communication result in positive outcomes, for the patient and you.

   Objective: Discuss special medical and legal considerations for managing behavioral emergencies.

7. a

   A panic attack is an intense fear that occurs for no apparent reason. A phobia is an irrational and constant fear of a specific activity, object, or situation (other than a social situation). An anxiety disorder is more intense than normal anxiety. Anxiety normally goes away after the stressful situation that caused it is over. An anxiety disorder lasts for months and can lead to phobias. Anxiety is a state of worry and agitation that is usually triggered by a vague or imagined situation.

Objective: Discuss the general factors that may cause an alteration in a patient's behavior.

8. c

Do not tape a patient's mouth closed. If the patient were to vomit, he could aspirate the vomitus into his lungs and die. It is acceptable to cover the patient's mouth with a disposable surgical mask because it is designed to allow adequate ventilation. If you choose to use an oxygen delivery device, you must turn the oxygen on and flow it at an appropriate rate.

Objective: Discuss the special considerations for assessing a patient with behavioral problems.

9. b

Once you have carefully evaluated and exhausted all other methods to control a potentially violent or harmful patient, restraining a patient should be coordinated and carried out quickly. Make sure all personnel involved in restraining a patient have taken the appropriate level of BSI precautions. Anticipate that the patient will attempt to spit. The use of "soft restraints" rather than handcuffs is essential. Patients in restraints often continue to fight even after they are restrained. Handcuffs may cause further injury.

Objective: Demonstrate various techniques to safely restrain a patient with a behavioral problem.

10. c

Depression is not limited to adults and adolescents. Children, too, may become depressed. The signs and symptoms of depression tend to differ according to age. Reactions to depression range from crying to acting out to use of drugs and alcohol to suicide attempts. Suicide attempts are not generally the first indicator that a patient is depressed; unfortunately it may be the first time that the patient is given the help he needs.

Objective: Discuss the characteristics of an individual's behavior that suggest that the patient is at risk for suicide.

11. b

Phobias are irrational and persistent fears. They do not come and go like panic attacks and are not characterized by a chronic depressed state. Rather, a phobia is a constant fear of something (such as heights, open spaces, tunnels, snakes, blood, or dentists). Avoiding the source of the fear allows phobic individuals to lead an otherwise normal life. When confronted with the particular fear, patients have been known to "shut down," stop all activity, and retreat inward.

Objective: Discuss the special considerations for assessing a patient with behavioral problems.

Matching

12.	E	23.	N
13.	O	24.	T
14.	R	25.	I
15.	C	26.	A
16.	M	27.	D
17.	J	28.	F
18.	U	29.	L
19.	S	30.	B
20.	Q	31.	K
21.	H	32.	P
22.	G		

Short Answer

33. Medical conditions that may cause changes in behavior include:

   - Poisoning
   - Central nervous system infection
   - Head trauma
   - Seizure disorder
   - Lack of oxygen (hypoxia)
   - Low blood sugar
   - Inadequate blood flow to the brain
   - Extremes of temperature (excessive cold or heat)

Objective: Discuss the general factors that may cause an alteration in a patient's behavior.

34. Obsessions are recurring thoughts, impulses, or images that cause the person anxiety. Examples of common obsessions include a fear of dirt or germs, extreme need for neatness, and doubts about whether an appliance was turned off.

Objective: N/A

35. Common signs and symptoms of an anxiety disorder include the following:

- Tiredness
- Headaches
- Muscle tension
- Muscle aches
- Difficulty swallowing
- Trembling
- Twitching
- Irritability
- Sweating
- Hot flashes

Objective: Discuss the special considerations for assessing a patient with behavioral problems.

36. Risk factors for suicide include the following:

- Previous suicide attempt(s)
- History of mental disorders, particularly depression

- History of alcohol and/or substance abuse
- Family history of suicide
- Family history of child maltreatment
- Feelings of hopelessness
- Impulsive or aggressive tendencies
- Barriers to accessing mental health treatment
- Loss (relational, social, work, or financial)
- Physical illness
- Easy access to lethal methods
- Unwillingness to seek help because of the stigma attached to mental health and substance abuse disorders or suicidal thoughts
- Cultural and religious beliefs; for example, the belief that suicide is a noble resolution of a personal problem
- Local epidemics of suicide
- Isolation, a feeling of being cut off from other people

Objective: Discuss the characteristics of an individual's behavior that suggest that the patient is at risk for suicide.

20 Obstetrics and Gynecology

READING ASSIGNMENT ▶ Read Chapter 20, pages 440 to 469 in your textbook.

Sum It Up

- The vagina is also called the *birth canal.* It is a muscular tube that serves as a passageway between the uterus and the outside of the body.
- The placenta is a specialized organ through which the fetus exchanges nourishment and waste products during pregnancy.
- The umbilical cord is the lifeline that connects the placenta to the fetus. It contains two arteries and one vein. The umbilical vein carries oxygen-rich blood to the fetus. The umbilical cord attaches to the umbilicus (navel) of the fetus.
- The amniotic sac is a membranous bag that surrounds the fetus inside the uterus. It contains fluid (amniotic fluid) that helps protect the fetus from injury.
- An abortion is the termination of pregnancy before the fetus is able to live on its own outside the uterus. A spontaneous abortion, also called a *miscarriage,* is the loss of a fetus as a result of natural causes. It usually occurs before the 20th week of pregnancy.
- An ectopic pregnancy occurs when a fertilized egg implants outside the uterus.
- Preeclampsia is a disorder of pregnancy that causes blood vessels to spasm and constrict. Preeclampsia usually occurs during the 3rd trimester of pregnancy. Eclampsia is the seizure phase of preeclampsia.
- Placenta previa occurs when the placenta attaches low in the wall of the uterus instead of at its top or sides. In this position, the placenta may cover all or part of the cervix (the entrance to the birth canal). Placenta previa can cause sudden, painless, bright red vaginal bleeding.
- Abruptio placentae occurs when a normally implanted placenta separates prematurely from the wall of the uterus (endometrium) during the last trimester of pregnancy. If the placenta begins to peel away from the wall of the uterus, bleeding occurs from the blood vessels that transfer nutrients to the fetus from the mother. The placenta may separate partially or completely. Partial separation may allow time for treatment of the mother and fetus. Complete separation often results in death of the fetus.

- A ruptured uterus is caused by the actual tearing (rupture) of the uterus. Uterine rupture can occur when the patient has been in strong labor for a long period, which is the most common cause. It can also occur when the patient has sustained abdominal trauma, such as a severe fall or a sudden stop in a motor vehicle collision.

- A pregnant patient's heart rate is normally slightly faster than usual. Her breathing rate is also slightly faster and more shallow than normal. Her blood pressure is often slightly lower than normal until the 3rd trimester. It is important to take vital signs in all patients. However, you will need to pay special attention to the pregnant patient's history and look for other signs that may suggest a potential problem.

- You must not visually inspect the vaginal area unless major bleeding is present or you anticipate that childbirth is about to occur. In these situations, it is best to have another healthcare professional or law enforcement officer present.

- An obstetric emergency is an emergency related to pregnancy or childbirth. It is frequently associated with bleeding. During childbirth, blood and amniotic fluid are expected and may splash. Therefore, in caring for a patient with an obstetric emergency, you should take BSI precautions and put on appropriate PPE. In addition to gloves, you should wear eye protection, a mask, and a gown.

- Labor is the time and process in which the uterus repeatedly contracts to push the fetus and placenta out of the mother's body. It begins with the first uterine muscle contraction and ends with delivery of the placenta. Delivery is the actual birth of the baby at the end of the second stage of labor.

- Women often have false labor pains about 2 to 4 weeks before delivery. False labor pains are called *Braxton-Hicks contractions.* These contractions help prepare the woman's body for delivery by softening and thinning her cervix.

- A woman in labor should be transported to the hospital unless delivery of the baby is expected within a few minutes. You must determine if there is time for the mother to reach the hospital or if preparations should be made for delivery at the scene.

- Meconium is material that collects in the intestines of a fetus and forms the first stools of a newborn. The presence of meconium in amniotic fluid results in fluid that is greenish or brownish-yellow rather than clear. It is an indication of possible fetal distress during labor.

- The steps for delivery and care of multiple babies, the mother, and placentas are the same as with the delivery of one baby.

- A premature infant is one born before the 37th week of gestation or weighing less than 5.5 pounds (2.5 kilograms). Premature babies are at increased risk for hypothermia and low blood sugar.

- Complicated deliveries include a prolapsed cord, breech birth, and limb presentation. A prolapsed cord is a condition where the cord presents through the birth canal before delivery of the head. It presents a serious emergency that endangers the life of the unborn fetus. A breech presentation occurs when the buttocks or lower extremities are low in the uterus and will be the first part of the fetus delivered. The newborn is at great risk for delivery trauma. A limb presentation occurs when a limb of the infant protrudes from the birth canal.

- Trauma to the external genitalia should be treated as other bleeding soft tissue injuries. Alleged sexual assault situations require initial and ongoing assessment and management, as well as psychological care.

▶ Tracking Your Progress

After reading this chapter, can you:	Page Reference	Objective Met?
• Identify the following structures: uterus, vagina, fetus, placenta, umbilical cord, amniotic sac, and perineum?	441	☐
• Identify and explain the use of the contents of an obstetrics kit?	445	☐
• Identify predelivery emergencies?	445	☐
• State indications of an imminent delivery?	454, 455	☐
• Differentiate the emergency medical care provided to a patient with predelivery emergencies from a normal delivery?	456	☐
• State the steps in the predelivery preparation of the mother?	456	☐
• Establish the relationship between BSI and childbirth?	455	☐
• State the steps to assist in the delivery?	455, 456	☐
• Describe care of the baby as the head appears?	457	☐
• Describe how and when to cut the umbilical cord?	457, 460	☐
• Discuss the steps in the delivery of the placenta?	461	☐
• List the steps in the emergency medical care of the mother after delivery?	460	☐
• Summarize neonatal resuscitation procedures?	458	☐
• Describe the procedures for the following abnormal deliveries: breech birth, prolapsed cord, limb presentation?	462, 463, 464	☐
• Differentiate the special considerations for multiple births?	465	☐
• Describe special considerations of meconium?	458	☐
• Describe special considerations of a premature baby?	465	☐
• Discuss the emergency medical care of a patient with a gynecological emergency?	466, 467	☐

True or False

Decide whether each statement is true or false. In the space provided, write *T* for true or *F* for false.

_____ 1. While assisting with a delivery, you observe the umbilical cord wrapped around the baby's neck. Attempts to slide the cord over the baby's head or shoulder are unsuccessful. You should now place two umbilical clamps or ties on the cord approximately 12 inches apart and then cut the cord between the two clamps.

_____ 2. When clearing a newborn's airway, suction the baby's nose first and then the mouth.

Multiple Choice

In the space provided, identify the letter of the choice that best completes the statement or answers each question.

_____ 3. The ovaries are responsible for
   a. stretching to adapt to the increasing size of a fetus.
   b. contracting to expel an infant from its mother's body.
   c. receiving and transporting the egg to the uterus.
   d. producing eggs and secreting hormones.

_____ **4.** In a normal pregnancy, the egg will travel to the uterus through the

  a. cervix.

  b. vagina.

  c. urethra.

  d. fallopian tubes.

_____ **5.** During delivery, especially very rapid deliveries, the tissue between the mother's anus and vagina may tear. This area is called the

  a. cervix.

  b. colon.

  c. perineum.

  d. labia majora.

_____ **6.** Your rescue crew has been dispatched to transport an assault patient from a crime scene. Local law enforcement personnel have secured the scene. Your patient is a 24-year-old woman complaining of head pain. She states she was jumped while jogging in the park and was hit in the head with a small bat. A police officer informs you the patient told her that she was raped. Appropriate interventions should include

  a. having the police officer transport the patient to the hospital to complete a "rape kit" examination.

  b. full spinal stabilization, oxygen therapy, focused history and physical examination, and transport.

  c. full spinal stabilization, oxygen therapy, focused history and physical examination to determine if a rape occurred, and transport.

  d. allowing the patient to bathe quickly, full spinal stabilization, focused history and physical examination, and transport.

_____ **7.** Your rescue crew has been called to the home of a 23-year-old female patient complaining of severe flu-like symptoms. She is 7 months pregnant with her first child. She informs you that she has been vomiting for the past 2 days and has a mild fever. She requests transport to a local clinic. You should position this patient

  a. on her left side.

  b. on her stomach (prone).

  c. flat on her back with her legs elevated.

  d. flat on her back with the head lower than the feet (Trendelenburg position).

_____ **8.** Your ambulance is transporting a 31-year-old pregnant woman who is $8\frac{1}{2}$ months pregnant with her first child. While en route to the hospital, the patient states she feels as if she has to move her bowels. When looking at the vaginal opening, you observe one of the infant's arms dangling from the birth canal. You should

  a. stop the ambulance and prepare for a "field" delivery.

  b. position the mother on her right side and rapidly transport to the hospital.

  c. position the mother in a head-down position with the pelvis elevated, and rapidly transport to the hospital.

  d. place the arm back in the birth canal, position the mother on her left side, and rapidly transport to the hospital.

Questions 9–11 pertain to the following scenario.

A 27-year-old woman says that her last menstrual period was 8 weeks ago but she has been spotting today. She is now having severe right lower quadrant abdominal pain that radiates to her shoulder. Her skin is pale, and she is sweating. Her heart rate is 132 beats per minute, her blood pressure is 80/50 mm Hg, and she feels faint.

_____ **9.** What condition do you suspect?

  a. Appendicitis

  b. Ectopic pregnancy

  c. Miscarriage

  d. Therapeutic abortion

_____ **10.** Where is the fertilized egg likely implanted in this patient?

  a. Abdomen

  b. Cervix

  c. Ovary

  d. Fallopian tube

_____ **11.** What emergency care measures should you take at this time?

  a. Administer oxygen.

  b. Give her sips of warm fluids.

  c. Lay her on her left side.

  d. Prepare for emergency delivery.

Questions 12–14 pertain to the following scenario.

Your rescue crew is called to the home of a 34-year-old woman whose bag of waters has broken. You arrive to find the patient supine on the floor of her apartment. The baby's head can be seen at the birth canal. You decide to remain on the scene and deliver the baby.

_____ 12. After the head has emerged from the birth canal, you should
   a. instruct the mother to give one last big push.
   b. suction the mouth and nose with a bulb syringe.
   c. apply gentle traction to the head to ease delivery of the shoulder.
   d. apply a pediatric oxygen mask to the baby and flow the oxygen at 5 L/min.

_____ 13. As soon as the entire baby has been delivered, you should immediately
   a. clamp the umbilical cord.
   b. clamp and cut the umbilical cord.
   c. begin warming, drying, and stimulating the baby.
   d. place the infant about 2-3 feet below the level of the birth canal.

_____ 14. Evaluation of this infant's condition after birth is conducted by using which of the following memory aids?
   a. AVPU   c. SAMPLE
   b. Apgar   d. A-NU-BABY

Questions 15–17 pertain to the following scenario.

Your rescue crew is dispatched to a motor vehicle collision on a local highway. Information at the time of dispatch is that there are three cars involved, and the accident "appears serious."

_____ 15. Your first action when arriving on the scene should be to
   a. perform a scene size-up.
   b. begin immediate extrication of all trapped patients.
   c. perform a primary survey on all critical patients.
   d. perform a rapid physical examination on all unconscious patients.

_____ 16. You are assigned to assess and treat a 32-year-old pregnant woman who was the driver of one of the vehicles involved. She tells you she was not wearing her seat belt and was traveling about 40 miles per hour when another car pulled out in front of her. She is alert and answering all questions appropriately. She is in severe distress. Which of the following findings would be consistent with an abruptio placentae?
   a. Elevated blood pressure, pedal edema, and severe headache
   b. Nausea, vomiting, elevated blood pressure, and subsequent seizures
   c. Painless bright red bloody discharge from the vagina and signs of shock
   d. Severe abdominal pain, dark red bloody discharge from the vagina, and signs of shock

_____ 17. Appropriate interventions for this patient would be
   a. to position the patient sitting upright and provide high-flow oxygen and rapid transport.
   b. to provide full spinal stabilization with the backboard tilted to the left, high-flow oxygen, and rapid transport.
   c. to position the patient on her left side and provide high-flow oxygen and transport slowly without lights or siren.
   d. to provide full spinal stabilization with the head of the backboard elevated, high-flow oxygen, and transport.

Questions 18–19 pertain to the following scenario.

Your ambulance crew is called to transport a 38-year-old woman complaining of vaginal bleeding. She is 38 weeks pregnant with her fifth child. Upon examination, you observe that the patient has lost about 200-300 mL of bright red blood in the last 10 minutes. According to the patient, her bag of waters has not ruptured. She denies any recent trauma or any pain associated with the bloody discharge. Her vital signs are as follows: pulse 116 beats/min with moderate strength, BP 108/72, respirations 16 breaths/min.

_____ 18. Which of the following is consistent with this patient's presentation?
    a. Eclampsia   **c.** Abruptio placentae
    b. Placenta previa   **d.** First stage of labor

_____ 19. Management of this patient should include
    a. instructing the patient to bear down and preparing for home delivery of the infant.
    b. inserting a tampon to stop the bleeding, administering oxygen by nonrebreather mask, positioning the patient on her left side, and transporting promptly.
    c. positioning the patient on her left side, administering oxygen by nonrebreather mask, and transporting promptly.
    d. placing the patient in a knee-chest position, inserting a gloved hand into the birth canal to create an airway for the infant, administering oxygen by nonrebreather mask, and transporting promptly.

Questions 20–22 pertain to the following scenario.

Your rescue crew is called to the scene of a 35-year-old woman complaining of a severe headache and blurred vision. You arrive to find the patient sitting in a darkened room. She states she is 8 months pregnant with her fourth child. She has received no prenatal care. On examination, you note that the patient's face is swollen and her blood pressure is 164/98.

_____ 20. Which of the following conditions would be consistent with your findings?
    a. Preeclampsia   **c.** Abruptio placentae
    b. Placenta previa   **d.** Ectopic pregnancy

_____ 21. The correct position and mode of transportation for this patient is
    a. patient on her left side, transport rapidly with lights and siren.
    b. patient in a knee-chest position, transport rapidly with lights and siren.
    c. patient on her left side, transport without lights and siren, and dim the lights in the patient area of the ambulance.
    d. patient on her back with her head lower than her feet (Trendelenburg), transport rapidly with lights and siren.

_____ 22. If this patient's condition worsens, she is at risk of
    a. having a seizure.   **c.** a diabetic emergency.
    b. placenta previa.   **d.** losing her feet because of inadequate circulation.

Sentence Completion

In the blanks provided, write the words that best complete each sentence.

23. A full-term baby's respiratory rate is normally between _____ and _____ breaths per minute.

24. A full-term baby's heart rate is normally between _____ and _____ beats per minute.

25. A breech birth occurs when the baby's _____ or _____ come out of the uterus first.

Matching

Match the key terms in the left column with the definitions in the right column by placing the letter of each correct answer in the space provided.

_____ 26. Spontaneous abortion

_____ 27. Abruptio placentae

_____ 28. Crowning

_____ 29. Labor

_____ 30. Blow-by oxygen

_____ 31. Ectopic pregnancy

_____ 32. Ovaries

_____ 33. Premature labor

_____ 34. Amniotic sac

_____ 35. Eclampsia

_____ 36. Acrocyanosis

_____ 37. Limb presentation

_____ 38. Menstruation

_____ 39. Preeclampsia

_____ 40. Delivery

_____ 41. Cervix

_____ 42. Incomplete abortion

_____ 43. Fallopian tube

_____ 44. Breech delivery

_____ 45. Meconium

_____ 46. Endometriosis

_____ 47. Placenta

_____ 48. Cephalic delivery

_____ 49. Placenta previa

_____ 50. Bloody show

_____ 51. Presenting part

A. Thick, sticky material that collects in the intestines of a fetus and forms the first stools of a newborn

B. The actual birth of the baby at the end of the 2nd stage of labor

C. A condition of pregnancy characterized by high blood pressure, swelling, protein in the urine, and seizures

D. A delivery in which an infant emerges head first from the birth canal

E. A condition that occurs when a fertilized egg implants outside the uterus

F. A condition that occurs when part or all of the placenta implants in the lower part of the uterus, covering the opening of the cervix

G. A condition in which uterine tissue is located outside the uterus, causing pain and bleeding

H. A condition of high blood pressure and swelling that occurs in some women during the 3rd trimester of pregnancy

I. Labor before a woman's 37th week of pregnancy

J. The narrow opening at the lower end of the uterus that connects the uterus to the vagina

K. The part of an infant that emerges first during delivery

L. The periodic discharge of blood and tissue from the uterus

M. The stage of birth when the infant's head is visible at the vaginal opening

N. Either of a pair of tubes that receive and transport the egg from the ovary to the uterus after ovulation

O. A delivery in which the presenting part of the infant is an arm or a leg instead of the head

P. Mucus and blood that may come out of the vagina as labor begins

Q. The loss of a fetus as a result of natural causes before the 20th week of pregnancy

R. Blueness of the hands and feet

S. The process in which the uterus repeatedly contracts to push the fetus and placenta out of the mother's body

T. Paired, almond-shaped organs in a woman's body that produce eggs

Continued

U. A specialized organ through which the fetus exchanges nourishment and waste products during pregnancy

V. A delivery in which the presenting part of the infant is the buttocks or feet instead of the head

W. Method of oxygen delivery in which the device used to deliver the oxygen does not make actual contact with the patient

X. The sac of fluid that surrounds the fetus inside the uterus

Y. A condition that occurs when a normally implanted placenta separates prematurely from the wall of the uterus during the last trimester of pregnancy

Z. An abortion in which part of the products of conception have been passed but some remain in the uterus

Short Answer

Answer each question in the space provided.

52. List three functions of the placenta.
   1.
   2.
   3.

53. Explain why a woman in late pregnancy should not lie flat on her back.

54. An infant's head is crowning. You see that the bag of waters has not broken. What should you do now?

55. Why is it very important to keep a newborn warm?

56. List three signs that suggest that the placenta is about to be delivered.
   1.
   2.
   3.

57. What sign or symptom distinguishes eclampsia from preeclampsia?

Answer Section

Chapter 20

True/False

1. False

If the cord is around the neck, gently loosen the cord and try to slip it over the baby's shoulder or head. If the umbilical cord is wrapped tightly around the baby's neck and cannot be loosened or is wrapped around the neck more than once, the cord must be removed. To do this, place two umbilical clamps or ties on the cord about 3 inches apart. Carefully cut the cord between the two clamps. Remove the cord from the baby's neck.

Objective: Describe how and when to cut the umbilical cord.

2. False

Suction the baby's mouth first to be sure there is nothing for the baby to suck into his lungs if he should gasp when you suction his nose.

Objective: Summarize neonatal resuscitation procedures.

Multiple Choice

3. d

The ovaries are paired, almond-shaped organs located on either side of the uterus. The ovaries perform two main functions: producing eggs and secreting hormones, such as estrogen and progesterone.

Objective: Identify the following structures: uterus, vagina, fetus, placenta, umbilical cord, amniotic sac, and perineum.

4. d

The egg is transported to the uterus through one of the fallopian tubes after ovulation. If fertilization occurs, the developing fetus (unborn infant) implants itself in the uterine wall and develops there.

Objective: Identify the following structures: uterus, vagina, fetus, placenta, umbilical cord, amniotic sac, and perineum.

5. c

The area between the anus and the vagina is the perineum. To help prevent tearing of the perineum, you may apply gentle pressure to the top of the infant's head as it emerges from the vagina. Be careful not to touch the fontanels, the areas of the skull that have not yet formed. The pressure you apply should not halt delivery of the infant, but control it. Colon is another term for the large intestine. The cervix is the neck of the uterus. During pregnancy, it contains the mucus plug that protects the uterus from the invasion of bacteria. The passage of the plug may account for a light bloody show in the 1st stage of labor. The labia majora is the term given to the outermost folds of skin that enclose the vulva.

Objective: Identify the following structures: uterus, vagina, fetus, placenta, umbilical cord, amniotic sac, perineum.

6. b

Spinal stabilization is indicated because of the trauma to the head. Here are some guidelines for dealing with alleged sexual assault. It is not your job to determine the truth of the patient's statements. It is also not your job to be judgmental or critical of the patient. You are dealing with a patient who has multiple injuries: an injured head, possible injuries to the pelvic area, and the very real injury to her psyche. Rape is a traumatic event, both physically and emotionally. Be professional and supportive. Be thorough in your history taking but not intrusive. Be supportive but not chatty. If available, have a crew member of the same gender interact with the patient. Be gentle and brief in conducting a physical examination. Examination of the patient's genitalia should be done only if profuse bleeding is present. If the suspected injury is not significant enough to require treatment, visualizing the area will only make the patient more uncomfortable and may result in the damage of important evidence. Make sure that your documentation is accurate and complete.

Objective: Discuss the emergency medical care of a patient with a gynecological emergency.

7. a

The preferred position for a pregnant (more than 20 weeks) patient is left lateral recumbent. Positioning the patient on the left side prevents the developing fetus from compressing the major blood vessels of the abdomen (abdominal aorta and inferior vena cava).

Objective: N/A

8. c

A limb presentation occurs when an arm or leg of the baby protrudes from the vagina before the head. This situation is a medical emergency because the baby cannot be delivered in this position. Prepare for immediate transport as soon as you recognize a limb presentation. Give oxygen to the mother and place her in the knee-chest position or on her left side with her hips and legs elevated to decrease pressure on the umbilical cord.

Objective: Describe the procedures for the following abnormal deliveries: breech birth, prolapsed cord, limb presentation.

9. b

Until proven otherwise, any female patient in her reproductive years who complains of severe one-sided (left or right) lower abdominal pain should be suspected of and treated for an ectopic pregnancy.

Objective: Identify predelivery emergencies.

10. d

An ectopic pregnancy occurs when a fertilized egg implants outside the uterus. An ectopic pregnancy is a medical emergency. The most common site where this occurs is inside a fallopian tube. An ectopic pregnancy that occurs in a fallopian tube is called a *tubal pregnancy*. Less commonly, the egg implants in the abdomen, cervix, or an ovary.

Objective: N/A

11. a

Treatment is geared toward slowing the progression of shock. Place the patient in a supine position, provide high-flow oxygen, and transport rapidly to an Emergency Department.

Objective: N/A

12. b

After the head emerges, instruct the mother to "breathe through" the next contraction until you can clear the infant's airway. Clear the airway with a bulb syringe. Make sure you depress (squeeze) the syringe before you put it in the infant's mouth and nose. Once the nose and mouth have been suctioned adequately, you may lower the infant's head slightly to ease delivery of the top shoulder. Then lift up slightly to deliver the bottom shoulder. The shoulders are the widest part of the infant's body. Once the shoulders are delivered, the delivery of the rest of the baby will be rapid. Be gentle but supportive as the infant emerges.

Objective: Describe care of the baby as the head appears.

13. c

Leave the infant at the level of the birth canal and immediately begin warming, drying, and stimulating the infant. Regardless of the infant's presentation (whether pink and crying or blue and slow to respond), warming, drying, and stimulating are the first steps in the resuscitation of a newborn.

Objective: Summarize neonatal resuscitation procedures.

14. b

Newborns are evaluated using the Apgar scale: *A*ppearance (color), *P*ulse (heart rate), *G*rimace (irritability), *A*ctivity (muscle tone), and *R*espirations (breathing rate). Each category is rated from 0 to 2 (with 2 being normal/healthy) for a total of 10 possible points. The scale is evaluated at 1 minute and 5 minutes after birth. If the 5-minute evaluation is less than 7, continue evaluating every 5 minutes. AVPU is a memory aid for assessing the level of consciousness for adults or children. SAMPLE is the history-taking acronym. A-NU-BABY is not an accepted acronym.

Objective: Summarize neonatal resuscitation procedures.

15. a

Your initial responsibility is to assess the scene. Your scene size-up should address the number of patients, the MOI, the need for additional resources, safety (for you, your crew, the patients, and bystanders), and BSI precautions. After the size-up, you can begin gaining access to and evaluating patients.

Objective: Determine if the scene is safe to enter.

16. d

Abruptio placentae may occur from trauma, high blood pressure, or multiple pregnancies. An abruptio placentae is the premature separation of the placenta from the uterine wall during the last trimester of pregnancy. Patients with this condition have severe abdominal pain. Bleeding may be present or absent depending on the location of the tear. Patients may also complain of decreased or absent fetal movement. Severe hypoxia slows the activity of the fetus.

Objective: Identify predelivery emergencies.

17. b

Because your patient has been involved in a motor vehicle collision, spinal stabilization is indicated. You must ensure that the fetus does not compress the blood vessels of the abdomen. To prevent this compression, tilt the entire backboard to the left. Provide high-flow oxygen and transport rapidly to the closest appropriate facility.

Objective: Identify predelivery emergencies.

18. b

The painless discharge of blood during the last trimester of pregnancy is most often associated with a placenta previa. Placenta previa develops if the placenta implants too low in the uterine wall. The lower portion of the uterus stretches and contracts in preparation for delivery. If the placenta has implanted in this area, it may tear. The fetus depends on the placenta for nourishment and oxygen.

Objective: Identify predelivery emergencies.

19. c

Although a "bloody show" is commonly associated with normal delivery (from the passage of the mucus plug), it is not normal for 200 for 300 mL of blood to be discharged before delivery of the infant. This patient should not be told to bear down because this may increase the size of the tear. Never place anything in the vagina (such as a tampon) because it hides the extent of bleeding. Apply sanitary napkins to the exterior of the vaginal opening to absorb the bleeding, provide high-flow oxygen, position the patient on her left side, and

transport rapidly. Retain used sanitary napkins for the hospital, as they indicate the extent of bleeding.

Objective: Identify predelivery emergencies.

20. a

Preeclampsia (also called *pregnancy-induced hypertension* or *toxemia of pregnancy*) is a disorder of pregnancy that causes blood vessels to spasm and constrict. Blood vessel constriction results in high blood pressure. It also decreases blood flow to the mother's organs, including the placenta. Less blood flow to the placenta usually means less oxygenated blood and nutrients reach the baby. In some cases, the baby may need to be delivered early to protect the health of the mother. Preeclampsia also causes changes in the blood vessels. These changes cause the mother's capillaries to leak fluid into her tissues. This results in swelling of the face, hands, and lower back. Other signs and symptoms include visual disturbances, headaches, irritability, and right upper quadrant abdominal pain.

Objective: Identify predelivery emergencies.

21. c

The appropriate position for this patient is left lateral recumbent. Although this patient has a serious medical complication, you must transport without lights and siren because stimulation from the flashing lights and loud siren may cause a seizure in this patient.

Objective: Identify predelivery emergencies.

22. a

Preeclampsia may deteriorate into eclampsia. Eclampsia is the seizure phase of preeclampsia. It is associated with a significant risk of death for the mother and fetus. Eclampsia is a medical emergency. During the active seizure, treat the mother as you would any other seizure patient and prevent the patient from injuring herself. After the seizure, position the patient on her left side, maintain an open airway (suctioning may be necessary), provide high-flow oxygen (by nonrebreather mask if breathing is adequate or by BM device if breathing is inadequate), and transport promptly but without excessive stimuli (lights or sirens).

Objective: Identify predelivery emergencies.

Sentence Completion

23. A full-term baby's respiratory rate is normally between __30__ and __60__ breaths per minute.

Objective: Summarize neonatal resuscitation procedures.

24. A full-term baby's heart rate is normally between __100__ and __180__ beats per minute.

Objective: Summarize neonatal resuscitation procedures.

25. A breech birth occurs when the baby's __buttocks__ or __feet__ come out of the uterus first.

Objective: Describe the procedures for the following abnormal deliveries: breech birth, prolapsed cord, limb presentation.

Matching

26.	Q	**39.**	H
27.	Y	**40.**	B
28.	M	**41.**	J
29.	S	**42.**	Z
30.	W	**43.**	N
31.	E	**44.**	V
32.	T	**45.**	A
33.	I	**46.**	G
34.	X	**47.**	U
35.	C	**48.**	D
36.	R	**49.**	F
37.	O	**50.**	P
38.	L	**51.**	K

Short Answer

52. The placenta is responsible for:
- Exchange of oxygen and carbon dioxide between the blood of the mother and fetus (the placenta serves the function of the lungs for the developing fetus)
- Removal of waste products
- Transport of nutrients from the mother to the fetus
- Production of a special hormone of pregnancy that maintains the pregnancy and stimulates changes in the mother's breasts, cervix, and vagina in preparation for delivery
- Maintaining a barrier against harmful substances

Objective: Identify the following structures: uterus, vagina, fetus, placenta, umbilical cord, amniotic sac, and perineum.

53. Avoid positioning the mother completely flat on her back because compression of the inferior vena cava and aorta can lower her blood pressure and decrease perfusion of the uterus.

Objective: Identify predelivery emergencies.

54. If the bag of waters does not break or has not broken, use your gloved fingers to tear it. Push the sac away from the infant's head and mouth as they appear.

Objective: State the steps to assist in a delivery.

55. Newborns lose heat very quickly because they are wet and suddenly exposed to an environment that is cooler than that inside the uterus. Quickly dry the baby's body and head to remove blood and amniotic fluid. Immediately remove the wet towel or blanket from the infant, and then quickly wrap the baby in a clean, warm blanket. Because most body heat is lost through the head, remember to cover the baby's head as soon as possible.

Objective: Summarize neonatal resuscitation procedures.

56. Signs indicating separation of the placenta include a gush of blood, lengthening of the umbilical cord, contraction of the uterus, and an urge to push. Encourage the mother to push to help deliver the placenta.

Objective: Discuss the steps in the delivery of the placenta.

57. If untreated, preeclampsia may progress to eclampsia. Eclampsia is the seizure phase of preeclampsia. Eclampsia is associated with a significant risk of death for the mother and fetus.

Objective: Identify predelivery emergencies.

Division 5

Trauma

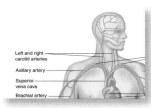

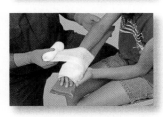

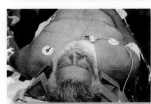

21 Bleeding and Shock

READING ASSIGNMENT ▶ Read Chapter 21, pages 471 to 485 in your textbook.

Sum It Up

- Perfusion is the circulation of blood through an organ or a part of the body. Shock (hypoperfusion) is the inadequate circulation of blood through an organ or a part of the body.

- A wound is an injury to soft tissues. A closed wound occurs when the soft tissues under the skin are damaged but the surface of the skin is not broken (for example, a bruise). An open wound results when the skin surface is broken (for example, a cut or scrape).

- Hemorrhage (also called *major bleeding*) is an extreme loss of blood from a blood vessel. It is a life-threatening condition that requires *immediate* attention. If it is not controlled, hemorrhage can lead to shock and potentially to death.

- Hemophilia is a disorder in which the blood does not clot normally. A person with hemophilia may have major bleeding from minor injuries and may bleed for no apparent reason. Some medications or a serious injury may also prevent effective clotting.

- Arterial bleeding is the most serious type of bleeding. The blood from an artery is bright red, oxygen-rich blood. A bleeding artery can quickly lead to the loss of a large amount of blood.

- Venous bleeding is usually easier to control than arterial bleeding because it is under less pressure. Blood lost from a vein flows as a steady stream and is dark red or maroon because it is oxygen-poor blood.

- Capillary bleeding is common because the walls of the capillaries are fragile and many are close to the skin's surface. Bleeding from capillaries is usually dark red. When a capillary is torn, blood oozes slowly from the site of the injury because the pressure within the capillaries is low. Capillary bleeding often clots and stops by itself within a few minutes.

- External bleeding is bleeding that you can see. Clotting normally occurs within minutes. However, external bleeding must be controlled with your gloved hands and dressings until a clot is formed and the bleeding has stopped.

- You must wear PPE when you anticipate exposure to blood or other potentially infectious material. HIV and the hepatitis virus are examples of diseases to which you may be exposed that can be transmitted by exposure to blood.
- Six methods may be used to control external bleeding. You must know the methods of external bleeding control that are approved by medical direction and your local protocol.
  — Applying direct pressure slows blood flow and allows clotting to take place.
  — Elevating a bleeding arm or leg may help control the bleeding. Do not elevate the extremity if pain, swelling, or deformity is present.
  — If bleeding continues from an arm or leg, pressure points (also called *pulse points*) may be used to slow severe bleeding.
  — A splint is a device used to limit the movement of an injured arm or leg and reduce bleeding. After applying the splint, make sure to check the patient's fingers (or toes) often for color, warmth, and feeling.
  — A pressure splint (also called an *air or pneumatic splint*) can help control bleeding from soft-tissue injuries or broken bones. It can also help stabilize a broken bone.
  — A tourniquet is a tight bandage that surrounds an arm or leg. It is used to stop the flow of blood in an extremity. A tourniquet should be used to control life-threatening bleeding in an arm or leg when you cannot control the bleeding with direct pressure.
- Internal bleeding is bleeding that occurs inside body tissues and cavities. A bruise is a collection of blood under the skin caused by bleeding capillaries. A bruise is an example of internal bleeding that is not life threatening.
- Shock is the inadequate flow of blood through an organ or a part of the body. Shock can be caused by failure of the body's pump (the heart), fluid (blood), or container (the blood vessels).
  — Cardiogenic shock can result if the heart beats too quickly or too slowly or if the heart muscle does not have enough force to pump blood effectively to all parts of the body.
  — Shock caused by severe bleeding is called *hemorrhagic shock*. The bleeding may be internal, external, or both.
  — Shock caused by a loss of blood, plasma, or other body fluid is called *hypovolemic shock.*
- Early (compensated) shock is often difficult to recognize. Remember to look for it and to consider the patient's MOI or the NOI when assessing your patient. Early shock is usually reversible if it is recognized and the patient receives emergency care to correct the cause of the shock.
- Late (decompensated) shock results when the patient's systolic blood pressure drops to less than 90 mm Hg. In this phase of shock, the body's defense mechanisms lose their ability to make up for the lack of oxygenated blood. The signs of late shock are more obvious than early shock, but late shock is more difficult to treat.
- Irreversible shock is also called *terminal shock.* You will feel an irregular pulse as the patient's heart becomes irritable and begins to beat irregularly. Permanent damage occurs to the vital organs because the cells and organs have been without oxygenated blood for too long. Eventually, the heart stops, breathing stops, and death results.

After reading this chapter, can you:	Page Reference	Objective Met?
• List the structures and functions of the circulatory system?	472	☐
• Differentiate between arterial, venous and capillary bleeding?	473	☐
• State methods of emergency medical care of external bleeding?	474	☐
• Establish the relationship between BSI and bleeding?	474	☐
• Establish the relationship between airway management and the trauma patient?	480	☐
• Establish the relationship between MOI and internal bleeding?	479	☐
• List the signs of internal bleeding?	479	☐
• List the steps in the emergency medical care of the patient with signs and symptoms of internal bleeding?	480	☐
• List signs and symptoms of shock (hypoperfusion)?	481, 482	☐
• State the steps in the emergency medical care of the patient with signs and symptoms of shock?	483	☐

Multiple Choice

In the space provided, identify the letter of the choice that best completes the statement or answers each question.

_____ **1.** An average adult man has a normal blood volume of about
  a. 3 to 4 L.   **c.** 5 to 6 L.
  b. 4 to 5 L.   **d.** 6 to 7 L.

_____ **2.** A 23-year-old man has been stabbed multiple times in his chest and abdomen. As you approach him and form your general impression, you see he is having difficulty breathing. There is a large pool of blood around him and his shirt is soaked with blood. After taking BSI precautions, you should first
  a. cover all wounds with a dressing.
  b. assess and manage the patient's airway and breathing.
  c. apply direct pressure to the most severe wounds.
  d. assess for signs of internal bleeding.

_____ **3.** A 22-year-old woman attempted suicide by slashing her left wrist. After taking BSI precautions, you find that the immediate life threat that is present is the bright red blood spurting from her left wrist. There is a large amount of blood on the floor around her. You apply a dressing with direct pressure to the wound but the wound is still bleeding. You should now
  a. apply a traction splint.
  b. apply a tourniquet.
  c. apply pressure at the femoral artery.
  d. place the patient on her back with her lower legs elevated 12 to 18 inches.

_____ **4.** Shock is generally attributed to failure of one of three components of the cardiovascular system: the pump (heart), the container (blood vessels), and the fluid (blood). Another name for failure of the pump is
  a. neurogenic shock.   **c.** hypovolemic shock.
  b. cardiogenic shock.   **d.** hemorrhagic shock.

_____ **5.** Which of the following regarding the response to shock in children and infants is correct?
  a. Children and infants will compensate much longer than adults.
  b. Children and infants will show the signs of shock much earlier than adults.
  c. Children and infants will show the signs of shock at the same rate as adults.
  d. Children and infants have healthy hearts and blood vessels and never go into shock.

_____ 6. Shock (hypoperfusion) is a condition that develops as a response to injury or insult. Which of the following organs will suffer damage earliest as a result of shock?
   a. The skin
   b. The brain
   c. The kidneys and liver
   d. The large muscles of the arms and legs

_____ 7. Your ambulance has been called to the home of an 8-month-old female patient. Her mother informs you the child has had diarrhea for the past three days and has refused her bottle for the past 36 hours. The child is pale, with a capillary refill time of 3 to 4 seconds. This child is most likely
   a. not in shock.
   b. in shock because of fluid loss.
   c. in shock because of pump failure.
   d. in shock because of container failure.

_____ 8. Which of the following is considered a late sign of shock?
   a. Altered mental status
   b. Rapid, shallow breathing
   c. Dropping blood pressure
   d. Persistent rapid, weak pulse

Questions 9–10 pertain to the following scenario.

Your rescue crew is called to a construction site for a 28-year-old man who cut his hand with a saw. You arrive to find the patient holding a blood-soaked towel over his left hand. He states that blood was "spurting out with every heart beat."

_____ 9. This type of bleeding is consistent with
   a. laceration of a vein.
   b. laceration of a tendon.
   c. laceration of an artery.
   d. laceration of a capillary bed.

_____ 10. The first step in controlling the bleeding associated with the injury is to apply
   a. a tourniquet.
   b. direct pressure at the injury site.
   c. pressure to the nearest pressure point.
   d. a blood pressure cuff to the upper arm and inflate until the bleeding stops.

Sentence Completion

In the blanks provided, write the words that best complete each sentence.

11. _____ shock is the most common type of shock.

12. _____ shock can result if the heart beats too quickly, too slowly, or if the heart muscle does not have enough force to pump blood effectively to all parts of the body.

13. In some EMS systems, the _____ _____ _____ can be used as a pressure splint to help control suspected severe bleeding in the abdomen or pelvis.

Matching

Match the key terms in the left column with the definitions in the right column by placing the letter of each correct answer in the space provided.

_____ 14. Anaphylactic shock

_____ 15. Dressing

_____ 16. Major bleeding

_____ 17. Internal bleeding

_____ 18. Tourniquet

_____ 19. Cardiogenic shock

A. Shock caused by a severe infection

B. An injury that occurs when the soft tissues under the skin are damaged but the surface of the skin is not broken

C. Another phrase for hemorrhage

Continued

_____ 20. Compound fracture

_____ 21. Hemophilia

_____ 22. Open wound

_____ 23. Hemorrhagic shock

_____ 24. Hypoperfusion

_____ 25. External bleeding

_____ 26. Closed wound

_____ 27. Wound

_____ 28. Hypovolemic shock

_____ 29. Bruise

_____ 30. Splint

_____ 31. Hemorrhage

_____ 32. Perfusion

_____ 33. Septic shock

_____ 34. Direct pressure

D. Circulation of blood through an organ or a part of the body

E. Shock caused by a severe allergic reaction

F. Bleeding that you can see

G. An injury in which the skin surface is broken

H. Firm force applied to a bleeding site with gloved hands or bandages to control bleeding

I. Bleeding that occurs inside body tissues and cavities

J. Shock

K. Shock that occurs when the heart muscle does not have enough force to pump blood effectively to all parts of the body

L. A device used to limit the movement of an injured arm or leg and reduce bleeding and discomfort

M. Shock caused by severe bleeding

N. A tight bandage that surrounds an arm or leg and that is used to stop the flow of blood in the extremity

O. A collection of blood under the skin caused by bleeding capillaries

P. A broken bone that penetrates the skin

Q. An injury to the soft tissues of the body

R. An extreme loss of blood from a blood vessel

S. Absorbent material placed directly over a wound

T. A disorder in which the blood does not clot normally

U. Shock caused by a loss of blood, plasma, or other body fluid

Short Answer

Answer each question in the space provided.

35. List the three stages of shock.

1.

2.

3.

36. What are the two most common causes of internal bleeding?

1.

2.

37. Complete the following table regarding the types of bleeding.

	Arterial	Venous	Capillary
Color			
Blood Flow			
Bleeding Control			

38. List the four major causes of container failure shock.

    1.

    2.

    3.

    4.

39. List four signs or symptoms of early shock.

    1.

    2.

    3.

    4.

40. Label the following major arteries and veins: aorta, axillary artery, brachial artery, coronary arteries, dorsalis pedis arteries, femoral arteries, inferior vena cava, left and right carotid arteries, popliteal arteries, radial artery, subclavian arteries, superior vena cava, tibial arteries, and ulnar artery.

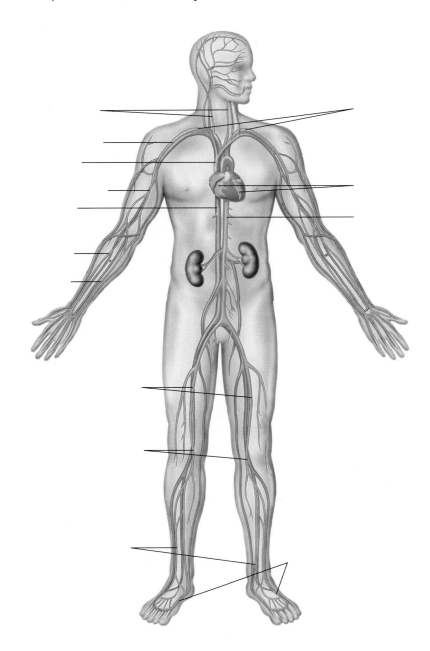

Answer Section

Chapter 21

Multiple Choice

1. c

An average adult man has a normal blood volume of about 5 to 6 L (5000-6000 mL).

Objective: List the structures and functions of the circulatory system.

2. b

Bleeding may be obvious when you approach a patient. However, remember that making sure the patient has an open airway and adequate breathing takes priority over other care. Stabilize the cervical spine if needed. During your assessment of the patient's circulation, control major (severe) bleeding.

Objective: State methods of emergency medical care of external bleeding.

3. b

Control bleeding by using direct pressure. If bleeding continues despite the use of direct pressure, your next steps to control bleeding must be guided by your medical director and local protocol. Some EMS systems use elevation, pressure points, and then a tourniquet if bleeding continues. In other EMS systems, a tourniquet is applied if direct pressure fails to control the bleeding.

Objective: State methods of emergency medical care of external bleeding.

4. b

Cardiogenic shock is shock brought on by the inability of the heart (the pump) to keep up with the body's demand. Neurogenic shock is container failure shock that occurs when the impulse from the brain to the arteries is cut off (such as when the spinal cord is damaged). In the absence of a nervous impulse, the vessels

of the body relax and dilate. When the vessels are fully dilated, the average body can hold approximately five times its normal volume of blood. Hypovolemic shock occurs from a loss of fluid, either blood or plasma. Hemorrhagic shock occurs from the loss of blood.

Objective: List signs and symptoms of shock (hypoperfusion).

5. a

Typically, children and infants have a more efficient compensatory mechanism than adults. Children can compensate for massive blood loss, for example, much longer than an adult can. In a previously healthy adult, a sudden episode of blood loss will usually not produce vital sign changes until the patient has lost from 15-30% of his blood volume. Then, the blood pressure will begin to creep down. Children may not show hemodynamic (blood pressure) compromise until 25% of the total blood volume is lost. By the time a child begins to show the more measurable signs of shock, he may be very deep into the progression of shock. Do not let a good blood pressure and healthy appearance fool you into undertreating a child.

Objective: List signs and symptoms of shock (hypoperfusion).

6. b

The brain, the heart, and the lungs are among the organs most sensitive to oxygen deprivation. Within 4 to 6 minutes, these organs will begin to suffer as a result of hypoperfusion. Because the brain is so sensitive to oxygen deprivation, one of the first signs of shock is an altered mental status (anxiety, restlessness, confusion). The skin and muscles will suffer damage after about 4 to 8 hours, and the kidneys and liver will suffer damage after about 45 to 90 minutes.

Objective: List signs and symptoms of shock (hypoperfusion).

7. b

A patient does not have to bleed to be in shock from fluid loss. The body may also become depleted of fluid by excessive sweating, urinating, vomiting, diarrhea, or burn injury.

Objective: List signs and symptoms of shock (hypoperfusion).

8. c

Decreasing blood pressure values are a late sign of shock. Altered mental status (anxiety, dizziness, restlessness) is an early sign because the brain is one of the first organs to be affected by hypoperfusion. Shallow, rapid breathing and a rapid, weak pulse are also early signs as compared to blood pressure.

Objective: List signs and symptoms of shock (hypoperfusion).

9. c

Arteries flow blood under high pressure (as compared to veins). Blood flowing through the arteries of the body is oxygenated and bright red. Therefore, arterial bleeds are characterized by the spurting of bright red blood. Veins carry deoxygenated blood from the cells of the body back to the heart. Deoxygenated blood is darker than oxygenated blood, and blood in veins does not flow under as high pressure as in arteries. Venous bleeding is characterized by the constant flow of dark red or maroon-colored blood. Capillaries are very small vessels. Red blood cells literally line up single file to flow through capillaries. Bleeding associated with capillary injury is an oozing of plasma with a scant amount of blood (like a "carpet burn").

Objective: Differentiate between arterial, venous, and capillary bleeding.

10. b

The first step to control bleeding is to apply direct pressure at the bleeding point. If needed, apply a pressure bandage using 4 × 4 gauze pads and an elastic bandage. Even if the blood flow is not completely stopped, the direct pressure

applied to the wound may be sufficient to slow the rate of blood loss so that the blood-clotting system can stop the hemorrhage. If applicable, splint the extremity to decrease movement.

Objective: State methods of emergency medical care of external bleeding.

Sentence Completion

11. **Hypovolemic** shock is the most common type of shock.

Objective: N/A

12. **Cardiogenic** shock can result if the heart beats too quickly, too slowly, or if the heart muscle does not have enough force to pump blood effectively to all parts of the body.

Objective: N/A

13. In some EMS systems, the **pneumatic antishock garment** (also called Military Antishock Trousers) can be used as a pressure splint to help control suspected severe bleeding in the abdomen or pelvis.

Objective: List the steps in the emergency medical care of the patient with signs and symptoms of internal bleeding.

Matching

14.	E	**25.**	F
15.	S	**26.**	B
16.	C	**27.**	Q
17.	I	**28.**	U
18.	N	**29.**	O
19.	K	**30.**	L
20.	P	**31.**	R
21.	T	**32.**	D
22.	G	**33.**	A
23.	M	**34.**	H
24.	J		

Short Answer

35. Shock occurs in stages:

   1. Early (compensated)
   2. Late (decompensated)
   3. Irreversible (terminal).

   Objective: List signs and symptoms of shock (hypoperfusion).

36. The most common causes of internal bleeding are:

   1. Injured or damaged internal organs
   2. Fractures, especially fractures of the femur and pelvis

   Objective: Establish the relationship between mechanism of injury and internal bleeding.

37.

	Arterial	Venous	Capillary
Color	Bright red	Dark red, maroon	Dark red
Blood Flow	Spurts with each heartbeat	Flows steadily	Oozes slowly
Bleeding Control	Difficult to control	Usually easier to control than arterial bleeding; bleeding from deep veins may be hard to control	Often clots and stops by itself within a few minutes

   Objective: Differentiate between arterial, venous, and capillary bleeding.

38. The four major causes of container failure shock are:

   1. Injury to the spinal cord (neurogenic shock)
   2. Severe infection (septic shock)
   3. Severe allergic reaction (anaphylactic shock)
   4. Severe drug reaction

   Objective: N/A

39. Signs and symptoms of early shock include:

   • Anxiety, restlessness
   • Thirst
   • Nausea or vomiting
   • Increased respiratory rate
   • Slight increase in heart rate
   • Pale, cool, moist skin
   • Delayed capillary refill in an infant or young child
   • Blood pressure in normal range

   Objective: List signs and symptoms of shock (hypoperfusion).

40.

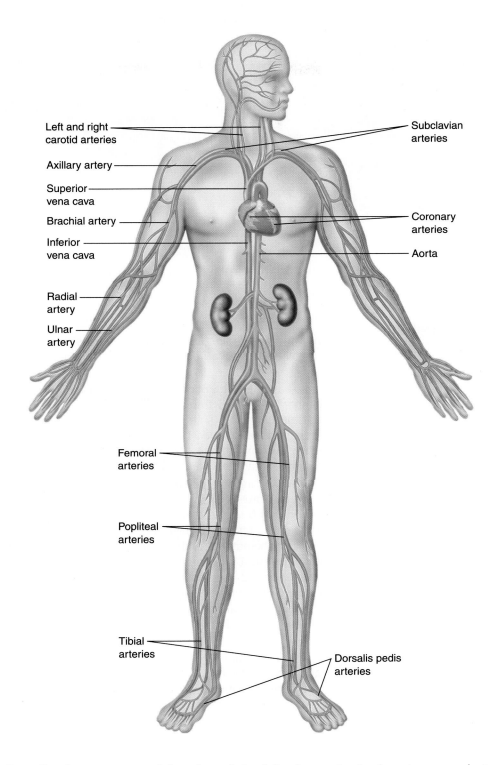

Left and right carotid arteries

Subclavian arteries

Axillary artery

Superior vena cava

Brachial artery

Coronary arteries

Inferior vena cava

Aorta

Radial artery

Ulnar artery

Femoral arteries

Popliteal arteries

Tibial arteries

Dorsalis pedis arteries

Objective: Describe the anatomy and function of the following major body systems: respiratory, circulatory, musculoskeletal, nervous, and endocrine.

READING ASSIGNMENT ▶   Read Chapter 22, pages 486 to 514 in your textbook.

Sum It Up

- The skin is the body's first line of defense against bacteria and other organisms, ultraviolet rays from the sun, harmful chemicals, and cuts and tears.
- Closed soft-tissue injuries occur because of blunt trauma. In blunt trauma, a forceful impact occurs to the body, but there is no break in the skin. In a closed soft-tissue injury, there is no actual break in the skin, but the tissues and vessels may be crushed or ruptured. When assessing a closed soft-tissue injury, it is important to evaluate surface damage and consider possible damage to the organs and major vessels beneath the area of impact.
- Closed soft-tissue injuries include contusions, hematomas, and crush injuries. A contusion is a bruise. In a contusion, the epidermis remains intact. Cells are damaged and blood vessels torn in the dermis. Localized swelling and pain are typically present. A buildup of blood causes discoloration (ecchymosis). A hematoma is the collection of blood beneath the skin. A larger amount of tissue is damaged compared with a contusion. Larger blood vessels are damaged. Hematomas frequently occur with trauma sufficient to break bones. Crush injuries are caused by a crushing force applied to the body. These injuries can cause internal organ rupture. Internal bleeding may be severe and lead to shock.
- Compartment syndrome is a compression injury. It develops when the pressure within a compartment causes compression and abnormal function of nerves and blood vessels. Unless the pressure is relieved within 6 to 8 hours, permanent nerve and muscle damage can result, leading to paralysis, loss of the limb, or even death.
- Crush syndrome can occur when a large amount of skeletal muscle is compressed for a long period. Crush syndrome should be considered when three criteria exist:
    1. Involvement of a large amount of muscle
    2. Compression of the muscle mass for a long period (usually 4 to 6 hours, although it may be as little as 1 hour)
    3. Compromised local blood flow
- In open soft-tissue injuries, a break occurs in the continuity of the skin. Because of the break in the skin, open injuries are susceptible to external

hemorrhage and infection. In an abrasion, the outermost layer of skin (epidermis) is damaged by shearing forces (e.g., rubbing or scraping). A laceration is a break in the skin of varying depth. A laceration may be linear (regular) or stellate (irregular). Lacerations may occur in isolation or with other types of soft-tissue injury. A puncture results when the skin is pierced with a pointed object such as a nail, pencil, ice pick, splinter, piece of glass, bullet, or a knife. An object that remains embedded in the open wound is called an impaled object. In an avulsion, a flap of skin or tissue is torn loose or pulled completely off. In a degloving avulsion injury, the skin and fatty tissue are stripped away. In an amputation, extremities or other body parts are severed from the body. In an open crush injury, soft-tissue and internal organs are damaged. These injuries may cause painful, swollen, deformed extremities. Internal bleeding may be severe.

- An evisceration occurs when an organ sticks out through an open wound. In providing care, do not touch or try to place the exposed organ back into the body. Carefully remove clothing from around the wound. Lightly cover the exposed organs and wound with a thick, moist dressing. Secure the dressing in place with a large bandage to keep moisture in and prevent heat loss.

- An impaled object is an object that remains embedded in an open wound. Do not remove an impaled object unless it interferes with CPR or is impaled through the cheek and interferes with care of the patient's airway. Control bleeding and stabilize the object with bulky dressings, bandaging them in place. Assess the patient for signs of shock and treat if present.

- In the case of an amputated body part, control bleeding at the stump. In most cases, direct pressure will be enough to control the bleeding. Ask an assistant to find the amputated part, as it may be able to be reattached at the hospital. Put the amputated part in a dry plastic bag or waterproof container. Carefully seal the bag or container and place it in water that contains a few ice cubes.

- There are three categories of burns:
  — A superficial (first-degree) burn affects only the epidermis. It results in only minor tissue damage (such as sunburn). The skin is red, tender, and very painful. This type of burn does not usually require medical care and heals in 2 to 5 days with no scarring.
  — A partial-thickness (second-degree) burn involves the epidermis and dermis. The hair follicles and sweat glands are spared in this degree of burn. A partial-thickness burn produces intense pain and some swelling. Blistering may be present. The skin appears pink, red, or mottled and is sensitive to air current and pressure. This type of burn usually heals within 5 to 35 days. Scarring may or may not occur, depending on the depth of the burn.
  — A full-thickness (third-degree) burn destroys both the epidermis and dermis and may include subcutaneous tissue, muscle, and bone. The color of the patient's skin may vary from yellow or pale to black. The skin has a dry, waxy, or leathery appearance. Because the skin is so severely damaged in this type of burn, it cannot perform its usual protective functions. Rapid fluid loss often occurs. Be ready to treat the patient for shock.

- The "rule of nines" is a guide used to estimate the affected body surface area. The rule of nines divides the adult body into sections that are 9% or are multiples of 9%. This guideline has also been modified for children and infants. To estimate the extent of a burn by using the rule of nines, add the percentages of the areas burned.

- A dressing is an absorbent material placed directly over a wound. A bandage is used to secure a dressing in place. A pressure bandage is a bandage

applied with enough pressure over a wound site to control bleeding.
Dressings and bandages serve the following functions:

—Help to stop bleeding
—Absorb blood and other drainage from the wound
—Protect the wound from further injury
—Reduce contamination and the risk of infection

▶ Tracking Your Progress

After reading this chapter, can you:	Page Reference	Objective Met?
• State the major functions of the skin?	488	☐
• List the layers of the skin?	488	☐
• Establish the relationship between BSI and soft-tissue injuries?	488	☐
• List the types of closed soft-tissue injuries?	488	☐
• Describe the emergency medical care of the patient with a closed soft-tissue injury?	491	☐
• State the types of open soft-tissue injuries?	492	☐
• Describe the emergency medical care of the patient with an open soft-tissue injury?	495, 496	☐
• Discuss the emergency medical care considerations for a patient with a penetrating chest injury?	496	☐
• State the emergency medical care considerations for a patient with an open wound to the abdomen?	496	☐
• Differentiate the care of an open wound to the chest from an open wound to the abdomen?	501	☐
• List the classifications of burns?	501	☐
• Define superficial burn?	501	☐
• List the characteristics of a superficial burn?	501	☐
• Define partial-thickness burn?	501	☐
• List the characteristics of a partial-thickness burn?	502	☐
• Define full-thickness burn?	502	☐
• List the characteristics of a full-thickness burn?	502	☐
• Describe the emergency medical care of the patient with a superficial burn?	505	☐
• Describe the emergency medical care of the patient with a partial-thickness burn?	505	☐
• Describe the emergency medical care of the patient with a full-thickness burn?	505	☐
• List the functions of dressing and bandaging?	508	☐
• Describe the purpose of a bandage?	509	☐
• Describe the steps in applying a pressure dressing?	510	☐
• Establish the relationship between airway management and the patient with chest injury, burns, blunt injuries, and penetrating injuries?	505	☐

After reading this chapter, can you:	Page Reference	Objective Met?
• Describe the effects of improperly applied dressings, splints and tourniquets?	510	☐
• Describe the emergency medical care of a patient with an impaled object?	497	☐
• Describe the emergency medical care of a patient with an amputation?	497	☐
• Describe the emergency care for a chemical burn?	506	☐
• Describe the emergency care for an electrical burn?	507	☐

True or False

Decide whether each statement is true or false. In the space provided, write *T* for true or *F* for false.

_____ **1.** Stop the burning process by applying cold water to a thermal burn for at least 15 minutes.

_____ **2.** Only partial-thickness and full-thickness burns are included when calculating the extent of a burn by using the rule of nines.

Multiple Choice

In the space provided, identify the letter of the choice that best completes the statement or answers each question.

Questions 3–4 pertain to the following scenario.

Your ambulance crew is called to the scene of an assault at a local pub. Local law enforcement has already secured the scene. You arrive to find your patient holding a dish towel over his left eye. He tells you he was cut with a broken bottle.

_____ **3.** While assessing the wound, you note it appears to be a straight cut parallel to the eyebrow and about 2-3 inches in length. You may classify this cut as

    a. a puncture.   **c.** an avulsion.

    b. a laceration.   **d.** an abrasion.

_____ **4.** To protect this wound from further contamination, you may put a(n) _____ over the wound and secure it with a _____.

    a. rag, duct tape   **c.** dressing, bandage

    b. bandage, dressing   **d.** occlusive bandage, dressing

_____ **5.** Your ambulance has been called to a local elementary school for a 9-year-old female who injured her eye. You find the patient in the nurse's office with a pencil imbedded in her eyeball. Appropriate treatment for this injury includes

    a. breaking off the end of the pencil, covering both eyes, positioning the patient sitting up, and transport.

    b. stabilizing the pencil with medical tape, covering both eyes, positioning the patient sitting up, and transport.

    c. stabilizing the pencil with a bulky dressing, covering both eyes, position the patient supine (on her back), and transport.

    d. attempting to remove the pencil once but stopping if resistance is met, covering both eyes, and transport.

_____ **6.** When treating an eye injury caused by a chemical burn, it is important to

    a. immediately cover both eyes.

    b. continuously irrigate with normal saline for at least 20 minutes.

    c. immediately attempt to neutralize the chemical by correcting its pH.

    d. continuously irrigate with bicarbonate of soda for at least 20 minutes.

_____ **7.** Calculate the percentage of BSA burned if the patient has burns covering both arms, the chest, and the abdomen.

    a. 18%   **c.** 36%

    b. 27%   **d.** 45%

_____ **8.** Your rescue crew has been called to the scene of a high-speed vehicle collision. While triaging the patients, you note that one patient has an eyeball dangling out of its socket (an extruded eyeball). Appropriate management of this injury includes

    a. replacing the eyeball to the socket and covering both eyes.

    b. submerging the eyeball in water and covering the affected eye.

    c. replacing the eyeball to the socket and covering the affected eye.

    d. covering the eyeball with a moist sterile dressing, protecting from further injury, and covering both eyes.

_____ **9.** You have been called to the home of a 3-year-old child who was burned while getting into a bathtub. His mother states the child burned himself getting into the bath when the water was too hot. The child is conscious and crying. Both legs show scald-type burns up to the buttocks. The percentage of BSA burned is

    a. 18%.   **c.** 45%.

    b. 28%.   **d.** 54%.

Questions 10–11 pertain to the following scenario.

Your ambulance has been called to the scene of a high-rise fire. You are assigned responsibility for a 66-year-old man with burns to his chest and arms. You note the jacket he is wearing is still smoldering. He is conscious and alert complaining of difficulty breathing and severe arm pain.

_____ **10.** Which of the following should be done first?

    a. Remove the patient's burning clothing.

    b. Attempt to calculate the total burn area.

    c. Cover the burns with a dry, sterile dressing.

    d. Begin high-flow oxygen therapy with a nonrebreather mask if breathing status is adequate.

_____ **11.** The burns to the patient's upper arms are red and blistered while the burns to the lower arms and hands are dry and leathery. The burns to the upper arms are most likely _____, while the burns to the lower arms are probably _____.

    a. 3rd degree, 1st degree   **c.** 1st degree, 2nd degree

    b. 1st degree, 3rd degree   **d.** 2nd degree, 3rd degree

Questions 12–14 pertain to the following scenario.

Your rescue crew is called to an apartment complex for a fight. Local law enforcement has secured the scene. Your patient is a 16-year-old male complaining of chest pain and severe difficulty breathing. He states that he was stabbed several times in the back. Upon examination, you find five stab wounds to the upper back and a knife protruding from one of the wounds. There is also a 3-inch laceration to the patient's lower left abdominal quadrant.

_____ **12.** The wounds on the patient's upper back should be covered with

    a. sterile gauze and wrap.

    b. occlusive dressing and elastic wrap.

    c. occlusive dressing taped on one side.

    d. occlusive dressing taped on three sides.

_____ **13.** According to bystanders, the knife's blade is about 3-4 inches long. About 1 inch of the blade is exposed; the rest is in the patient. You should

    a. stabilize the knife with bulky dressings and secure it in place.

    b. seat the knife (push it in the remaining 1 inch), then secure it in place.

    c. remove the knife if it compromises the ability to immobilize the patient's spine.

    d. attempt to remove the knife once, but stop and secure it in place if you meet any resistance.

_____ 14. While examining the abdominal injury, you note a loop of what appears to be intestine is hanging out about 2 inches. Appropriate management of this injury includes
   a. pushing the loop back into the abdominal cavity.
   b. covering the loop with dry, sterile gauze and securing with tape.
   c. covering with a large, sterile dressing moistened with sterile saline, securing with a large bandage, and preventing heat loss.
   d. covering the loop with an occlusive dressing, applying ice packs or cool compresses, and securing with a gauze wrap.

Sentence Completion

In the blanks provided, write the words that best complete each sentence.

15. A(n) _____ is the most common type of closed wound.

16. A _____ burn affects only the epidermis and results in only minor tissue damage.

17. An occlusive dressing prevents _____ from entering a wound.

Matching

Match the key terms in the left column with the definitions in the right column by placing the letter of each correct answer in the space provided.

_____ 18. Epidermis

_____ 19. Rule of nines

_____ 20. Impaled object

_____ 21. Puncture wound

_____ 22. Ecchymosis

_____ 23. Open soft-tissue injury

_____ 24. Compartment syndrome

_____ 25. Superficial burn

_____ 26. Bandage

_____ 27. Penetrating chest injury

_____ 28. Abrasion

_____ 29. Full-thickness burn

_____ 30. Avulsion

_____ 31. Paresthesias

_____ 32. Fascia

_____ 33. Evisceration

_____ 34. Soft tissues

_____ 35. Laceration

_____ 36. Pressure bandage

_____ 37. Fasciotomy

_____ 38. Closed soft-tissue injury

_____ 39. Circumferential burn

_____ 40. Anesthesia

A. Material, such as roller gauze, that is applied snugly to create pressure on a wound and hold a dressing in place over it

B. A localized collection of blood beneath the skin caused by a tear in a blood vessel

C. Abnormal sensations such as tingling, burning, numbness, or a "pins-and-needles" feeling

D. Damage to the outermost layer of skin (epidermis) by shearing forces (such as rubbing or scraping)

E. Layers of the skin and the fat and muscle beneath them

F. An object that remains embedded in an open wound

G. A break in the skin of varying depth that may be linear (regular) or stellate (irregular)

H. A burn that involves the epidermis and dermis

I. A guide used to estimate the affected BSA of a burn

J. A burn in which the epidermis and dermis are destroyed

K. Outermost skin layer

L. The protrusion of an organ through an open wound

Continued

_____ **41.** Partial-thickness burn

_____ **42.** Hematoma

_____ **43.** Air embolism

M. A compression injury that develops when the pressure within a compartment causes compression and abnormal function of nerves and blood vessels

N. A soft-tissue injury that results when the body is struck by a blunt object; there is no break in the skin, but the tissues and vessels beneath the skin surface are crushed or ruptured

O. A burn that affects only the epidermis

P. Without sensation

Q. A soft-tissue injury in which a break occurs in the skin

R. Swelling from a burn that encircles an extremity

S. A break in the skin over the chest wall

T. A tough sheet of fibrous tissue that covers the skeletal muscles of the body

U. Material used to secure a dressing in place

V. Discoloration of the skin that occurs as blood leaks from torn vessels into the surrounding tissue

W. The entry of air into the circulation through a blood vessel that is torn and exposed to the air

X. A soft-tissue injury in which a flap of skin or tissue is torn loose or pulled completely off

Y. Piercing of the skin with a pointed object such as a nail or ice pick

Z. A surgical procedure in which a physician cuts the tough sheet of fibrous tissue covering a muscle to relieve pressure

Short Answer

Answer each question in the space provided.

44. The mother of a 12-year-old boy is anxious because her son's nose won't stop bleeding. She says her son has a history of allergies but is otherwise healthy. The nosebleed started about 15 minutes ago. You find the boy standing in the bathroom of his home holding a bloody towel to his face. After taking BSI precautions, you perform a primary survey. No life-threatening injuries are present. How will you care for the patient's nosebleed?

45. A 33-year-old man was found unresponsive in an apartment fire. The patient is breathing and has a pulse. List four signs or symptoms that should alert you to possible airway problems in this patient.

1.

2.

3.

4.

46. What is the most urgent type of injury to the eye?

47. A 25-year-old man has been stabbed in the abdomen. Your assessment reveals abdominal organs are protruding from the wound.

a. What is the name of this type of injury?

b. Describe how you will care for the injury.

48. List four types of open wounds.

1.

2.

3.

4.

49. List the "five Ps" of compartment syndrome.

1.

2.

3.

4.

5.

50. List four factors that affect the severity of a burn.

1.

2.

3.

4.

Answer Section

Chapter 22

True/False

1. False

   Keep in mind that even after being removed from the heat source, burned tissue will continue to burn. You can help limit the progression of a surface burn injury if you can rapidly cool the burn shortly after it happens. Stop the burning process with clean, room temperature water for no more than 1-2 minutes. Cooling the burn for more than 2 minutes can cause a critical loss of body heat and shock.

   Objective: Demonstrate the steps in the emergency medical care of a patient with burns.

2. True

   The rule of nines is a guide used to estimate the affected BSA. The rule of nines divides the adult body into sections that are 9% or are multiples of 9%. The rule of nines has been modified for children and infants. Only partial-thickness and full-thickness burns are included when the extent of a burn is calculated.

   Objective: List the classifications of burns.

Multiple Choice

3. b

   Lacerations are characterized by a break in the skin of varying depth that may be linear or irregular. A puncture is a wound created when a pointed object pierces the skin. Whereas a laceration is a "slashing" type of injury, a puncture is a "stabbing" type of injury. An avulsion is characterized by a flap of skin or tissue at the injury site. An abrasion occurs because of rubbing or scraping, such as a "skinned knee."

   Objective: State the types of open soft-tissue injuries.

4. c

   Dressings cover wounds, and bandages hold dressings in place. Rags may be used in extreme cases when sterile dressings cannot be found; however, avoid the use of duct tape in circumstances in which the tape must contact the patient's skin because duct tape may cause further trauma during removal. Occlusive dressings are used to form an airtight seal. This is not necessary with a simple laceration.

   Objective: List the functions of dressing and bandaging.

5. c

   The eyeball is filled with two different fluids: The anterior (front) chamber is filled with aqueous humor while the posterior chamber is filled with vitreous humor. Imagine the eye socket is like a cup. Positioning the patient supine maximizes the holding capacity of the cup. Stabilizing the pencil with bulky dressings and covering both eyes are critical to ensuring that further harm does not occur from the movement of the pencil or the eye.

   Objective: Demonstrate the steps in the emergency medical care of a patient with an impaled object.

6. b

   Chemical injuries to the eyes are considered the most urgent eye injury. Immediate and continuous irrigation of the affected eye(s) is critical to the long-term outcome for the patient. Twenty minutes is the minimum amount of time required for irrigation. Preferably, you should continuously irrigate the eye until transfer of care at the receiving facility. If only one eye is affected, irrigate away from the unaffected eye. You may need to assist in opening the eye to facilitate irrigation. Open the eye by gently rolling the lid back. Make sure that you have provided for your safety. The minimum level of personal protective clothing for this type of patient is medical gloves, arm protection, and face protection (such as goggles and mask). Individual chemicals may dictate the necessity for a higher level of protection.

Objective: Describe the emergency care for a chemical burn.

7. c

The rule of nines for an adult divides the body into regions that equal 9% of the total body surface area (or a multiple of 9%). The head and each arm are given a value of 9%. The anterior trunk (chest and abdomen), the posterior trunk (the back), and each leg are given a value of 18%. The genitalia is considered 1%. This patient's percentage of BSA burned is 36%.

Objective: List the classifications of burns.

8. d

Replacing the eyeball may cause further damage and would increase the opportunity for infection. Do not attempt to replace misplaced body parts. Instead, you should attempt to keep the eyeball moist and protected.

Objective: N/A

9. b

The rule of nines differs for children and infants because their heads are proportionally larger than the heads of adults. The head is given twice the adult value, or 18%. The anterior chest, posterior chest, arms, and genitalia remain the same values while the legs are given a value of 14% each rather than 18%. This patient's percentage of BSA burned is 28%. Something about the characteristics of this burn should catch your attention: If the water was too hot, why would the patient put both legs completely under the surface of the water? The "story" from the parent does not make sense. When treating injured dependent patients (such as children, older adults, mentally challenged), be aware that abuse exists. While it is not the role of an EMT to investigate abuse, it is your responsibility to notify the appropriate agency (law enforcement or medical direction) of circumstances that suggest abuse.

Objective: Demonstrate the steps in the emergency medical care of a patient with burns.

10. a

Your immediate concern should be to protect the patient from further harm. This means stopping the burning process and moving the patient to a safe place. Calculating the burn area, applying sterile dressings, and initiating oxygen therapy should be done only after ensuring the safety of the patient. *Note:* While oxygen is not flammable, it does support and accelerate combustion. Do not use oxygen around an open or smoldering flame.

Objective: Demonstrate the steps in the emergency medical care of a patient with burns.

11. d

Partial-thickness burns, also known as *second-degree burns,* are characterized by painful red or mottled skin that ultimately develops blisters. Both the epidermis and dermis are damaged in a partial-thickness burn, whereas a superficial burn involves damage only to the epidermis. Full-thickness burns, also known as *third-degree burns,* may appear white, brown, or charred. Because the dermal layer is destroyed in full-thickness burns, no pain is associated with these burns (the nerves that sense pain in the skin are located in the dermal layer); however, a full-thickness burn is usually associated with superficial and partial-thickness burns, which are painful.

Objective: List the classifications of burns.

12. d

Air will always follow the path of least resistance. If there is a hole in the chest wall, air will enter the hole during inhalation. This air may become trapped in the chest cavity, leading to life-threatening compromise (pneumothorax or tension pneumothorax). An airtight barrier is critical. Sealing the occlusive dressing on three sides creates an airtight seal while allowing an avenue (the unsecured fourth side) for trapped air to escape.

Objective: Describe the emergency medical care of the patient with an open soft-tissue injury.

13. a

The proper technique for securing an impaled object is to wrap the object with bulky dressing, then secure the bulky dressing. Pushing the knife in any further may cause additional harm. Removing the knife to perform spinal immobilization is not appropriate. In this case, spinal immobilization would be indicated since the possibility exists that the spinal cord may have been lacerated. However, you must improvise immobilization to facilitate transporting the patient with the knife in place (possibly immobilize the patient on his side).

Objective: Describe the emergency medical care of a patient with an impaled object.

14. c

Never touch or attempt to replace exposed abdominal organs. Protect the organs from further harm by applying a large sterile dressing moistened with sterile water or saline over the area. Retain moisture and preserve body heat by securing with a large bandage. Replacing the organs in the abdomen increases the risk of infection. Allowing the organs to dry out or freeze may result in surgical removal of the affected section of bowel.

Objective: Describe the emergency medical care of the patient with an open soft-tissue injury.

Sentence Completion

15. A **contusion** (bruise) is the most common type of closed wound.

Objective: List the types of closed soft-tissue injuries.

16. A **superficial** (first-degree) burn affects only the epidermis and results in only minor tissue damage.

Objective: List the characteristics of a superficial burn.

17. An occlusive dressing prevents **air** from entering a wound.

Objective: List the functions of dressing and bandaging.

Matching

18.	K	31.	C
19.	I	32.	T
20.	F	33.	L
21.	Y	34.	E
22.	V	35.	G
23.	Q	36.	A
24.	M	37.	Z
25.	O	38.	N
26.	U	39.	R
27.	S	40.	P
28.	D	41.	H
29.	J	42.	B
30.	X	43.	W

Short Answer

44. Have him sit up and lean his head forward. This will help keep blood from draining into the back of his throat. Pinch the fleshy part of his nostrils together with your thumb and two fingers for 15 minutes.

Objective: State methods of emergency medical care of external bleeding.

45. Signs and symptoms that suggest a possible airway problem include facial burns, soot in the nose or mouth, singed facial hair or nasal hair, swelling of the lips or inside the mouth, coughing, inability to swallow secretions, and a hoarse voice.

Objective: Establish the relationship between airway management and the patient with chest injury, burns, blunt and penetrating injuries.

46. A chemical burn is the most urgent eye injury. The damage to the eye depends on the type and concentration of the chemical, length of exposure, and elapsed time until treatment.

Objective: Describe the emergency care for a chemical burn.

47. a. Evisceration

b. Do not touch or try to replace the exposed organ. Carefully remove clothing from around the wound. Cover the exposed organs and wound by applying a thick, moist dressing lightly over the organs and wound. Secure the dressing in place with a large bandage to retain moisture and prevent heat loss. Place the patient in a position of comfort if no spinal injury is suspected. Keep the patient warm. Assess for signs of shock and treat if present.

Objective: State the emergency medical care considerations for a patient with an open wound to the abdomen.

48. Types of open wounds:

- Abrasion
- Laceration
- Penetration/puncture wound
- Avulsion
- Amputation
- Open crush injury

Objective: State the types of open soft-tissue injuries.

49. The "five Ps" of compartment syndrome:

1. *P*ain on passive stretching of the muscle
2. *P*aralysis (or weakness)
3. *P*aresthesias
4. Increased *p*ressure
5. Diminished *p*eripheral *p*ulses

Objective: N/A

50. The severity of a burn is determined by a number of factors:

- The depth of the burn (how deeply the burn penetrates the skin)
- The extent of the burn (how much of the body surface is burned)
- The location of the burn
- The patient's age
- Medical or surgical conditions present before the burn
- Associated factors (such as the MOI)

Objective: N/A

23 Musculoskeletal Care

READING ASSIGNMENT ▶ Read Chapter 23, pages 515 to 543 in your textbook.

Sum It Up

- The mechanism of injury to bones and joints can be caused by direct forces, indirect forces, and twisting forces:
  - A direct force causes injury at the point of impact.
  - An indirect force causes injury at a site other than the point of impact.
  - A twisting force causes one part of an extremity to remain in place while the rest twists. Twisting injuries commonly affect the joints such as ankles, knees, and wrists. Twisting forces cause ligaments to stretch and tear.
- Injuries to bones and joints may be open or closed:
  - In an open injury, the skin surface is broken. An open injury increases the risk of contamination and infection. These injuries can also result in serious blood loss.
  - In closed injuries of bones and joints, the skin surface is not broken. The injury is often painful, swollen, and deformed.
- A fracture is a break in a bone. If a bone is broken, chipped, cracked, or splintered, it is said to be fractured.
- A dislocation occurs when the ends of bones are forced from their normal positions in a joint.
- A subluxation, which is a partial dislocation, means the bone is partially out of the joint. A complete dislocation means it is all the way out. Dislocations and subluxations usually result in temporary deformity of the joint and may result in sudden and severe pain.
- A sprain is a stretching or tearing of a ligament, the connective tissue that joins the end of one bone with another. Sprains are classified as mild, moderate, and severe.
- A strain is a twisting, pulling, or tearing of a muscle or tendon. A muscle strain usually occurs when a muscle is stretched beyond its limit. A strain often occurs near the point where the muscle joins the tough connective tissue of the tendon.
- Most sprains and strains can be treated with the RICE technique:
  - **R**est
  - **I**ce
  - **C**ompression
  - **E**levation

- In assessing extremity injuries, check the **p**ulse, **m**ovement, and **s**ensation (PMS) in each extremity.
- A splint is a device used to limit movement of a body part (immobilize) to prevent pain and further injury.
  —In some situations, the patient will have already splinted the injury by holding the injured part close to his body in a comfortable position. Using the body as a splint is called a *self-splint* or *anatomic splint*.
  —Before splinting an injured hand or foot, place it in the position of function. The natural position of the hand at rest looks as if you were gently grasping a small object, such as a baseball.
- Rigid splints are made of hard material, such as wood, strong cardboard, or plastic. This type of splint is useful for immobilizing injuries that occur to the middle portion (midshaft) of a bone. Some rigid splints are padded, but others must be padded before they are applied to the patient.
- Semi-rigid (flexible) splints are very useful for immobilizing joint injuries. These splints can be molded to the shape of the extremity. Examples include the SAM splint and aluminum ladder splints. Semirigid splints can be used in combination with other splints, such as a sling and swathe.
- Soft splints are flexible and useful for immobilizing injuries of the lower leg or forearm. Examples of soft splints include a sling and swathe, blanket rolls, pillows, and towels.
  —A sling and swathe is used to immobilize injuries to the shoulder, collarbone, or upper arm bone. A triangular bandage is often used to make a sling. A swathe is a piece of soft material used to secure the injured extremity to the body.
- A traction splint is a device used to immobilize a closed fracture of the thighbone. This type of splint maintains a constant steady pull on the bone. A traction splint keeps broken bone ends in a near-normal position.
  —A unipolar traction splint has one pole that provides external support for the injured leg.
  —A bipolar traction splint uses two external poles, one on each side of the injured leg, to provide external support
- A pneumatic splint requires air to be pumped in or suctioned out of it. An air splint, vacuum splint, and the PASG are examples of pneumatic splints. A pneumatic splint is placed around the injured area and is inflated (air splint or PASG) or deflated (vacuum splint) until it becomes firm.

▶ Tracking Your Progress

After reading this chapter, can you:	Page Reference	Objective Met?
• Describe the function of the muscular system?	516	☐
• Describe the function of the skeletal system?	516	☐
• List the major bones or bone groupings of the spinal column, the thorax, the upper extremities, and the lower extremities?	517	☐
• Differentiate between an open and a closed painful, swollen, deformed extremity?	521	☐

After reading this chapter, can you:	Page Reference	Objective Met?
• State the reasons for splinting?	526	☐
• List the general rules of splinting?	527	☐
• List the complications of splinting?	526	☐
• List the emergency medical care for a patient with a painful, swollen, deformed extremity?	525	☐

True or False

Decide whether each statement is true or false. In the space provided, write *T* for true or *F* for false.

_____ **1.** Most muscles are attached to bones by tendons.

_____ **2.** Ice should be applied to a sprain or strain for 40 minutes and removed for 20 minutes.

_____ **3.** Before being applied to a patient, a splint should be padded to prevent pressure and discomfort.

Multiple Choice

In the space provided, identify the letter of the choice that best completes the statement or answers each question.

_____ **4.** When immobilizing an extremity, it is important to check pulses
  a. after the splint is applied.
  b. before the splint is applied.
  c. before and after the splint is applied.
  d. during immobilization of the affected extremity.

Questions 5–7 pertain to the following scenario.

Your rescue crew is called to the scene of a collision of a car and motorcycle and assigned responsibility to treat the motorcyclist. Bystanders state that a vehicle T-boned the motorcyclist at about 35 miles per hour. He was wearing a helmet and is found lying on the ground screaming in pain. As you approach, he tells you that his right leg is "all messed up."

_____ **5.** Which of the following should be done first?
  a. Begin splinting the right leg.
  b. Remove the patient's helmet.
  c. Perform a primary survey.
  d. Perform a rapid trauma assessment.

_____ **6.** After the appropriate assessment and interventions, you consider the use of a traction splint for the patient's right leg. Which of the following is an indication for use of the traction splint?
  a. An isolated pelvic injury with no damage to the leg
  b. An isolated knee injury with no damage to the pelvis
  c. An isolated mid-thigh injury with no joint or lower leg injuries present
  d. An isolated lower leg injury with no joint or upper leg injuries present

_____ **7.** When securing the traction splint to the patient, there are three basic points of attachment: the groin, the leg, and the ankle. The proper order for securing the device is
  a. groin, then ankle, and finally leg.
  b. groin, then leg, and finally ankle.
  c. ankle, then leg, and finally groin.
  d. leg, then ankle, and finally groin.

_____ **8.** Which of the following indicates an open fracture?
- **a.** A wound over the injury
- **b.** No pulse distal to the inury
- **c.** Severe deformity
- **d.** A cool and pale extremity

Questions 9–12 pertain to the following scenario.

Your ambulance crew is called to the scene of a motor vehicle collision. A 41-year-old woman crashed her motorcycle when she hit a patch of ice in the road. She was wearing a helmet and is complaining of severe right leg pain. She tells you the motorcycle came down on her leg when she crashed. You observe deformity and swelling at the middle of her thigh. She is also complaining that she felt her right knee "pop" when she went down.

_____ **9.** Which of the following procedures takes priority?
- **a.** Perform a rapid trauma assessment.
- **b.** Begin stabilizing the patient's spine.
- **c.** Obtain a SAMPLE history from the patient.
- **d.** Assess distal motor, sensory, and circulation and begin splinting the affected limb.

_____ **10.** After exposing the entire limb, you notice that the patient is wearing a gold hoop anklet (a bracelet on the ankle). It is slightly larger than the diameter of the ankle and does not appear to be affected by swelling. You should
- **a.** remove the jewelry.
- **b.** leave it in place unless it is affecting circulation.
- **c.** leave the anklet in place as a gauge to monitor distal swelling.
- **d.** place ice packs on the foot and ankle to ensure that swelling does not disturb circulation past the anklet.

_____ **11.** Which of the following devices should be used to immobilize this patient?
- **a.** A backboard
- **b.** A traction splint
- **c.** A traction splint and backboard
- **d.** A traction splint, PASG, and a backboard

_____ **12.** After properly treating this patient, you reassess her injuries. You are able to palpate a distal pulse on the top of the patient's right foot. You should
- **a.** mark this spot with an ink pen.
- **b.** attempt to palpate a blood pressure in the extremity.
- **c.** leave your hand in the same spot throughout transport.
- **d.** mark this spot by scratching the skin at the pulse site until it turns red.

Sentence Completion

In the blanks provided, write the words that best complete each sentence.

13. A shoulder injury typically involves three bones: the _____, the _____, and the _____.

14. Splinting an elbow injury requires immobilization of the _____ (the bone above the injury) and the _____ and _____ (the bones below the injury).

15. The three major parts of a skeletal muscle are the _____, the _____, and the _____.

16. The two main divisions of the skeleton are the _____ and the _____ skeleton.

Matching

Match the key terms in the left column with the definitions in the right column by placing the letter of each correct answer in the space provided.

_____ 17. Origin

_____ 18. Anatomic splint

_____ 19. Fibula

_____ 20. Body

_____ 21. Manubrium

_____ 22. Phalanges

_____ 23. Insertion

_____ 24. Metacarpals

_____ 25. Axial skeleton

_____ 26. Patella

_____ 27. Shoulder girdle

_____ 28. Sprain

_____ 29. Traction splint

_____ 30. Tendons

_____ 31. Appendicular skeleton

_____ 32. Metatarsals

_____ 33. Dislocation

_____ 34. Growth plate

_____ 35. Pelvis

_____ 36. Position of function

_____ 37. Radius

_____ 38. Skeletal muscle

_____ 39. Swathe

_____ 40. Subluxation

_____ 41. Pelvic girdle

_____ 42. Strain

A. The bones of the fingers and toes

B. Forceful movement of the ends of bones from their normal positions in a joint

C. The bony arch formed by the clavicles and scapulae

D. Voluntary muscle

E. The bone that lies next to the tibia along the outer side of the lower leg

F. The bone on the thumb (lateral) side of the forearm

G. The uppermost portion of the breastbone

H. The natural position of the hand or foot at rest

I. Stretching or tearing of a ligament

J. The movable attachment of a muscle to a bone

K. An area of growing tissue near each end of a long bone in children and adolescents

L. The flat, triangular, movable bone that forms the anterior part of the knee

M. Using the body as a splint

N. The bones that enclose and protect the organs of the pelvic cavity

O. A piece of soft material used to secure an injured extremity to the body

P. Strong cords of connective tissue that stretch across joints

Q. A dislocation that fully or partially returns to its normal alignment without intervention

R. The upper and lower extremities, shoulder girdle, and pelvic girdle

S. The bones that form the support for the palm of the hand

T. A device used to maintain a constant, steady pull on a closed fracture of the femur

U. Twisting, pulling, or tearing of a muscle

V. The stationary attachment of a skeletal muscle to a bone

W. The bony ring formed by three separate bones that fuse to become one in an adult

X. The main part of a skeletal muscle

Y. The part of the skeleton that includes the skull, spinal column, sternum, and ribs

Z. The bones that form the part of the foot to which the toes attach

Short Answer

Answer each question in the space provided.

43. List four functions of the skeletal system.

1.

2.

3.

4.

44. What is a dislocation?

45. RICE is a technique used to treat sprains and strains. Explain the meaning of each of these letters.

R =

I =

C =

E =

46. What are the three most common signs and symptoms of a musculoskeletal injury?

1.

2.

3.

47. List four reasons for splinting a musculoskeletal injury.

1.

2.

3.

4.

48. List three hazards of improper splinting.

1.

2.

3.

49. What three things should you assess before and after applying a splint?

1.

2.

3.

50. List three types of splints.

1.

2.

3.

Answer Section

Chapter 23

True/False

1. **True**

   Most skeletal muscles are attached to bones by means of tendons. Tendons create a pull between bones when muscles contract. The tendons of many muscles cross over joints, which contributes to the stability of the joint.

   Objective: Describe the function of the muscular system.

2. **False**

   Apply ice to a sprain or strain for 20 minutes and then remove it for 40 minutes. Follow this rotation hourly. Ice reduces blood flow into the affected area, which in turn reduces swelling.

   Objective: List the emergency medical care for a patient with a painful, swollen, deformed extremity.

3. **True**

   Pad a rigid or semi-rigid splint before applying it. Padding helps lessen patient discomfort caused by pressure, especially around bony areas.

   Objective: List the general rules of splinting.

Multiple Choice

4. **c**

   Assess the presence of pulses, movement, and sensation in each of your patient's extremities *before* and *after* immobilization.

   Objective: List the general rules of splinting.

5. **c**

   Immediately after the scene size-up (which should include BSI precautions), you should begin the primary survey to assess the patient's mental status, airway, breathing, and circulation condition as well as any life-threatening conditions that may exist. Removing the helmet may be appropriate if it complicates assessment of the airway. A rapid trauma assessment should be performed after the primary survey assessment for unresponsive patients. Because this patient is conscious, a focused exam should follow the primary survey.

   Objective: List the emergency medical care for a patient with a painful, swollen, deformed extremity.

6. **c**

   Traction splints are indicated for use in the lower extremity if the injury is isolated to the mid-thigh (mid-femur). The device reduces the pain associated with mid-thigh fractures and also reduces the chance of further tissue damage. The device should not be applied if there is any significant injury to the lower leg, the knee, or the pelvis because the force of traction necessary to stabilize a thigh injury may increase the extent of trauma to these other body areas.

   Objective: List the general rules of splinting.

7. **a**

   First, the traction splint is secured to the anchor point of the body, the groin. Once it is anchored to the body, the ankle hitch is applied and the traction increased until the amount of mechanical traction equals the amount of manual traction being applied by a second rescuer. Once the splint is adjusted correctly for the amount of traction necessary, the leg straps should be applied. Avoid applying leg straps directly over the kneecap or the injury site, as they may interrupt the flow of blood to the lower leg or aggravate the injury.

   Objective: List the emergency medical care for a patient with a painful, swollen, deformed extremity.

8. a

If the continuity of the skin is broken at or near the injury site, then the wound is classified as open. Any open wound over a fracture site indicates the possibility of an open fracture. Open wounds present an additional hazard to the patient because contaminants can now enter the body. When treating open injuries, you must cover them with a sterile dressing before splinting.

Objective: Differentiate between an open and a closed painful, swollen, deformed extremity.

9. b

Spinal stabilization is a high priority and should begin during the primary survey as you address airway. It is not necessary to secure the patient to a long backboard before beginning the SAMPLE history, nor should you move the patient until distal neurovascular status is assessed in all limbs. However, the MOI makes it necessary to immediately begin manual stabilization of the spine.

Objective: Describe the implications of not properly caring for potential spine injuries.

10. a

Don't wait for distal jewelry to become a problem before you address it. Remove the jewelry, ask the patient where she would like it kept (pocket, purse, with a friend, etc.), and then show her that you are putting it there. You must be extremely careful when handling valuables (jewelry, wallets, purses, and money)—if they are misplaced, some patients may blame you. Professionalism and good communication skills with the patient allow you to avoid unpleasant situations.

Objective: List the general rules of splinting.

11. a

Traction splints are indicated for closed, painful, swollen, deformed mid-thigh injuries (sometimes referred to as a *midshaft femur fracture*) with no joint or lower leg injury. This patient informed you that her knee "popped" when she crashed. You must assume that the joint has been damaged, and the traction splint is contraindicated. A backboard should be used to immobilize the entire body. If permitted by local protocol, a PASG may be used to help control suspected severe bleeding in the abdomen or pelvis that is accompanied by hypotension.

Objective: List the emergency medical care for a patient with a painful, swollen, deformed extremity.

12. a

Marking the pulse point with a pen allows you to quickly reassess distal circulatory status. It is not practical to keep your finger on the pulse throughout the entire transport nor is it necessary to assess a distal blood pressure.

Objective: List the emergency medical care for a patient with a painful, swollen, deformed extremity.

Sentence Completion

13. A shoulder injury typically involves three bones: the **collarbone (clavicle)**, the **shoulder blade (scapula)**, and the **upper arm bone (humerus)**.

Objective: List the major bones or bone groupings of the spinal column, the thorax, the upper extremities, and the lower extremities.

14. Splinting an elbow injury requires immobilization of the **humerus** (the bone above the injury) and the **radius** and **ulna** (the bones below the injury).

Objective: List the general rules of splinting.

15. The three major parts of a skeletal muscle are the **insertion**, the **body**, and the **origin**.

Objective: Describe the anatomy and function of the following major body systems: respiratory, circulatory, musculoskeletal, nervous, and endocrine.

16. The two main divisions of the skeleton are the **axial** and the **appendicular** skeleton.

Objective: Describe the anatomy and function of the following major body systems: respiratory, circulatory, musculoskeletal, nervous, and endocrine.

Matching

17. V		**27.** C	
18. M		**28.** I	
19. E		**29.** T	
20. X		**30.** P	
21. G		**31.** R	
22. A		**32.** Z	
23. J		**33.** B	
24. S		**34.** K	
25. Y		**35.** W	
26. L		**36.** H	

37.	F	40.	Q
38.	D	41.	N
39.	O	42.	U

Short Answer

43. The skeletal system:

   • Gives the body shape, support, and form
   • Works with muscles to provide for body movement
   • Stores minerals such as calcium and phosphorus
   • Produces red blood cells
   • Protects vital internal organs
     —The skull protects the brain.
     —The rib cage protects the heart and lungs.
     —The lower ribs protect most of the liver and spleen.
     —The spinal canal protects the spinal cord.

   Objective: Describe the function of the skeletal system.

44. A dislocation occurs when the ends of bones are forced from their normal positions in a joint. A partial dislocation (subluxation) means the bone is partially out of the joint. A complete dislocation means it is all the way out.

   Objective: N/A

45. RICE stands for *R*est, *I*ce, *C*ompression, and *E*levation.

   Objective: List the emergency medical care for a patient with a painful, swollen, deformed extremity.

46. The three most common signs and symptoms of a musculoskeletal injury are

   1. Pain
   2. Deformity
   3. Swelling

   Objective: List the emergency medical care for a patient with a painful, swollen, deformed extremity.

47. The reasons for splinting include the following:

   • Limit motion of bone fragments, bone ends, or dislocated joints
   • Lessen the damage to muscles, nerves, or blood vessels caused by broken bones
   • Help prevent a closed injury from becoming an open injury
   • Lessen the restriction of blood flow caused by bone ends or dislocations compressing blood vessels
   • Reduce bleeding resulting from tissue damage caused by bone ends
   • Reduce pain associated with the movement of the bone and the joint
   • Reduce the risk of paralysis resulting from damaged nerves or spinal cord

   Objective: State the reasons for splinting.

48. The hazards of improper splinting include the following:

   • The compression of nerves, tissues, and blood vessels from the splint
   • A delay in transport of a patient with a life-threatening injury
   • Distal circulation that is reduced as a result of the splint's being applied too tightly to the extremity
   • Aggravating the musculoskeletal injury
   • Causing or aggravating tissue, nerve, vessel, or muscle damage from excessive bone or joint movement

   Objective: List the complications of splinting.

49. Before and after applying a splint, you should assess (1) distal pulses, (2) movement, and (3) sensation in the injured extremity.

   Objective: List the general rules of splinting.

50. Types of splints include the following:

   • Anatomic/self-splint
   • Rigid/semi-rigid splints
   • Soft splints
   • Pneumatic splints

   Objective: State the reasons for splinting.

CHAPTER

24 Injuries to the Head and Spine

READING ASSIGNMENT ▷ Read Chapter 24, pages 544 to 572 in your textbook.

Sum It Up

- Most spinal injuries occur to the cervical spine. The next most commonly injured areas are the thoracic and lumbar spine. A spinal column injury (bony injury) can occur with or without a spinal cord injury. A spinal cord injury can also occur with or without an injury to the spinal column. The spinal cord does not have to be severed in order for a loss of function to occur.

- Compression fractures of the spine result in weakened vertebrae. A compression fracture can occur with or without a spinal cord injury.

- Distraction occurs when the spine is pulled apart. When the spine is distracted, ligaments and muscles are overstretched or torn and the vertebrae are pulled apart.

- An injury to the spinal cord may be complete or incomplete:
  — A complete spinal cord injury occurs when the spinal cord is severed. The patient has no voluntary movement or sensation below the level of the injury. Both sides of the body are equally affected.
    • Paraplegia is the loss of movement and sensation of the lower half of the body from the waist down. Paraplegia results from a spinal cord injury at the level of the thoracic or lumbar vertebrae.
    • Quadriplegia (also called *tetraplegia*) is a loss of movement and sensation in both arms, both legs, and the parts of the body below the area of injury to the spinal cord. Quadriplegia results from a spinal cord injury at the level of the cervical vertebrae.
  — With an incomplete spinal cord injury, some parts of the spinal cord remain intact. The patient has some function below the level of the injury. With this type of injury, there is a potential for recovery because function may be only temporarily lost.

- The signs and symptoms of a possible spinal injury include the following:
  — Tenderness in the injured area
  — Pain associated with movement (Do *not* ask the patient to move in order to see if he has pain. Do *not* move the patient to test for a pain response.)
  — Pain independent of movement or palpation along the spinal column
  — Pain down the lower legs or into the rib cage
  — Pain that comes and goes, usually along the spine and/or the lower legs

273

- —Soft-tissue injuries associated with trauma to the head and neck (cuts, bruises)
- —Numbness, weakness, or tingling in the extremities
- —A loss of sensation or paralysis below the site of injury
- —A loss of sensation or paralysis in the upper or lower extremities
- —Difficulty breathing
- —A loss of bladder or bowel control
- —An inability of the patient to walk, move his extremities, or feel sensation
- Manual stabilization of the head and neck is also called *in-line stabilization*. Manual stabilization of the head and neck helps prevent further injury to the spine.
- As an EMT, you may need to apply a rigid cervical collar (also called a *C-collar*) in treating a spinal injury. When used alone, a rigid cervical collar does not immobilize. For effective immobilization, a rigid collar must be used with manual stabilization or a spinal immobilization device, such as a backboard.
- A log roll is a technique used to move a patient from a facedown or side-lying position to a face-up position while maintaining the head and neck in line with the rest of the body. This technique is also used to place a patient with a suspected spinal injury on a backboard.
- A long backboard helps stabilize the head, neck, torso, pelvis, and extremities. It is used to immobilize patients found in a lying, standing, or sitting position.
- A short backboard helps to immobilize a patient's head, neck, and torso. It can also be used as a long backboard for a small child. Examples include vest-type devices and rigid, short backboards.
- An injury to the scalp may occur because of blunt or penetrating trauma. When injured, the scalp may bleed heavily. In children, the amount of blood loss from a scalp wound may be enough to produce shock.
- The skull protects the brain from injury. However, damage to the skull can cause damage to the brain. Skull injuries may occur from blunt or penetrating trauma. Significant force, such as a severe impact or blow, can result in a skull fracture.
- A head injury may be open or closed:
  - —In an open head injury, the scalp is not intact and the risk of infection is increased. Broken bones or foreign objects forced through the skull can cut, tear, or bruise the brain tissue itself.
  - —In a closed head injury, the skull remains intact. However, the brain can still be injured by the forces or objects that struck the skull. The forces that impact the skull cause the brain to move within skull. The brain strikes the inside of the skull, which causes injuries to the brain tissue.
- A concussion is a traumatic brain injury that results in a temporary loss of function in some or all of the brain. A concussion occurs when the head strikes an object or is struck by an object. The injury may or may not cause a loss of consciousness. A headache, loss of appetite, vomiting, and pale skin are common soon after the injury.
- A cerebral contusion is a brain injury in which brain tissue is bruised and damaged in a local area. Bruising may occur at both the area of direct impact (coup) and on the side opposite (contrecoup) the impact.
- A subdural hematoma usually results from tearing of veins located between the dura and the cerebral cortex after an injury to the head. Blood builds up in the space between the dura and the arachnoid layer of the meninges.

- An epidural hematoma involves a rapid buildup of blood between the dura and the skull. An epidural hematoma often involves the tearing of an artery, usually the middle meningeal artery.
- An intracerebral hematoma is a collection of blood within the brain. Signs and symptoms depend on the area of the brain involved, the amount of bleeding, and associated injuries.
- An altered or decreasing mental status is the best indicator of a brain injury.
- To treat a patient with head injury, use the following steps:
  —Conduct a scene size-up, ensure safety, and put on appropriate PPE. Evaluate the MOI.
  —Perform a primary survey and ask an assistant to manually stabilize the patient's head and neck while you continue your exam.
  —Closely monitor the patient's airway, breathing, pulse, and mental status.
  —Perform a physical examination.
  —Dress and bandage any open wounds
  —Immobilize the patient's spine.

▶ Tracking Your Progress

After reading this chapter, can you:	Page Reference	Objective Met?
• State the components of the nervous system?	546	☐
• List the functions of the central nervous system?	546	☐
• Define the structure of the skeletal system as it relates to the nervous system?	547	☐
• Relate MOI to potential injuries of the head and spine?	547, 564	☐
• Describe the implications of not properly caring for potential spine injuries?	549	☐
• State the signs and symptoms of a potential spine injury?	551	☐
• Describe the method of determining whether a responsive patient may have a spine injury?	552	☐
• Relate the airway emergency medical care techniques to the patient with a suspected spine injury?	553	☐
• Describe how to stabilize the cervical spine?	551	☐
• Discuss indications for sizing and using a cervical spine immobilization device?	555	☐
• Establish the relationship between airway management and the patient with head and spine injuries?	555, 564	☐
• Describe a method for sizing a cervical spine immobilization device?	555	☐
• Describe how to log roll a patient with a suspected spine injury?	555	☐
• Describe how to secure a patient to a long spine board?	555	☐
• List instances when a short spine board should be used?	559	☐
• Describe how to immobilize a patient by using a short spine board?	559	☐
• Describe the indications for the use of rapid extrication?	559	☐
• List steps in performing rapid extrication?	559	☐

After reading this chapter, can you:	Page Reference	Objective Met?
• State the circumstances in which a helmet should be left on the patient?	564	☐
• Discuss the circumstances in which a helmet should be removed?	564	☐
• Identify different types of helmets?	564	☐
• Describe the unique characteristics of sports helmets?	564	☐
• Explain the preferred methods to remove a helmet?	564	☐
• Discuss alternative methods for removal of a helmet?	564	☐
• Describe how the patient's head is stabilized to remove the helmet?	564	☐
• Differentiate between how the head is stabilized with a helmet and how it is stabilized without a helmet?	564	☐

Multiple Choice

In the space provided, identify the letter of the choice that best completes the statement or answers each question.

_____ 1. You are assessing a patient who hit his head on the steering wheel. You note some clear drainage coming from his left ear. What should you do next?
   a. Place a loose sterile dressing over the ear.
   b. Apply direct pressure to the ear to stop the flow.
   c. Place a cotton ball or other absorbent dressing in the ear.
   d. Have the patient turn his head to the left to prevent the drainage from coming out of his left ear.

_____ 2. A bluish discoloration behind the ear is known as
   a. Battle's sign.
   b. raccoon's sign.
   c. Cushing's sign.
   d. Heimlich's sign.

_____ 3. Which of the following statements regarding facial trauma is true?
   a. Patients with facial trauma should not be given oxygen.
   b. Never suction the mouth of a patient with facial trauma.
   c. Patients with suspected facial bone fractures should have an oral airway inserted to protect their airway.
   d. Injuries to the face may complicate airway management because of increased salivation and decreased movement.

_____ 4. Your rescue crew has been called to a motor vehicle collision. Upon arrival at the scene, you observe that a passenger van has rear-ended a 4-door sedan. Your patient is a 47-year-old woman complaining of neck pain. Although the patient denies the use of alcohol or drugs, her speech is slurred and her breath smells of alcohol. On the basis of this MOI, when can you definitively rule out the possibility of spinal column or cord damage?
   a. During the primary survey
   b. If the patient is able to walk without difficulty
   c. During the secondary survey
   d. Only after examination by the receiving medical facility

_____ 5. Your ambulance crew is called to the scene of a motor vehicle collision near a railroad track. You arrive to find one vehicle positioned on the tracks. A train is approaching and less than 2 minutes from the scene. Your patient is unconscious and may have severe spinal compromise. This is an indication for
   a. positioning the ambulance between the train and the victim's car.
   b. rapid extrication, possibly without the use of any immobilization device.
   c. use of a cervical collar and long backboard for extrication and immobilization.
   d. use of a cervical collar and short backboard for extrication and immobilization.

_____ **6.** Which of the following is true regarding the sizing of cervical collars?

  a. It is better to have a collar too big than one too small.
  b. It is better to have a collar too small than one too big.
  c. An improperly-sized cervical collar may do more harm than good.
  d. If you do not have the correct size, do not attempt to stabilize the cervical spine.

Questions 7–8 pertain to the following scenario.

Your ambulance crew is called to the scene of a motor vehicle collision in the parking lot of a local mall. You arrive to find your patient, a 57-year-old man, sitting behind the steering wheel with his seat belt still in place. He tells you that another vehicle hit his car head on at less than 10 miles per hour. The other vehicle has fled the scene. The patient is complaining of severe lower back pain. After evaluation, you decide to use a vest-type extrication device.

_____ **7.** Which of the following should you do first?

  a. Apply a cervical collar.
  b. Position the device behind the patient.
  c. Maintain manual in-line stabilization of the head and spine.
  d. Assess pulses, motor function, and sensation in the upper and lower extremities.

_____ **8.** There are three different body regions that a vest-type extrication device attaches to: the head, the chest, and the legs/groin. In which order should the straps be secured?

  a. Head, chest, legs/groin   **c.** Chest, legs/groin, head
  b. Head, legs/groin, chest   **d.** Legs/groin, chest, head

Questions 9–10 pertain to the following scenario.

Your rescue crew is called to the scene of a "motorcycle down." You arrive to find one patient in the middle of the street lying on his back. Bystanders inform you that a vehicle bumped the patient's motorcycle, then fled the scene. The speed limit in the area is 45 mph.

_____ **9.** After taking the appropriate BSI measures, you assess your patient's mental status and find him to be unresponsive. Which of the following would be an indication that his helmet must be removed?

  a. Helmets are always removed.
  b. The helmet must be removed if it does not have a face shield.
  c. The helmet must always be removed if you are going to stabilize the spine.
  d. The helmet must be removed if it interferes with your ability to assess the airway.

_____ **10.** It takes a minimum of two EMTs to remove a helmet properly. Which of the following statements regarding helmet removal is correct?

  a. The helmet should be cut away with trauma scissors.
  b. The patient's head should be turned to the side to facilitate removal of the helmet.
  c. The helmet should be removed in one swift motion as soon as the chin strap is released.
  d. The patient's head should be supported so that it does not drop to the backboard when the helmet is removed.

Matching

Match the key terms in the left column with the definitions in the right column by placing the letter of each correct answer in the space provided.

_____ 11. Concussion

_____ 12. Medulla oblongata

_____ 13. Cerebrum

_____ 14. Autonomic nervous system

_____ 15. Epidural hematoma

_____ 16. Log roll

_____ 17. Cushing's triad

_____ 18. Dura mater

_____ 19. Midbrain

_____ 20. Paraplegia

_____ 21. Cerebrospinal fluid

_____ 22. Sensory nerves

_____ 23. Spinal cord

_____ 24. Meninges

_____ 25. Pons

_____ 26. Cranial nerves

_____ 27. Arachnoid layer

_____ 28. Intracerebral hematoma

_____ 29. Cerebral contusion

_____ 30. Motor nerves

_____ 31. Quadriplegia

_____ 32. Pia mater

_____ 33. Subdural hematoma

_____ 34. Corpus callosum

_____ 35. Central nervous system

_____ 36. Spinal nerves

A. Delicate inner layer of the meninges that clings gently to the brain and spinal cord

B. Loss of movement and sensation of the lower half of the body from the waist down

C. The brain and spinal cord

D. A clear liquid that acts as a shock absorber for the brain and spinal cord and provides a means for the exchange of nutrients and wastes among the blood, brain, and spinal cord

E. Nerves that carry responses _from_ the brain and spinal cord, stimulating a muscle or organ

F. A buildup of blood in the space between the dura and the arachnoid layer of the meninges that usually results from tearing of veins located between the dura and the cerebral cortex after an injury to the head

G. Nerves that send signals _to_ the brain about the activities of the different parts of the body relative to their surroundings

H. A part of the brainstem that connects parts of the brain with one another by means of tracts and influences respiration

I. Three findings that indicate increasing intracranial pressure in a head-injured patient

J. A brain injury in which brain tissue is bruised and damaged in a local area

K. A part of the brainstem that acts as a relay for auditory and visual impulses

L. Loss of movement and sensation in both arms, both legs, and the parts of the body below an area of injury to the spinal cord

M. A technique used to move a patient from a facedown or side-lying position to a face-up position while keeping the head and neck in line with the rest of the body

N. A collection of blood within the brain

O. The largest part of the brain, made up of two hemispheres

P. Middle meningeal layer with delicate fibers resembling a spider's web

Q. Tough, durable, outermost layer of the meninges that adheres to the inner surface of the cranium

Continued

R. Nervous tissue that extends from the base of the skull down the back and is responsible for relaying electrical signals to and from the brain and peripheral nerves

S. Any of 31 pairs of nerves that branch from the spinal cord

T. Division of the PNS that has receptors and nerves concerned with the internal environment; controls the involuntary system of glands and smooth muscle and functions to maintain a steady state in the body

U. Three layers of connective tissue coverings that surround the brain and spinal cord

V. A part of the brainstem that extends from the pons and is continuous with the upper portion of the spinal cord

W. Twelve pairs of nerves that connect the brain with the neck and structures in the chest and abdomen

X. A traumatic brain injury that results in a temporary loss of function in some or all of the brain

Y. Collection of nerve fibers in the brain that connect the left and right cerebral hemispheres

Z. A buildup of blood between the dura and the skull that often involves the tearing of an artery; usually the middle meningeal artery

Short Answer

Answer each question in the space provided.

37. List the three areas of the spine that are most commonly injured.
   1.
   2.
   3.

38. What is a log roll and when is this technique performed?

39. List the components of Cushing's triad.

40. What is Cushing's triad?

Answer Section

Chapter 24

Multiple Choice

1. a

If fluid is seen in the ears, do not attempt to stop the flow. Cover the ear with a loose, sterile dressing.

Objective: N/A

2. a

A bluish discoloration behind the ear (Battle's sign) is a sign of a possible skull fracture. It is important to remember that swelling or discoloration behind the ears may not be seen for hours after the injury.

Objective: N/A

3. d

Facial fractures may cause an increase in the production of saliva, and because of the fracture, the ability to swallow the saliva becomes impaired. Constant attention to airway status must be maintained. Anticipate the need for frequent suctioning. An oral airway may be inserted if the patient is unconscious and does not have a gag reflex; however, the insertion of an oral airway does not replace the need to constantly reevaluate the patient's airway status.

Objective: Establish the relationship between airway management and the patient with head and spine injuries.

4. d

EMTs should not "clear" the spine of any patient complaining of neck or back pain unless such a protocol exists within their EMS system and their medical director permits BLS personnel to perform this function. This is true regardless of the position the patient is found in (standing, sitting, walking, etc.). If the patient is complaining of traumatic neck pain, you should immediately begin manual in-line stabilization until full spinal stabilization is accomplished.

Objective: Relate MOI to potential injuries of the head and spine.

5. b

This scene is immediately unsafe for the patient and the crew. You should attempt to perform rapid extrication of the patient. Remember that the safety of yourself and your crew comes before the safety of the patient. If adequate time does not exist to rapidly extricate the patient, do not stay in the hazard area! Rapid extrication should be performed when there is an immediate threat to life, such as in the following situations: altered mental status, inadequate breathing, shock (hypoperfusion), unsafe scene, and situations in which a patient blocks your access to another, more seriously injured patient.

Objective: Describe the indications for the use of rapid extrication.

6. c

You should apply a rigid cervical collar only if it fits properly. If you are not able to properly size a patient with a cervical collar, it is better to use an improvised device rather than a cervical collar of the wrong size. If the collar is too tight, it can apply pressure on the blood vessels in the patient's neck and reduce blood flow. If the collar is too loose, it can cover the patient's chin and mouth, causing an airway obstruction. If it is too loose, it will also not adequately stabilize the head and neck. A collar that is too short will not provide adequate stabilization because the patient's head can move forward. A collar that is too tall will not provide adequate stabilization because the patient's head will be moved backward by the collar. It can also force the jaw closed, limiting access to the airway. You can improvise a collar by using towel rolls, blanket rolls, or rolled-up clothing.

Objective: Describe a method for sizing a cervical spine immobilization device.

7. c

After taking BSI precautions, begin manual stabilization of the patient's head and spine. This is best achieved by positioning a rescuer behind the patient to hold the patient's head and neck with both hands. Then, evaluate motor function, sensation, and circulation in all four extremities. The neck should then be visualized and palpated for injury and a cervical collar put on. The patient is positioned, and the device is then placed behind the patient for application.

Objective: Describe how to immobilize a patient by using a short spine board.

8. c

The correct order for securing a vest-type extrication device to the patient is the chest (generally there are three chest/abdomen straps), the legs/groin (one strap for each leg), then the head (one strap for the forehead and one for the chin). Make sure that any voids (spaces) are padded. The device should not be so tight that breathing or opening the mouth is impaired.

Objective: Describe how to immobilize a patient by using a short spine board.

9. d

You should *remove a helmet* in these circumstances:

- You are unable to assess and/or reassess the patient's airway and breathing.
- The helmet limits your ability to adequately manage the patient's airway or breathing.
- The helmet does not fit properly, allowing excessive head movement within the helmet.
- You cannot properly stabilize the patient's spine with the helmet in place.
- The patient is in cardiac arrest.

Objective: Discuss the circumstances when a helmet should be removed.

10. d

Removing a helmet is a carefully coordinated effort between two knowledgeable rescuers. Strict attention must be paid to ensure that the spine is not manipulated. The head and spine should be maintained in a neutral in-line position throughout the procedure. The use of a cutting device should be avoided as it increases the length of time necessary to remove the helmet and the possibility of manipulating the spine.

Objective: Describe how the patient's head is stabilized to remove the helmet.

Matching

11.	X	**24.**	U
12.	V	**25.**	H
13.	O	**26.**	W
14.	T	**27.**	P
15.	Z	**28.**	N
16.	M	**29.**	J
17.	I	**30.**	E
18.	Q	**31.**	L
19.	K	**32.**	A
20.	B	**33.**	F
21.	D	**34.**	Y
22.	G	**35.**	C
23.	R	**36.**	S

Short Answer

37. The three most commonly injured areas of the spine are the following:

1. Cervical (neck) spine—most commonly injured
2. Thoracic (chest) spine
3. Lumbar (low back) spine

Objective: Relate MOI to potential injuries of the head and spine.

38. A log roll is a technique used to move a patient from a facedown or side-lying position to a face-up position while maintaining the head and neck in line with the rest of the body. This technique is also used to place a patient with a suspected spinal injury on a backboard.

Objective: Describe how to log roll a patient with a suspected spine injury.

39. Cushing's triad:

    1. Increased systolic blood pressure

    2. Abnormal breathing pattern

    3. Decreased heart rate

Objective: Relate MOI to potential injuries of the head and spine.

40. Cushing's triad is a series of three findings (increased systolic blood pressure, abnormal breathing pattern, and decreased heart rate) that, when present in a head-injured patient, suggest the presence of increased intracranial pressure. It is very important to recognize these signs. When they are present, you must move quickly and transport rapidly to the closest appropriate facility.

Objective: N/A

25 Injuries to the Chest, Abdomen, and Genitalia

READING ASSIGNMENT ▶ Read Chapter 25, pages 573 to 589 in your textbook.

Sum It Up

- Chest injuries are categorized as closed or open injuries. In closed chest injuries, no break occurs in the skin over the chest wall. These injuries are usually the result of blunt trauma. Underlying structures, such as the heart, lungs, and great vessels, may sustain significant injury. In open chest injuries, a break occurs in the skin over the chest wall. These injuries result from penetrating trauma, such as gunshot wounds, stabbings, or an impaled object.

- Rib fractures are a common injury. Fractures of ribs 1 and 2 are associated with significant trauma. Fractures of ribs 9-11 on the left are associated with rupture of the spleen. Fractures of ribs 5-9 on the right associated with injury to the liver.

- Flail chest occurs when three or more adjacent ribs are fractured in two or more places or when the sternum is detached. The section of the chest wall between the fractured ribs becomes free-floating because it is no longer in continuity with the thorax. This free-floating section of the chest wall is called a *flail segment*. The flail segment does not move with the rest of the rib cage when the patient attempts to breathe (paradoxical movement).

- A pneumothorax is a collection of air or gas outside the lung, between the lung and the chest wall. In a simple pneumothorax, air enters the chest cavity, causing a loss of negative pressure and a partial or total collapse of the lung.

- A spontaneous pneumothorax is a type of pneumothorax that does not involve trauma to the lung. It is usually caused by the rupture of a bleb (a small air- or fluid-filled sac) in the lung. A primary spontaneous pneumothorax occurs in people with no history of lung disease. A secondary spontaneous pneumothorax most often occurs as a complication of lung disease, such as COPD, asthma, pneumonia, tuberculosis, or lung cancer.

- An open pneumothorax is also called a *sucking chest wound*.

- A tension pneumothorax is a life-threatening condition in which air enters the pleural cavity during inspiration and progressively builds up under pressure. The flap of injured lung acts as a one-way valve, allowing air to enter the pleural space during inspiration but trapping it during expiration. The injured lung collapses completely. Pressure rises, forcing the trachea, heart, and major blood vessels to be pushed toward the opposite side. Shifting of the major blood vessels causes them to kink, resulting in a backup of blood into the venous system. The backup of blood into the venous system results in JVD, decreased blood return to the heart, and signs of shock.

- A hemothorax is a collection of blood in the pleural cavity that may result from injury to the chest wall, the major blood vessels, or the lung because of penetrating or blunt trauma. A hemothorax is often seen with a simple or tension pneumothorax. A massive hemothorax is blood loss of more than 1500 mL in the chest cavity.

- Cardiac tamponade usually occurs because of penetrating chest trauma, but it can also occur because of blunt trauma to the chest. Cardiac tamponade occurs when blood enters the pericardial sac. The blood in the pericardial sac compresses the heart, decreasing the amount of blood the heart can pump out with each contraction. The patient's signs and symptoms depend on how quickly blood collects in the pericardial sac.

- Traumatic asphyxia occurs because of a severe compression injury to the chest, such as compression of the chest under a heavy object or between a vehicle's seat and steering wheel. Blood backs up into the veins, venules, and capillaries of the head, neck, extremities, and upper torso, resulting in capillary rupture.

- A pulmonary contusion is bruising of the lung. In a pulmonary contusion, the alveoli fill with blood and fluid because of bruising of the lung tissue. As a result, the area of the lung available for gas exchange is decreased.

- A myocardial contusion is bruising of the heart muscle. Signs and symptoms of a myocardial contusion include chest pain or discomfort, increased heart rate, and (possibly) an irregular heart rhythm.

- The severity of an open pneumothorax depends on the size of the wound. If the diameter of the chest wound is more than 2/3 the diameter of the patient's trachea, air will enter the chest wound rather than through the trachea with each breath. Promptly close the chest wound with an airtight (occlusive) dressing. Plastic wrap and petroleum gauze are examples of dressings that may be used. Make sure that the dressing is large enough so that it is not pulled into the wound during inspiration. Tape the dressing on three sides. If signs and symptoms of a tension pneumothorax develop after an airtight dressing has been applied, release the dressing.

- Types of abdominal injuries include open injuries, in which the skin is broken, and closed injuries, in which the skin is not broken. If hollow abdominal organs are cut or rupture, their contents spill into the abdominal cavity, causing inflammation. Severe bleeding may result if a solid organ is cut or ruptures.

- Injuries to the external male genitalia include cuts, bruises, penetrating objects, amputations, and avulsions.

- The internal female genitalia are rarely injured except in the pregnant patient or in cases of sexual assault with penetration. Injuries to the external female genitalia usually result from straddle injuries or sexual assault.

▶ Tracking Your Progress

After reading this chapter, can you:	Page Reference	Objective Met?
• List the contents of the chest cavity?	575	☐
• List two classifications of chest injuries?	575	☐
• State the signs and symptoms and describe the emergency care for:	577, 578, 579, 580,	☐
• Rib fractures	581, 582, 583, 584, 585	
• Flail chest		
• Simple pneumothorax		
• Tension pneumothorax		
• Hemothorax		
• Cardiac tamponade		
• Traumatic asphyxia		
• Pulmonary contusion		
• Myocardial contusion		
• Open pneumothorax		
• State the signs and symptoms of a possible abdominal injury?	586	☐
• Describe the emergency care for a patient with a possible abdominal injury?	587	☐
• Describe the emergency care for injuries to the external male genitalia?	587	☐
• Describe the emergency care for injuries to the external female genitalia?	588	☐

True or False

Decide whether each statement is true or false. In the space provided, write *T* for true or *F* for false.

_____ **1.** If exposed abdominal organs are present, you should make at least one attempt to reinsert them into the abdominal cavity.

_____ **2.** Rib fractures are more common in children than in adults.

_____ **3.** All ribs are connected to the sternum by cartilage.

_____ **4.** Paradoxical movement is probably most readily seen in an unresponsive patient.

Multiple Choice

In the space provided, identify the letter of the choice that best completes the statement or answers each question.

_____ **5.** Which of the following best describes paradoxical chest movement?
- **a.** Bruising of the lung
- **b.** Two or more adjacent ribs broken in two or more places
- **c.** A crackling sensation under the fingers felt while palpating the chest
- **d.** A part of the chest wall moves in an opposite direction of the rest of the chest wall during breathing

_____ **6.** Your ambulance crew is called to a local high school for a 16-year-old male who was assaulted. Upon arrival, your patient is found in the nurse's office. He is holding his chest on the left side and appears to be experiencing severe discomfort. The nurse tells you that the patient was kicked in the chest several times. Which of the following findings would be consistent with a myocardial contusion?

    a. The patient is coughing up blood.

    b. Lung sounds are absent on the left side.

    c. The patient's pulse is rapid and irregular.

    d. The patient's trachea is deviated to the right.

_____ **7.** The abdomen contains both solid and hollow organs. The liver, for example, is considered solid whereas the stomach is considered hollow. Perforation of a solid abdominal organ is most commonly associated with

    a. paralysis.

    b. severe hemorrhage.

    c. tension pneumothorax.

    d. inflammation and infection.

_____ **8.** Your rescue crew is called to a local park for a male assault victim. Upon arrival, your patient is found lying on the ground moaning in pain. He does not speak English, and you are unable to understand what he is trying to explain to you. Which of the following physical findings would be consistent with an abdominal injury?

    a. The patient's abdomen is large and soft.

    b. The patient is coughing up bright red blood.

    c. The patient's blood pressure is high and his pulse rate is low.

    d. The patient is in the fetal position and appears to be in shock.

_____ **9.** Your rescue crew has been called to the scene of a sexual assault. Local law enforcement personnel have secured the scene. The police inform you that while trying to commit a rape, a 34-year-old man had his penis severed from his body. The amputated body part is on the ground. The patient is bleeding lightly from the groin. Appropriate management includes

    a. controlling bleeding with a tourniquet, leaving the amputated part at the crime scene, and transporting the patient to the Emergency Department.

    b. controlling bleeding with a tourniquet, packing the amputated part in a bag filled with ice, and transporting the patient and the bag to the Emergency Department.

    c. controlling bleeding with direct pressure, submerging the amputated part in a cup of water, and transporting the patient and the cup to the Emergency Department.

    d. controlling bleeding with direct pressure, wrapping the amputated part in sterile gauze, placing it in a plastic bag to keep it cool, and transporting the patient and the bag to the Emergency Department.

_____ **10.** Your rescue crew is called to a local recreation area for a 23-year-old woman who injured herself while mountain biking. The patient states that she slipped off the seat while going over a bump and landed on the bar. She tells you that there is a 1-inch laceration between her vagina and anus. You observe a slow stream of blood from her groin. Appropriate management of this injury includes

    a. applying ice directly to the wound.

    b. packing the vaginal opening with sterile gauze.

    c. controlling bleeding with external pressure and sterile gauze.

    d. protecting the patient's modesty by not evaluating or treating the injury.

Questions 11–14 pertain to the following scenario.

Your rescue crew is called to the scene of a motor vehicle collision. Your patient is a 42-year-old woman complaining of severe chest pain. She was not wearing a seat belt when she crashed her car into a light pole. She is responsive and denies any past medical history.

_____ **11.** Which of the following statements made by the patient would be consistent with a rib fracture?

    a. "The pain in my chest radiates down my left arm."

    b. "The chest pain is a dull, squeezing sensation."

    c. "The chest pain started just before the accident."

    d. "The chest pain is worse when I take a deep breath."

_____ 12. When evaluating this patient's anterior chest wall, you observe redness and swelling on her lower right chest wall. There are no open wounds to the chest wall. You should be suspicious of damage to the

  a. liver.   c. bladder.
  b. spleen.   d. kidneys.

_____ 13. Appropriate management of this patient should include

  a. positioning the patient her left side, administering oxygen by nonrebreather mask, and transporting.
  b. covering the chest wall with an occlusive dressing, administering oxygen by nonrebreather mask, and transporting.
  c. providing full spinal stabilization, administering oxygen by nonrebreather mask, encouraging the patient to cough or breathe deeply, and transporting.
  d. providing full spinal stabilization, administering oxygen by nonrebreather mask, applying tape around the chest wall to stabilize the right side, and transporting.

Matching

Match the key terms in the left column with the definitions in the right column by placing the letter of each correct answer in the space provided.

_____ 14. Subcutaneous emphysema

_____ 15. Pulmonary contusion

_____ 16. Cardiac tamponade

_____ 17. Hematuria

_____ 18. Pneumothorax

_____ 19. Bleb

_____ 20. Secondary spontaneous pneumothorax

_____ 21. Flail chest

_____ 22. Traumatic asphyxia

_____ 23. Open pneumothorax

_____ 24. Mediastinal shift

_____ 25. Hemoptysis

_____ 26. Simple pneumothorax

_____ 27. Hematemesis

_____ 28. Primary spontaneous pneumothorax

_____ 29. Tracheal deviation

_____ 30. Hemothorax

_____ 31. Tension pneumothorax

_____ 32. Crepitation

_____ 33. Myocardial contusion

A. A life-threatening condition in which air enters the pleural cavity during inspiration and progressively builds up under pressure

B. Air trapped between layers of skin

C. Vomiting blood

D. A collection of air or gas outside the lung and between the lung and the chest wall

E. A condition in which air enters the chest cavity, causing a loss of negative pressure (vacuum) and a partial or total collapse of the lung

F. Bruising of the heart

G. Blood in the urine

H. A collection of blood in the pleural cavity that may result from injury to the chest wall, the major blood vessels, or the lung caused by penetrating or blunt trauma

I. Shifting of the heart and major blood vessels from their normal position

J. Shifting of the trachea from its normal midline position

K. A small air- or fluid-filled sac

L. A collection of air or gas outside the lung and between the lung and the chest wall that most commonly occurs in tall, thin men between the ages of 20 and 40

M. Bruising of the lung

Continued

N. A collection of air or gas outside the lung and between the lung and the chest wall that most often occurs as a complication of lung disease

O. Coughing up blood

P. A condition in which two or more adjacent ribs are fractured in two or more places or when the sternum is detached

Q. A crackling sensation heard and felt beneath the skin caused by bone ends grating against each other

R. A condition that occurs when blood enters the pericardial sac because of laceration of a coronary blood vessel, a ruptured coronary artery, laceration of a chamber of the heart, or a significant cardiac contusion

S. The entry of air through an open wound in the chest wall into the pleural cavity

T. A condition that occurs because of a severe compression injury to the chest resulting in a backup of blood into the veins, venules, and capillaries of the head, neck, extremities, and upper torso and subsequent capillary rupture

Short Answer

Answer each question in the space provided.

34. List six signs or symptoms of a tension pneumothorax.

1.

2.

3.

4.

5.

6.

35. Briefly explain the two types of spontaneous pneumothorax.

36. List two common signs or symptoms of a spontaneous pneumothorax.

1.

2.

37. What is a hemothorax?

38. Explain what happens in traumatic asphyxia.

39. List four signs or symptoms of traumatic asphyxia.
1.
2.
3.
4.

Answer Section

Chapter 25

True/False

1. False

   If exposed abdominal organs are present, do not attempt to reinsert them into the abdominal cavity. Cover them with a moist, sterile dressing.

   Objective: State the emergency medical care considerations for a patient with an open wound to the abdomen.

2. False

   Children are less likely to sustain rib fractures than adults are because a child's chest wall is more flexible than that of an adult.

   Objective: State the signs and symptoms and describe the emergency care for rib fractures, flail chest, simple pneumothorax, tension pneumothorax, hemothorax, cardiac tamponade, traumatic asphyxia, pulmonary contusion, myocardial contusion, and open pneumothorax.

3. False

   All but two of the ribs are connected by cartilage to the sternum in the front.

   Objective: Describe the anatomy and function of the following major body systems: respiratory, circulatory, musculoskeletal, nervous, and endocrine.

4. True

   Paradoxical movement is probably most readily seen in an unresponsive patient. In patients with thick or muscular chest walls, it may be difficult to observe paradoxical movement. In some conscious patients, spasm and splinting of the chest muscles may cause paradoxical motion to go unnoticed.

   Objective: State the signs and symptoms and describe the emergency care for rib fractures, flail chest, simple pneumothorax, tension pneumothorax, hemothorax, cardiac tamponade, traumatic asphyxia, pulmonary contusion, myocardial contusion, and open pneumothorax.

Multiple Choice

5. d

   Paradoxical chest movement is uneven chest movement. When paradoxical movement is present, a part of the chest wall moves in an opposite direction of the rest of the chest wall during breathing. This finding is a sign of a flail segment. When the patient breathes in, the flail segment is drawn inward instead of moving outward. When the patient breathes out, the flail segment moves outward instead of moving inward. Bruising of the lung is a pulmonary contusion. Two or more adjacent ribs broken in two or more places describes a flail segment. Subcutaneous emphysema is a crackling sensation under the fingers felt while palpating the chest. It feels and sounds like crisped rice cereal.

   Objective: N/A

6. c

   A cardiac contusion results when the heart tissue is bruised because of blunt-force trauma. A cardiac dysrhythmia (irregular heartbeat) may result. This is a potentially life-threatening injury and requires prompt treatment (high-concentration oxygen therapy) and rapid transport. Coughing up blood suggests damage to the lung tissue or air passages. Absent or diminished breath sounds are consistent with a pneumothorax. Tracheal deviation is a very late sign of a tension pneumothorax.

   Objective: State the signs and symptoms and describe the emergency care for rib fractures, flail chest, simple pneumothorax, tension pneumothorax, hemothorax, cardiac tamponade, traumatic asphyxia, pulmonary contusion, myocardial contusion, and open pneumothorax.

7. b

The solid organs of the abdominal cavity (the spleen, liver, pancreas, and kidneys) are extremely vascular structures. Damage to these organs commonly results in significant blood loss. The abdominal organs may be injured by either penetrating or blunt trauma. For example, unrestrained patients in MVCs are highly susceptible to spleen damage from striking the steering wheel during impact. Paralysis is most commonly associated with nerve damage, whereas a tension pneumothorax is a thoracic (chest) injury.

Objective: State the signs and symptoms and describe the emergency care for rib fractures, flail chest, simple pneumothorax, tension pneumothorax, hemothorax, cardiac tamponade, traumatic asphyxia, pulmonary contusion, myocardial contusion, and open pneumothorax.

8. d

Sometimes your best indicator of injury and level of distress will be the patient's initial presentation. Patients with abdominal injuries will commonly assume the fetal position (lying on the side with the legs drawn up). Not all people with large abdomens have an abdominal injury (obviously), and a soft abdomen is a normal finding. Rigidity, however, may suggest injury. Coughing up blood is generally associated with an injury to the respiratory tract.

Objective: State the signs and symptoms and describe the emergency care for rib fractures, flail chest, simple pneumothorax, tension pneumothorax, hemothorax, cardiac tamponade, traumatic asphyxia, pulmonary contusion, myocardial contusion, and open pneumothorax.

9. d

Amputated genital organs are treated like any other amputation injury, with a more concerned emphasis placed on patient modesty and privacy. Bleeding should be controlled with direct pressure. Cold packs (not direct ice application) may relieve pain and swelling. The amputated body part should be wrapped in sterile gauze, placed in a bag, kept cool, and transported with the patient. As with all crime scenes, you must communicate closely with local law enforcement personnel.

Objective: Describe the emergency care for injuries to the external male genitalia.

10. c

This injury is treated like any other soft-tissue injury: Apply direct pressure with a sterile dressing.

Protecting the patient's modesty is important; however, not treating the patient because of the location of the injury is inappropriate. If possible, have a female rescuer examine and treat this injury. Be professional. Ice should never be applied directly to any wound because of the possibility of tissue damage. Vaginal bleeding should not be treated with the internal application of gauze or any other product in the prehospital setting.

Objective: Describe the emergency care for injuries to the external female genitalia.

11. d

Fractured ribs will cause an increase in discomfort during normal breathing. To compensate for this, patients will commonly breathe faster and more shallowly (almost like a panting dog). The pain associated with rib fractures is localized and sharp, unlike typical cardiac-type chest pain. Dull, squeezing pain; pain that radiates down the arms; or pain that started before the injury should all be considered cardiac (heart) in origin until proven otherwise in at the hospital.

Objective: State the signs and symptoms and describe the emergency care for rib fractures, flail chest, simple pneumothorax, tension pneumothorax, hemothorax, cardiac tamponade, traumatic asphyxia, pulmonary contusion, myocardial contusion, and open pneumothorax.

12. a

The liver is located just underneath the lower right rib cage. Fractures of ribs 5-9 on the right side may result in laceration of the liver. Fractures of ribs 9-11 on the left side may result in laceration of the spleen. The kidneys may be lacerated by posterior (backside) rib fractures. The bladder may be lacerated if the pelvis is fractured.

Objective: State the signs and symptoms and describe the emergency care for rib fractures, flail chest, simple pneumothorax, tension pneumothorax, hemothorax, cardiac tamponade, traumatic asphyxia, pulmonary contusion, myocardial contusion, and open pneumothorax.

13. c

The MOI indicates that spinal stabilization should be performed. Providing high-concentration oxygen should maximize oxygen delivery. To keep the lungs properly inflated, the patient should be encouraged to breathe deeply or cough. Simple rib fractures do not generally necessitate rapid (lights and siren) transport.

Objective: N/A

Matching

<table>
<tr><td>14.</td><td>B</td><td>24.</td><td>I</td></tr>
<tr><td>15.</td><td>M</td><td>25.</td><td>O</td></tr>
<tr><td>16.</td><td>R</td><td>26.</td><td>E</td></tr>
<tr><td>17.</td><td>G</td><td>27.</td><td>C</td></tr>
<tr><td>18.</td><td>D</td><td>28.</td><td>L</td></tr>
<tr><td>19.</td><td>K</td><td>29.</td><td>J</td></tr>
<tr><td>20.</td><td>N</td><td>30.</td><td>H</td></tr>
<tr><td>21.</td><td>P</td><td>31.</td><td>A</td></tr>
<tr><td>22.</td><td>T</td><td>32.</td><td>Q</td></tr>
<tr><td>23.</td><td>S</td><td>33.</td><td>E</td></tr>
</table>

Short Answer

34. Signs and symptoms of a tension pneumothorax include:

- Cool, clammy skin
- Increased pulse rate
- Cyanosis (late sign)
- JVD
- Decreased blood pressure
- Severe respiratory distress
- Agitation, restlessness, anxiety
- Bulging of intercostal muscles on the affected side
- Decreased or absent breath sounds on the affected side
- Tracheal deviation toward the unaffected side (late sign)
- Possible subcutaneous emphysema in the face, neck, or chest wall

Objective: N/A

35. There are two types of spontaneous pneumothorax. A primary spontaneous pneumothorax occurs in people with no history of lung disease. This condition most commonly occurs in tall, thin men between the ages of 20 and 40. It rarely occurs in persons older than 40 years.

A secondary spontaneous pneumothorax most often occurs as a complication of lung disease. COPD is the most common underlying disorder. Other lung diseases associated with this condition include asthma, pneumonia, tuberculosis, and lung cancer. A secondary spontaneous pneumothorax usually occurs in older persons.

Objective: N/A

36. Although they depend on the size of the pneumothorax, common signs and symptoms include a sudden onset of chest pain on the affected side, shortness of breath, an increased respiratory rate, and a cough. The patient's chest pain may be described as dull, sharp, or stabbing.

Objective: N/A

37. A hemothorax is a collection of blood in the pleural cavity that may result from injury to the chest wall, the major blood vessels, or the lung caused by penetrating or blunt trauma.

Objective: N/A

38. Traumatic asphyxia occurs because of a severe compression injury to the chest, such as compression of the chest under a heavy object or between a vehicle's seat and steering wheel. Blood backs up into the veins, venules, and capillaries of the head, neck, extremities, and upper torso, resulting in capillary rupture. The skin of the head and neck becomes deep red, purple, or blue. This characteristic finding is called *hooding* or a *purple cape* by EMS professionals.

Objective: N/A

39. Signs and symptoms of traumatic asphyxia include:

- JVD
- Swelling of the tongue and lips
- Eyes that may appear bloodshot and bulging
- Deep red, purple, or blue discoloration of the head and neck (hooding)
- Low blood pressure once the compression is released
- Skin below the level of the crush injury that remains pink (unless other injuries are present)

Objective: N/A

Infants and Children

26 Infant and Child Emergency Care

READING ASSIGNMENT ▶ Read Chapter 26, pages 591 to 620 in your textbook.

Sum It Up

- The age classification of infants and children is the following:
  - —Newly born: birth to several hours after birth
  - —Neonate: birth to 1 month
  - —Infant: 1 to 12 months of age
    - Young infant: 0 to 6 months of age
    - Older infant: 6 months to 1 year of age
  - —Toddler: 1 to 3 years of age
  - —Preschooler: 4 to 5 years of age
  - —School-age child: 6 to 12 years of age
  - —Adolescent: 13 to 18 years of age
- Perform a primary survey. Begin by forming a general impression of an infant or child from "across the room." Quickly determine if the child appears sick or not sick. Quickly assess:
  - —*Appearance*. A child should be alert and responsive to his surroundings.
  - —*(Work of)* Breathing. With normal breathing, both sides of the chest rise and fall equally. Breathing is quiet and painless and occurs at a regular rate.
  - —*Circulation*. Visual signs of circulation relate to skin color, obvious bleeding, and moisture. If the child's skin looks pale, mottled, flushed, gray, or blue, proceed immediately to the primary survey.
- Once your general impression is complete, perform a hands-on ABCDE assessment to determine if life-threatening conditions are present. In a responsive infant or child, use a toes-to-head or trunk-to-head approach. This approach should help reduce the infant or child's anxiety.
- During your primary survey, find the answers to these five questions:
  1. Is the child awake and alert?
  2. Is the child's airway open?
  3. Is the child breathing?
  4. Does the child have a pulse?
  5. Does the child have severe bleeding?
- If a child is unable to speak, cry, cough, or make any other sound, his airway is completely obstructed. If the child has noisy breathing, such as snoring or gurgling, he has a partial airway obstruction. You will need to intervene if the child has a complete airway obstruction.

- In children, pulse regularity normally changes with respirations (increases with inspiration, decreases with expiration).

- Use the carotid artery to assess the pulse in an unresponsive child older than 1 year of age. Feel for a brachial pulse in an unresponsive infant. Feel for a pulse for about 10 seconds. If there is no pulse, or if a pulse is present but the rate is less than 60 beats/min with signs of shock, you must begin chest compressions.

- In infants and children, it is important to compare the pulse of the central blood vessels (such as the femoral artery) with those found in peripheral areas of the body (such as the feet). They should feel the same. If they do not, a circulatory problem is present.

- Assess capillary refill in children 6 years of age or younger. Delayed capillary refill may occur because of shock or hypothermia, among other causes.

- Assess blood pressure in children older than 3 years of age. In children 1 to 10 years of age, the following formula may be used to determine the lower limit of a normal systolic blood pressure: 70 + (2 $\times$ child's age in years) = systolic blood pressure. The lower limit of normal systolic blood pressure for a child 10 or more years of age is 90 mm Hg. The diastolic blood pressure should be about 2/3 the systolic pressure.

- The most common medical emergencies in children are respiratory emergencies. Upper airway problems usually occur suddenly. Lower airway problems usually take longer to develop. Respiratory distress is an increased work of breathing (respiratory effort). Respiratory failure is a condition in which there is not enough oxygen in the blood and/or ventilation to meet the demands of body tissues. Respiratory failure becomes evident when the patient becomes tired and can no longer maintain good oxygenation and ventilation. Respiratory arrest occurs when a patient stops breathing.

- Cardiopulmonary arrest results when the heart and lungs stop working. When respiratory failure occurs together with shock, cardiopulmonary failure results. Cardiopulmonary failure will progress to cardiopulmonary arrest unless it is recognized and treated promptly.

- A seizure is a temporary change in behavior or consciousness caused by abnormal electrical activity in one or more groups of brain cells. Status epilepticus is recurring seizures without an intervening period of consciousness. Status epilepticus is a medical emergency that can cause brain damage or death if it is not treated.

- The most common causes of an altered mental status in a pediatric patient are a low level of oxygen in the blood, head trauma, seizures, infection, low blood sugar, and drug or alcohol ingestion. Any patient with an altered mental status is in danger of an airway obstruction. Be prepared to clear the patient's airway with suctioning.

- SIDS is the sudden and unexpected death of an infant. The cause of SIDS is not clearly understood.

- Injuries are the leading cause of death in infants and children. If the child is not alert or the MOI suggests that the child experienced trauma to the head or neck, stabilize the child's spine. Making sure the child's airway is open and clear of secretions is the most important step in managing a trauma patient. Extremity injuries should be stabilized by immobilizing the joint above and below the fracture site. Remember to assess pulses, motor function, and sensation in the affected extremity before and after immobilization.

- Child maltreatment is an act or failure to act by a parent, caregiver, or other person as defined by state law that results in physical abuse, neglect, medical neglect, sexual abuse, and/or emotional abuse. It is also defined as an act or failure to act that presents an impending risk of serious harm to a child.

— Physical abuse refers to physical acts that caused or could have caused physical injury to the child. Examples of physical abuse include burning, hitting, punching, shaking, kicking, beating, or otherwise harming a child.

— Neglect is the failure to provide for a child's basic needs. Neglect can be medical, physical, educational, or emotional. Medical neglect is a type of maltreatment caused by failure of the caregiver to provide for the appropriate healthcare of the child although financially able to do so.

— Sexual abuse is inappropriate adolescent or adult sexual behavior with a child. To be considered child abuse, these acts have to be committed by a person responsible for the care of a child (for example, a babysitter, parent, or daycare provider) or related to the child. If a stranger commits these acts, it is considered sexual assault and is handled by the police and criminal courts.

- Psychological maltreatment is a pattern of caregiver behavior that conveys to children that they are worthless, flawed, unloved, unwanted, endangered, or only of value in meeting another's needs. This type of maltreatment includes verbal abuse, emotional abuse or neglect, psychological abuse, and mental injury.

- When providing care for an infant or child who is ill or injured because of neglect or abuse, show a professional and caring attitude for the patient. Report known or suspected child abuse as required by law in your state. Carefully document your physical exam findings as well as your observations of the child's environment. Document the caregiver's comments exactly as stated and enclose them in quotation marks. Your documentation must reflect the facts and not your opinion of what may or may not have occurred. Report your findings to appropriate personnel when transferring patient care. After the call, assess your own emotional needs. A discussion with other personnel involved in the call may be helpful.

- Infants and children with special needs include many different types of children. Examples of these patients include premature babies with lung disease, babies and children with heart disease, infants and children with nervous system disease, and children with chronic disease or altered function from birth.

▶ Tracking Your Progress

After reading this chapter, can you:	Page Reference	Objective Met?
• Identify the developmental considerations for the following age groups: —Infants?	593	☐
—Toddlers?		
—Preschoolers?		
—School-age children?		
—Adolescents?		
• Describe differences in anatomy and physiology of the infant, child and adult patient?	595, 596, 597	☐
• Differentiate the response of the ill or injured infant or child (age specific) from that of an adult?	598	☐
• Indicate various causes of respiratory emergencies?	604	☐
• Differentiate between respiratory distress and respiratory failure?	604	☐

After reading this chapter, can you:	Page Reference	Objective Met?
● List the steps in the management of foreign body airway obstruction?	604	☐
● Summarize emergency medical care strategies for respiratory distress and respiratory failure?	605	☐
● Identify the signs and symptoms of shock (hypoperfusion) in the infant and child patient?	608	☐
● Describe the methods of determining end-organ perfusion in the infant and child patient?	604, 603	☐
● State the usual cause of cardiac arrest in infants and children versus adults?	606	☐
● List the common causes of seizures in the infant and child patient?	608	☐
● Describe the management of seizures in the infant and child patient?	608	☐
● Differentiate between the injury patterns in adults, infants, and children?	612	☐
● Discuss the field management of the infant and child trauma patient?	613	☐
● Summarize the indicators of possible child abuse and neglect?	615	☐
● Describe the medical-legal responsibilities in suspected child abuse?	616	☐
● Recognize the need for debriefing after a difficult infant or child transport?	612	☐

Multiple Choice

In the space provided, identify the letter of the choice that best completes the statement or answers each question.

_____ 1. Your rescue crew is called to the scene of an 8-month-old male patient who was found unresponsive in his crib. He is warm to the touch and was last observed playing in the crib only 10 minutes before your arrival. When assessing this patient's airway, you should perform a

    a. a head tilt–chin lift maneuver.
    b. a jaw thrust without head tilt maneuver.
    c. a head tilt–chin lift maneuver without hyperextending the neck.
    d. a head tilt–chin lift maneuver while hyperextending the neck.

Questions 2–4 pertain to the following scenario.

You are dispatched for a "sick child." When you arrive, you find a 7-year-old who is having difficulty breathing.

_____ 2. Which of the following accurately reflects your primary survey priorities when assessing this child?

    a. Determine pulse, get medical history, count breathing rate
    b. Assess mental status, determine breathing effectiveness, count pulse rate
    c. Count pulse rate, perform head-to-toe exam, determine breathing rate
    d. Get medical history, count breathing rate, assess mental status

_____ 3. Which breathing assessment would be abnormal for this child?

    a. Breathing is at a regular rate of 16 breaths per minute
    b. Breathing is noisy, and you hear a whistling sound
    c. Neck muscles are relaxed, and the child is lying flat
    d. Skin is pink, warm, and dry

_____ 4. Which is an appropriate initial method to assess circulation in this child?

    a. Assess skin color of the nail beds, mouth, and eyelids.
    b. Count the pulse for 5 seconds and multiply by 12.
    c. Press on the nail bed or forehead to check capillary refill.
    d. Take the blood pressure in both arms.

_____ **5.** Which of the following statements is true regarding the pediatric patient?

    a. Poisonings are the leading cause of death in infants and children.

    b. Airway and breathing problems are common with head injuries.

    c. Penetrating trauma is the most common mechanism of serious injury in the pediatric patient.

    d. Injury patterns seen in children are identical to those seen in an adult.

_____ **6.** A 3-year-old child had what her mother described as a seizure while watching TV on the couch. She is now very sleepy and is breathing at a rate of 24 breaths per minute. What should you do?

    a. Assist ventilations

    b. Elevate her legs

    c. Immobilize the child on a spine board

    d. Place the child in the recovery position

_____ **7.** Your ambulance crew is called to a long-term care facility for a 6-year-old male patient with breathing difficulty. Upon arrival, a care provider informs you that the patient is on a ventilator connected to a tracheostomy at the base of his neck. He is not able to breathe well on his own, and it appears that the ventilator is malfunctioning. While a replacement ventilator is being retrieved, the broken one is disconnected. Once disconnected, the patient begins breathing shallowly at 4 breaths/min. You should

    a. begin CPR.

    b. provide blow-by oxygen at the tracheostomy at 15 L/min.

    c. ventilate through the tracheostomy tube using a BM device at 20 respirations/min.

    d. ventilate through the tracheostomy tube using a nonrebreather mask at 12 respirations/min.

Questions 8–10 pertain to the following scenario.

Your ambulance crew is called to the home of a 4-month-old female infant with difficulty breathing and a history of an upper respiratory infection. You arrive on scene to find this patient pale and sleepy in her father's arms. There is a considerable amount of thick, yellow discharge coming from the patient's nose.

_____ **8.** To open the airway of this patient, you should

    a. perform a jaw thrust without head tilt maneuver.

    b. hyperextend the head and neck.

    c. place the patient's chin on her chest.

    d. place the head in a neutral position.

_____ **9.** Which of the following is true regarding this patient's airway and breathing?

    a. The tongue is proportionally smaller in children than in adults.

    b. An early sign of infant respiratory distress is a slow respiratory rate (bradypnea).

    c. It is a common but insignificant finding for children this age to grunt during exhalation.

    d. Children this age are obligate nose breathers, and the patient may not open her mouth to breathe if the nose is obstructed.

_____ **10.** After assessing the airway, you determine a need for suctioning. Which of the following is a correct guideline for suctioning this patient's nasal passages?

    a. Use a rigid catheter and suction for no more than 3 to 5 seconds.

    b. Use a bulb syringe and suction on insertion for no more than 5 seconds.

    c. Use a bulb syringe and suction on withdrawal for no more than 10 seconds.

    d. Use a rigid catheter and suction on insertion for no more than 15 seconds.

Questions 11–12 pertain to the following scenario.

Your rescue crew is called to the home of a 2-year-old male child with shortness of breath. You arrive to find this patient conscious and alert in his mother's arms. She informs you that her son has a 3-day history of a productive cough and runny nose. He is not presently taking any medications.

_____ **11.** To make the child more at ease with your presence, you should

    a. introduce yourself and try to hold him.

    b. develop a rapport with the patient's mother.

    c. inspect the patient's airway with a pen light.

    d. separate the mother and child and perform a primary survey.

_____ **12.** When performing a physical examination, you should
   a. attempt to hold the patient for better control.
   b. examine the trunk before examining the head.
   c. speak in a harsh tone that demands respect and submission.
   d. explain the entire procedure to the child before beginning the examination.

_____ **13.** Your ambulance crew is called to the home of an 8-year-old girl who fell from her bicycle. This is the fourth time this month you have been to the same house for an injured child. The patient initially tells you she fell off her bike but then changes her story. Her body is covered with bruises in different stages of healing. You suspect the child has been physically abused. You should
   a. question the child about the possible abuse.
   b. question the parents about their discipline habits and document your findings.
   c. treat and transport the patient, document your findings, and express your concerns to the Emergency Department physician.
   d. treat the child and transport only if medically necessary. If the child is not transported, start keeping a detailed log about your suspicions.

_____ **14.** Your rescue crew is called to the home of a 2-year-old boy with difficulty breathing. Upon your arrival, the patient's mother tells you the patient's tracheostomy tube "sounds clogged and he is having difficulty getting his breath." You assess the patient's airway and breathing and determine that suctioning is necessary. You should
   a. provide oxygen before and after suctioning and suction for no more than 10 seconds per attempt.
   b. remove the tracheostomy tube, clean it in sterile water or normal saline, then put it back in place.
   c. attempt to dislodge the obstruction with abdominal thrusts (Heimlich maneuver).
   d. provide oxygen by nonrebreather mask and transport with lights and siren to the closest appropriate facility.

Questions 15–18 pertain to the following scenario.

Your rescue crew is called to the home of a 3-year male patient with difficulty breathing. Upon arrival, his father tells you that he has had a cold with a slight fever for the past 2 days. The patient is responsive, alert, and sitting on his mother's lap. He does not appear to be happy with your presence.

_____ **15.** When interacting with this patient, you should
   a. set him on your lap for proper assessment.
   b. tell him, "Be good, big boys don't cry," if he begins crying.
   c. use a doll or stuffed animal to ask questions and perform the physical exam.
   d. use medical terms when explaining what you are about to do to temporarily confuse the child into letting you treat him.

_____ **16.** Assessing heart rate and lung sounds
   a. is unnecessary and may only agitate the child more.
   b. should be done by the parents so that the patient does not become overly agitated.
   c. should be performed at the conclusion of your physical assessment to decrease the child's anxiety.
   d. should be performed immediately with the patient in his mother's arms because agitation may change the results.

_____ **17.** Upon auscultation of lung sounds, you note wheezing in all lung fields. He has mild accessory muscle use to assist with inhalation and exhalation. You conclude that he is in need of oxygen therapy. The child becomes very agitated when you attempt to strap a nonrebreather mask to his face. Your best option for providing oxygen to the patient is
   a. use a nasal cannula flowing oxygen at 15 L/min.
   b. have his mother hold a nonrebreather mask near his face and blow-by oxygen at 10-15 L/min.
   c. take the regulator off the portable oxygen bottle, crack the oxygen open, place the bottle near the patient, and saturate the immediate area with pure oxygen.
   d. draw a happy face on a Styrofoam cup, insert oxygen supply tubing through the base of the cup, flow the oxygen at 10-15 L/min, and have the patient hold the cup near his face.

_____ 18. A very late sign of severe respiratory distress for this patient would be that

    a. his pulse rate is 120 beats per minute.

    b. he screams and cries throughout transport to the hospital.

    c. he is breathing 30 times per minute with audible wheezes.

    d. he is breathing 8 times per minute, and wheezes are no longer audible.

Matching

Match the key terms in the left column with the definitions in the right column by placing the letter of each correct answer in the space provided.

_____ 19. Respiratory failure

_____ 20. Tracheostomy

_____ 21. Peripherally inserted central catheter

_____ 22. Psychological maltreatment

_____ 23. Coining

_____ 24. Neglect

_____ 25. Respiratory arrest

_____ 26. Gastrostomy tube

_____ 27. Sudden infant death syndrome

_____ 28. Sexual abuse

_____ 29. Apparent life-threatening event

_____ 30. Mongolian spots

_____ 31. Ventricular shunt

_____ 32. Physical abuse

_____ 33. Shaken baby syndrome

_____ 34. Impetigo

_____ 35. Stoma

_____ 36. Hydrocephalus

A. Failure to provide for a child's basic needs

B. An episode in which an infant was about to die, but was found early enough for successful resuscitation

C. A surgically created opening

D. A special catheter placed directly into the stomach for feeding

E. A healing remedy practiced by some cultures in which a coin is heated in hot oil and then rubbed along the patient's spine to heal an illness

F. A condition in which there is an excess of CSF within the brain

G. Inappropriate adolescent or adult sexual behavior with a child

H. A drainage system used to remove excess CSF in a patient who has hydrocephalus

I. The creation of a surgical opening into the trachea through the neck, with insertion of a tube to aid passage of air or removal of secretions

J. The sudden and unexpected death of an infant that remains unexplained after a thorough case investigation, including performance of a complete autopsy, examination of the death scene, and review of the clinical history

K. An IV line often used for neonates, young children, or patients requiring relatively short-term IV therapy for the delivery of medications and nutritional solutions directly into the venous circulation

L. Acts that caused or could have caused physical injury to the child

M. A condition in which there is not enough oxygen in the blood and/or ventilation to meet the demands of body tissues

N. A severe form of head injury that occurs when an infant or child is shaken by the arms, legs, or shoulders with enough force to cause the baby's brain to bounce against his skull

Continued

O. A pattern of caregiver behavior that conveys to children that they are worthless, flawed, unloved, unwanted, endangered, or only of value in meeting another's needs

P. Bluish areas usually seen in non-Caucasian infants and young children that may be mistaken for bruises

Q. An absence of breathing

R. A contagious bacterial skin infection that can look like a burn

Short Answer

Answer each question in the space provided.

37. What is the leading cause of death in infants and children?

38. List four signs of physical abuse.
1.
2.
3.
4.

39. List five possible causes of altered mental status.
1.
2.
3.
4.
5.

40. List three possible causes of an increased heart rate in an infant or child.
1.
2.
3.

41. What is the formula used to approximate the lower limit of systolic blood pressure in children 1 to 10 years of age?

42. What is shaken baby syndrome?

Answer Section

Chapter 26

Multiple Choice

1. c

The airways of infants are extremely delicate. Hyperextending the airway may cause the trachea to become damaged and swell (leading to further airway complications). When opening the airway of an infant, the patient's head should be placed somewhere between the neutral position (no extension—looking straight up while lying supine) and the "sniffing position" (nose slightly elevated up from the neutral position).

Objective: Identify and describe the airway anatomy in the infant, child and the adult.

2. b

Your primary survey priorities include assessing the patient's level of responsiveness, noting the need for spinal precautions. Then assess the patient's ABCs, reassess mental status, and expose the patient as necessary for a more thorough physical exam.

Objective: N/A

3. b

Normal breathing is quiet, painless, and occurs at a regular rate. Noisy breathing is abnormal breathing. Remember to approach the patient immediately and begin your focused assessment if the patient:

- Looks as if he is struggling (laboring) to breathe
- Has noisy breathing
- Is breathing faster or more slowly than normal
- Looks as if his chest is not moving normally

Objective: Distinguish between methods of assessing breathing in the adult, child, and infant patient.

4. a

While assessing the patient's pulse, quickly check the patient's skin. Assessing the patient's skin condition can provide important information about the flow of blood through the body's tissues (perfusion). Assess perfusion by evaluating skin color, temperature, condition (moist, dry).

Objective: Describe normal and abnormal findings when assessing skin color.

5. b

Airway and breathing problems are common with head injuries. The most common cause of a low oxygen level in the unresponsive head injury patient is the tongue obstructing the airway. Injuries are the leading cause of death in infants and children. Blunt trauma is the most common mechanism of serious injury in the pediatric patient.

The injury pattern seen in a child may be different from that seen in an adult. For example, if an adult is about to be struck by an oncoming vehicle, he will typically turn away from the vehicle. This results in injuries to the side or back of the body. In contrast, a child will usually face an oncoming vehicle, resulting in injuries to the front of the body. In an MVC, an unrestrained infant or child will often have head and neck injuries. Restrained passengers often have abdominal and lower spine injuries. Child safety seats are often improperly secured, resulting in head and neck injuries. Contributing factors to pediatric motor vehicle–related injuries include failure to use (or improper use of) passenger restraints, inexperienced adolescent drivers, and alcohol abuse.

Objective: Differentiate between the injury patterns in adults, infants, and children.

6. d

A patient who has had a seizure is likely to be confused and/or sleepy after a seizure. If no spinal injury is suspected, place the patient in the recovery position to allow gravity to help any secretions in the mouth drain out. Suction the child's mouth if necessary and administer oxygen.

Objective: Describe the management of seizures in the infant and child patient.

7. c

This patient needs full ventilatory assistance. Connect a BM device directly to his tracheostomy tube and begin ventilating with high-concentration oxygen. The correct rate is 12 to 20 ventilations/min (once every 3 to 5 seconds). CPR would only be necessary if the patient were apneic and pulseless. Blow-by oxygen or nonrebreather mask therapy would not be viable options because of the patient's profoundly slow respiratory rate.

Objective: N/A

8. d

A "sleepy" presentation in a distressed child is not a good sign. Infants and children do not generally become sleepy until their compensatory mechanisms are about to fail. The correct manner in which to position an infant's airway is to place the head in a neutral position or with the head slightly elevated ("sniffing" position). Hyperextending the neck may result in kinking of the patient's delicate trachea. Placing the chin on the chest may cause the tongue to obstruct the airway. Because there is no indication or history of trauma, the jaw thrust without head tilt maneuver would not be necessary.

Objective: Describe the steps in performing the head tilt–chin lift.

9. d

Until about 6 months of age, infants are obligate nose breathers. They depend on an open nasal passage for breathing. If the nasal passage is obstructed, these infants may not "think" to breathe through their mouths. The tongue is proportionately larger in children and infants than adults. A slow respiratory rate is a late and worrying sign of distress. Infants and children compensate for distress much longer than adults, but when they crash, they crash fast. Do not wait for measurable signs of injury or illness before starting treatment. Grunting with each exhalation is a significant sign of possible respiratory collapse. If grunting is present and breathing is adequate, provide high-flow oxygen by nonrebreather mask and continuous

reassessment. If breathing is inadequate, assist ventilations with a BM device and supplemental oxygen.

Objective: Describe differences in anatomy and physiology of the infant, child, and adult patient.

10. c

Bulb syringes are excellent for suctioning nasal and oral secretions in infants. You should provide oxygen before and immediately after suctioning. To correctly use the bulb syringe, you must first depress the bulb, then insert the tip gently in the patient's mouth or nose, and finally release the bulb. Remove the syringe from the airway, depress the bulb, and repeat as necessary. Do not suction for more than 10 seconds per attempt and provide supplemental oxygen between suctioning attempts if possible. (Do not suction a newborn for more than 3 to 5 seconds per attempt.)

Objective: Describe the techniques of suctioning.

11. b

At this age, children are very attached to their parents and caregivers. You are a perceived threat. If you show that the parent trusts you, the child may open up to you. Attempting to hold him, sticking a light in his eyes, or separating him from his mother may be disastrous (not necessarily for the child's health, but for your ability to evaluate him).

Objective: Identify the developmental considerations for the following age groups: infants, toddlers, preschool, school age, and adolescent.

12. b

A child may watch and interact if you assess the abdomen and chest first. If you go straight to the patient's head, again you will be perceived as a threat to his safety. Whenever possible, have the parent or caregiver hold the patient during the examination. Children understand tone of voice at a very young age. Use a gentle tone and simple explanations. Overexplaining your intentions may only confuse and upset the child. Be gentle, nonthreatening, and kind. Use praise or rewards, such as stickers or a "glove balloon."

Objective: Identify the developmental considerations for the following age groups: infants, toddlers, preschool, school age, and adolescent.

13. c

If you suspect abuse, all efforts should be made to transport the child to an appropriate facility. Attempt to gather as much information as possible without appearing too pushy. It is difficult not to get emotionally involved when a child has been injured, but your professionalism may be the key to getting the matter handled appropriately. If you suspect abuse and the parents/caregiver refuses transport, discretely contact medical direction and law enforcement as per local protocol. Make sure that your documentation of the incident is complete, accurate, and without drawn conclusions or personal bias.

Objective: Describe the medical-legal responsibilities in suspected child abuse.

14. a

As with all pediatric patients, you should suction for a maximum of 10 seconds, and oxygen therapy should be provided between suctioning attempts. A flexible (soft) catheter is generally used to clear obstructed tracheostomy tubes. Remember to suction only on withdrawal, not on insertion. If you have problems or questions, consult medical direction. If the patient is in severe respiratory distress and you are unable to correct the obstruction, request ALS assistance or immediately begin rapid transport.

Objective: Describe the techniques of suctioning.

15. c

Many times a child would much rather answer questions posed to him by a familiar "friend." In these cases, a doll or stuffed animal can be invaluable. Not only will the child answer your questions, but you also can develop a playful, nonthreatening relationship with the patient. Taking a noncritical patient away from a parent or caregiver is generally unnecessary. You should be suspicious if a child doesn't put up a fight when being separated from a loved one, as this is not typical for children from 6 months to about 12 years and may be a sign that the patient is more seriously injured or ill than you thought.

Objective: Identify the developmental considerations for the following age groups: infants, toddlers, preschool, school age, and adolescent.

16. d

Ideally, you would like to assess the patient's heart rate and breathing status while the patient is at rest, not when he is crying or otherwise stimulated. Having a parent or caregiver assess lung sounds is not feasible; however, you may allow the parent to mock an assessment first to show the patient that there is no threat or pain involved with your treatment.

Objective: Identify the attributes that should be obtained when assessing breathing.

17. b

If the child won't tolerate a nonrebreather mask strapped to his face, blow-by high-concentration oxygen is your next best option. A nonrebreather mask or paper cup may be useful; however, you should avoid using products like Styrofoam because pieces of the cup may chip off and create an airway problem. Never attempt to use an oxygen bottle without a functioning regulator as oxygen is stored under pressure (at over 2000 psi) and may be very hazardous.

Objective: Identify a nonrebreather face mask and state the oxygen flow requirements needed for its use.

18. d

Wheezing is an abnormal lung sound that requires a certain amount of air to be moving in and out of the lungs to create the whistling sound. Wheezing may stop if the narrowing of the airway is reversed or if the amount of air moving in and out decreases to the extent that a whistle is no longer audible. For this particular scenario, the absence of wheezing combined with the slow respiratory rate is a very worrisome sign of impending respiratory arrest. While it may try your nerves more, crying is a much better sign than sleepiness or silence in a sick child.

Objective: Differentiate between respiratory distress and respiratory failure.

Matching

19.	M	**23.**	E
20.	I	**24.**	A
21.	K	**25.**	Q
22.	O	**26.**	D

27.	J	32.	L
28.	G	33.	N
29.	B	34.	R
30.	P	35.	C
31.	H	36.	F

Short Answer

37. Injuries are the leading cause of death in infants and children. Blunt trauma is the most common mechanism of serious injury in the pediatric patient.

Objective: N/A

38. Signs of physical abuse include:

- Multiple bruises in various stages of healing
- Human bite marks
- Inflicted burns: "stocking-like" burns with no associated splash marks; usually present on the buttocks, genitalia, or extremities
- Circular burns from a cigarette or cigar
- Rope burns on wrists
- Burns in the shape of a household utensil or appliance, such as a spoon or iron
- Fractures
- Head, face, and oral injuries
- Abdominal injuries
- Injury inconsistent with the history or developmental level of the child

Objective: Summarize the indicators of possible child abuse and neglect.

39. Possible causes of altered mental status include:

- Low level of oxygen in the blood (hypoxia)
- Head trauma
- Seizures (including the postictal phase)
- Infection
- Shock
- Low blood sugar
- Drug or alcohol ingestion
- Abuse
- Fever
- Respiratory failure

Objective: N/A

40. Bleeding, vomiting, diarrhea, shock, fever, anxiety, pain.

Objective: N/A

41. The formula used to approximate the lower limit of systolic blood pressure in children 1 to 10 years of age is 70 + (2 × age in years).

Objective: Describe the methods to assess blood pressure.

42. Shaken baby syndrome is a severe form of head injury. It occurs when an infant or child is shaken by the arms, legs, or shoulders with enough force to cause the baby's brain to bounce against his skull. Just 2 to 3 seconds of shaking can cause bruising, swelling, and bleeding in and around the brain. It can lead to severe brain damage or death.

Objective: N/A

Division 7

Operations

READING ASSIGNMENT ▶ Read Chapter 27, pages 622 to 641 in your textbook.

Sum It Up

- Preparations for an emergency call include having the appropriate personnel and equipment and an emergency response vehicle that is ready for use. Minimum staffing requirements for an ambulance include at least one EMT in the patient compartment. Two EMTs are preferred. Emergency transport vehicles are required to carry specific types and quantities of medical equipment to be "certified" as an ambulance. In addition to basic medical supplies, nonmedical supplies include personal safety equipment as required by local, state, and federal standards, and preplanned routes or comprehensive street maps. Daily inspections of the emergency response vehicle and its equipment are necessary to ensure it is in proper working order.

- In the dispatch phase of an EMS response, the patient or a witness reports the emergency by calling 9-1-1 or another emergency number. EMD receives the call and gathers information from the caller. The dispatcher then activates (dispatches) an appropriate EMS response based on the information received.

- En route to the reported emergency, begin to anticipate the knowledge, equipment, and skills you may need to provide appropriate patient care. Notify the dispatcher that you are responding to the call. Determine the responsibilities of the crewmembers before arriving on the scene.

- Laws pertaining to the proper methods of responding to an emergency vary from state to state. In general, most states require emergency vehicle operators to obey all traffic regulations unless a specific exemption has been made and documented in statute. Most states allow for such an exemption "as long as it does not endanger life or property." In addition, these exemptions are typically only granted when a true emergency exists. A true emergency is a situation in which there is a high possibility of death or serious injury and the rapid response of an emergency vehicle may lessen the risk of death or injury.

- When driving in emergency mode, the operator of an emergency vehicle must drive with due regard for the safety of others on the roadway. Due regard means that, in similar circumstances, a reasonable and responsible person would act in a way that is safe and considerate of others. Emergency vehicles should never operate at a speed greater than is warranted by the nature of the call or the condition of the patient that you are transporting.

This speed must also not be greater than traffic, road, and weather conditions allow. All emergency vehicle warning systems should be used as intended by the manufacturer and must be in operation during an emergency response. All emergency vehicle warning systems must be functioning in the prescribed manner before entering any intersection.

- Escorts and multiple-vehicle responses are extremely dangerous. They should be used only if emergency responders are unfamiliar with the location of the patient or receiving facility. Provide a safe following distance (generally a minimum of 500 feet). Stop and then proceed through any intersection as directed by the standard right-of-way guidelines.

- While approaching the scene, be cautious, and look for dangers. Position the emergency vehicle with careful consideration of potential dangers such as fire, hazardous materials, downed power lines, crowds, heavy traffic flow, and potential violence. When you arrive on the scene, notify the EMD of your arrival. Before initiating patient care, put on appropriate PPE. Determine the MOI or nature of the patient's illness. Ask for additional resources before making patient contact and institute the Incident Command System if needed. When it is safe to do so, gain access to the patient. Perform a primary survey and provide essential emergency care.

- If patient transport is needed, prepare the patient. Ask for assistance with lifting and moving the patient to the ambulance. Secure the patient to the stretcher and lock the stretcher in place. Ensure outside compartment doors are closed and secure.

- During transport, remember that your safety must be your priority. Wearing a seatbelt is one way to ensure your safety. Notify the dispatcher when you are leaving the scene. Perform ongoing patient assessments during transport. Complete your PCR and contact the receiving facility, if possible, using a standardized medical reporting format.

- Notify the dispatcher as soon as you arrive at the receiving facility. Give a verbal report to the hospital staff. Notify the dispatcher when you are en route to your station and again when you arrive. Clean and disinfect the vehicle and equipment as needed in preparation for the next call. Replace supplies used during the run. Notify the dispatcher when your tasks are complete and you are ready for another call.

- Air medical transport may be necessary when the condition of one or more patients is critical. If your unit is designated to land the helicopter, you will need to locate a secure landing zone. You must locate an area that is easily controlled for traffic and pedestrians. You should allow at least 100 feet by 100 feet to land any helicopter. The area should be free of overhead obstacles such as wires, trees, and light poles. It should also be free of debris and should be relatively level. The ground should be clear of rocks and grooves and must be firm enough to support the aircraft.

▶ Tracking Your Progress

After reading this chapter, can you:	Page Reference	Objective Met?
• Discuss the medical and nonmedical equipment needed to respond to a call?	624	☐
• List the phases of an ambulance call?	627, 632, 634, 636, 637	☐

After reading this chapter, can you:	Page Reference	Objective Met?
• Describe the general provisions of state laws relating to the operation of the ambulance and privileges in any or all of the following categories?	629	☐
—Speed		
—Warning lights		
—Sirens		
—Right of way		
—Parking		
—Turning		
• List contributing factors to unsafe driving conditions?	630	☐
• Describe the considerations that should by given to:	631, 632	☐
—Request for escorts?		
—Following an escort vehicle?		
• Intersections?	629	☐
• Discuss "due regard for the safety of others" while operating an emergency vehicle?	627	☐
• State what information is essential in order to respond to a call?	632	☐
• Discuss various situations that may affect response to a call?	625	☐
• Differentiate among the various methods of moving a patient to the unit on the basis of injury or illness?	636	☐
• Apply the components of the essential patient information in a written report?	637	☐
• Summarize the importance of preparing the unit for the next response?	637	☐
• Identify what is essential for completion of a call?	637	☐
• Distinguish among the terms cleaning, disinfection, high-level disinfection, and sterilization?	637	☐
• Describe how to clean or disinfect items following patient care?	637	☐

Multiple Choice

In the space provided, identify the letter of the choice that best completes the statement or answers each question.

_____ 1. Which of the following statements regarding vehicle operations is correct?
   a. The use of lights and siren automatically grants you the right of way.
   b. The light bar on the top of the vehicle is the most visible warning device on the vehicle.
   c. The standard rules of the road apply, even if you are in the emergency response mode.
   d. Most drivers will not yield the right of way when they notice your approach with lights and siren.

_____ 2. When establishing a landing zone for a medical helicopter, the minimum size of the area secured should be:
   a. 20 feet by 40 feet.   b. 100 feet by 100 feet.
   c. 200 feet by 200 feet.   d. 500 feet by 500 feet.

_____ 3. Before approaching a medical helicopter, you should
   a. move to the uphill side.
   b. wait until signaled to approach by the flight crew.
   c. extinguish cigarettes when within 25 feet of the aircraft.
   d. raise your arms above your head to get a better feel for the height of the rotor blades.

_____ 4. Which of the following is correct regarding the operation of lights and siren for emergency response?
   a. Lights and siren should be used simultaneously when operating in the emergency response mode.
   b. Flashing lights must be used continuously, and the siren should be activated at intersections to control traffic.
   c. In the emergency response mode, activating the lights and siren is necessary only when operating in extremely heavy traffic conditions.
   d. When operating in the emergency response mode, lights and siren should be turned on when local laws are being broken and shut down when local laws are being obeyed.

Questions 5–9 pertain to the following scenario.

Your rescue crew has been called to the scene of a serious multi-vehicle collision on a local interstate highway. Several rescue units have been dispatched. As you get closer to the scene, you find yourself driving behind another responding rescue crew.

_____ 5. Both units are responding with lights and sirens activated. You should
   a. maintain a minimum following distance of at least 200 feet.
   b. select a different route to the scene even if it delays your response time.
   c. follow as close to the lead vehicle as possible to maximize your visibility when entering intersections.
   d. use a different siren or audible tone to help motorists distinguish a multiple-vehicle response.

_____ 6. While responding to the emergency scene
   a. you must wear your seat belt at all times.
   b. you must wear your seat belt only if you are driving the vehicle.
   c. you need not wear your seat belt because you are using the red lights and siren to avoid a collision.
   d. you must wear your seat belt only if you are riding in a rear-facing seat ("jump" seat).

_____ 7. As you approach an intersection, the light is red for your direction of travel. You should
   a. slow to 20–25 miles per hour and proceed through the intersection.
   b. come to a complete stop, wait until the light changes to green, then proceed through the intersection.
   c. come to a complete stop, ensure traffic has stopped in all directions, then proceed through the intersection.
   d. proceed through the intersection, maintaining no more than 10 miles per hour above the posted speed limit.

_____ 8. As you approach the scene, you observe that one of the involved vehicles has caught on fire. What is the minimum distance you should park your rescue vehicle from the fire (assuming you do not have the training or responsibility for firefighting functions)?
   a. 100 feet   b. 200 feet
   c. 2,000 feet   d. 1 mile

_____ 9. Assuming you are the first unit to arrive at the scene, which of the following responsibilities should be addressed first?
   a. Gain access to all patients.
   b. Notify the dispatcher of your arrival at the scene.
   c. Perform a primary survey of all patients to determine care priorities.
   d. Provide essential emergency care to stabilize patients and prepare them for transport.

_____ 10. Your patient is a 31-year-old woman with an open head injury. Your crew provides prompt, efficient treatment, and the patient is transported to an appropriate facility. You have restocked your supplies and are prepared to return to service. Upon returning to the vehicle, you observe a small amount of blood on the handle of your door. Your best course of action would be to
   a. drive the vehicle through a commercial car wash.
   b. immediately scrub away the blood with undiluted household bleach.
   c. have the vehicle put out of service until an OSHA-approved vendor decontaminates it.
   d. put on appropriate PPE and personally decontaminate the handle with a bleach and water solution.

Matching

Match the key terms in the left column with the definitions in the right column by placing the letter of each correct answer in the space provided.

_____ 11. Intermediate-level disinfection

_____ 12. True emergency

_____ 13. Decontamination

_____ 14. Low-level disinfection

_____ 15. High-level disinfection

_____ 16. Sterilization

_____ 17. Emergency response

A. A method of decontamination that destroys all microorganisms including highly resistant bacterial spores

B. A situation in which there is a high possibility of death or serious injury and the rapid response of an emergency vehicle may lessen the risk of death or injury

C. Operation of an emergency vehicle while responding to a medical emergency

D. A method of decontamination that destroys most bacteria and some viruses and fungi, but not tuberculosis bacteria or bacterial spores

E. The use of physical or chemical means to remove, inactivate, or destroy bloodborne pathogens on a surface or item to the point where they are no longer capable of transmitting infectious particles and the surface or item is considered safe for handling, use, or disposal

F. A method of decontamination that destroys all microorganisms except large numbers of bacterial spores

G. A method of decontamination that destroys tuberculosis bacteria, vegetative bacteria, and most viruses and fungi, but not bacterial spores

Short Answer

Answer each question in the space provided.

18. Where do most accidents involving emergency response vehicles occur?

19. List four important areas to consider when placing an emergency vehicle at the scene of an emergency.
    1.
    2.
    3.
    4.

20. List six contributing factors to unsafe driving conditions.
    1.
    2.
    3.
    4.
    5.
    6.

Answer Section

Chapter 27

Multiple Choice

1. c

Headlights are the most visible warning devices on an emergency vehicle because they are mounted at the eye level of other drivers. Use caution during any response that uses lights and siren because of the "excitement factor."

Objective: Discuss various situations that may affect response to a call.

2. b

If your unit is designated to land a helicopter, you will need to locate a secure landing zone. You must locate an area that is easily controlled for traffic and pedestrians. You should allow at least 100 feet by 100 feet to land any helicopter. The area should be free of overhead obstacles such as wires, trees, and light poles. It should also be free of debris and should be relatively level. The ground should be clear of rocks and grooves and must be firm enough to support the aircraft.

Objective: N/A

3. b

Communications are crucial during helicopter operations. One rescuer should be assigned the responsibility of securing the landing zone and communicating with the aircraft crew. Securing a LZ may require additional personnel, especially in populated areas. Only essential personnel should approach the aircraft. Before approaching, rescue personnel should be granted permission to enter the LZ area by either direct radio contact or hand signals by the flight crew. Approaches should be made from the front of the aircraft and from the downhill side (if applicable). Do not raise anything above your head as you approach. Stay as low as feasible. Secure any objects that maybe blown away (hat, papers, blankets, etc.) before approaching the aircraft.

Objective: Describe the roles and responsibilities related to personal safety.

4. a

All visual and audible warning devices should be activated when driving in the emergency response mode. Avoid turning the siren on and off repeatedly as you may surprise drivers by your sudden, unsuspected approach. There may be circumstances when operating the siren is not desired, such as when driving through a residential neighborhood in the middle of the night. Common sense and local protocol should prevail. However, if you are going to turn off the siren, you should consider turning off the flashing lights as well, thus returning to a "normal" response mode.

Objective: Discuss "due regard for the safety of others" while operating an emergency vehicle.

5. d

Provide a safe following distance (generally a minimum of 500 feet). Stop and then proceed through any intersection, using standard right-of-way guidelines. Check your agency's policy regarding the use of siren and/or lights in these situations. Some agencies do not want them used because they may confuse other drivers. Other agencies specify that a different siren time and/or tone must be used to help other motorists distinguish multiple emergency vehicles.

Objective: Describe the considerations that should be given to a request for escorts, following an escort vehicle, and intersections.

6. a

During transport, remember that your safety must be your priority. Wearing a seat belt is one way to ensure your safety. While some people may consider it cumbersome to wear a seat belt during transport, your risk of injury increases if you are not restrained. All passengers and patients should also be properly secured. Infants and children should always be appropriately secured.

Objective: Describe the roles and responsibilities related to personal safety.

7. c

Although it is not necessary to wait for the light to change to green, waiting until all vehicles in all lanes of traffic yield the right-of-way is absolutely necessary. Failure to operate with due regard for the safety of others may have detrimental effects on your health, the health of others, and your long-term financial and professional stability. Reckless, aggressive driving does not make a significant difference in response times and should never be tolerated.

Objective: Discuss "due regard for the safety of others" while operating an emergency vehicle.

8. a

You should park a minimum of 100 feet upwind of any burning vehicle. If the vehicle is very large or involves some other hazard, you would obviously want to increase your safety zone. A minimum safety zone of 2,000 feet should be observed at hazardous materials incidents.

Objective: Discuss various situations that may affect response to a call.

9. b

When you arrive at the scene, you should notify the dispatcher of your arrival and provide a brief on-scene report to other emergency vehicles responding to the scene. Your report could be as simple as, "Rescue 10 is on scene. Three-car collision with trapped patients. Appears serious." This brief report allows responding units to plan their actions and prepare for special assignments en route (such as extrication duties, firefighting, special approach considerations, or ALS-level care). This on-scene notification should be followed by the scene size-up, which includes BSI precautions, scene safety control, and determination of the MOI. Next, you must gain access to the patients, perform primary surveys, provide emergency care, and prepare the patients for transport. If the number and/or severity of the patients outweighs your initial on-scene resources, triage should begin as part of the scene size-up.

Objective: List the correct radio procedures in the following phases of a typical call: to the scene, at the scene, to the facility, at the facility, to the station, and at the station.

10. d

A strong solution of household bleach should remove and/or kill any biological contaminant, especially on something nonporous like a metal handle. Be sure to readdress BSI during any decontamination procedure. In this situation, you should, as a minimum, wear disposable gloves.

Objective: Describe how to clean or disinfect items following patient care.

Matching

11. G	**15.** F
12. B	**16.** A
13. E	**17.** C
14. D	

Short Answer

18. Most accidents involving emergency response vehicles occur in intersections.

Objective: List contributing factors to unsafe driving conditions.

19. There are four things to consider when placing an emergency vehicle at the emergency scene:

1. Scene safety
2. Traffic volume and flow
3. Egress from the scene
4. Distance from the patient(s) or scene.

Objective: N/A

20. Contributing factors to unsafe driving conditions:

- Escorts
- Road surface
- Excessive speed
- Reckless driving
- Weather conditions
- Multiple-vehicle response
- Inadequate dispatch information and unfamiliarity with the location
- Failing to heed traffic warning signals
- Disregarding traffic rules and regulations
- Failing to anticipate the actions of other motorists
- Failing to obey traffic signals or posted speed limits

Objective: List contributing factors to unsafe driving conditions.

28 Gaining Access

Sum It Up

- Extrication is the process of removing machinery from around a patient to facilitate patient care and transport. The EMT on the extrication scene has an important role both as a care provider for the patient and a support member for the extrication team. Base the extrication on the patient's condition to ensure that the techniques used will provide the fastest access and best egress for the patient from the vehicle.

- Protective clothing that is appropriate for the situation must be worn during extrication. This includes protective boots, pants, a coat, eye protection, a helmet, and gloves. Respiratory protection may also be needed.

- Scene size-up is an important step in the extrication process. A proper scene size-up will reveal any hazards present and also give a good indication of the number of persons injured, the types of injury, and which patient or patients require medical attention first.

- Once on the scene, fire apparatus should be parked in the fend-off position, which involves parking your unit downward from the scene and in such a way that allows traveling vehicles to strike your unit and not crew members.

- Stabilization is the process of rendering a vehicle motionless in the position in which it is found. The purpose of stabilization is to eliminate potential movement of a vehicle (or structure) that may cause further harm to entrapped patients or rescuers.

- Simple extrication is the use of hand tools in order to gain access and extricate the patient from the vehicle. Complex extrication involves the use of powered hydraulic rescue tools such as cutters, spreaders, and rams. The patient's level of entrapment will determine whether the extrication will fall into a simple or complex category.

- Four levels of entrapment are possible during a motor vehicle crash. The first level is no entrapment. Light entrapment means that a door or some other object will need to be opened or moved to get the patient out. Moderate entrapment is more involved, requiring removal of doors or the roof. Heavy entrapment is the highest level of entrapment and involves any situation that is above and beyond moderate entrapment.

- Disentanglement is the moving or removing of material that is trapping a victim.
- Continue your education beyond the information contained in this chapter in order to provide the best care for your patient and maintain and improve your skills as you gain more experience in EMS.

▶ Tracking Your Progress

After reading this chapter, can you:	Page Reference	Objective Met?
• Describe the purpose of extrication?	643	☐
• Discuss the role of the EMT in extrication?	643	☐
• Identify what equipment for personal safety is required for the EMT?	643	☐
• Define the fundamental components of extrication?	643	☐
• State the steps that should be taken to protect the patient during extrication?	646	☐
• Evaluate various methods of gaining access to the patient?	645	☐
• Distinguish between simple and complex access?	647	☐

True or False

Decide whether each statement is true or false. In the space provided, write *T* for true or *F* for false.

_____ 1. Cutters, spreaders, and rams are examples of tools used during a simple extrication.

_____ 2. All persons involved in an extrication operation should wear protective clothing.

_____ 3. Equipment for stabilization involves the use of hammers, hacksaws, cutters, and spreaders.

_____ 4. When attempting to gain access to a patient, it is best to use the path of least resistance first.

Multiple Choice

In the space provided, identify the letter of the choice that best completes the statement or answers each question.

_____ 5. Before removing a patient from a vehicle during extrication, what step should be taken?
  a. Take a full set of vital signs   **c.** Maintain spinal stabilization
  b. Bandage all wounds   **d.** Obtain a complete history and perform a physical exam

Questions 6–10 pertain to the following scenario.

Your rescue crew is called to the scene of motor vehicle collision on a local 4-lane highway. Information at time of dispatch indicates that there are at least five vehicles involved. The posted speed limit is 55 miles per hour. The crash has occurred 45 miles from the nearest hospital.

_____ 6. Which of the following duties should be performed first?
  a. Gain access to the most critically injured patients
  b. Triage patients according to the severity of their injuries
  c. Determine the number of patients, the types of injuries, and additional resource needs
  d. Assess the mental, airway, breathing, and circulation status of all patients, and begin treating life-threatening conditions

_____ 7. One of the vehicles has come to rest on its side. There is one occupant in the vehicle. Before gaining access and assessing the occupants, you should consider

   a. removing the vehicle's battery.
   b. siphoning the fuel from the tank.
   c. cribbing the vehicle with wedges and boards.
   d. checking to see if the patient can get out of the vehicle without assistance.

_____ 8. After access has been made to this patient, you determine that he is critically injured and showing late signs of shock. Which of the following should you consider?

   a. Requesting a medical helicopter
   b. Application of an AED
   c. Spinal stabilization with a vest-type extrication device
   d. Rocking the vehicle back over onto its wheels to facilitate rapid extrication

_____ 9. To gain full access to this patient, you must go through one of the windows. Which of the following techniques would be indicated?

   a. Break either the front or rear window.
   b. Cover the patient with a blanket and break the front windshield.
   c. Cover the patient with a blanket and break a window far from the patient's location.
   d. Cover the patient with a blanket and break the closest windshield to the patient's location.

_____ 10. Once you have gained access to this patient, which of the following should be done first?

   a. Check for a pulse
   b. Perform a primary survey
   c. Perform a rapid trauma assessment
   d. Apply a nonrebreather mask connected to supplemental oxygen

_____ 11. As an EMT, which of the following is your primary responsibility during extrication?

   a. Communicating with the dispatcher
   b. Coordinating the rescue operation
   c. Operating the rescue tools
   d. Protecting the patient

Matching

Match the key terms in the left column with the definitions in the right column by placing the letter of each correct answer in the space provided.

_____ 12. Complex extrication

_____ 13. Fend-off position

_____ 14. Extrication

_____ 15. Stabilization

_____ 16. Disentanglement

_____ 17. Simple extrication

A. The process of removing machinery from around a patient to facilitate patient care and transport

B. The use of powered hydraulic rescue tools such as cutters, spreaders, and rams to gain access and extricate the patient from the vehicle

C. The moving or removing of material that is trapping a victim

D. Parking an emergency vehicle downward from the scene and in such a way that allows traveling vehicles to strike the vehicle and not crew members

E. The use of hand tools in order to gain access and extricate the patient from the vehicle

F. The process of rendering a vehicle motionless in the position that it is found in

Short Answer

Answer each question in the space provided.

18. List three examples of equipment that may be used for vehicle stabilization.

1.

2.

3.

19. Explain the 5-10-20 rule regarding strike zones from undeployed airbags.

20. Explain what is meant by the phrase "simple extrication."

21. List three examples of tools used during a simple extrication.

1.

2.

3.

22. List five possible hazards that you should be cautious of while on scene.

1.

2.

3.

4.

5.

23. List two examples of tools used during a complex extrication.

1.

2.

24. List the four levels of entrapment that are possible during an MVC.

1.

2.

3.

4.

25. What is the fend-off position?

26. Describe three situations that may require complex access.

27. State the steps that should be taken to protect the patient during extrication.

Answer Section

Chapter 28

True/False

1. False

Simple extrication is the use of hand tools in order to gain access and extricate the patient from the vehicle. Simple hand tools include tools such as hammers, hacksaws, battery-operated saws, and pry bars.

Objective: Distinguish between simple and complex access.

2. True

Remember that your personal safety is your priority on every call. Protective clothing that is appropriate for the situation must be worn during extrication. This includes protective boots, pants, a coat, eye protection, a helmet, and gloves. Respiratory protection may also be needed if there is the possibility of particulates from the extrication process entering the nose or mouth. Hearing protection may also be necessary depending on the amount of noise on the scene. If there is any possibility of a fire, structural firefighting gear should be worn. Additional protection may be required for bloodborne and airborne pathogens. Always wear the PPE that will give you the most protection from the hazards present at the extrication scene.

Objective: Identify what equipment for personal safety is required for the EMT.

3. False

Complex extrication involves the use of powered hydraulic rescue tools such as cutters, spreaders, and rams. Equipment for stabilization may include cribbing and wedges, airbags, step chocks, come-alongs (hand winches), hydraulic rams, jacks, and/or chains. Simple extrication

involves the use of tools such as hammers, hacksaws, battery-operated saws, and pry bars.

Objective: Distinguish between simple and complex access.

4. True

Gaining access to the patient inside of an entangled vehicle should be accomplished as soon as safely possible after arriving on the scene. Use the path of least resistance. Try opening each door, roll down windows, or have the patient unlock doors.

Objective: Distinguish between simple and complex access.

Multiple Choice

5. c

Before removing the patient from the vehicle during extrication, maintain spinal stabilization.

Objective: Discuss the role of the EMT in extrication.

6. c

The scene size-up is your first responsibility at the scene. Some of the components of the scene size-up include determining the number of patients, the types of injuries, the need for additional resources, the number of vehicles, and the extent of damage to the vehicles. An important aspect of the size-up is the concern for the safety of yourself, your crew, the patient(s), and bystanders. Do not forget that BSI is part of the scene size-up. Gaining access to, triaging, and assessing patients all occur after the scene size-up.

Objective: Evaluate the role of the EMT in the multiple casualty situation.

7. c

This vehicle is not secure in its present position (on its side). Before accessing the patient, rescue personnel should immediately begin stabilizing the vehicle with wedges, chocks, jacks, etc. Removing the battery may actually slow your extrication efforts if an electric seat in the vehicle needs to be moved to access the patient more fully. Siphoning fuel from the tank may actually increase the possibility of explosion or exposure. Patients involved in MVCs should not be asked to crawl free of the wreckage unless imminent danger exists (such as if the vehicle is on fire).

Objective: Define the fundamental components of extrication.

8. a

With the closest hospital 45 miles from the accident scene, it is safe to say that ground transport will exceed 15 minutes. This patient is in critical condition, and rapid transportation to an appropriate facility is just as vital as is rapid stabilization. The patient's condition warrants rapid extrication. The use of a vest-type extrication device would be appropriate if the patient's condition is stable. The AED may be applied if the patient is apneic and pulseless; currently, this is not the case. Rocking the vehicle back onto its wheels would compromise the patient's spinal stabilization and could aggravate any injury that exists.

Objective: Describe the indications for the use of rapid extrication.

9. c

Ideally, you should break a window remote from the patient. Modern passenger car side and rear windows are made of tempered glass. When broken, tempered glass fractures into hundreds of small rounded pieces rather than large shards of glass. The front windshield, however, is made of laminated safety glass. This glass is much more difficult to remove because the plates of glass are bonded to a clear laminate. Perhaps the best way to remove the front windshield is to remove the frame and rubber seal, and then pop the window out. In any case, patients should be covered during extrication. Putting a rescuer in with the patient is ideal. Extrication can be very noisy and frightening for patients of any age. Close communication with the patient is essential.

Objective: State the steps that should be taken to protect the patient during extrication.

10. b

Once access is made, a primary survey should be performed. If the patient is unconscious or conscious but has an altered mental status, a rapid trauma assessment should follow the primary survey. If the patient is conscious and alert, a focused history and physical examination should follow the primary survey.

Objective: Discuss the reason for performing a focused history and physical exam.

11. d

EMTs are responsible for giving necessary care to the patient before extrication and making sure that the patient is removed in a way that minimizes further injury. Some EMTs are also responsible for extrication procedures.

Objective: Discuss the role of the EMT in extrication.

Matching

12.	B	15.	F
13.	D	16.	C
14.	A	17.	E

Short Answer

18. Equipment for stabilization may include cribbing and wedges, airbags, step chocks, come-alongs (hand winches), hydraulic rams, jacks, and/or chains.

    Objective: Define the fundamental components of extrication.

19. The 5-10-20 rule is the standard rule regarding strike zones from undeployed airbags. This means that you should be at least 5 inches away from the side airbags, 10 inches away from the driver's side airbag, and 20 inches from the passenger side airbag.

    Objective: Define the fundamental components of extrication.

20. Simple extrication is the use of hand tools in order to gain access and extricate the patient from the vehicle.

    Objective: Distinguish between simple and complex access.

21. Simple hand tools include tools such as hammers, hacksaws, battery-operated saws, and pry bars.

    Objective: Distinguish between simple and complex access.

22. Possible hazards that you should be cautious of while on scene:

- Traffic at the scene
- Gasoline spills
- Hazardous materials
- Exposed or downed electrical wires
- Fire or possibility of fire
- Explosive materials
- Unstable vehicle or structure
- Environmental conditions (heavy rain, heavy snow fall, flash floods)

Objective: Define the fundamental components of extrication.

23. Complex extrication involves the use of powered hydraulic rescue tools such as cutters, spreaders, and rams.

Objective: Distinguish between simple and complex access.

24. Four levels of entrapment are possible during an MVC:

1. No entrapment
2. Light entrapment
3. Moderate entrapment
4. Heavy entrapment

Objective: Define the fundamental components of extrication.

25. The fend-off position involves parking your unit downward from the scene and in such a way that allows traveling vehicles to strike your unit and not crew members. This provides protection to crew members while they are working on the scene.

Objective: Describe the roles and responsibilities related to personal safety. Discuss the roles and responsibilities of the EMT toward the safety of the crew, the patient, and bystanders.

26. Complex access requires the use of tools, special equipment, and special education. Examples of situations that may require complex access include high-angle rescue, basic vehicle rescue, water and ice rescue, confined space rescue, and building collapse rescue.

Objective: Distinguish between simple and complex access.

27. After you have gained access into the vehicle, the next step should be to provide protection for the patient. A heavy tarp or other type of cover specially designed for rescue purposes should be used to protect the patient, and respiratory protection should be used if there is a concern of particulates entering the respiratory tract. It is important to remember that the patient does not understand the extrication process and can become frightened by the sounds and procedures occurring around them. It is often desirable for a rescuer working in the interior of the vehicle to provide psychological support from underneath the tarp during the extrication. This will also give you the opportunity to assess the patient continuously throughout the extrication process

Objective: State the steps that should be taken to protect the patient during extrication.

29 Special Response Situations

READING ASSIGNMENT ▶ Read Chapter 29, pages 657 to 660 in your textbook.

Sum It Up

- As defined by the NFPA, a hazardous material is any substance that causes or may cause adverse effects on the health or safety of employees, the general public, or the environment.
- A hazardous substance can be identified using a number of resources:
  —U.S. DOT Emergency Response Guidebook
  —UN classification numbers
  —NFPA 704 placard system
  —UN/DOT placards
  —Shipping papers
  —MSDSs
- The first phase of dealing with a hazardous materials incident is recognizing that one exists. As always, your personal safety is your priority in any emergency scene. If there is no risk to you (and you are properly trained and equipped to do so), remove patients to a safe zone. The safe zone (also called the *cold zone*) is an area safe from exposure or the threat of exposure. The warm zone is a controlled area for entry into the hot zone. It also serves as the decontamination area after exiting the hot zone. All personnel in the warm zone must wear appropriate protective equipment. The hot zone is the danger zone.
- An MCI may also be called a *multiple-casualty incident* or *multiple-casualty situation* (MCS). An MCI is any event that places a great demand on resources—equipment, personnel, or both.
- The START triage system is used by many systems in dealing with MCIs. START stands for *Simple Triage And Rapid Treatment*. On the basis of your assessment findings, you categorize each patient according to one of four categories. Color-coded triage tags that correspond with these categories are placed on the patient and used to identify the level of injury sustained.
- The JumpSTART triage system was developed for use with children. It specifies how the four color-coded tags are applied to pediatric patients.
- The NIMS was created to provide a consistent nationwide template that allows all governmental, private-sector, and nongovernmental agencies to work together during domestic incidents. The ICS is an important part of

NIMS. ICS is a standardized system developed to assist with the control, direction, and coordination of emergency response resources. The ICS can be used at an incident of any type and size.

- An IC is the person who is responsible for managing all operations at the incident site. Depending on the size of the incident, the IC may assign to others the authority to perform certain activities. Scene operations may be broken down into groups, such as treatment and extrication.

- If you arrive on the scene of an MCI where the ICS has been established, report to the command post. Find out who the IC is. Identify yourself and your level of training. Follow the directions given by the IC about your assignment.

▶ Tracking Your Progress

After reading this chapter, can you:	Page Reference	Objective Met?
• Explain the EMT's role during a call involving hazardous materials?	652	☐
• Describe what the EMT should do if there is reason to believe that there is a hazard at the scene?	653	☐
• Describe the actions that an EMT should take to ensure bystander safety?	653	☐
• State the role the EMT should perform until appropriately trained personnel arrive at the scene of a hazardous materials situation?	653	☐
• Break down the steps to approaching a hazardous situation?	653	☐
• Discuss the various environmental hazards that affect EMS?	652	☐
• Describe the criteria for a multiple casualty situation?	658	☐
• Evaluate the role of the EMT in the multiple casualty situation?	658, 659	☐
• Summarize the components of basic triage?	658	☐
• Define the role of the EMT in a disaster operation?	659	☐
• Describe basic concepts of incident management?	659	☐
• Explain the methods for preventing contamination of self, equipment, and facilities?	653, 657	☐
• Review the local mass casualty incident plan?	657	☐

Multiple Choice

In the space provided, identify the letter of the choice that best completes the statement or answers each question.

Questions 1–6 pertain to the following scenario.

Your rescue crew is called to the scene of a 22-year-old man who has been "burned" (according to the information at time of dispatch). You arrive at an industrial complex to find your patient standing in an assembly area. Bystanders state that a container of dry chlorine powder burst open and covered the patient. The material is used for pool maintenance and is all over the patient and his immediate area. The shipping container information states that the product may cause irritation to the skin and mucous membranes. You call for a Hazmat team. Their estimated time to the scene is 20 minutes. Your crew has taken BSI precautions with gloves, eye, and respiratory protection and gowns.

_____ 1. Your best course of action will be to
   a. form a general impression and primary survey.
   b. wait until the Hazmat team arrives.
   c. remove the patient, your crew, and the bystanders from the area.
   d. begin irrigating the patient with water to remove the gross contaminants.

_____ 2. As performed by trained personnel, the first step in decontaminating this patient should be
   a. immediate irrigation with water.
   b. immediate removal of all dry powder.
   c. neutralization of the acid with a corresponding base (such as lye).
   d. immediate submersion of the patient in a chemical bath of bicarbonate of soda and water.

_____ 3. Which of the following is correct regarding the decontamination of this patient?
   a. All clothing and jewelry must be removed before or during irrigation.
   b. The patient must strip down to his underwear before or during irrigation.
   c. The patient should change into clean clothes if available before or during irrigation.
   d. The patient should be decontaminated with his clothes on so the clothing becomes decontaminated as well.

_____ 4. After continuous irrigation, the patient begins to complain of left eye discomfort. He states that his eye is burning and itching. Appropriate treatment for this complaint would be to
   a. cover the left eye with a moistened, sterile gauze pad.
   b. lay the patient on his left side and continuously irrigate the left eye until arrival at the hospital.
   c. lay the patient on his right side and continuously irrigate the left eye until arrival at the hospital.
   d. have the patient submerse his head in a container of water and bicarbonate of soda until the discomfort is relieved.

_____ 5. Which of the following would suggest that this patient may have inhaled some chlorine powder?
   a. Abdominal cramping
   b. Nausea and vomiting
   c. Blisters on the chest and neck area
   d. Difficulty breathing, with crackles (rales)

_____ 6. Appropriate management of this patient en route to the hospital would be continuous irrigation and
   a. no oxygen because of an explosion hazard.
   b. low-flow oxygen (nasal cannula at 4 to 6 L/min).
   c. high-flow oxygen (nonrebreather mask at 15 L/min).
   d. high-flow oxygen (nonrebreather mask at 15 L/min) and application of occlusive dressings to all burned areas.

Questions 7–10 pertain to the following scenario.

Your rescue crew is called to assist another rescue crew at the scene of a chemical spill. The first arriving rescue crew attempted to rescue an unconscious male from an "empty" processing vat. When you arrive, you find the patient and three rescuers unconscious in a large metal vat. The vat is about 8 feet tall by 6 feet square and open on the top. There is no unusual odor in the immediate area.

_____ 7. The unconscious rescuers are wearing firefighter turn-out clothing without a SCBA. This is also known as what level of protection?
   a. Level 1
   b. Level A
   c. Level D
   d. Level 0

_____ 8. An on-site foreman informs you that the worker was cleaning the vat with "XYZ SpeedeeKleen Cleanser." What document should the company have on hand that provides specific, detailed information about the chemical name, physical properties, fire and explosion hazard, and emergency first aid treatment?

    a. UN/DOT placard   **c.** MSDS

    b. Receipt of purchase   **d.** _Emergency Response Guidebook_

_____ 9. Additional information about the specific chemical may be rapidly obtained by contacting

    a. the UN.

    b. the company that shipped the chemical.

    c. the Emergency Department of a local hospital.

    d. CHEMTREC.

_____ 10. While investigating the chemicals involved in this incident, you decide to establish safety zones. The zone immediately surrounding the danger area is referred to as the

    a. hot zone.   **c.** Level-1 zone.

    b. red zone.   **d.** Level-A zone.

Questions 11–13 pertain to the following scenario.

Your ambulance crew is called to the scene of a "5-car pileup" on a local highway. Information at time of dispatch indicates that several people have been injured seriously. En route you request that a paramedic ambulance and the local fire department respond as well. When you arrive at the scene, you observe that 14 people have been injured in the collision. Their injuries range from minor to life-threatening. The other responding units are still about 8 minutes from the scene.

_____ 11. The initial on-scene needs far outweigh your initial resources. Which of the following is true about triaging this scene?

    a. CPR on a deceased patient takes priority over triage.

    b. Triage should wait until paramedics arrive at the scene.

    c. You should immediately begin full physical assessments on all patients.

    d. You should immediately begin triaging all patients rather than treating any one seriously injured patient.

_____ 12. During triage, which of the following patients should be considered the lowest priority at this scene?

    a. A 34-year-old man with swelling and deformity at the right arm and left lower leg.

    b. A 51-year-old woman who is pulseless and apneic with blood coming from both ears.

    c. A 24-year old woman complaining of chest pain after striking the steering wheel with her upper torso.

    d. A 60-year old man who is up and walking around the scene. He is awake but does not know his name, nor does he recall the accident.

_____ 13. Which of the following patients should be treated and transported first?

    a. A 24-year-old woman with blistering scald burns to one arm and both upper legs.

    b. A 74-year-old woman who was ejected from her vehicle. She is pulseless and apneic.

    c. A 13-year-old male complaining of abdominal pain who is showing the signs of shock.

    d. A 27-year-old man complaining of neck pain. He is unable to feel or move his arms or legs.

Questions 14–15 pertain to the following scenario.

The NFPA has developed a standard system of hazardous chemical identification. This system employs a diamond-shaped diagram divided into four quadrants, each with a different color.

_____ 14. The red portion of the diagram refers to

    a. a health hazard.

    b. a flammability hazard.

    c. a reactivity/stability hazard.

    d. the level of protective clothing required for entry into the scene.

15. A placard with a "1" rating in the blue field indicates that the substance

   a. will not burn.
   b. is extremely flammable.
   c. is slightly hazardous to your health.
   d. may detonate; vacate the area if material is exposed to fire.

Matching

Match the key terms in the left column with the definitions in the right column by placing the letter of each correct answer in the space provided.

_____ **16.** Triage

_____ **17.** National Incident Management System

_____ **18.** Warm zone

_____ **19.** Mass casualty incident

_____ **20.** Hazardous material

_____ **21.** Cold zone

_____ **22.** Decontamination (decon)

_____ **23.** Hot zone

_____ **24.** Incident commander

_____ **25.** Chemical protective clothing

_____ **26.** Exclusion zone

_____ **27.** Material safety data sheets

A. An identified safety zone at a hazardous materials incident that is an area safe from exposure or the threat of exposure and that serves as the staging area for personnel and equipment

B. Documents required by OSHA to be kept on site anywhere where chemicals are used

C. A standardized system that provides a consistent nationwide template allowing governmental, private-sector, and nongovernmental agencies to work together during domestic incidents

D. An identified safety zone at a hazardous materials incident that contains the hazardous material (contaminant)

E. Sorting multiple victims into priorities for emergency medical care or transportation to definitive care

F. A substance (solid, liquid, or gas) that, when released, is capable of creating harm to people, the environment, and property

G. Physical and/or chemical processes used at a hazardous materials incident to reduce and prevent the spread of contamination from persons and equipment

H. Any event that places a great demand on resources—equipment, personnel, or both

I. The person who is responsible for managing all operations during domestic incidents

J. Another name for the hot zone at a hazardous materials incident

K. An identified safety zone at a hazardous materials incident that serves as a controlled area for entry into the hot zone and where most operations take place

L. Materials designed to protect the skin from exposure by either physical or chemical means

Short Answer

Answer each question in the space provided.

28. List the four categories used in the START triage system.

1.

2.

3.

4.

29. List the four areas evaluated during a primary survey using the START triage system.

1.

2.

3.

4.

30. You are called to the scene of a multiple casualty incident. The ICS has been established. What should you do first when you arrive at the scene?

31. List three examples of chemical protective clothing.

1.

2.

3.

32. When should Level A personal protective equipment be used?

33. List four resources that may be used to identify a hazardous material substance.

1.

2.

3.

4.

Answer Section

Chapter 29

Multiple Choice

1. c

Do not assume that, because you have some prehospital education about treating exposed patients, you are capable of or expected to be able to manage a hazardous materials incident. Once you recognize that your "medical" incident has a "hazardous materials" element, immediately return to the scene size-up mode. Ensure the safety of yourself, your crew, the patient, and all potential patients (bystanders). Call for available resources (fire department, Hazmat team, on-site specialists, local public safety department, local public health department, etc.). Find out what your particular resources are *before* you encounter a hazardous materials incident.

Your scene assessment reveals that you, your crew, the patient, and the bystanders may be harmed by staying in the immediate area. In all cases in which your location may put you in harm's way, you need to move as quickly as the situation warrants. Because the patient is conscious and standing, it would be appropriate for you to instruct him to follow you out of the area. Have all bystanders leave the area but direct them to a site different than the one to which you are directing the patient. Remember: As long as the patient is contaminated, everywhere he goes is contaminated until proven otherwise.

Objective: State the role the EMT should perform until appropriately trained personnel arrive at the scene of a hazardous materials situation.

2. b

Because the patient is covered in a dry product, you should attempt (or instruct the patient) to sweep off the material. Immediate and continuous irrigation with water should follow. Never attempt to "correct" a product's pH to reduce an injury or burn. Do not add an acid to an alkali or vice versa. The result could be fatal. The only substance you should use to irrigate is water.

Objective: Explain the EMT's role during a call involving hazardous materials.

3. a

Protecting a patient's modesty and privacy is important; however, when decontaminating a patient, all clothing must be removed, including jewelry, wigs, toupees, or other body adornments. Do not be concerned with decontaminating these things as your efforts should be directed toward saving the patient. Do not transport the clothing or other effects with the patient—they are contaminated. If you are concerned about the safety of valuables, ensure that law enforcement personnel secure the entire area from nonessential personnel. Allowing the patient to wear "clean" clothing during the decontamination may only result in ineffective decontamination. If bystanders and nonessential personnel are removed from the area, you have met the privacy concerns of the patient to the best of your ability.

Objective: Explain the EMT's role during a call involving hazardous materials.

4. b

The correct method for treating an eye exposure is to have the patient lie down and continuously irrigate the affected eye with water or normal saline solution. The affected eye is lowered so that contaminants are not washed into the unaffected eye. If both eyes are affected, you may position the patient on either side. Laying the patient flat may cause the contaminated irrigation fluid to run down the face toward the nose and mouth.

Objective: N/A

5. d

The signs and symptoms of inhaled poisoning include difficulty breathing; crackles, or rales (typically from damage to the lungs leading to leaking fluid in the lung space); chest pain; cough or hoarseness (typically from damage to the larynx); dizziness (typically from shock and inadequate oxygenation); and headache, confusion, seizures, or altered mental status (typically from inadequate oxygen delivery to the brain). Abdominal cramping, vomiting, and nausea generally accompany ingested poisoning incidents. Blisters on the chest and neck area suggest an absorbed poisoning incident.

Objective: List signs and symptoms associated with poisoning.

6. c

Continuously irrigate to ensure that most of the contaminants are washed away. *Caution*: Your patient may become extremely cold during continuous irrigation. The ideal way to warm the patient without stopping irrigation is to use the heater in the transport vehicle. Monitor your patient closely for signs of hypothermia, especially if severe burns are present. Oxygen should be delivered by nonrebreather mask at 15 L/min.

Objective: Describe the steps in the emergency medical care for the patient with suspected poisoning.

7. c

Level D PPE provides limited body protection and no respiratory protection. These rescuers should have done a better job in sizing up the scene and recognizing potential hazards. Obviously, they ignored or downplayed the assessment of the MOI. Instead of helping to resolve the situation, they became part of the problem, and it may have cost them their lives. This scenario is based on countless similar real-life incidents. Remember that personal safety is your priority!

Objective: Break down the steps to approaching a hazardous situation.

8. c

MSDSs are the first responding emergency crew's best friend. Each MSDS contains valuable information about a specific chemical. UN/DOT placards and the *Emergency Response Guidebook* provide only generic information about similar types of chemicals. OSHA law mandates that businesses have immediate access to MSDSs for all chemicals used or stored on site.

Objective: Describe what the EMT should do if there is reason to believe that there is a hazard at the scene.

9. d

CHEMTREC provides a 24-hour hotline for product information and emergency response protocols. CHEMTREC is particularly useful as a resource for identifying the chemical components of a substance on the basis of the product's trade name. In this example, CHEMTREC may be able to provide information with regard to the ingredients and hazards of XYZ SpeedeeKleen Cleanser.

Objective: Describe what the EMT should do if there is reason to believe that there is a hazard at the scene.

10. a

The hot zone should encompass the contamination area and potential contamination area. Therefore the hot zone size may be influenced by ambient temperature, wind direction, and terrain, as well as the characteristics of the contaminant. Only personnel with the appropriate level of PPE should enter the hot zone. Personnel entering the hot zone should have a specific purpose—no freelancing in the hot zone! The warm zone is a control area for entry into the hot zone. Also, personnel leaving the hot zone are decontaminated in the warm zone. The appropriate level of PPE must be observed in the warm zone. The cold zone is a safe area intended for support personnel and unused resources. The general public should be kept out of the cold zone.

Objective: Explain the EMT's role during a call involving hazardous materials.

11. d

The most knowledgeable EMS professional arriving on the scene first should assume the responsibility of scene triage. "Fully" assessing each patient requires too much time and resources and is not a component of triage. Treating patients (such as performing CPR) is not a component of triage. Triage is a system of rapidly assessing each patient so that he may be "tagged" according to his priority. Typically, triage procedures evaluate three patient factors: breathing status, heart rate, and level of consciousness. Patients are categorized according to this brief assessment. Once resources have arrived to begin treating patients, assigned tasks should be based on the triage patient categorization.

Objective: Evaluate the role of the EMT in the multiple casualty situation.

12. b

The woman who is pulseless and apneic with blood coming from both ears should be categorized as the lowest priority. The woman complaining of chest pain and the man who has an altered mental status should be considered the highest priority. The man with arm and leg trauma should be considered an intermediate priority.

Objective: Summarize the components of basic triage.

13. c

Patients showing signs of shock are considered a high priority, especially given the fact that this patient is young. Young patients do not typically show signs of shock until their compensatory mechanisms begin to crash rapidly. Burn patients without airway compromise and spinal injury patients are a second priority. Again, patients who are not breathing and are pulseless are a last priority.

Objective: Summarize the components of basic triage.

14. b

The red quadrant of the NFPA 704 diamond refers to flammability hazard. The blue quadrant refers to health hazards whereas the yellow quadrant refers to reactivity hazards. The white quadrant contains information regarding special hazard concerns such as water reactivity or radioactivity. The three colored quadrants rate hazards on a scale of 1 to 4, with 4 being the highest level of hazard. The white quadrant contains symbols or words that indicate special hazard considerations, if applicable.

Objective: Describe what the EMT should do if there is reason to believe that there is a hazard at the scene.

15. c

The blue field refers to health hazard, and a rating of 1 indicates that only a slight health hazard exists. A 0 rating would indicate that there is no hazard present. A 4 rating would indicate that an extreme health hazard exists and only trained personnel with proper attire should enter the hazard area.

Objective: Describe what the EMT should do if there is reason to believe that there is a hazard at the scene.

Matching

16. E		**22.** G	
17. C		**23.** D	
18. K		**24.** I	
19. H		**25.** L	
20. F		**26.** J	
21. A		**27.** B	

Short Answer

28. 1. Red: immediate
2. Yellow: delayed
3. Green: ambulatory
4. Black: dead or nonsalvageable

Objective: Summarize the components of basic triage.

29. Four areas are evaluated during the primary survey using the START system:

1. Ability to walk (ambulatory)
2. Respiration
3. Perfusion
4. Mental status

Objective: Summarize the components of basic triage.

30. If you arrive on the scene of a multiple casualty incident where the ICS has been established, report to the command post. Find out who the IC is and identify yourself and your level of training. Follow the directions given by the IC about your assignment.

Objective: Evaluate the role of the EMT in the multiple casualty situation.

31. CPC is designed to protect the skin from exposure by either physical or chemical means. Examples of CPC classes include gas-tight encapsulating suits, liquid-splash protective suits, permeable protective suits, nonhazardous chemical protective clothing, and other protective apparel, such as chemically resistant hoods, gloves, and boots.

    Objective: List the PPE necessary for each of the following situations: hazardous materials, rescue operations, violent scenes, crime scenes, exposure to bloodborne pathogens, and exposure to airborne pathogens.

32. Level A PPE is a vapor protective suit that is encapsulated. It provides the highest available level of respiratory, skin, and eye protection from solid, liquid, and gaseous chemicals. It is intended for situations in which chemical(s) have been identified and pose high levels of hazards to the respiratory system, skin, and eyes.

Objective: List the PPE necessary for each of the following situations: hazardous materials, rescue operations, violent scenes, crime scenes, exposure to bloodborne pathogens, and exposure to airborne pathogens.

33. Resources that may be used to identify a hazardous material include the following:

- U.S. DOT *Emergency Response Guidebook*
- UN classification numbers
- NFPA 704 placard system
- UN/DOT placards
- Shipping papers
- Material safety data sheets

Objective: Explain the EMT's role during a call involving hazardous materials.

Division 8

Advanced Airway (Elective)

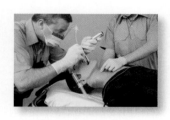

30 Advanced Airway Techniques

READING ASSIGNMENT ▶ Read Chapter 30, pages 662 to 680 in your textbook.

Sum It Up

- In some states, advanced airways may be inserted by EMTs who have been properly instructed in their use and who receive ongoing education to ensure skill competency. Advanced airways include the ETC (or Combitube) and the ET tube. Insertion of an ET tube requires visualization of the structures of the upper airway. Insertion of a Combitube does not.
- An ET tube is a plastic tube that is open at both ends and designed for insertion into a patient's trachea. Endotracheal intubation is the placement of an ET tube into a patient's trachea to keep the airway open.
- Indications for endotracheal intubation include the following:
  —Prolonged artificial ventilation is required
  —Adequate artificial ventilation cannot be achieved by other methods
  —The patient is unresponsive and has no cough or gag reflex
  —The patient is unable to protect his own airway (cardiac arrest, unresponsive)
- The average size ET tube for an adult man is 8.0-8.5 mm i.d. For an adult woman, the average size is 7-8 mm i.d. The "emergency rule" is that a 7.5 mm i.d. ET tube will fit most adults in an emergency. When selecting the proper size ET tube for the pediatric patient, you should use a length-based tape.
- There is a high incidence of misplaced and displaced tracheal tubes in the prehospital setting. Current resuscitation guidelines recommend that if your transport time is short, oxygenation and ventilation of a patient with a BM device is recommended over endotracheal intubation.
- A straight laryngoscope blade is placed under the epiglottis. The tip of a curved blade is placed into the vallecula.
- Infants and children are at increased risk of accidental ET tube displacement. Movement of the head or movement of the ET tube less than 2 centimeters can displace the ET tube.
- The measurement of exhaled CO_2 levels is called *capnometry*. In patients who have adequate perfusion, the use of an exhaled CO_2 detector is considered the most reliable method for verifying tube placement. In a patient who has poor perfusion, an exhaled CO_2 detector may not be reliable.
- Use at least two methods to confirm ET tube placement. Methods used should include a combination of assessment methods (such as breath sounds, chest rise and fall) and mechanical methods (such as the use of an exhaled CO_2

detector and/or esophageal detection device). Ongoing assessments are essential to ensure proper position of the tube.

- Before using an exhaled CO_2 detector to confirm ET tube placement, ventilate the patient at least six times. This is done to quickly wash out any CO_2 that may have entered the patient's esophagus and stomach with BM ventilation. Patient movement is a primary cause of displaced tubes. Be sure to reassess chest wall motion and breath sounds, and use a CO_2 detector after every major move.
- An EDD is an inexpensive, easy-to-use tool that may be used as an aid in confirming the position of an ET tube.
- The Combitube is called a *dual-lumen airway* because it consists of two (esophageal and tracheal) tubes. This permits ventilation if the tube is inserted into the esophagus (most common) or into the trachea. After the Combitube is inserted, the cuffs on the device are inflated with air and the patient is ventilated through the tube with a bag-mask device.
- In the prehospital setting, indications for insertion of an NG/OG tube include an unresponsive patient and the inability to artificially ventilate a patient because of gastric distention.

► Tracking Your Progress

After reading this chapter, can you:	Page Reference	Objective Met?
• Identify and describe the airway anatomy of the infant, child, and the adult?	664	☐
• Differentiate between the airway anatomy of the infant, child, and the adult?	664	☐
• Explain the pathophysiology of airway compromise?	664, 665	☐
• Describe the proper use of airway adjuncts?	665	☐
• Review the use of oxygen therapy in airway management?	665	☐
• Describe the indications, contraindications, and technique for insertion of nasogastric tubes?	678	☐
• Describe how to perform the Sellick maneuver (cricoid pressure)?	665	☐
• Describe the indications for advanced airway management?	666	☐
• List the equipment required for endotracheal intubation?	666	☐
• Describe the proper use of the curved blade for endotracheal intubation?	668	☐
• Describe the proper use of the straight blade for endotracheal intubation?	668	☐
• State the reasons for and proper use of the stylet in endotracheal intubation?	668	☐
• Describe the methods of choosing the appropriate size ET tube for an adult patient?	667	☐
• State the formula for sizing an infant or child endotracheal tube?	667	☐
• List complications associated with advanced airway management?	674	☐
• Define the various alternative methods for sizing the infant and child endotracheal tube?	667	☐
• Describe the skill of endotracheal intubation in the adult patient?	669	☐

After reading this chapter, can you:	Page Reference	Objective Met?
• Describe the skill of endotracheal intubation in the infant and child patient?	669	☐
• Describe the skill of confirming endotracheal tube placement in the adult, infant and child patient?	672	☐
• State the consequence of and the need to recognize unintentional esophageal intubation?	672	☐
• Describe the skill of securing the endotracheal tube in the adult, infant, and child patient?	671	☐

Multiple Choice

In the space provided, identify the letter of the choice that best completes the statement or answers each question.

Questions 1–6 pertain to the following scenario.

Your rescue crew is called to the home of a 56-year-old man complaining of chest pain. Upon arrival, you find the patient supine in bed. He is not breathing and does not have a palpable pulse. CPR is initiated. En route to the hospital, you decide to perform endotracheal intubation.

_____ 1. Before intubating this patient, you should
   a. provide high-flow oxygen therapy by nonrebreather mask at 15 L/min.
   b. provide high-flow oxygen therapy by nonrebreather mask at 25 L/min.
   c. ventilate the patient with a BM device and supplemental oxygen at a rate of 10 to 12 breaths per minute.
   d. ventilate the patient with a BM device and supplemental oxygen at a rate of 30 breaths per minute.

_____ 2. What size ET tube should you initially use for this adult male patient?
   a. 6 mm i.d.   c. 8 mm i.d.
   b. 7 mm i.d.   d. 9 mm i.d.

_____ 3. You decide to use a size 4 curved laryngoscope blade. The laryngoscope handle should be held in your _____ hand, and the tip of the blade should be placed into the patient's _____.
   a. Left, vallecula   c. Left, glottic opening
   b. Right, vallecula   d. Right, glottic opening

_____ 4. While intubating this patient, what can be done to reduce the likelihood of vomiting and aspiration of stomach contents?
   a. Cricoid pressure   c. Abdominal thrusts
   b. Chest compressions   d. Insertion of an oral airway

_____ 5. Once the endotracheal tube is in position, you must confirm proper placement. When auscultating with a stethoscope, which of the following correctly reflects the first place that you should listen to confirm correct placement?
   a. The left lateral chest wall   c. The left anterior chest wall
   b. Over the epigastrium   d. The right anterior chest wall

_____ 6. Initially, the ET tube appears to have been placed properly. However, on arrival at the receiving facility and removal of the patient from the ambulance, you reassess lung sounds and hear no air movement over the left chest wall. You should
   a. immediately remove the ET tube.
   b. ventilate at a faster rate (30 to 40 ventilations per minute).
   c. deflate the balloon and gently withdraw the tube a short distance.
   d. insert another ET tube on the left side of the original tube.

_____ 7. There are several anatomical differences between adults and children/infants. For example, the narrowest aspect of the adult upper airway is the glottic opening at the vocal cords. For children and infants, the narrowest aspect of the upper airway is the

   a. pharynx.   **c.** cricoid cartilage.

   b. esophagus.   **d.** thyroid cartilage.

Sentence Completion

In the blanks provided, write the words that best complete each sentence.

   8. You have inserted a Combitube into a patient's airway. You should fill the pharyngeal balloon with _____ mL of _____.

   9. In an adult man, the average ET tube depth is _____ cm at the lips and _____ cm at the teeth.

   10. In an adult woman, the average ET tube depth is _____ cm at the lips and _____ cm at the teeth.

Matching

Match the key terms in the left column with the definitions in the right column by placing the letter of each correct answer in the space provided.

_____ **11.** Thyroid cartilage

_____ **12.** Esophagus

_____ **13.** Endotracheal intubation

_____ **14.** Orogastric tube

_____ **15.** Glottic opening

_____ **16.** Cricoid cartilage

_____ **17.** Esophageal detector device

_____ **18.** Laryngoscope

_____ **19.** Epiglottis

_____ **20.** Capnometry

_____ **21.** Esophageal-tracheal Combitube

_____ **22.** Nasogastric tube

_____ **23.** Endotracheal tube

_____ **24.** Stylet

A. A long, flexible tube that is passed through the mouth and into the stomach

B. The measurement of exhaled CO_2 levels

C. A plastic tube that is open at both ends and designed for insertion into a patient's trachea

D. The space between the vocal cords

E. A flexible plastic-coated wire that is inserted into an ET tube to provide stiffness and shape to the tube

F. The placement of an ET tube into a patient's trachea to keep the airway open

G. A dual-lumen airway that consists of two tubes, permitting ventilation if the tube is inserted into the esophagus or into the trachea

H. A special flap of cartilage that covers the trachea during swallowing so that food or liquids do not enter the lungs

I. An instrument that consists of a handle and blade that are made of plastic or stainless steel and used to visualize the space between the vocal cords

J. The only complete ring of cartilage in the larynx

K. The largest cartilage of the larynx

L. A long, flexible tube that is passed through the nose, into the posterior nasopharynx, down the esophagus, and into the stomach

M. An inexpensive, easy-to-use tool used as an aid in confirming the position of an ET tube

N. The muscular tube about 9 inches long (in adults) that is a passageway for food

Short Answer

Answer each question in the space provided.

25. Where does an ET tube that is inserted too far will generally end up?

26. Once ventilation stops to intubate a patient, how much time do you have to successfully place the ET tube and restart ventilation?

27. What is the "emergency rule" that pertains to adult endotracheal tube sizing?

28. List three indications for endotracheal intubation.
1.
2.
3.

29. List the equipment and supplies necessary to perform endotracheal intubation.

30. What is the Murphy eye on an endotracheal tube?

31. After intubating a patient, you inflated the pilot balloon. Why is it important to remember to unhook the syringe from the inflation valve?

32. When selecting the proper size ET tube for the pediatric patient, you should use a length-based tape. If a length-based tape is not available, you can use two formulas to estimate the correct ET tube size for children 1 to 10 years of age. List the correct formula to use for a cuffed ET tube and an uncuffed ET tube.
1. Cuffed ET tube:
2. Uncuffed ET tube:

Answer Section

Chapter 30

Multiple Choice

1. c

   Before intubating, ventilate the patient at a rate of 10 to 12 breaths/min. If the patient is not breathing, a nonrebreather mask is not an appropriate device to use to administer supplemental oxygen.

   Objective: Review the use of oxygen therapy in airway management.

2. c

   The average size ET tube for an adult man is 8.0–8.5 mm i.d. For an adult woman, the average size is 7-8 mm i.d. The "emergency rule" is that a 7.5 mm i.d. ET tube will fit most adults in an emergency.

   Objective: Describe the methods of choosing the appropriate size ET tube for an adult patient.

3. a

   The laryngoscope should be held in the left hand and the laryngoscope blade inserted in the right side of the patient's mouth. The laryngoscope blade is used to sweep the tongue to the patient's left to move the tongue out of the way. The curved laryngoscope blade is designed to follow the natural curvature of the tongue. The tip of the curved blade fits into the vallecula (the "valley" formed by the base of the tongue and the base of the epiglottis). Upward pressure on the vallecula lifts the epiglottis, exposing the glottic opening. The straight blade is used to directly lift the epiglottis and expose the glottic opening.

   Objective: Describe the skill of endotracheal intubation in the adult patient.

4. a

   During intubation, application of cricoid pressure (the Sellick maneuver) may be helpful. Cricoid pressure reduces the likelihood that the patient will vomit by preventing the introduction of air into the stomach, which often leads to distention and vomiting.

   Objective: Describe the skill of endotracheal intubation in the adult patient.

5. b

   When initially confirming placement of the tube (and while making sure with one hand that the ET tube does not move), place your stethoscope over the upper portion of the patient's stomach (epigastrium). With the stethoscope on the epigastrium, have an assistant attach the bag-mask device to the ET tube and begin positive-pressure ventilation. You should not hear gurgling or air entry over the epigastrium. If gurgling or air entry is heard over this area, you most likely have intubated the esophagus instead of the trachea. Remove the ET tube *immediately*, attach a mask to the bag-mask device, and provide BM ventilation.

   Objective: Describe the skill of confirming endotracheal tube placement in the adult, infant, and child patient.

6. c

   After intubation and upon discovering the absence (or diminution) of breath sounds over one side of the chest (typically the left side), immediately assess the depth of the ET tube by looking at the centimeter markings at the patient's gumline. Base your interventions on these findings. An ET tube inserted too far will usually go down the right mainstem bronchus. This may occur during the initial intubation attempt or because of excessive patient movement without careful management of the

ET tube. If the ET tube is in the right mainstem bronchus, assessment of the patient will reveal breath sounds heard over the right lung and diminished lung sounds over the left. To correct this problem, deflate the cuff and gently pull the tube back slightly (about a centimeter at a time) while artificially ventilating and auscultating over the left chest. Stop when breath sounds appear equal on both sides of the chest. Reinflate the cuff and secure the ET tube in place. Note the markings on the tube at the upper teeth or gum line and record.

Objective: Describe the skill of confirming ET tube placement in the adult, infant, and child patient.

7. c

Because the cricoid cartilage is the narrowest part of the upper airway of an infant and young child, intubation of children is different from intubation of adults. In adults, the ET tube is advanced until the inflatable cuff is just past the glottic opening (vocal cords). The ET tube cuff is then inflated. In infants and young children, ET tubes without inflatable cuffs are often used because of the narrow diameter of the trachea. The cricoid cartilage provides a natural cuff for the ET tube. Extreme care should be taken to secure the ET tube in children because of the susceptibility of these tubes to displacement.

Objective: Differentiate between the airway anatomy of the infant, child, and the adult.

Sentence Completion

8. You have inserted a Combitube into a patient's airway. You should inflate the pharyngeal balloon with **100** mL of **air**. (If you were using the Combitube SA, you would inflate the pharyngeal balloon with 85 mL of air.)

Objective: N/A

9. In an adult man, the average ET tube depth is **23** cm at the lips and **22** cm at the teeth.

Objective: Describe the skill of endotracheal intubation in the adult patient.

10. In an adult woman, the average ET tube depth is **22** cm at the lips and **21** cm at the teeth.

Objective: Describe the skill of endotracheal intubation in the adult patient.

Matching

11.	K	18.	I
12.	N	19.	H
13.	F	20.	B
14.	A	21.	G
15.	D	22.	L
16.	J	23.	C
17.	M	24.	E

Short Answer

25. An ET tube that is inserted too far has a tendency to go down the right mainstem bronchus because it is shorter, wider, and straighter than the left.

Objective: Describe the skill of endotracheal intubation in the adult patient.

26. Once ventilation stops, you have 30 seconds to complete the intubation and resume ventilating the patient.

Objective: Describe the skill of endotracheal intubation in the adult patient.

27. The "emergency rule" is that a 7.5 mm i.d. ET tube will fit most adults in an emergency.

Objective: Describe the methods of choosing the appropriate size ET tube for an adult patient.

28. Indications for endotracheal intubation include the following:

- Prolonged artificial ventilation is required.
- Adequate artificial ventilation cannot be achieved by other methods.
- The patient is unresponsive and has no cough or gag reflex.
- The patient is unable to protect his own airway (cardiac arrest, unresponsive).

Objective: Describe the indications for advanced airway management.

29. Equipment and supplies for endotracheal intubation include:

- PPE, including gloves, mask, and goggles
- Oxygen supply
- BM device
- Suction equipment
- Laryngoscope handle with batteries
- Laryngoscope blades

- ET tubes (size needed plus $\frac{1}{2}$ size larger and $\frac{1}{2}$ size smaller)
- Stylet
- 10-mL syringe to inflate the ET tube cuff (if present)
- CO_2 detector and/or esophageal detector device
- Pulse oximeter
- Tape or commercial ET tube holder to secure the tube

Objective: List the equipment required for endotracheal intubation.

30. The distal tip of an ET tube is beveled to ease passage of the tube between the vocal cords. There is an opening on the side of the ET tube opposite the beveled tip. This opening is called the *Murphy eye.* It helps prevent complete obstruction of the tube if the tip of the ET tube should become blocked.

Objective: Describe the skill of endotracheal intubation in the adult patient.

31. After the patient is intubated, you will inflate the pilot balloon with air using a 10-mL syringe. This in turn inflates the cuff and seals the trachea. After inflating the cuff, you must remember to unhook the syringe or the air will escape out of the cuff and go back into the syringe.

Objective: Describe the skill of endotracheal intubation in the adult patient.

32. When selecting the proper size ET tube for the pediatric patient, you should use a length-based tape. The tape provides all recommended ET tube sizes, blade sizes, vital signs, and other information for children who weigh up to about 35 kg. If a length-based tape is not available, you can use the following formulas to estimate the correct ET tube size for children 1 to 10 years of age:

1. (age in years/4) + 3 = *cuffed* ET tube size (mm i.d.)
2. (16 + age in years)/4 or (age in years/4) + 4 = *uncuffed* ET tube size (mm i.d.)

Objective: State the formula for sizing an infant or child ET tube.

A Cardiopulmonary Resuscitation

READING ASSIGNMENT ▶ Read Appendix A, pages 681 to 701 in your textbook.

True or False

Decide whether each statement is true or false. In the space provided, write *T* for true or *F* for false.

_____ 1. To ensure an accurate reading, no one should be allowed to touch a patient once the "analyze" button has been depressed on an AED.

_____ 2. Once started, CPR should be stopped only if effective breathing and circulation have returned.

Multiple Choice

In the space provided, identify the letter of the choice that best completes the statement or answers each question.

_____ 3. The airways of infants and children differ from the airways of adults. To properly open the airway of an infant you must
  a. tilt the head to one side.
  b. place the head in a neutral position.
  c. hyperextend the head and neck more than that of an adult.
  d. place the infant's chin on his chest and open the mouth as wide as possible.

_____ 4. Which of the following is an inappropriate method to clear a patient's airway?
  a. Suctioning   **c.** Blind finger sweeps
  b. Finger sweeps   **d.** Recovery position

_____ 5. Chest compressions should be performed for an adult, infant, or child at a rate of about
  a. 30 compressions/min.   **c.** 100 compressions/min.
  b. 80 compressions/min.   **d.** 200 compressions/min.

Sentence Completion

In the blanks provided, write the words that best complete each sentence.

6. When providing rescue breathing for an adult, give 1 breath every _____ seconds, which is _____ breaths/min.

7. When providing rescue breathing for an infant or child, give 1 breath every _____ seconds, which is _____ breaths/min.

Short Answer

Answer each question in the space provided.

8. List three situations in which chest thrusts may be used to relieve an upper airway obstruction.

1.

2.

3.

9. List the three categories of upper airway obstruction.

1.

2.

3.

10. Explain why it is important to keep your hands away from the bottom of the breastbone (xiphoid process) when performing CPR or abdominal thrusts.

Answer Section

Appendix A

True/False

1. True

When the adhesive electrodes are attached to the patient's chest, the AED "looks" at the patient's heart rhythm and analyzes it. Some AEDs require the operator to press an "analyze" control to start rhythm analysis while others automatically begin analyzing the patient's rhythm when the pads are attached to the patient's chest. While the AED is in analyze mode, it is taking multiple "looks" at the patient's rhythm. Although the AED has safety filters that check for false signals (such as radio transmissions, poor electrode contact, 60-cycle interference, and loose electrodes), it is important that there be no movement around the patient during this time to ensure that the AEDs analysis of the patient's rhythm is accurate.

2. False

You should stop CPR only if:

- Effective breathing and circulation have returned
- The scene becomes unsafe
- You are too exhausted to continue
- You transfer patient care to a healthcare professional with equal or higher certification
- A physician assumes responsibility for the patient

Multiple Choice

3. b

The airway of a child is more pliable than the airway of an adult. To open the airway of an infant or child, place the patient in a supine position with the head in a neutral (looking straight forward). Hyperextending the neck may cause the trachea to kink (much like a drinking straw bent too far). Placing the chin on the chest and opening the mouth as wide as possible are not acceptable techniques.

4. c

Blind finger sweeps should never be performed. Doing so may cause the object to become further lodged in the patient's throat.

5. c

For an adult, infant, or child in cardiac arrest, give chest compressions at a rate of about 100 compressions/min.

Sentence Completion

6. When providing rescue breathing for an adult, give 1 breath every **5 to 6** seconds, which is **10–12** breaths/min.

7. When providing rescue breathing for an infant or child, give 1 breath every **3 to 5** seconds, which is **12 to 20** breaths/min.

Short Answer

8. Chest thrusts may be used to relieve an upper airway obstruction in
   1. An obese adult
   2. A woman in the later stages of pregnancy
   3. Infants

9. The three categories of airway obstruction are:
   1. Partial airway obstruction with good air exchange
   2. Partial airway obstruction with poor air exchange
   3. Complete airway obstruction

10. Do not place your hands on the patient's ribs or on the bottom of the breastbone (xiphoid process). The xiphoid process can easily be broken off the breastbone and cut underlying organs, such as the liver.

B   Older Adults

READING ASSIGNMENT ▶ Read Appendix B, pages 702 to 706 in your textbook.

True or False

Decide whether each statement is true or false. In the space provided, write *T* for true or *F* for false.

_____ 1. When communicating with a hearing-impaired patient, speak more slowly and loudly so that the patient can understand you.

_____ 2. A patient who has a sudden vision impairment requires immediate transport to the closest appropriate facility.

_____ 3. Older adults have reduced pain perception.

Multiple Choice

In the space provided, identify the letter of the choice that best completes the statement or answers each question.

_____ 4. To determine an older adult's normal level of responsiveness, it is best to

    a. ask a family member or neighbor to give you this information.
    b. contact the patient's physician for this information.
    c. assume that the patient's mental status is impaired.
    d. contact your billing department for this information from previous PCRs.

_____ 5. Which of the following strategies will help you to effectively care for a person who is visually impaired?

    a. Call the person by name each time you speak to him.
    b. Have the family relay information to the patient.
    c. To guide the patient in walking, push him.
    d. Speak loudly to the patient.

Answer Section

Appendix B

True/False

1. False

A common mistaken belief of some emergency care professionals is that you must speak more slowly and loudly for the patient to understand you. Not only does this not work, it may actually confuse the patient. When you speak more slowly than normal, you have a tendency to overemphasize the way you move your mouth when you speak. This can lead to a greater misunderstanding if the patient is trying to read your lips. Try not to drastically change the way you speak. Use your normal tone of voice and speak at your normal speed—as if you were carrying on a conversation with any other patient.

2. True

A patient may have a visual impairment caused by a medical emergency, a traumatic injury, or a preexisting condition. As a general rule, a patient who has a *sudden* change in vision needs immediate transport to the closest appropriate medical facility. Vision changes may be due to a lack of oxygen to the brain. They may also result from physical damage to the eyes, the optic nerve, or even the brain. If the vision disturbance is due to a preexisting condition, continue with your assessment and treatment.

3. True

Because pain sensation can be lessened or absent in older adults, the patient can easily misjudge how serious his condition is.

Multiple Choice

4. a

It may be difficult for you to find out whether the patient's symptoms are due to a medical emergency, an ongoing (chronic) medical problem, or a part of normal aging. To help find out what the patient's normal mental status is, ask someone who knows the patient to give you this information. For example, ask a family member or neighbor how the patient appears to him today. Ask the family, "What is different today? Is he confused? Behaving inappropriately? Having hallucinations? Does his speech sound normal to you?" Then ask the person providing information to compare how your patient appears today with how he was 2 or 3 days ago.

5. a

When you speak to a blind patient, address him by name. In guiding a patient who is blind, you should offer the patient your arm and lead him— do not push, pull, or grab a blind patient.

C IV Monitoring

READING ASSIGNMENT ▶ Read Appendix C, pages 707 to 713 in your textbook.

True or False

Decide whether each statement is true or false. In the space provided, write *T* for true or *F* for false.

_____ **1.** When a hollow needle that also serves as the catheter is used for IV therapy, the needle remains in place.

_____ **2.** Warm, red skin around an IV insertion site is most likely due to an air embolism.

Multiple Choice

In the space provided, identify the letter of the choice that best completes the statement or answers each question.

_____ **3.** The administration of a liquid substance, such as IV fluids or medications, directly into the venous circulation is known as

    a. IV monitoring.   **c.** IV cannulation.

    b. IV therapy.   **d.** venipuncture.

_____ **4.** Which of the following is considered a "large-bore" IV needle?

    a. 16 gauge   **c.** 20 gauge

    b. 18 gauge   **d.** 24 gauge

_____ **5.** Your patient is to receive 250 mL of IV fluid over 30 minutes. The IV administration set delivers 10 drops (gtt) per mL. How many drops per minute (gtt/min) should this patient receive?

    a. 42   **c.** 100

    b. 83   **d.** 125

Answer Section

Appendix C

True/False

1. True

   A hollow needle IV catheter is also called a
   butterfly catheter, scalp vein needle, or *winged
   infusion set.* When this type of IV catheter is
   used, the ALS provider holds onto the wings of
   the device and then pierces the patient's skin
   with the metal needle. Once the vein has been
   entered, the needle remains in place and is
   secured with tape.

2. False

   An embolism can occur when air, blood, or any
   other foreign material enters the bloodstream
   through the IV site. Although it is considered
   uncommon, an air embolism may be fatal to an
   ill person at volumes reported to be less than
   30 mL of air. The general signs and symptoms
   of an embolus may include low blood pressure;
   cyanosis; a weak, rapid pulse; complaint
   of shortness of breath; and possible loss of
   consciousness. Phlebitis (inflammation of a vein)
   may occur simply because a foreign body (the IV
   catheter) is present. The patient's skin may be
   warm and red around the IV site. The patient's
   extremity may be swollen, and the patient may
   complain of throbbing pain in the limb. If any
   of these complications occur, immediately notify
   ALS personnel.

Multiple Choice

3. b

   IV therapy is the giving of a liquid substance,
   such as IV fluids or medications, directly into the
   venous circulation.

4. a

   The smaller the number, the larger the diameter.
   IV needles that have a gauge of 16 or less are
   considered "large-bore" IV catheters. An ALS
   provider will use a 12-, 14-, or 16-gauge IV needle
   when a large volume of fluid must be given over a
   short period or when he anticipates the patient's
   condition may quickly worsen.

5. b

   Using the formula *volume* $\times$ *drop factor* $\div$ *minutes,*
   you should get a figure of 83.3 gtt/min. You
   should round the gtt/min, which, in this case, is
   83 gtt/min.

D Weapons of Mass Destruction

READING ASSIGNMENT ▶ Read Appendix D, page 714 to 721 in your textbook.

Multiple Choice

In the space provided, identify the letter of the choice that best completes the statement or answers each question.

_____ **1.** A blister agent is an example of a(n)

     a. biological weapon.   **c.** nuclear weapon.

     b. chemical weapon.   **d.** explosive.

_____ **2.** Cyanide is an example of a

     a. nerve agent.   **c.** blood agent.

     b. blister agent.   **d.** choking agent.

Short Answer

Answer each question in the space provided.

3. List four common types of biological agents.

1.

2.

3.

4.

4. List six categories of weapons of mass destruction that a terrorist might use.

1.

2.

3.

4.

5.

6.

5. Fill in the missing information.

Disease/Agent	Group/Type
	Biological/virus/category A
Botulism/enterotoxin B/ricin	
	Rickettsia/category B
	Category C
Sarin, soman, tabun, VX	
	Blister agents
Cyanide, arsine, hydrogen chloride	
Chlorine, phosgene	
	Irritants

Answer Section

Appendix D

Multiple Choice

1. b

   Blister agents are types of chemical weapons. Their effects are like those of a corrosive chemical like lye or a strong acid. They can cause severe burns to the eyes, skin, and tissues of the respiratory tract.

2. c

   Cyanide is an example of a blood agent. It causes rapid respiratory arrest and death by blocking oxygen absorption in cells and organs through the bloodstream.

Short Answer

3. There are four common types of biological agents:

   1. Bacteria
   2. Viruses
   3. Rickettsia
   4. Toxins

4. There are six main categories of WMD. B-NICCE is a simple way to remember these categories:

   1. *Biological*
   2. *Nuclear/radiological*
   3. *Incendiary*
   4. *Chemical*
   5. *Cyber/technological*
   6. *Explosive*

5.

Disease/Agent	Group/Type
Anthrax, ebola, smallpox, plague, tularemia, VHEs	Biological/virus/category A
Botulism/enterotoxin B/ricin	Toxin
Q fever	Rickettsia/category B
Napha virus, hanta virus	Category C
Sarin, soman, tabun, VX	Nerve agents
Distilled mustard, nitrogen mustard	Blister agents
Cyanide, arsine, hydrogen chloride	Blood agents
Chlorine, Phosgene	Choking agents
Mace, pepper spray, tear gas	Irritants

Rural and Frontier EMS

READING ASSIGNMENT ▶ Read Appendix E, page 722 to 725 in your textbook.

True or False

Decide whether each statement is true or false. In the space provided, write *T* for true or *F* for false.

_____ **1.** Prehospital care is provided in most rural and frontier areas of the United States by full-time, paid Paramedics.

_____ **2.** Logging, hunting, and fishing are among the least hazardous occupations in the United States.

Short Answer

3. List four reasons why the number of EMS volunteers in rural and frontier areas may be decreasing.

1.

2.

3.

4.

4. List two "nontraditional" settings in which EMS professionals are being used in some rural and frontier communities.

1.

2.

5. List three reasons why the response time to a 9-1-1 call may be longer in a rural or frontier area than in an urban area.

1.

2.

3.

Answer Section

Appendix E

True/False

1. False

   In rural and frontier settings, the level of Emergency Medical Responder and EMT prehospital care is more likely to be available than advanced-level care. This situation is partly due to the costs, time, and travel needed to obtain advanced level training.

   Individuals who do become AEMTs and Paramedics often do not remain in the rural or frontier area after their training is finished. Low call volumes in some areas make it difficult for some advanced care professionals to keep up their skills. Continuing education opportunities may be limited and training resources (including qualified instructors) are often scarce.

2. F

   Many rural and frontier residents are employed in some of the most hazardous occupations in our country—logging, mining, farming, fishing, and hunting. Work-related deaths occur more frequently among these groups of workers than among workers as a whole.

SHORT ANSWER

3. The number of interested EMS volunteers may be decreasing because of:

   - The increasing necessity for a two-wage-earner household prohibits voluntarism
   - Limited or lack of pay for EMS positions
   - Significant risks in providing EMS care

   - The belief that there is increased personal liability when providing EMS care
   - Lack of EMS leadership in the community
   - Limited or lack of funding for training, equipment and supplies
   - Increased number of nursing homes and routine transfer calls instead of emergency calls

   Some rural and frontier communities are using EMS professionals in doctors' offices, health clinics, hospice, and home health settings.

4. Some rural and frontier communities are using EMS professionals in:

   - doctor's offices
   - healthcare clinics
   - hospice
   - home health settings

5. Response times in the rural or frontier setting may be long as a result of:

   - Delay in volunteers' response from home or work (or failure to respond)
   - The physical distance that must be covered
   - The type of transportation that must be used (land, air, water)
   - The type and condition of the roadway, airway, or water
   - Bad weather

   Limited access to communications may delay detection and reporting of a need for emergency care. When traveling on land, unpredictable road conditions (including unmarked roads) can delay the arrival of EMS professionals on the scene.